The Villa of the Papyri at Herculaneum

Sozomena

Studies in the Recovery of Ancient Texts

Edited
on behalf of the Herculaneum Society

by

Alessandro Barchiesi, Robert Fowler,
Dirk Obbink and Nigel Wilson

Vol. 1

De Gruyter

The Villa of the Papyri at Herculaneum

Archaeology, Reception, and Digital Reconstruction

Edited by

Mantha Zarmakoupi

De Gruyter

ISBN 978-3-11-048222-5
e-ISBN 978-3-11-021543-4
ISSN 1869-6368

Library of Congress Cataloging-in-Publication Data

The Villa of the Papyri at Herculaneum : archaeology, reception, and digital reconstruction / edited by Mantha Zarmakoupi.
p. cm. – (Sozomena: studies in the recovery of ancient texts)
Includes bibliographical references and index.
ISBN 978-3-11-048222-5 (hardcover : alk. paper)
1. Villa of the Papyri (Herculaneum) 2. Dwellings – Italy – Herculaneum (Extinct city) 3. Herculaneum (Extinct city) – Antiquities. 4. Excavations (Archaeology) – Italy – Herculaneum (Extinct city) I. Zarmakoupi, Mantha, 1975–.
DG70.H5V56 2010
937'.72564–dc22 2010046157

Bibliographic information published by the Deutsche Nationalbibliothek

The Deutsche Nationalbibliothek lists this publication in the Deutsche Nationalbibliografie; detailed bibliographic data are available in the Internet at http://dnb.d-nb.de.

Printing: Hubert & Co. GmbH & Co. KG, Göttingen
∞ Printed on acid-free paper

Printed in Germany

www.degruyter.com

Contents

Introduction

MANTHA ZARMAKOUPI

Excavated for the first time in the 18th century by means of underground tunnels, the Villa of the Papyri has been profoundly influential in the field of Classical Studies. Not only do the collection of papyri from the Villa form the only intact library to survive from Greco-Roman antiquity, but the sculptural decoration of the Villa also contributed to the development of Winckelmann's aesthetic theories and made a significant impact on the study of Classical Art. The unique character of the finds, as well as the inaccessibility of the Villa itself after the end of the excavations contributed to the creation of a myth around the site and more specifically around its finds and ownership. In the 1990s, after over two centuries of inaccessibility during which Weber's plan was the only tangible reference to the Villa's architecture, new excavations brought more of this fascinating site to light. The new excavations, conducted in 1994–1998 by Infratecna and after 2007 by the Archaeological Superintendency of Pompeii, have enriched our knowledge and understanding of the Villa of the Papyri. The papers presented in this volume give a comprehensive account of the new excavations, for the first time in English, and provide an overview of new research on the Villa.

In the first two chapters the new excavations are presented. Antonio De Simone discusses the process of re-discovering the Villa in the 1980s and analyzes the results of the first open-air excavations of 1994–1998. These show that the Villa was more extensive and monumental than previously thought, and demonstrate that it is exemplary of the monumental luxury villas that fronted the Bay of Naples in the first century B.C.E. and the first century C.E. Maria Paola Guidobaldi and Domenico Esposito discuss the most recent excavations conducted at the Villa and present the new finds from the Villa, including the decoration of room (I) of the *basis villae* and the wooden furniture lined with ivory that present Dionysian-related scenes. The study of the construction techniques, pavements and wall paintings enables us to assess the chronology of the Villa and date its first phase to the third quarter of the first century B.C.E. Furthermore, Guidobaldi tackles the issues involved in the management and restoration of this fragile site that in some areas lies almost 4 m below the current sea level.

Chapters three and four discuss the wall paintings and sculptural collection of the Villa. Eric Moormann assesses his previous work on the fragments of wall paintings found in the 18th-century to analyze the overall chronology of the wall paintings at the Villa. As in other opulent villas and houses from the Campanian region, owners appreciated and retained Second Style decorations side by side with the new fashions of the Fourth Style. Carol Mattusch analyzes the sculptural collection found at the Villa and goes beyond the traditional concept of a sculptural program to look more deeply at the industry of sculpture and at the means by which these art-works found homes.

The following two chapters examine the papyri found at the Villa. In chapter five, Mario Capasso re-examines the question of the Villa's owner(s) by assessing the research and scholarship on the archaeology of the Villa and attempts to bridge the approaches of archaeologists and papyrologists to the question. In the next chapter, David Sider presents the attempts and methods used to open and read the papyrus rolls from the Villa in the 18th and 19th centuries and discusses the nature of the library of the Villa. The specialized library of mainly Greek Epicurean texts must have been part of a larger library of both Greek and Latin texts.

The reception of the Villa in the 18th and 20th centuries is addressed in the next two chapters. Kenneth Lapatin discusses the genesis of J. Paul Getty's idea to build a replica of the Villa of the Papyri in Malibu, California, in order to house his art collection. The association of the Villa with Julius Caesar's father-in-law appealed greatly to the tycoon and the limited information about the Villa's architecture allowed the interpretative leeway necessary for the realization of his vision. Dana Arnold uses Derridean concepts to point to the fragmentary way that the Villa was accessed and understood in the 18th century. The codified representation of the Villa's underground spaces by Weber is indicative of the ways in which the scientific graphic conventions were a means to codify knowledge about architecture and archaeology at the time.

The last two chapters address the real and virtual reconstructions of the Villa of the Papyri. Diane Favro focuses on the real re-birthing of the Villa of the Papyri as the Getty Villa to address the history of reconstructions and their sensorial "stigma." Her analysis of responses to the sensorial delights of the Getty Villa sheds light on the academic dichotomy between scientific/conceptual (i. e., good) and sensorial (i. e., bad) approaches that lingers in the fields of architectural and art history as well as archaeology. Mantha Zarmakoupi presents the *Virtual reality digital model of the Villa of the Papyri project* to address the ways in which such models may be used to document and investigate archaeological sites. By presenting a reconstruction that distinguishes between known and hypothetical structures, this project aims to provide a research and educational tool for the Villa.

This volume is the outcome of a conference that was held in Oxford in September 2007 on *The archaeology, reception and digital reconstruction of the Villa of the Papyri*. I would like to thank the British Academy and the Oxford Classics Faculty Board for their support and the Friends of Herculaneum Society for generously sponsoring the conference. I am indebted to Robert Fowler and Dirk Obbink for their assistance and support for the conference as well as for the production of the present volume. I am particularly grateful to Robert Fowler for checking the English translations of the Italian texts. Furthermore, I would like to thank Elisa Perego and Veronica Tamorri for translating the first two chapters from Italian to English.

At the time of the conference, the most recent excavations by the Archaelogical Superintendency of Pompeii were underway at the Villa. I am grateful to Maria Paola Guidobaldi and Domenico Esposito for agreeing to present the results of their work in this volume.

New York, May 2010
Mantha Zarmakoupi

Rediscovering the Villa of the Papyri

ANTONIO DE SIMONE

Introduction

More than twenty years have passed since the discovery of the Villa of the Papyri at Herculaneum in October 1986, and ten years separate us from the accomplishment of the first *sub divo* works in the period spanning from 1994 to 1998. Despite the new information provided by the recent investigation, the majority of the studies on the Villa are still based on the 18th-century documentation. However, the period between the discovery of the Villa in 1986 and the present day proved useful for the overall assessment of what has been done so far – both confirming the relative accuracy of the 18th-century exploration and raising the possibility of collecting all the data needed to gain a whole picture of the Villa by means of a thorough excavation.[1]

Recent excavations[2]

In the preface to the first volume of *Cronache Ercolanesi* in 1971, Marcello Gigante stated anew the idea of locating the Villa, and expressed hope for its identification and excavation.[3] At the beginning of the 1980 s the discovery of the boat by the ancient seashore and of the bodies of numerous victims, trapped in the hardened mud of 79 C.E., brought new knowledge of great archaeological importance. Gigante's wish now seemed prophetic. It is no coincidence that in 1980 Carlo Knight and Andrea Jorio published their study on the location of the Villa,

1 I would like to thank Prof. Robert Fowler and Dr. Mantha Zarmakoupi who invited me to the conference entitled "Villa of the Papyri: archaeology reception and digital reconstruction" held in Oxford on September 22nd and 23rd 2007.

2 Referred as Infratecna excavation or "New Excavations" by Infratecna elsewhere in this volume. (Ed.)

3 Gigante 1971, 5.

which identified the 18th-century entrance to the tunnels "Ciceri 1" as well as the area above the Villa, known as the "Bosco degli Agostiniani" in the 18th century.[4] Knight and Jorio's publication signalled a real change in focus, since it contextualized the Villa within its surrounding territory. Since 1765 when the Bourbon exploration was interrupted, research on the Villa was conducted within the walls of museums and archives and was focused on the finds from the Villa, the papyri and sculptures.[5] The architectural analysis of the Villa was included only in a few studies and was limited to the discussion of the plan proposed by Weber (fig. 1),[6] and the history of the 18th-century excavations was reconstructed on the basis of contemporary documents. Now for the first time the object of study – with appreciable results – was the location of the Villa.

In 1982 the Ministry of Culture set up a working group to prepare a feasibility study on the excavation of the Villa. The working group, privileging a geotechnical approach, proposed the construction of four new access shafts, equipped with mechanical lifts, in order to access the ancient level and locate the Villa, and on the basis of the outcome of this investigation to initiate a second project for the excavation of the Villa by means of galleries.[7] The aforementioned proposal puzzled archaeologists who privileged a methodology grounded in the principles of historical topography. In 1983, a group of archaeologists from the University of Naples Federico II, informally led by Attilio Stazio,[8] assessed the existing evidence and proposed to conduct a preliminary survey of the surroundings of the Villa in order to identify the 18th-century access shafts (wells) and start the new exploration through them.

Subsequently the Ministry incorporated these investigations into a more comprehensive project to manage all the archaeological areas

4 Knight and Jorio 1980.

5 An example of this persisting research attitude is a recent work by C.C. Mattusch. Her study is valuable and of great importance for the study of the sculptures. The study of the overall architectural context is on the other hand limited, despite the importance of the recent finds. See *Mattusch*, 12–28, 51–54.

6 Comparetti and De Petra 1883 (repr. 1972) (henceforth *CDP*), Mustilli 1956 (repr. 1983), Sauron 1980.

7 The project proposal, mentioned by Gullini (1985, 7) was elaborated by Arrigo Croce, a Geotechnical Engineer and Lecturer at the University of Naples. I have a copy of the project but I was not able to find any trace of it in the archives.

8 S. Adamo Muscettola, A. De Simone and L. Scatozza were also part of this group.

around Vesuvius.[9] Many experts from the Ministry were involved in the preliminary survey as well as in the realization of the project. The feasibility study for the excavation of the Villa was entrusted directly to the Archaeological Superintendency of Pompeii and several investigations were conducted between 1986 and 1990 towards the completion of this task.[10]

Firstly, it was necessary to re-examine the 18th-century documentation in order to reconstruct the works carried out in the 18th century.[11] By chronologically correlating sundry documents we were able to identify the excavated areas, locate the entrances to the tunnels and contextualize the surviving data.

The re-examination of the 18th-century documentation involved contemporary maps such as the ones drawn by the Duke of Noia[12] and by La Vega.[13] These plans showed the 18th-century topography

---

9 On the overall results of the project see *Progetto Pompei.*

10 The Records (Atti) are deposited in the Archives of the Archaeological Superintendency of Pompeii. In order to reconstruct the history of the excavations it is useful to indicate exhaustively the administrational acts which document the work. The folder is named "Esplorazioni archeologiche, indagini geologiche sul territorio di Ercolano inclusi gli espropri e le occupazioni necessarie per lo studio di fattibilità per lo scavo di Villa dei Papiri" and includes the following reports: "Perizia no. 105 del 22/4/1986, disposta con Decreto Ministeriale 1/7/1986, registrata alla Corte dei Conti il 31/1/1987 Reg. 5 F1 372;" "Perizia no. 165 del 21/4/1987, approvata con Decreto Ministeriale del 5/7/1988" and "Perizia 165/VAR del 29/7/1988, approvata con Decreto Ministeriale del 5/10/1988;" and "Perizia suppletiva dell'aprile del 1989." On the work undertaken see Franchi dell'Orto (ed.) 1990, 72–73, 126–127, figs. 83–86.

11 The archive research took place in the following archives: Archivio di Stato di Napoli (Fondi: Archivio Borbone; Casa Reale Antica; Casa Reale Amministrativa); Società Napoletana di Storia Patria (Fondi: Fondo Avellino; Fondo Cuomo; Ms XXB 19 bis); Archivio Storico della Soprintendenza Archeologica di Napoli e Caserta. The documents recovered are almost entirely published in the following works: Venuti 1748; Fiorelli 1878–1780, I, 233–273, II, 228–234, IV, 164–212, IV, 164–212; *CDP*; Ruggiero 1885; Ruggiero 1888; Gallavotti 1940; Maiuri 1958; Pannuti 1983; *Fonti Ercolano Stabia*; *Pompei Ercolano Stabiae Oplontis*; Guadagno 1986. For an exhaustive summary of archival sources see McIlwaine 1988, 59–63. For the documents concerning the history of the excavations see Parslow 1995, 77–106.

12 De Seta 1975, vol. 1, 145–209, vol. 2, pl. 28.

13 The two maps have been edited by F. and P. La Vega and engraved by A. Cataneo. They are published in Rosini (1797) and accompanied by the following captions: Pl. I, Topografia dei villaggi di Portici, Resina e Torre del Greco, e di porzione de' loro territori, per quanto serve a rischiarare altra Carta dell'an-

and the reconstruction of the ancient terrain, on the basis of the wells and tunnels explored at that time. Furthermore, an 18th-century map kept at the National Archive of Naples enabled the reconstruction of the property boundaries at the time of the Bourbon excavations.[14] This map gave names of landowners, some of whom, as contemporary documents show, received payment for damages caused by the exploration.[15]

On the basis of this information, the traces of the 18th-century exploration were identified on the modern landscape and a survey of the access shafts was carried out.[16] This work followed up an earlier attempt by Maiuri in 1927,[17] mentioned in the Records (Atti) of the archives of the Superintendency.[18] The investigation enabled the identification of a well located between the property of Nicola Iacumino and

tico stato dell'agro ercolanese; Pl. II, Topographia Herculanensis, qua eius agri facies, prout olim, antequam celeberrima Vesuvii eructatione, anno primo Titi Imperatoris obrueretur, erat spectabilis, ex varia multiplicum adgestionum altitudine et situ investigata exhibetur.

14 Archivio di Stato di Napoli, Piante e disegni, X 22. Published in Allrogen-Bedel and Kammerer-Grothaus 1983, 85 and fig. 1.

15 This is the case of Nicola Iacumino who received several payments from November 12th 1752 to October 24th 1761, as stated in the Ms 2.6.2 of the Fondo Cuomo held by the Società Napoletana di Storia Patria (doc. 2, from f. 76 v. to f. 94 v.).

16 The drawings realized during these preliminary explorations are stored in the "Archivio Disegni" of the Archaeological Superintendency of Pompeii under the following classification codes: P/870: Villa dei Papiri. Topographia Herculanensis; P/870a: Ubicazione di Villa dei Papiri; P/870b: Villa dei Papiri. Mappa topografica della città di Napoli e de' suoi contorni. Elaborazione della mappa del Duca di Noja (1775) sulla base della topografia odierna; P/870c: Villa dei Papiri. Stato dei luoghi al 1986; P/871: Villa dei Papiri. Topografia di Portici e Resina. Elaborazione della mappa di F. e P. La Vega (1797) sulla base della topografia odierna; P/871a: Villa dei Papiri. Portici e dintorni. Elaborazione della mappa conservata all'Archivio di Stato di Napoli, Piante e disegni, X 22 (anteriore al 1740) sulla base della topografia odierna; P/872: Villa dei Papiri. Pianta di una parte della moderna Resina. Elaborazione della pianta Tascone (1885) sulla base della topografia odierna; P/873: Villa dei Papiri. Pianta e sezione del Pozzo Veneruso; P/874: Villa dei Papiri. Ipotesi ricostruttive della linea di costa da Portici a Ercolano; P/876: Villa dei Papiri. Rilievo planovolumetrico dei luoghi; P/879: Villa dei Papiri. Planimetria: perimetro della Villa e pozzi di discesa.

17 The exploration of the access shafts was pursued before the *sub divo* excavation of the urban area, since it proved to be a necessary pre-excavation investigation.

18 De Simone 1987; Conticello 1987; Conticello and Cioffi 1990.

the garden of the Agostiniani Scalzi (which we called "Veneruso 1" after its 18th-century owner) through which we eventually entered the Villa on October 16th 1986, over 200 years after the Bourbon exploration.

After entering the Villa through the "Veneruso 1" shaft we located and reopened an older access, the "Ciceri 1" shaft at a cellar under Cortese's house in Via Roma (Municipality of Portici), which gives access to the area of the Belvedere of the Villa (fig. 2). Through "Ciceri 1" we followed a tunnel that starts from the Belvedere up to the north-western limit of the Big Pool and the "Ciceri 2" shaft. However, we had to interrupt the exploration in October 1988 for safety reasons, given the long distance needed to exit from the "Ciceri 1" shaft. From the "Veneruso 1" shaft a new exploration was started. This concerned the tunnels starting around the *tablinum* and reaching the south-west limit of the big pool, and going along the *gruta derecha* in the opposite direction until the so-called library, Room "V" in Weber's map (fig. 1). The room was extensively dug during the 18th-century exploration and then filled with three large supporting walls made of volcanic stones. Few fragments of wood, polished on both sides, were found that probably belonged to shelves where papyri were stored.

The new exploration of the Villa through the galleries was essential in order to gain information concerning the state of preservation of the complex, to evaluate whether it was possible to go on with further excavations and to locate correctly the monument on the landscape. The operation enabled the Ministry of Culture to preserve the area and declare on May 23rd 1990 the Bourbon shafts as well as "the buildings dating to the Roman period and belonging to the ancient Villa of the Pisoni or Villa of the Papyri in the Municipality of Herculaneum (Na) that came to light during the exploration of the tunnels and located only recently" property of the State.

From 1986 to 1990 geological samplings were carried out to define the features of the subsoil, which were useful for the creation of the excavation project of the Villa.[19]

---

19 Geo-seismic prospecting has been carried out through 59 profiles and mechanical prospecting of 24 core samples as well as by measuring the ground water levels. The charts documenting the results of these investigations are stored in the "Archivio Disegni" of the Archaeological Superintendency of Pompeii and are labelled as follows: P/875: Villa dei Papiri. Rappresentazione geologica dei luoghi; P/877: Villa dei Papiri. Planimetria: stendimenti microsismici;

Several results have been gained between 1983 and 1990:

- the structures which survived the destructive Bourbon exploration appeared to be still noteworthy both on the quantitative and qualitative side. Their direct investigation by means of a *sub divo* excavation allowed a different interpretation of the archaeological and architectural data compared to the one offered by the partial and problematic 18th-century documentation available up to that point.
- the results of the geophysical investigations showed a height difference of the ancient area surrounding the Villa of more than 10 m from one end to the other, demonstrating the existence of a slope or a cliff.[20] It appears that the Villa was built on a hillside between Vesuvius and the sea in a position that was extremely favourable for taking advantage of the climate and the view of the landscape.
- the complexity of the observed structures excluded the possibility of exploration through tunnels, whose network in the 18th century had already caused disturbance. Excavating by means of tunnels served then to retrieve artefacts rapidly for the, then new, Bourbon museum, but this method is no longer suitable for modern archaeological investigations, which require the use of a stratigraphic methodology based on a top-down reading of archaeological layers.
- the soil lying on top of the Villa is constituted by heterogeneous materials, and is therefore not compatible with an excavation by means of tunnels. Indeed, the Villa is covered by consolidated mud, the result of the 79 C.E. eruption on top of which are materials deposited after several subsequent eruptions, such as the extremely flaky lava layer of the 1632 eruption.

The results obtained allow some considerations:

- the exposed archaeological area of the ancient city of Herculaneum is delimited on the south-west and south-east by its own natural border; on the north-east, beyond the *decumanus maximus*, by the impassable boundary of the modern city.
- on the north-west the border is formed by the Vico del Mare, beyond which are the furthest *insulae* of the ancient city – partially known from the 18th-century documentation – below land that is

P/878: Villa dei Papiri. Planimetria: sondaggi geognostici condotti e relative sezioni. Cioffi 1993, 655–658.

20 Cioffi 1993, 655–658.

for the most part still free of modern buildings. Immediately beyond these is the Villa of the Papyri.

- the only way to expand our knowledge of the ancient city was to resume exploration in this direction. This would also throw light on the definition of public spaces in the central area of the ancient city, which remain obscure despite notable recent contributions such as those of Pagano.[21]

Another consideration regarding the excavation of the Villa became clear. The multiplicity of interpretations, often divergent, of the character of the monument demonstrated the limit of studies based solely on the 18th-century documentation. Therefore exploration of the Villa by means of excavation, quite apart from the hope of finding other parts of the Library, seemed to be the only way to define the nature of the monument's architecture, which is unique for its central position on the Bay of Naples, and quite unusual for its dimensions and composite character.

It thus seemed necessary to conjoin the excavation of the Villa with that of the north-west sector of the city, with the aim of restoring to the scientific community and the wider public the vision of an integral urban organism, physically connected with the adjacent suburb.

The excavation had to be conducted proceeding inland from the sea. In 79 C.E. Vesuvius covered the area with a remarkable volume of material, cascading down the slope and dragging towards the sea pieces and entire sections of buildings located on the mountain. Excavating in the other direction would have entailed the loss of valuable knowledge. It is no coincidence that Maiuri himself proceeded in a similar manner when he started excavating the city in 1926.

The resumption of excavations at Herculaneum, including the Villa, was presented as a long-term undertaking to be conducted in stages, the first of which involved the parts of the city and the Villa closest to the coast, with the intention of tackling the regions further inland in subsequent decades. The project was therefore intended as the first stage of a more wide-ranging activity with the aim of restoring the entire city and excavating the whole north-west sector of Herculaneum including the excavation *sub divo* of the Villa of the Papyri.

On the basis of the results of the investigation carried out so far and the considerations mentioned above, the Ministry of Culture and the

---

21 Pagano 1996.

Archaeological Superintendency of Pompeii drew up a project entitled "Restauro e riuso, valorizzazione dell'area archeologica di Ercolano," which was instituted by the Ministry on March 29th 1990.

The project envisaged the restoration of the seafront of the city and the area of the suburban baths, reopening access to the Villa from the archaeological site of Herculaneum through a gallery realized in the 1980 s and installing sump pumps (fig. 3). A further aim of the project was to buy the land from the front of the north-west *Insula* of the city up to the atrium quarter of the Villa of the Papyri in order to conduct future excavations in this area.[22]

The planned work was carried out between 1991 and 1998, as it was scheduled in the original project. The first phase of the work (1991–1994) took place in the part of the city located on the seaside, with the repair of the suburban area of the *sacelli* and the Baths. Furthermore, another ramp exiting the city was unearthed. This ramp was the continuation of the third cardo and next to the House of the Inn. During this phase of the project, an excavation of the area outside the bastion of the House of Aristides was completed.[23]

Results of the excavation

During the second phase of the project (1994–1998), the excavation involved the front of the north-west *Insula* of Herculaneum and the Villa of the Papyri.[24] The work conducted on the Villa of the Papyri was limited to the western part of the atrium. The north-west *Insula* of Herculaneum (fig. 4), extending over an area of about 2,300 m^2 on a slope rising about 16–17 m, is located outside the defensive walls of the original settlement. Its location is clear evidence of the partial or total obliteration of the defensive walls as well as of the novel arrangement of the new residential units built beyond their limits. This sector of the city was not known by the Bourbon explorers and therefore was not included in the schematic reconstruction of the urban layout in La Vega's second map.[25] The composition of the structures reveals a pro-

22 De Simone 1998.

23 A complete description of the whole intervention can be found in De Simone et al. 1998.

24 Referred as 1996–1998 excavations elsewhere in this volume. (Ed.)

25 Rosini 1797, Pl. II.

gression of the city towards the sea of about 40 m from the west façade of the House of Aristides and suggests the presence of a promontory with landing areas, which reminds us of the one described by Dionysus of Halicarnassus as safe for every season (*Ant. Rom.* 1.35). The progression of the city towards the sea is particularly evident in the case of the building near the House of Aristides, which projects towards the shore far beyond the limit of the area explored so far. This projection of the building dates back to the late Republican period and is characterized by a series of arched and rectangular niches (fig. 5). Unfortunately, the lack of preservation after the excavations resulted in the collapse of these structures (fig. 6).

No evidence of architectural structures was found to the north of the aforementioned urban area because of a morphological depression. This gap was also noticed by other scholars,[26] who suggested that one of the two *fluvia* mentioned by Sisenna may have been located in this area (Sisenna, fr. 53, 54, Peter *HR Rel*). The depression indicates a remarkable discontinuity between the city and the Villa of the Papyri and highlights the suburban nature of the Villa despite its vicinity to the city.

The excavation of the Villa brought to light the western part of the atrium quarter as well as the south-west prospect of the *basis villae* underneath it. The continuation of the excavation to the south revealed the existence of a monumental complex of the Villa, located 9 m below the atrium level and projecting toward the sea.[27]

The results of the excavation carried out in the 1990s are presented below. The first part of the report is devoted to the re-examination of the atrium, the second examines the *basis villae*, and the third the monumental complex on the lower terrace.

I. The atrium quarter

The atrium quarter of the Villa occupies a prominent position with a panoramic view of the sea, constituting the main level of a complex, which extends over several terraces at different elevations.

26 Guadagno 1993, n. 77; Pagano 1993, 146.

27 For a more detailed account of the results of the excavation and the analysis of the Villa, see De Simone and Ruffo 2002 and 2003.

The study of this sector resulted, in the first instance, in identifying architectural and structural elements known from the 18th-century documentation, and determining their state of preservation. Weber's plan appeared to be accurate on the whole, except for some details concerning the systems of passage between the different rooms and for the incorrect perimeter of room "o," which was located near the eastern corner of the atrium. Notwithstanding the destructive nature of the 18th-century exploration, the walls in many places are preserved to a maximum height of about 2.9 m; they thus prove useful for the interpretation of the arrangement of the original building.

The atrium sector is about 102 Roman feet wide (fig. 7). This measurement includes both the width of the central atrium and the width of the two large triclinia adjacent to it. The well-balanced distribution of the space suggests the existence of careful planning preceding the construction of the building.

Sixteen rooms of the atrium sector and a portion of the tripartite portico surrounding the atrium sector on the side of the sea were located and dug. The overall measure of the excavated area is approximately 750 m^2 (fig. 8). All the rooms are decorated with mosaics. The sixteen rooms were: atrium (c) with its two *alae* (d, e); *tablinum*-exedra (b); three corridors (h, n, t); two rooms on the eastern corner (o, p); three spacious triclinia (i, l, q) and four "halls" (f, g, r, s), all accessible from the surrounding portico.

The fragments of the walls preserve wall paintings impressive for their quality as well as for the sophistication of their execution. The decoration can be mainly attributed to the Second Style and is therefore contemporaneous to the construction of the building. The pavement decoration, wholly preserved in situ, consists of black and white as well as polychrome mosaics with geometric decorations, and can be dated between the late Republican and early Imperial periods.[28]

The walls located in the excavated area were mainly built of *opus reticulatum* faced with tufa blocks; the external supports, the doorframes of the *alae* and the interior corners were constructed in brickwork; and the doorframes of the inner rooms were built of *opus vittatum* made of tuff blocks. The masonry of the excavated portion displays a uniform execution, as there are no examples of gap-filling or separate abutting sections.

28 De Simone and Ruffo 2004.

These structural features have been recognized at the point where the rooms of the atrium quarter connected to the large peristyle, and reveal a substantial homogeneity between the two main parts of the Villa, which therefore must be contemporaneous. On the basis of finds and analysis of the excavated part, the Villa fits in the context of elaborate luxury residences built between 60 B.C.E. and 40 B.C.E., in the period of the greatest expansion of the Second Style. An obvious unity of architectural and decorative idiom informs these buildings in Campania, Latium, and Etruria, in suburban, pseudo-urban, and coastal contexts, but also in more productive areas. Comparisons can be found in well-known complexes such as the Villa of the Mysteries at Pompeii, the Villa A at Torre Annunziata, the Villa of Fannius Synistor at Boscoreale, the Villa of the Volusii at Lucus Feroniae, the Villa of Via Nomentana and the Villa Settefinestre in the *ager cosanus*.

II. The *basis villae*

The 18th-century exploration was limited to the main level of the Villa. The investigation did not go beyond the pavement of the main level, except from a small area near the Belvedere – where a previously excavated small portion of a wall under the level of the pavement was identified during the preliminary survey (1986–1988). The almost total absence of tunnels and the compact character of the pyroclastic layers under the main level known from Weber's plan further confirmed that the 18th-century exploration did not penetrate this level. On the basis of the data collected during the re-exploration of the tunnels, we were expecting to uncover a terrace structure supporting the Villa, which may have been built on a slope looking towards the gulf. Indeed, the excavation revealed the presence of a *basis villae*, on top of which the main level of the Villa was built. The façade of the *basis villae* was brought to light for a length of 25 m and to a height of about 4 m. The evidence thus obtained suggests that the *basis villae* had the same extent as the Villa's atrium quarter.

The monumental façade attests the presence of a first lower level corresponding to the south-west sector of the atrium (fig. 9). The wall of the façade is covered with white plaster, made with abundant marble powder. It has five openings, four of which are crowned by *oculi*, originally closed with glass slabs (fig. 10).

The openings give access to rooms beneath the portico of the atrium quarter. A partial and brief survey took place in the first room from the north-west, room (I) (fig. 11). Room (I) is 3.85 m deep and connected with other rooms located to its north-west and north-east. This is indicated by the presence of doors on the corresponding north-west and north-east walls. The room is decorated with a black and white mosaic pavement and with fine paintings, dating to the transitional phase between the Third and Fourth Styles (fig. 12; see also Guidobaldi and Esposito in this volume, figs. 25–26).[29] The wall and floor decorations, particularly elegant and sophisticated, indicate that the rooms had a domestic function and excluded the possibility that they served as a living area for the servants, as attested in other parts of the Villa.[30] The presence of an inner door of communication on the rear north-east wall suggests the presence of another series of rooms, located at the back of those lining the façade and below the rooms opening on to the portico on the upper level of the atrium quarter. Furthermore, it seems also likely that the rooms of the lower level did not extend towards the north-east interior of the Villa body like the ones of the upper level, suggesting that these rooms were the result of the adaptation of the Villa's structures to the sloping terrain. It is likely that this arrangement did not extend beyond the north-east limit of the *tablinum*-exedra and the nearby rooms.

A structure has been uncovered near the north-west edge of the façade, at the corner with the limit of the excavation area, which was only partially investigated because of its location. The structure has a curved profile (fig. 13; see also Guidobaldi and Esposito in this volume, fig. 32) featuring two wide rectangular windows and its covering was lined in cocciopesto that seems to be connected with a cocciopesto floor. Only a part of this floor, located outside the windowsill of the first window at the north-west, was investigated. This structure suggests the presence of yet another level, below the one immediately under the atrium quarter (fig. 14).[31]

---

29 For the results of further excavations of the first lower level of the *basis villae* see Guidobaldi and Esposito in this volume, 33–42.

30 This is the case of the rooms of Villa Arianna at Stabiae placed below the main level.

31 For further investigations of the second level of the *basis villae* see Guidobaldi and Esposito in this volume, 42–44.

The observation of these elements reveals a *basis villae* articulated on several levels and a monumental configuration of architectural forms towards the sea with a strong scenographic character. This was quite unexpected and totally unforeseeable on the basis of the 18th-century documentation.

III. The lower terrace (VPSO area)[32]

Further structures belonging to a monumental section protruding towards the sea were exposed. They were situated to the south of the Villa, at a distance of about 23 m from the front of the *basis villae* and at an elevation of 9 m below the main level of the Villa (fig. 15). The partial excavation prevented us from understanding the full extent of the area. Only the south-west and south-east outer limits of a terrace, arranged as a 20 cm high parapet, were found. For the purposes of my research I will designate this monumental section as the lower terrace.

The 18.35 m wide terrace is parallel to the main building of the Villa, to which it must be related considering its position, orientation, importance of structure and decoration, but also because of the architectural and decorative grandeur of the structure and its overall height.

On the terrace, in a central alignment, there is a building of which only the foundation remains. It was a large room covered by a flat roof that collapsed entirely under the weight of the eruption (fig. 16). Examination of the collapse of the structure reveals that the building was a large hall, 8.90 m. wide. The sumptuousness and the opulence of the whole building are attested by some of the surviving wall decorations.

At the interior east and south corners of the hall there were two quadrangular brick bases, whose marble cladding was found in an extremely fragmentary state; traces of an irregular concave depression marked its upper surface (fig. 17). These bases supported two female statues, of the types of "Sciarra Amazon" (fig. 18) and "Hera Borghese" (fig. 19), which were discovered outside the structure near the corners (fig. 20).[33] The symmetrical arrangement of the statue bases within

32 For the results of further excavations of the lower terrace see Guidobaldi and Esposito in this volume, 45–50.

33 De Simone 2000, 22–23; Gasparri 2005, 51–59.

the room allows the hypothesis that there were other statues in the corners on the north-east side of the room, opposite to the explored area. The discovery of these two masterpieces also suggests that other statues may be still buried in the unexplored areas of the Villa, complementing the rich collection discovered in the course of the 18th-century exploration.

Interpretation of the results

The re-examination of the Villa after the new excavation allows us to think about new hypotheses on the dating of the structures. The studies of the Villa preceding the excavation were primarily summarized in the work of Wojcik.[34] About the dating of the structure, she agrees with the conclusions offered by Mustilli and places the Villa of the Papyri "in the category of pseudo-urban villas characteristic of Campania;" identifying the original nucleus in the atrium quarter, dating to the first half of the first century B.C.E., and the addition of the big peristyle to the original nucleus by the end of the century. Both Mustilli and Wojcik, whose analyses of the Villa were based on the 18th-century documentation only, interpret the structural evolution of the Villa of the Papyri on the basis of a development scheme known from other villas. The analysis of the Villa's architectural and decorative features, made available by the *sub divo* excavation, enables us to establish that the monument was an essentially unitary undertaking, to be dated close to 60 B.C.E. The construction of the Villa on a slope forced designers to articulate it on more than one level; for structural reasons, the construction needed to be done unitarily. This is demonstrated by the following considerations: the two parts of the Villa – the so-called "quarter of the atrium" and the "quarter of the big peristyle" are joined together by a series of rooms, including room "XVI" in Weber's plan. Room "XVI" is open on three sides and one of them fits perfectly in the architectonic composition of the peristyle (see Guidobaldi and Esposito in this volume, fig. 3). The mosaic pavement of this room was removed during the 18th century exploration and is known only by Weber's documentation (fig. 21)[35] published in table no. X in the book by Ruggiero.[36]

34 *Wojcik.*

35 The drawing is stored in the Archivio Disegni della Soprintendenza archeologica di Pompei under no. P/61715.

36 Ruggiero 1885, pl. X, 1.

The mosaic belongs to the Second Style and therefore has an early dating. The *emblema* is formed by a meander with labyrinthic motif, with squares and double swastikas represented in perspective, and the meander circumscribes a pattern of rhomboidal *sectilia*, forming cubes in perspective.

The best location to fully perceive the perspective is from the big peristyle and this demonstrates that room "XVI" in Weber's plan and the big peristyle were planned and realized together. A parallel for the chronology, considering the use of the decorative elements and the composition, is offered by the pavement of *tablinum* 33 of the House of the Faun in Pompeii (figs. 22–23) where, similarly to the Villa in Herculaneum, the perception of the perspective in the decoration of the pavement forces the observer to be in one exact point (fig. 24).[37]

The onsite investigation of the atrium quarter enabled us to define the function of its adjacent portico. It is important to recall that the 18th-century exploration was not carried out beyond this area. The interaxal distance of the columns corresponding to rooms (s) and (b) is big so as to guarantee the view of the panorama. Room (b), which is the main transition between the atrium and the portico, is configured as a sort of *tablinum*-exedra rather than as a large *fauces*, acting as a panoramic opening to the sea and not just as an entrance to this part of the Villa. Atrium (c), the least preserved part of the excavated area, is expanded by *alae* and is directly related to the *tablinum*-exedra. It seems therefore inappropriate to speak of an atrium, which usually has a function of access and linking, but rather of a "grand hall," with clear analogies in prestigious residences located along the coast, such as the Villa of Arianna at Stabiae.

Still, the most important result arising from the recent investigation is certainly the new understanding of the Villa's vertical dimension along its western seaward prospect. Here I may mention that the most accepted theories, supported also by the recent re-exploration of the Bourbon tunnels, posited a large blind course of masonry to support the structure. It is now legitimate to speak of a three-dimensional monument as opposed to a horizontal or two-dimensional one that has been handed down merely for two centuries on the basis of Weber's plan.

The open-air excavation has shown four different architectonic levels, including the main one (fig. 25). The main level of the Villa studied in the 18th century stands at an altitude of 11 m. Since the ancient

37 *PPM* 1–10, vol. 5, 108–111, figs. 31–34.

ground level was about 5 m deeper, we should fix the height of the main floor in antiquity at 16 m above sea level. The levels underlying the main level of the Villa are adapted to the natural slope, showing progressively smaller dimensions. These rooms were probably for household activities.

The second level, which has a height of about 5 m, starting from 6 m above sea level, corresponding to 11 m above the ancient shore level, is represented by the aforementioned façade of the *basis villae*. The third level has an apsidal forepart. To the same level pertains the building noted as "lower terrace," with its floor at 2.30 m above sea level, that is 7.30 m above the ancient shore level. From this height starts the fourth level and from here it was possible to access the beach, through a staircase at the south-east edge of the lower terrace.

Marcello Gigante identified a reference to the Villa in an epigram of the *Palatine Anthology* attributed to Philodemus.[38] The subject was recently re-examined by Mario Capasso.[39] The epigram reads as follows:

> Ἤδη καὶ ῥόδον ἐστὶ καὶ ἀκμάζων ἐρέβινθος
> καὶ καυλοὶ κράμβης, Σωσύλε, πρωτοτόμου
> καὶ μαίνη σελαγεῦσα καὶ ἀρτιπαγὴς ἁλίτυρος
> καὶ θριδάκων οὔλων ἀφροφυῆ πέταλα.
> Ἡμεῖς δ' οὔτ' ἀκτῆς ἐπιβαίνομεν οὔτ' ἐν ἀπόψει
> γινόμεθ' ὡς αἰεί, Σωσύλε, τὸ πρότερον·
> καὶ μὴν Ἀντιγένης καὶ Βάκχιος ἐχθὲς ἔπαιζον,
> νῦν δ'αὐτοὺς θάψαι σήμερον ἐκφέρομεν.
> (*Anth. Pal.* 9.412)

> "Here already are the rose, the ripe chickpea, the small first-cut cabbages, O Sosylus, the shining sardine, the freshly curded salted cheese, and the frothy leaves of curly lettuce. But we will not go up on the headland; nor, as always Sosylus, in the past times, do we find ourselves at the belvedere. Yesterday Antigenes and Bacchius were still playing, and today we are accompanying them to the burial." (Transl. by D. Obbink)[40]

The passage is very suggestive; the pain for the death of the friends is coupled with the sorrow of being unable to ascend again to the *acté*, the Promontory, which is the highest point of the coast, where the *apopsis*, the Belvedere of the Villa is built, where they frequently used to meet. In the beautiful frame of an enchanted landscape, in which the

38 Gigante 1988, 54; Gigante 1990, 69–79.
39 Capasso 1991, 35.
40 In D. Obbink's translation of Gigante 1990: *Philodemus in Italy* (Ann Arbor 1995), 55.

Villa plays a central role, the brightness of the gulf and the Epicurean delight in little things ease the pain of death, its longing and deep melancholy.

The excavation has shown the Villa to be built on several levels, following the natural slope; this picture of the Villa was wonderfully prefigured by the philological mastery of Marcello Gigante.

The discovery of the lower terrace shows that the Villa could not be limited to a one-directional scheme of about 250 m, as was suggested by Weber's reconstruction, but involved also a second line of development in the opposite direction to that already known, from inland seaward. Such a scheme, at right angles to the slope, suggests a scenic arrangement of the complex, articulated on several levels, downhill from the part explored in the 18th century. This arrangement has counterparts in known elements of important monumental residences fronting on the Bay of Naples,[41] which precisely through their connection to the sea afforded the seafarer a natural and privileged perspective, asserted their identity and ensured their recognition. Specifically in the area struck by the eruption of 79 C.E. one may mention, for instance, remarkable complexes such as the villas of Stabiae[42] and sites on the suburban edge of Herculaneum such as Villa Sora[43] and Villa of Ponte di Rivieccio.[44]

The above-mentioned villas are artificial scenographies, but fit entirely within the natural setting of the bay of Naples. The villas are the contexts for rich furnishings such as frescoes, precious objects, refined sculptures and, in the case of the Villa of the Papyri, a great library.[45] I believe that the Villa and its contents together can recall the fashionable *asiatica luxuria* introduced into Roman society from the beginning of the second century B.C.E. and renewed after the conquests made by Sulla.[46] In the Greek world *tryphé*, which corresponds with *luxuria*, represents the distinctive sign of the gods and their houses; in the Hellenistic world the term was subsequently adopted for the kings who inherited Alexander's divine character. Pliny ascribes the origin of the phenomenon to the events related to the inheritance of the king-

41 D'Arms 1970 and 1981, ch. 4, "Luxury, Productivity and Decline: Villa Society on the Bay of Naples," 72–96; Pappalardo 2000; Ciardiello 2007.
42 De Simone 2002.
43 Pagano 1991.
44 Pagano 1994.
45 Mielsch 1999, 89–98.
46 On specific aspects of the *luxuria* in Campania see Pesando 1997, 221–263.

dom of Pergamon, the destruction of Carthage and the victory over Achaea.[47] Pliny remembers also that in Rome statues are made in bronze, but before they were made in wood or terracotta.[48] The assumption of this lifestyle by Roman society is well attested, for example in the moralistic reaction initiated by Cato, which caused the exile of Scipio, as well as in several references against the *luxus* in buildings by Vitruvius.

I personally believe that the Hellenistic *tryphé*, interpreted as an aspiration to regal houses, becomes stronger in the *asiatica luxuria* of the Roman world, in which the improved construction techniques allowed the creation of buildings which have no comparison in the Greek world. Furthermore, novel and typically Roman is a certain sensibility for the use of illusionistic effects in order to widen the domestic spaces, as well as the integration of architecture in natural settings, either by modifying the existing landscape or by constructing an artificial one.[49] The Bay of Naples, the *crater ille delicatus* in Cicero's own definition (*Att.* 2.8.2), was the ideal scenario to carry out such architectural projects.

The Villa of the Papyri is one of the clearest and most significant examples of this phenomenon of regal residences, due to the presence of the library and the collection of sculptures. The investigation carried out so far envisions an exceptional architectural complex in the tradition of Roman *asiatica luxuria*. Further excavations are likely to cast light upon this phenomenon, which deserves a more precise definition.

The decision to continue the Herculaneum excavation is in the hands of the Public Administrators and the Managers of the Ministry of Culture who will act on the basis of archaeological as well as territorial and urban considerations related to appropriate scientific and professional concerns.[50] We can only express personal evaluations on the basis of the experience gained during the 1990s excavation. Naturally, the most important decision is whether to start a new excavation, especially considering the expected results. I believe it is fair to signal the existence of prominent opposite opinions to those I propose below.[51]

47 Plin. *HN* 33.1.48: *Asia, primum deviata, luxuriam misit in Italiam.*

48 Plin. *HN* 34.34: *usque ad devictam Asiam, unde luxuria.*

49 Purcell 1987.

50 Quilici and Longobardi 2007.

51 Guzzo 1998 and 1999.

The earlier excavation of the Villa of the Papyri, which was considered one of the most important archaeological achievements of the 18th century, revealed the presence of one level of a large building complex, 250 m long and 40 m wide. The recent excavations have demonstrated that the Villa is much wider than 40 m and has four levels, three of which are preserved as they appeared at the time of the eruption in 79 C.E.

During the 18th-century excavation, about 80 sculptures were unearthed. It has now been confirmed that the Villa preserves other statues.

It has often been questioned whether other papyri, apart from the ones discovered in the 18th century, are still to be found in the Villa. Examining the position where the papyri were recovered one could hypothesize that part of the collection was being moved from their possible original locations, an issue already considered by other scholars.[52] The distribution of the papyri in various rooms of the Villa and the variability of their grouping, loose or in portable cupboards (fig. 26), suggest that an attempt was made in antiquity to save the papyri by carrying them along an escape route through the rooms of the underlying levels, leading to the beach. So we can imagine the presence of other papyri along this path.

Compared to the uncertainties that the Bourbon exploration raised, the results of the recent investigations can only create expectations that will be hopefully satisfied by further excavations.

Excavating the Villa is not a simple operation, considering a number of problems such as the urban context within which the site is located and the thickness of the volcanic debris covering the area. The extreme complexity of the situation raises concern and issues about the feasibility of the archaeological investigation.

However, part of the site has already been exposed and only the mountainside limits of the monument are covered by modern buildings, while the access from the sea front is completely free.

Furthermore, a new excavation is not incompatible with the modern town of Herculaneum. The surrounding area is in huge decay and asks for projects and interventions. Some projects are already in progress, and others are scheduled such as the restoration of the 18th-century villas in Miglio d'Oro, the redevelopment of the area of Pugliano and the repair of important parts of the urban road network such as Via 4 No-

---

52 Longo Auricchio and Capasso 1987.

vembre and Via Resina. In the context of these activities a new excavation of the Villa and the north-west *Insula* of Herculaneum could be used as stimulus for a process of redefinition of the entire sea-side of the modern town, offering to the modern inhabitants and tourists the real perception of the ancient landscape, which includes the city of Herculaneum together with its suburb where the Villa of the Papyri lies (fig. 27).[53]

53 De Simone 2007a, 80–83.

New Archaeological Research at the Villa of the Papyri in Herculaneum

MARIA PAOLA GUIDOBALDI, DOMENICO ESPOSITO

Introduction

The area of the "New Excavations" ("Scavi Nuovi"), which included the portion of the Villa of the Papyri already unearthed, was officially handed over to the Archaeological Superintendency of Pompeii on the third of August 1999. The excavation and the organization of the site had been up to this point conducted by Infratecna and had been left unfinished. Unfortunately, no necessary planning had been made to guarantee the conservation of the structures and finds after their excavation. Once the area was made available to the Superintendency, it became clear that there was an immediate need for the conservation of structures and finds of the site. The problems that we faced as well as the resources needed to deal with these problems were enormous. The work required in order to ensure the long-term management and enhancement of this complicated site is, it must be stated, immense.

The ancient structures uncovered so far lie about 30 m below the modern ground level: such is the incredible thickness of the volcanic material from the Vesuvius that surrounds the excavation on every side. It forms an enormous wall, on top of which stand the greenhouses, gardens and houses of modern Ercolano, including the Council House.

The environmental situation is complicated by the fact that the level of the ancient beach was about 4 m below the current sea level due to the eruption and the violent phenomena related to it. The archaeological area of Herculaneum is also affected by the water table as the excavations have gone below the level of the ancient shoreline. This can be seen both along the western edge of the ancient city, which corresponds to the ancient beach, and in the area of the New Excavations. The work of drying out both areas affected by ground water, where rainwater obviously gathers as well, can only be carried out by pumps in constant action. The complete efficiency of this system is a vital condition for any conservation or preservation activity, public access and, of course, any further excavation.

The first task of the Superintendency was therefore to plan and install a new and efficient water pumping system, which allowed the water to be removed from the area in March 2002. Once the water had been removed, preliminary urgent draining of the area was carried out. In addition, other works were conducted towards the restoration of the site and its presentability to the public. Furthermore, a visitor route was put in place to allow group visits, which began on the first of March 2003 with a booking system; shortly afterwards audio-guides were also made available.

Visits were temporarily suspended in July 2007, when new works began for the excavation, conservation and enhancement of the area. These were carried out by the Superintendency and financed by the European Community within its Regional Operative Program (P.O.R.) for the Campania Region.

The main aim of these works, particularly those relating to the actual archaeological excavation, was therefore to determine where it was most urgent to improve the general management of the area, to attempt to make the archaeological structures understandable, and to ensure that future planning for managing and restoring the site would be arranged in the best possible way, considering its current form and dimensions.

The large scale of the site as well as the amount of work needed to complete, restore and maintain the already excavated areas posed great problems for the effective management of the site. The general situation was further complicated by the particular shape and position of the site. The first task was to reorganize and improve the water drainage system. Furthermore, it was necessary to rebuild and increase the storage spaces for archaeological material that were erected by Infratecna. The new storage spaces enabled the proper organization of around eight hundred and fifty crates of material from the 1996–1998 excavations, which were duly cleaned and photographed. Only after this large-scale preliminary systemization is it possible to conduct scientific classification of the archaeological finds. Protective shelters were also constructed for all the excavated archaeological structures that were exposed. Finally, a walkway is being built halfway up the escarpment, taking advantage of an artificial platform made during the previous excavations, that will be used both for maintaining the escarpment as well as for creating visitor routes overlooking the site.

The complete publication of the works carried out in the entire area of the New Excavations appeared in 2009 in the *Vesuviana* and a more complete graphic and photographic record will be available in the *Fasti Archeologici on line FOLD&R*. A summary concerning the Villa of the Papyri only appeared in the *Cronache Ercolanesi* in 2009.[1] The English version of this summary is offered in the present publication thanks to the kind invitation of the editor, whom we would like to thank.

The main excavation was carried out between July 2007 and the end of March 2008. The areas of the Villa involved in the excavation are the following (fig. 1): A) the atrium quarter and the Bourbon tunnels on the Villa's main storey; B) the first lower level of the *basis villae*; C) the second lower level of the *basis villae*; D) the terrace with monumental structures overlooking the sea, that is the VPSO area of the Infratecna Excavation.[2] The excavation, directed by the authors of the present article and conducted and documented on the field with great competence and professionalism by Domenico Esposito, has produced results beyond expectation. As will be explained below, the main novelties concern the first lower level of the *basis villae* and the terrace with monumental structures, whose architectural arrangement – albeit still partially unknown in respect of its original setting – now appears significantly different from what was envisaged on the basis of the previous excavation. Further elements of novelty concern the decorative phases and the use of the Villa after the first important building phase that is ascribed to the Second Style period. This phase has been dated by Domenico Esposito to the third quarter of the first century B.C.E., which is in agreement with the chronology proposed by Valeria Moesch for the main core of the sculpture collection of the Villa. On the basis of the structures unearthed so far, the Villa seems to have been much more complex and monumental than previously envisaged, with at least two floors, whose residential use is demonstrated, and a third one for which use as a residential area is probable but not attested (respectively, the main storey and the first lower level of the *basis villae*, and the second lower level of the *basis villae*); and then a grand pavilion with a large rectangular swimming pool that led directly to the beach through a small staircase that faded into and mingled with the natural rock.

At the end of significant, but not definitive, preparatory work carried out during the 2000–2006 Campania P.O.R., we can assess the

1 Guidobaldi et al. 2009; Guidobaldi and Esposito 2009.

2 See below n. 67.

area of the New Excavations with the full confidence that we have properly deployed the available resources to bring a major part of the excavation to a sufficient level of conservation as well as archaeological and architectural understanding. From the latest work, as mentioned earlier, we have obtained not only new fundamental information concerning the Villa's planning, chronology, building as well as decorative phases (not to mention the two monumental complexes now correctly identified as *Insula* I and the north-western *Insula* of the ancient city), but also concrete elements of knowledge with which to organize the next excavations within the actual boundaries of the site as well as possible further enlargements of the area under study. Any short- and medium-term goals relating at least to the Villa of the Papyri must include the completion of the excavation, together with the restoration of the decorative apparatus and the study and publication of all the rooms of the first lower level of the *basis villae*; the repair of the bay-window pertaining to the second lower level of the *basis villae*; the complete excavation of the façade of the Villa at these two levels; the identification of the foundation of the *basis villae* through minor excavation surveys; the repair, cleaning and documentation of the tunnels leading towards the rectangular peristyle; as well as the excavation, and contextual *anastylosis*, of the collapsed structures of the terrace pertaining to the VPSO area.

Even from this brief and limited list – which does not include the equally fundamental and probably even more expensive works necessary for the complete analysis, restoration and evaluation of the thermal baths complex of the north-west *Insula* and the residential building of *Insula* I – we may grasp the resources that will be necessary to find and the effort that must be invested in order to ensure the conservation and the public display of this extraordinary monument as well as the effective management of this extremely fragile, vulnerable and complex archaeological site.

Maria Paola Guidobaldi

The Villa of the Papyri

A.1. The atrium quarter (figs. 2–3)

Very precise interventions have been carried out in the Villa's atrium quarter. The aim of these works was to conclude the excavation of some of the rooms and to clean part of the Bourbon tunnels explored at the end of the 1980 s,[3] in order to obtain a more coherent understanding of the structures explored so far.

The excavation of corridor (h), which connected wing (e) with portico (a) and had two side openings towards rooms (g) and (i), was not conducted at the time of the Infratecna Excavation. The corridor was still full of the backfilling material of a Bourbon tunnel that ran at its entire length, as indicated by Weber's plan. Corridor (h) was cut at its west section, near the openings towards rooms (g) and (i), by a perpendicular tunnel, which ran through the rooms located near portico (a) (that is, rooms s, t, f, b, g, h, i). To avoid possible landslides and the collapse of the structure, the tunnel had been closed with a retaining wall erected with waste material,[4] especially lava fragments and *cubilia* from the collapsed walls found in the stratigraphy cut by the tunnels. Such material is commonly used by the quarry workers ("cavamonti") (fig. 4). The backfilling of the tunnel consisted almost exclusively of wall painting fragments, the majority of which dated to the Second Style, but some also dated to the Fourth Style. The presence of wall painting fragments in the filling of the tunnel suggests that the Bourbon workers used materials taken from the nearby rooms. The walls of corridor (h) were built in *opus reticulatum* with 8–10 cm wide irregularly arranged *cubilia*; they were extensively damaged and in a number of cases the wall surface was missing. Near the opening leading to *ala* (e), the walls of the corridor were cut by a second tunnel which ran in a north-south direction.

Corridor (h) is furnished with mosaics in the *opus tessellatum* technique, or "woven style," where white regular cubic *tesserae* form a white background of oblique courses that is characterized by the irregular dot-

3 On these excavations see De Simone et al. 1998; De Simone and Ruffo 2002, 2003, 2005; De Simone 2007b; and De Simone in this volume.

4 This is the Bourbon wall (MB12) identified at the time of the Infratecna Excavation. See the *Diari di scavo Infratecna*, 100, which can be found at the Ufficio Scavi in Ercolano.

ting of black *tesserae*, limestone fragments and coloured marbles, and can be ascribed to the Second Style (fig. 5).[5] The mural decoration has survived only near the opening to *ala* (e), over the opening made by the Bourbon tunnel. In the upper zone only a panel with a faded and blackened red background is recognizable.[6] The panel of the middle zone is surmounted by a pink curtain held up by a rope depicted as a row of black dots, and above the rope the blue sky is visible.[7] In correspondence to the east end of the south wall a red vertical fascia is painted.

A second excavation was carried out in room (g), where a layer of residual collapsed material of about 1 m^2 was still piled up at its south-east corner. This layer contained the collapsed wall paintings which once decorated that corner of the room (figs. 6–7).[8] A pink pilaster marked the end of the east wall. The pilaster was composed of a series of parallelepipedal drums separated by thin planking undercuts rendered in violet. Identical pilasters were painted at the four corners of the room, in order to give the impression that the pilasters were coupled. On the south wall, the decorative scheme featured a high plinth composed of two superimposed bands, black and dark brown respectively.[9] Above this plinth, there was a dado featuring violet orthostats, placed parallel to the viewer of the wall painting, alternating with yellow ones, placed perpendicular to the viewer of the wall painting, supported by green mouldings. The dado supports a green podium, above which the central tableau is arranged. The latter displays a wall with a red-brown background in a foreshortened view, in which a small double lancet window

5 De Simone and Ruffo 2005, 168.

6 The same phenomenon can be recognized also on the walls of the atrium of the Villa of the Mysteries, where the orthostats of the central tableau had a red background painted with *minium*, which tarnished and displays today a blackened surface.

7 The motif of the curtain that partially discloses the sky behind is very common in the decorative apparatus of the late Second Style. One of the most significant examples is the decoration of the *oecus tetrastylus* (4) of the House of the Silver Wedding. See *PPM* 3, 760, fig. 181.

8 It must be noted that due to the extreme frailty of the stratigraphic context and the complexity of the intervention aimed at recovering the plaster fragments, the excavation was carried out by the restorers with the help of the archaeologist in order to reconstruct the decorative apparatus. It was therefore possible to recover all the collapsed plaster fragments and to reconstruct almost completely the decorative scheme on the south-east corner of the wall.

9 Actually, the black band was painted on a brown background shared with the dark brown band.

enclosed within an ochre yellow frame is painted. The sky visible through the double lancet window gives the impression of an open space. A rich festoon of leaves hangs down from the window and supports a yellow *taenia*. The wall is surmounted by a gilded cornice featuring a shelf. The cornice is embellished with a frieze composed of floral corollas alternating with figures of stylized dragons that support the shelf. The upper part of the wall is supposed to be open with a window, framed on the left by a red cinnabar pilaster with a gilded listel which supports a rich entablature featuring a cornice with denticulations. The latter is crowned with a frieze characterized by a yellow and light blue background that includes a series of masks alternating with dragon-shaped supports that sustain a shelf with red small arches. A panelled ceiling in perspective that is visible behind this rich entablature suggests the presence of another room. The large opening above the gilded shelf is mainly occupied by a *pinax,* in perspective, with two half-closed wickets, which allow one to see a female standing figure wearing a yellow mantle and a blue-grey dress with green and golden hues. The panel in perspective was framed on the right, near the centre of the decorative scheme, by a pink pilaster whose shaft was adorned with a rectangular cavity. The pilaster was connected to a red cinnabar cornice. Unfortunately, the rest of the decoration is missing.[10] On the east wall, the surviving portion of the decorative scheme is more reduced. The plinth and the angular pilaster that frames the wall are identical to the ones on the south wall. The dado, however, takes the shape of a golden-yellow base embellished with a yellow-beige moulding at the bottom, a simple epistyle and an upper cornice featuring a shelf. The dado is also characterized by two *avant-corps* decorated with *Nikai Tropaiophoroi* figures on the main side (fig. 8).[11] The central tableau is positioned at the base of the dado. However, only the decoration painted on the lower part of the wall's south section is still visible. This part of the wall is characterized by a bordeaux-violet red background adorned with painted columns and pillars. Columns with cylindrical fluted shafts and violet Attic bases are placed on the *avant-corps*. A pillar

10 The author is currently studying all the fragments recovered during the old and new excavation campaigns in order to reconstruct the decorative scheme of the entire room.

11 The corresponding *avant-corps* on the other side of the wall was discovered at the time of the Infratecna Excavation, but after that it has completely vanished. See De Simone and Ruffo 2003, 295.

leaning on a grey moulded base was painted almost at the south edge of the wall. The pink parallelepipedal shaft of this pillar displays a rectangular cavity adorned inside with rows of flowers, each flower embellished with eight red and violet petals.

Some fragments of the stucco decoration from the wall's final part and the false ceiling have been recovered during the excavation.[12]

Minor cleaning interventions have been carried out in atrium (c). During the clean-up of the *impluvium* basin, it has been possible to identify the imprints of the slabs removed at the time of the Bourbon excavation in the mortar bed of the *impluvium*. There is also evidence of the passage of a tunnel, which seems to stop at the northern border of the *impluvium*.

Three minor clearing surveys were carried out at the openings towards *tablinum* (b) and *alae* (d) and (e). During these surveys the remains of mosaics adorning the thresholds of these rooms, which were removed during the Bourbon exploration, were recovered.[13]

A limited excavation survey was carried out in room (s) to verify the presence of the pavement.[14] The survey, carried out along the east wall, confirmed that the pavement of the room, in *opus tessellatum*, must have rested upon a flat floor supported by wooden beams, which collapsed at the time of the 79 C.E. eruption.[15] It is probable, therefore, that the floor is still *in situ*, but subsided under several dozens of centimetres of collapsed material.

---

12 The most significant stucco fragments include: the fragment of a cornice with a double smoothed fascia surmounted by a Ionic *kyma* and a white upper section; three fragments of mouldings characterized by a significant projection (at least 20 cm) and decorated with a complex scheme of brackets and lacunars; finally, a fragment pertaining to the ceiling decoration. The latter, which is difficult to relate to any specific section of the ceiling, consists of a cylindric element adorned with a row of elongated triangles and surmounted by a double annulet. An ovoid pointed protuberance enclosed within a corolla or a crown of leaves leans on the annulet. The shape of this object is reminiscent of that of a *thyrsus*.

13 It is probable that these thresholds can be recognized among some of the flooring now stored in the apartments of the Reggia of Portici. Pagano 2001, esp. 337–338 and figs. 5–8.

14 This small portion of pavement had been already identified at the time of the Infratecna Excavation. De Simone and Ruffo 2003, 299.

15 *Diario di scavo Infratecna*, 4-2-1997; De Simone and Ruffo 2003, 299.

A.2. The Bourbon tunnels

The partial exploration of the Bourbon tunnels conducted between 1986 and 1990 aimed to verify the information obtained from Weber's plan and to evaluate the real extension of the Villa's ancient remains in anticipation of a possible *sub divo* excavation. The results of these first attempts were very rewarding, with the exploration of large part of the *gruta derecha* – the tunnel that runs throughout the entire Villa, from the belvedere to the sector of room "V" in Weber's plan – and the so-called library, where the shelves with the papyri were found. Before the open-air excavation of the Villa, the results of these first surveys were partially published in a preliminary form.[16] During the present works of restoration of the atrium quarter, we have cleaned up the Bourbon tunnels that depart from the area of the so-called Pozzo Veneruso and the ones that depart from room (q), which is almost completely excavated, go through Weber's room "o," as far as the north and west ambulatories of the square peristyle, and reach Weber's room "V" through the *gruta derecha*'s terminal section (fig. 9).

The first room accessible through the tunnels is the room indicated by the letter "o" in Weber's plan (fig. 10). The tunnel, which runs from east to west, was excavated along the north side of the room and therefore runs in parallel with the north wall. The north wall is not visible as it is hidden by a Bourbon retaining wall built up with stones, *cubilia* and fragments of roof tiles and pantiles. The west wall was in communication with the adjacent *oecus* (q) through an opening framed with doorposts in *opus vittatum*.[17] The room's flooring is in white *tessellatum*, composed of 1 cm wide *tesserae* forming an oblique course, enclosed within a frame of black *tesserae* inserted between two bands of white *tesserae* with a straight course and a marginal one, towards the edges of the room, of white *tesserae* with an oblique course. At the centre of the floor there is an *emblema* made of black and white *tessellatum*, with *tesserae* forming a straight course and reproducing a net of meanders, swastikas and inscribed squares. The *emblema* was enclosed within a triple frame composed of two bands of black *tesserae* on a white background with a straight course. The two bands frame another fascia in poly-

16 De Simone 1987; Budetta 1988; Conticello and Cioffi 1990.

17 This opening is not signalled in Weber's plan which reports a sort of a niche instead.

chrome *tessellatum* with red, orange, white, black and grey *tesserae* with an oblique course (fig. 11).

Room "o" was characterized by a large opening leading towards the square peristyle. The opening's threshold was decorated with a black and white *tessellatum* mosaic that featured a lozenge-shaped motif enclosed within a double fascia of black *tesserae* (fig. 12).

Beyond this threshold it is possible to reach the north-west corner of the square peristyle (fig. 13). In this area of the excavation it is not possible to recognize structures related to the elevation of the porticoes, the only exception being the north and west colonnades. The columns were built in *opus testaceum*, with tufa bases and capitals carved separately (fig. 14). The bases of the columns are characterized by the Attic profile, while the capitals probably belong to the Ionic typology with four faces. This is demonstrated by the tufa fragment of an Ionic capital found in the filling of the tunnel, which runs along the gutter of the north ambulatory of the square peristyle.[18] The columns were coated with white stucco, which rendered the flutes of the shaft.

The colonnade's flooring is strongly compressed in the centre along the lengthwise axis. The pavement is in white *tessellatum* with *tesserae* placed in an oblique course and embellished by parallel rows of small black crosses. The pavement is framed on the two sides by a fascia of black *tesserae* enclosed within two bands of white *tesserae* in an oblique course. The intercolumniations were decorated with pavements of polychrome *tessellatum* with white, red, orange, black, grey/green limestone rectangular *tesserae* (circa 2 x 1 cm) placed on a basket weave pattern (fig. 15).[19] At some spots, especially along the north ambulatory,

---

18 Half of a tufa four-faced capital, whose dimensions are identical with the capitals of the square peristyle's columns, has been discovered in the deposit of the materials that were recovered during the excavation of the sector of the atrium. Unfortunately, it was not possible to identify the precise area of provenance of this material. The tufa capital is characterized by a squared abacus supported by stylized volutes. Large palmettes framing an Ionic *kyma* are inserted where the volute meets the echinus. An annulet decorated with a row of astragali runs below the *kyma*. For a complete review of this specific typology of capitals, which were widespread in Pompeii and the area of the Vesuvius, see Napoli 1950. Four-faced Ionic capitals are represented in the Second Style paintings from room (11) and (23) of Villa A at Torre Annunziata and in the painting recently discovered on the Padiglione Cavaliere of the Castello Aragonese in Baia: Miniero 2007, 167, fig. 18

19 A comparison is offered by the pavement of *cubiculum* (i) from the House of the Trojan Sacellum (Casa del Sacello Iliaco) and by the pavement of colonnade

these thresholds display evidence of small repairs carried out with black and white square *tesserae* placed on a grid pattern.

The passage to the garden was signalled by a narrow threshold of "bardiglio di Luni" marble. A watercourse runs at the foot of this threshold. The watercourse consists of a series of tufa slabs with a central hollow and a lateral flat parapet. At the west corner of the peristyle a shallow pool is visible whose basement of tufa slabs is enclosed within a slightly raised border.[20] The latter is at the same level of the border of the watercourse (fig. 16). The pool is related to a fountain that consists of a round marble basin – about 85 cm in diameter – and a small supporting small pillar.[21] The fountain was located in front of the bronze herm of the Doryphoros (NM 4885). The herm and its supporting pillar have been found at the west corner of the square peristyle.[22]

The tunnel that goes through the south-west wing of the square peristyle runs along the west side of the portico at its north-west part, from which transverse segments depart towards the intercolumniations of the portico with the purpose of finding statues. The fragment of a lead *fistula* is visible in one of these tunnels. It was probably removed from its original location and brought to the peristyle's floor during the 18th century (fig. 17). In correspondence to the central intercolumniation of the south-west wing of the portico, the tunnel turns eastward and after this point runs next to and in parallel with the columns, which have survived up to 50 cm in height, up to the intersection with the peristyle's south wing (figs. 18–19).

The excavation carried out in the 1980 s from the south corner of the peristyle explored a segment of the *gruta derecha* as far as room "V" in Weber's plan. This area is one of the most intensively explored during the 18th century, and it is therefore extremely difficult to identify the scanty remains of the structures that are still in place. This difficulty is increased by the fact that the walls of the *gruta derecha* are completely covered with supporting pilasters and retaining walls made up of lava

(14) from House of M. Fabius Rufus in Pompeii. *PPM* 1, 1990, 310, figs. 49–50; *PPM* 7, 1997, 960, fig. 23.

20 This basement is 1.80 m wide. The other sides are not visible because they are still unexcavated.

21 "Habiendose hallado tambien en la propria gruta una fuente, cuya taza tiene tres palmos y tres onzas de diametro, y una columnilla con su base." See *Noticia* = *CDP*, 160 = Pannuti 1983, 321.

22 Weber's plan, *Quarta Explicacion*, m = *CDP*, 223 and 160; finally, see V. Moesch in Gudiobaldi 2008, 268, cat. n. 73; Moesch 2008, 78.

and tufa slabs, *cubilia* and fragments of roof tiles and pantiles. Furthermore, all the pavements of this area were systematically removed in the 18th century. Just beyond the south-east wing of the peristyle, it is possible to recognize the so-called *respiradero*, a shaft constructed under Weber's direction for the ventilation of the underground galleries, that was closed together with the tunnels at the end of the excavations. After the *respiradero*, the gallery is reinforced by two walls surmounted by an arch. The space following this arch must correspond to the room just before the so-called library. A mosaic pavement was probably removed from this room.[23] Finally, it is possible to enter room "V," the so-called library, where the shelves with the majority of the papyri recovered from the Villa were stored at the time of the 79 C.E. eruption (fig. 20). The room is now mainly occupied by four large masonry pillars that support the vault of the tunnel, which is cut in a stepped profile in order to better sustain the weight of the earth above and allow the excavators to investigate the entire room. At the moment it is possible to see only a limited part of the south and east walls. Both of them are cut in their lower section by tunnels that branch out to the surrounding rooms. The walls were built in *opus reticulatum* with 7–9 cm wide *cubilia*. Only a small part of the east wall is visible, which is located between two supporting pillars erected at the time of the Bourbon excavation. In this part it is still possible to detect part of the masonry with the facing in *opus reticulatum* of the side towards the room to the east (fig. 21). In the upper part of the wall it is possible to see, in section, large fragments belonging to a collapsed floor in *opus caementicium* with the remains of a cocciopesto pavement. The remains of the floor are mixed with lapilli, fragments of plaster and of an amphora. It is therefore probable that – as already noted in other parts of the Villa – the upper stories were occupied by storage spaces. The south wall is cut by a tunnel and a series of small round holes (the so-called *pruebas*) are visible on the wall's ridge. These holes were excavated in the volcanic deposit to search for other materials (fig. 22). The room, therefore, was systematically deprived of its furniture and decorations. As indicated in the 18th-century excavation report, the mosaic flooring,

23 Weber's plan, V Explication, VII. According to De Petra, the number VII, which is not included in the piñata, may correspond to the dotted square between numbers V and VI. *CDP*, 224, n. 3.

which included a quadrangular central *emblema* in polychrome *tessellatum*, was also removed.[24]

B. The rooms pertaining to the first lower level of the *basis villae*

The west façade of the Villa was unearthed for a length of circa 25 m during the Infratecna Excavation. The excavation revealed the presence of at least two other floors arranged on artificial terraces under the main storey. The existence of these further architectural levels was impossible to envisage on the basis of the Bourbon plans only. At the first lower level of the *basis villae*, located 6.20 m above sea level, the façade, covered with smooth white plaster, is marked by large quadrangular windows. Four of these windows are surmounted by splayed *oculi* (fig. 23). Inside, only a very limited sector of room (I) – located near the north-west corner of the *basis villae* – was explored during the Infratecna Excavation.[25] The excavation was carried out from the window by maintaining the height of the windowsill. At the end of the Infratecna Excavation, a limited part of the east wall and an even more limited part of the north wall were explored and the pavement was identified 90 cm below the windowsill level through a minor excavation survey (see De Simone in this volume, fig. 12). We decided to extend our exploration at least as far as the second, from the north, window that is visible on the façade of the Villa, in order to clarify the arrangement of the first lower level of the *basis villae* and to understand whether the latter consisted of a series of rooms or a windowed corridor, which was hypothesized on the basis of comparison with other buildings from Pompeii.[26] The excavation of room (I) has left no doubt that the first lower level of the *basis villae* did not contain a windowed corridor but a series of at least six rooms. Although these rooms are almost completely filled with the pyroclastic flow deposit, due to the scaffolding

24 "Y habiendo yo observado ayer tarde al tempo que se ha acavado de limpiar la referida estancia, en que estaban los papiros, que se ha descubierto en la misma un bellisimo pavimento de mosaico, que el pedaso de medio de diversos colores puede corrtarse sano de 8 pal^s. en cuadro […]." *CDP*, 170, report dating to the 25 August 1754.

25 Cfr. De Simone and Ruffo 2002, 330–332; 2003, 301–302.

26 M.P. Guidobaldi has suggested that the first lower level of the Villa may have consisted of a windowed corridor similar to that identified in M. Fabius Rufus' urban villa in Pompeii. Guidobaldi in Pesando and Guidobaldi 2006a, 398.

erected to restore the façade plaster, it was possible to identify through the *oculi* the character of the covering of the rooms, which was constructed in *opus caementicium*: in the case of the second room from the north the covering consists of a flat floor covered with painted plaster; in the case of rooms (IV) and (V), the covering consists of a series of vaults oriented in an east-west direction; and in the case of rooms (II) and (IV), some stucco cornices have survived near the lunettes.[27]

The excavation of room (I) was technically difficult and required circa 3 months of work. The room was completely filled up with two overlapping pyroclastic flow deposits which had resulted in the simultaneous collapse of the majority of the stuccoes of the vault. The stucco fragments lie in a sub-horizontal position inside the volcanic stratum – mainly between the first and the second deposits – and had often collapsed in several overlapping and overturned layers.[28] The excavation of the room reached the level of the windowsill that opens onto the façade of the *basis villae*. This window is still the only access available to the room.[29] A further excavation is needed to reach the floor level, which was identified 90 cm below the windowsill level at the time of the Infratecna Excavation.

Room (I) is rectangular (3.80 m x 7.30 m) and composed of two different spaces, an antechamber and a hall or alcove (fig. 24). Two windows opened at the west wall, the window from which the excavation started, and a second window which at the time of the eruption was closed and covered with painted plaster. Two openings are visible on the opposite east wall; they preserve burned wooden doorposts and architraves – probably belonging to windows shared with the rooms located at the back that are not yet excavated. The actual door was located on the north-west corner of the room, which was therefore accessible

27 The covering of room (IV) is decorated with a denticulate motif, which may date back to the primitive Second Style decorative phase of the Villa.

28 The stuccoes have been excavated thanks to the constant and essential support of the restorers, who isolated and recovered each single fragment and at the same time consolidated and cleaned the surface of the stuccoes and of the paintings that were progressively unearthed during the excavation of the vault and the walls.

29 At the time of the excavation, this window still had its jambs as well as three of the four casements of the window-shutter. De Simone and Ruffo 2002, 330–331; 2003, 302.

from rooms located at the north part of the Villa.[30] These rooms are obviously not yet excavated since room (I) forms the limit of the present open-air excavation.

The antechamber is characterized by a ribbed vaulted ceiling, while the hall displays a round vault with a north-south orientation (figs. 25–26). The *oculus* located above the west wall window may have been closed by a small sliding shutter. The burned remains of its frame and sliding shutter have been recovered there.[31]

On the basis of the remains unearthed in the antechamber during the Infratecna Excavation, the wall decoration of room (I) had been dated to a transition phase between the Third and Fourth Style.[32] The completion of the excavation of the room has revealed the presence of a series of overlapping layers of paintings pertaining to different decorative phases dating between the second half of the first century B.C.E. and 79 C.E.

The dado is characterized by a black background and is separated by the central tableau through two narrow listels, respectively white and green. The middle section has a paratactic structure, composed of a series of five panels on the long walls and three panels on the short walls that have a yellow background – turned red.[33] The panels are framed by red cinnabar cornices placed between pairs of white listels (fig. 24). Green fascias are depicted at the corners of the four walls. The panels are decorated on the inside with narrow brown fascias, embellished

30 These rooms should develop at least as far as the line of rooms (s, t, f, b, g, h, i), where it is possible to recognize a phenomenon of collapse of the structures. Furthermore, the pavement of hall (s) rested upon a flat floor supported by beams, clear evidence of the presence of another room under the hall. The arrangement of these rooms is similar to the disposition of the rooms from the first lower level of M. Fabius Rufus' house in Pompeii.

31 Similar systems of shuttering were widespread both in Herculaneum and Pompeii. For example, in the case of Pompeii, see the House of the Ephebe, room (a); the House of Pinarius Cerialis, *triclinium*; Praedia Iulia Felix, room (97); House of the Painters at Work (IX, 12), room (5). In the case of Herculaneum, see House of the Alcove, room (23); House of the Stags, room (26).

32 De Simone and Ruffo 2002, 332; 2003, 302. The same hypothesis was also advanced by M.P. Guidobaldi in Pesando and Guidobaldi 2006a, 398; see also Moormann in this volume, 72 and 78.

33 On each wall, the ochre yellow background of the panels turned red because of the dehydration that the exceptional temperature of the eruption caused. The original hue of the wall background is still partially visible on the south-east corner of the room. Even there, however, the yellow colour presents traces of red.

with stylized vegetal and floral motifs painted in white with overlapping green hues. Paintings featured at the centre of each panel. The central panel of the south wall is decorated with the small reproduction of a villa and the lateral panels display vignettes with flying Cupids. Only one painting has survived on the east wall, in the centre of the last panel on the right, which shows a pigeon standing on a parallelepipedal base covered with flowers. On the west wall, only the painting in the central panel has survived. The painting was just sketched and displays a bird. The panels of the middle zone were separated by narrow compartments with a black background framed by pairs of vegetal *thyrsi* which enclose an elegant decoration. On the south wall, these compartments are surrounded by pairs of outstretched garlands, embellished with white small flowers, which frame vegetal *thyrsi*, from which *rhyta* and Pan-pipes hang down. The *rhyta* and the flutes are separated by panels surrounded by concave pale blue cornices, which contain vignettes with airborne swans, while an octagon with a small mask of the Gorgon type is depicted in the centre. These compartments are surmounted by a small drum in perspective.

On the long walls, the black compartments are surrounded by couplets of vegetal *thyrsi* that support a shell-shaped ceiling. Segments of outstretched garlands are depicted on the inside of the compartments. The garlands are embellished with white and pink small flowers and are connected to each other by ribbons, from which volutes ending in alternatively erect and pendulous floral corollas depart. The outstretched garlands are separated by three medallions with green cornices surrounded by couplets of pink listels. The medallions contain figures of flying Cupids. The panels of the central tableau are crowned with a brown listel that is surmounted by a white fascia. The white fascia is adorned with a row of suspended lotus flowers that alternate with stylized bell-shaped kraters. Above the white fascia, there is a second red cinnabar fascia that is surmounted by a narrow white stucco moulding frame.

The stucco cornice is surmounted by a frieze with a violet background adorned with a series of palmettes enclosed within heart-shaspirals. The palmettes alternate with suspended lotus flowers and are surrounded by stylized floral vine branches. The frieze is crowned with a white stucco moulding. The moulding is decorated with a trefoil Lesbian *kyma* and an indented fascia, which supports the ceiling. The ceiling is surmounted by a smooth crowning on which runs a second Lesbian *kyma*.

The lunette decoration has survived on the room's back wall and on the antechamber's east wall. The decoration, on a white background, is framed at the bottom by an horizontal brown-violet fascia while the arch is surrounded by a red fascia enclosed within a narrow yellow line embellished with palmettes, stylized corollas and a row of green drops (fig. 26). The lunette is decorated on the inside with a pair of crossed vegetal *thyrsi*, from which a *rhyton* and a tambourine hang down. A violet cloth rests upon the *thyrsi* and falls down in three large oval lobes, which are surrounded by an indigo frame. The indigo frame is enclosed within a pair of yellow listels that are decorated with rows of stylized corollas and palmettes. Flying Cupids are depicted in the centre of the drape's lobes. The entire composition is surrounded by three pairs of twigs.

The ceiling of this room is divided into the antechamber and the hall areas. The vault of the antechamber is decorated with frescoes of the transitional Third/Fourth Style. However, only a small portion of the paintings located at the east edge of the central scheme has survived (fig. 25). The central part of the composition is almost completely lost. Only the red cornice adorned with a tapestry border surrounding the central panel has survived. The central panel was probably lozenge-shaped. It is enclosed within a series of vegetal twigs on a white background, from which masks hang down. The panel is also inscribed within an octagon, with four concave sides and four straight sides. The concave sides are framed by dark green fascias embellished with heart-shaped elements, while the straight sides are decorated with small panels with Egyptian blue background that featured Cupids. The panels rest upon an ovoid element decorated with a suspended palmette located between red heart-shaped volutes on a dark green background. The four pendentives of the vaults are decorated with vegetal *thyrsi* in a pyramidal form. The *thyrsi* depart from a Pan's head, whose beard ends in caulis-shaped motives. The *thyrsi* stand out against pairs of square panels that are superimposed by an ovoid form and are decreasing in size. Grapevine racemes depart from the panels on both sides. *Pinakes* enclosed within boxes featuring pairs of theatre masks are placed between the two panels. Under the *thyrsi*, a triangular area with a white background and a red frame features a vignette with an airborne bird.

The vault's decoration is surmounted by an Egyptian blue frieze, on which swans and other airborne birds stand out.[34] The frieze is framed by a pair of fascias, of which the internal one is red and the external one is violet. A stucco cornice surrounds the entire composition. The stucco cornice is embellished with a series of lotus buds framed by pairs of S-spirals located between two smooth mouldings.[35]

The hall is characterized by a vaulted stucco ceiling dating to the first decorative phase of the Villa – the Second Style (fig. 27). The rich decorative scheme embellished with lacunars is surrounded by a smooth double ribbing and a cornice decorated with ovoli. The diverse panels are characterized by a bright polychrome decoration. Red, Egyptian blue and light blue colours are employed for the background of the lacunars and for the listels framing the different cornices.

The decorative scheme features parallel fascias that alternate with square panels embellished with acanthus inflorescences and rectangular panels. The acanthus inflorescences frame either lozenge-shaped panels with a central rosette surrounded by a Lesbian *kyma* or square metopes embellished with large corollas surrounded by cornices with 'sea waves' motive. In the central section of the vault, which is almost completely collapsed, there are panels decorated with rectangular frames enclosed by triangles with inscribed lozenges decorated with vegetal motifs.

The most interesting element of the entire composition is a pair of rectangular panels, from which only the panel on the east side of the vault has survived. The panels are surrounded by an Ionic *kyma* and decorated with a white stucco frieze that represents a pile of weapons on a red background (fig. 28).[36] The weapons are represented with extreme accuracy.[37] Some weapons of the Hellenistic tradition are attested and some eastern and "barbarian" weapons, but especially prominent are weapons typical in North Europe. Defensive weapons include: a breastplate with corset, two greaves, nine helmets and fourteen shields. Offensive weapons include: a two-edged axe, a *gorytos* with a sheaf of arrows, two swords, a *machaira* and three spears. It is possible to recognize different typologies of shields: the flat round shield with a round-studded

34 Unfortunately, the figures of the birds are almost completely invisible due to their precarious conditions of conservation.

35 The stucco frame on the west wall displayed the same motif, roughly engraved in the fresh stucco without adopting any stamp.

36 Polito 1998.

37 The entire composition seems to have been hand-made, without the adoption of any mould. The use of the stick is widespread.

umbo;[38] the mixtilinear shield with a central umbo;[39] the oval shield with a spindle-shaped spine or a central umbo;[40] the rectangular shield,[41] and its semi-cylindrical variant with a spindle-shaped spine; the hexagonal shield;[42] the Amazon pelta, both in the variant with one concavity[43] and in the variant with two concavities; and, finally, a rare figure-of-eight shield with two concavities.

All the shields present incised decorations realized with the stylus, mainly lozenges containing bundles of lightning bolts, volutes with opposed S-shaped motifs and radial decorations for the round shields. The borders of the shields are decorated with round studs. The helmets are mainly of the type that has a hemispheric crown with nape shield, cheek pieces and a movable frontal reinforcement. Some examples are decorated with crests. The following are distinguished among the offensive weapons: two short swords with the hilt characterized by a hemispheric knob,[44] a *machaira,*[45] a two-edged axe and a *gorytos* full of arrows, which make reference to the Amazons or at least to the East. A trumpet (*carnyx*) ending with the head of a fantastic/imaginary animal, probably a dragon,[46] appears in the left part of the frieze.

The frieze decorated with weapons from the Villa of the Papyri belongs to a well-known figurative tradition, although in its genre it is a *unicum*. In fact the motif of the pile of weapons surely reproduce famous models, dating to the late Hellenist period, such as the friezes that dec-

38 This shield, of probable Nordic or Celtic origin, spread in Roman friezes from the end of the Republican period. Polito 1998, 40.

39 This shield, of probable Nordic origin, is present in Roman friezes dating between the late Republican and early Imperial period. Polito 1998, 40.

40 Polito 1998, 42.

41 This kind of shield was widespread during the late Republic and rarely also during the Imperial time. Polito 1998, 43.

42 This typology of shield is considered to be Germanic, or at least characteristic of the Northern populations. Polito 1998, 43

43 This is especially present in Roman friezes dating back to the late Republican and the early Imperial periods. Polito 1998, 45.

44 This kind of sword could be a *gladius*, a weapon introduced in the Roman army at the end of the Republican period. However, it can be also related to the gladiatorial ambit and the Northern populations. It generally appears in late Republican and proto-Imperial friezes only. Polito 1998, 55, 202, fig. 142, 168, figs. 109, 170 and 112.

45 Polito 1998, 54.

46 Polito 1998, 59. It is peculiar that a very similar motif, the protome of a bird or a dragon projecting from an acanthus tuft, is in one of the panels located in the lower part of the ceiling.

orated the balustrades of the porticoes of the sanctuary of Athena Polias in Pergamon.[47] Numerous and relevant are the comparisons with the carved friezes from both public and private monuments that started to spread in Rome starting from the late Republican period.[48]

Much rarer are the comparisons with friezes depicting weapons that are painted or realized in stucco. The most interesting example is offered by the friezes with painted weapons on the walls of the atrium of the Villa of the Mysteries in Pompeii, dating to around 80 B.C.E.[49] These friezes framed wooden *pinakes* – now completely lost – which probably celebrated war campaigns.[50] A similar frieze, mainly composed of weapons from the Western barbaric world, decorated the walls of cubiculum (q) from the House of the Trojan Sacellum (Casa del Sacello Iliaco) in Pompeii. This house was originally joined to the House of the Cryptoporticus, where the room from which the house took its name was decorated with a coffered ceiling with polychrome stucco featuring, as an isolated motive in the centre of the lacunars, oval shields and *sicae*.[51]

Single weapons motifs are also included in the stucco decoration of the lacunars pertaining to the libraries and other rooms of the House of Augustus[52] and in the coffered ceiling from the so-called Villa of Galba at Frascati.[53] The aforementioned examples date to between the third quarter and the end of the first century B.C.E. The paintings and the stuccoes of the House of the Cryptoporticus and of the House of the Trojan Sacellum date to between 40 and 25 B.C.E. The stucco frieze from room (I), as well as all the Second Style decorations recovered so far from the Villa, can be consistently dated to phase IIa of the Second Style, according to the classification of Beyen.[54] It is therefore possible

---

47 Polito 1998, 90–95, with previous bibliography.

48 See the numerous examples in Polito 1998, esp. 121–189.

49 On the chronology of the Second Style frescoes from the Villa of the Mysteries see Esposito 2007, esp. 448–453.

50 Polito 1998, 127–129; Esposito 2007, 461–462.

51 Polito 1998, 131, fig. 63.

52 On the weapons motifs that embellished the ceilings of libraries (8) and (8bis) as well as of other rooms from the House of Augustus see Polito 1998, 129–130, figs. 56–62.

53 Polito 1998, fig. 64.

54 Beyen 1938–1960.

to suggest a date between 40 and 25 B.C.E. for the Second Style decorative phase of the Villa of the Papyri as well.[55]

The paintings and stuccoes decorating the walls and ceiling of room (I) from the first lower level of the *basis villae* underwent at least two phases of restoration and repair. The wall decoration was completely renovated during the Claudian period and can be dated to the final phase of the Third Style.[56] The most convincing comparisons, both for the general scheme and the decorative details, are with the paintings of the House of M. Lucretius Fronto in Pompeii,[57] the House of the Tuscan Colonnade (Casa del Colonnato Tuscanico) at Herculaneum[58] and the Villa of the Pisanella (Villa della Pisanella) at Boscoreale.[59] All these examples date to phase IIb of the Third Style, according to the classification of Bastet and de Vos.[60]

The Third Style paintings from room (I), however, show clear evidence that further works of restoration were still taking place at the time of the eruption. In the centre of the east wall, the workers were still applying some red paint on the fascia between the central tableau and the frieze (fig. 29).[61] On the west wall, the central panel of the central zone features a small unfinished picture of a bird that was still in the sinopia stage. The same unfinished condition is also noticed in the stuccoes of the ceiling. In fact, the excavation enabled us to observe that whereas the east half of the vault was completed the west half was not. The large panel with weapon trophies on the west side of the vault was

55 For the chronology of the Second Style of the Villa of Papyri see also Moormann in this volume, 65–71.

56 The paintings from room I can be dated to phase IIb of the Bastet and de Vos classification, or can at least be related to those paintings of transition to the Claudian Age dating between 35 and 45 C.E. according to the Ehrhardt classification. Bastet and De Vos 1979, 62–99; Ehrhardt 1987, 93–132.

57 Peters 1993.

58 Manni 1974, 16–20, tabl. IV-VIII.1; Esposito 2005, 138–141.

59 Bastet 1977; Bastet and De Vos 1979, 68–69.

60 On the chronology of the paintings from the House of M. Lucretius Fronto see Peters 1993, 276–277. On the chronology of the paintings from the Villa of the Pisanella in Boscoreale see Bastet 1976, Bastet and De Vos 1979, 68–69. On the chronology of the paintings from the House of the Tuscan Colonnade see Manni 1990, 137–139; Bastet 1976; Bastet and De Vos 1979, 69 and 89, n. 124; Ehrhardt 1987, 128–132, 151; Esposito 2005, 138.

61 It is also significant the great difference in the execution of the motif with lotus flowers and kraters, which indicates that at least two different painters were restoring the frescoes of the room.

even lacking the entire composition – the only exception being the tip of a spear featuring at the upper left corner (fig. 30). The same situation has also been noticed in the antechamber, where the decoration of the vault is almost complete on the east half while the west half is still unfinished (fig. 25). The excavation has shown exceptional evidence that the painters were still working on the paintings at the time of the eruption. In fact the remains of a wooden structure, which was probably a scaffolding, were recovered at the base of the walls (fig. 31).

It is therefore clear that at the moment of the 79 C.E. eruption restoration works were still carried out in room (I) of the *basis villae*, probably in order to restore the damage caused to the building by the increasing and violent seismic activity that must have preceded the final explosion of Vesuvius.

C. The rooms of the second lower level of the *basis villae*

The floor of first lower level of the *basis villae* is indicated by a stringcourse on the façade of the Villa (height 24 cm; depth 26 cm), which suggests the presence of a further level. During the Infratecna Excavation, a structure protruding in respect to the front of the *basis villae* was discovered at the west end of the façade (fig. 32). This apsidal or at least curvilinear *avant-corps* is marked by a series of large windows (1.75 m wide; 1.40 m high).[62] The windows are framed by posts in *opus vittatum,* which are protected by wooden *antepagmenta* (7 cm wide), and are crowned with wooden architraves (7 cm high) and flat arches in *opus vittatum,* in which small tufa blocks and tiles alternate. The windows are closed by pairs of wooden shutters secured to the *antepagmenta* through bronze hinges that were reinforced with bronze plates fixed on them through iron nails. The windowsill consists of a flat arch in *opus vittatum* (40 cm high) coated with a layer of hydraulic mortar (3 cm thick). There is a second row of windows under the flat arches. The windows of the lower row have the same dimensions

62 At the time of the Infratecna Excavation it was possible to see only the upper part of two windows. During the last 10 years, however, the ground water infiltrations has caused a continuous landslide of the pyroclastic filling, undermining the stability of this notable architectural feature to the point that it has been necessary to shore it up. On the other hand, the partial emptying of the pyroclastic filling due to these water infiltrations has revealed new elements of this structure and have enabled its more accurate understanding.

as the windows of the upper row. They are closed at the bottom by a 1.50 m high windowsill, which is placed on a curvilinear base coated with hydraulic mortar. Only a small part of the windowsill is visible in the section of the excavation.

The *avant-corps* was therefore an imposing and airy 5.50 m high bow window structure.[63] It was furnished with ten windows arranged on two levels, all of which were bolted at the time of the eruption. Inside the bay-windows the space is still almost entirely filled up with volcanic material. However, it is possible to see a small portion of the south wall, which seems to be covered with white undecorated plaster. The roof, as already signalled by the previous excavators,[64] was composed of a flat cocciopesto floor with a related border in *opus caementicium* that rested upon a wooden planking. The latter was sustained by round beams (diameter: circa 22 cm) arranged at a regular distance (circa 45 cm). The cocciopesto floor reached the front of the Villa's atrium more or less at the same level of the pavement of the rooms located on the first lower level of the *basis villae* and in continuity with a moulding that operated as a string-course frame between the two levels.

At the opposite end of the façade to the bow window structure, the cleaning operation has revealed for the first time the presence of a circular cocciopesto layer with an oblique course.[65] This layer is part of a cone shaped ceiling belonging to another *avant-corps* that must have articulated the design of the Villa's façade. Also in this case, the structure was probably not higher than the string-course located between the first and the second lower levels of the *basis villae*.[66]

Finally, the articulation of the façade of the Villa of the Papyri is further defined by another element that was found in the area located immediately south-west of the façade of the *basis villae*. In this area, inside the area of the excavation, a 50 cm long portion of the white plastered façade has been discovered. This small portion of the front is located at a

63 The appearance of this bow window is very similar to that of room (62) from the House of M. Fabius Rufus in Pompeii. However, the dimensions and proportions of the bow window from the Villa of the Papyri were even more monumental.

64 De Simone and Ruffo 2002, 330; 2003, 301.

65 This structure was very difficult to detect also because it was dismantled at the ground level.

66 Unfortunately, at the time of the present intervention it has been impossible to carry out the excavation beyond this point. For this reason we have preferred to signal the existence of this structure for future research.

slightly lower level in respect to the string course and therefore pertains to the second lower level of the *basis villae*, to which the bow window structure located at the north-west corner of the façade also belongs. A square window opens into this wall, which is almost completely invisible, except for a short segment of the upper part that is covered with a wooden cornice. The window opening lit up a vaulted room, which is now almost completely filled up with volcanic material.

The window opening is crowned with a smooth entablature (50 cm high), which is surmounted by a sharp projecting moulding (40 cm high). The latter consists of three superimposed stucco cornices, framed by pairs of listels and separated by smooth fascias.[67] The moulding is crowned with a string-course whose upper margin has a slightly convex curvilinear profile. Two superimposed cocciopesto layers (18 cm and 12 cm thick respectively) rest upon the moulding margin (fig. 33).

From the partial observation of this interesting architectural element, it is clear that the part of the Villa of the Papyri located to the south-west of the atrium is arranged in a series of vaulted rooms which may have supported an uncovered area, possibly a terrace.[68]

67 The first two cornices are almost completely identical in their dimensions (height: 6 cm; width of the decorative motif between two lotus buds: 9.5 cm) and are characterized by a decorative motif of upright palmettes inscribed within semicircles and separated by lotus buds (Riemenschneider 1986, ornament 141). The third cornice is slightly smaller than the others (height: 4 cm; width of the decorative motif: 8.5 cm) and is decorated with erected palmette separated by pendulous lotus buds within "S" volutes.

68 It must be noted that this area was explored at the time of the Bourbon excavation. The Bourbon tunnels are clearly reported in Weber's map. De Petra suggests that this area was the one excavated between August and December 1755 and January and April 1756 and identified as a "giardino co' dolii" (garden with dolia) (red numbers 13, 42, 43). A small artificial ditch which brought water to the large terracotta dolia ("un canaletto fabbricato che portava l'acqua in vari grandi dolii di terracotta") was discovered in this area in January 1758 (red no. 42 in Weber's map: see *CDP*, 234).

D. The terrace with monumental structures (VPSO area)

A large rectangular terrace was unearthed at the south-west of the Villa of the Papyri during the Infratecna Excavation.[69] The terrace is oriented north-east/south-west and is therefore coaxial to the Villa. This structure is located 2.50 m above sea level and after the present excavation can be almost positively identified as the part of the Villa built nearest to the ancient shoreline (figs. 34–35).

The terrace, which is not yet completely unearthed, measures 22.50 m along the south-west front and 15 m along the north edge, while the wall that encloses the terrace at the south has been excavated for a length of circa 8 m.[70] The east limit of the terrace is still unknown. The excavation of this feature will require the reconfiguration of the routes of circulation and visit that are unfortunately, but necessarily, arranged on the basis of the ramps formed during the first open-air excavation. These ramps lie on collapsed structures that are still unexcavated. However, if we take into account the presence – upstream – of the south-west portion of the façade of the *basis villae*, which is located between the atrium quarter and the area of the lower terrace, it is possible to suggest that the lower terrace itself must have been a square structure of circa 22.50 m width.

The flooring of the terrace consists of a bed in *opus caementicium*, with the only exception of a small area of red cocciopesto pavement that has survived near the south part of the west wall of room VPSO (a). This cocciopesto layer dates to the construction phase of the terrace and appears to have been almost completely dismantled at the time of the eruption. In the south-west area of the terrace a dismantled wall with a north-east/south-west direction has been recognized. This wall runs alongside the west wall of room VPSO (a), as far as the wall that encloses the terrace at the south. The latter, which is coated with red plaster on the side facing the terrace, has survived only up to 80 cm in height. A heap of earth and stones was piled against this wall, clear

69 During the Infratecna Excavation, this area was labelled VPSO (**V**illa dei **P**apiri area **S**ud-**O**vest). A large room located within the terrace, to which we turn later, was labelled VPAB. During the present excavation, we have maintained the label VPSO to indicate the entire lower terrace. Nonetheless, we have also chosen to identify with small letters all the different areas recovered during the excavation. It must be noted that the VPAB room of the Infratecna Excavation has been labelled VPSO (a) and the terrace which surrounds it VPSO (b).

70 This 42 cm thick wall is built in *opus reticulatum*.

evidence that there were construction and restoration works in progress in this area as well at the time of the eruption.

A big room located at the centre of the lower terrace was found during the Infratecna Excavation, of which only the south-west corner was excavated, for an area of circa 50 m^2.[71] The room is a large rectangular hall constructed in *opus reticulatum* with yellow tufa *cubilia* (7 cm a side). The pilasters, straight arches and relieving arches of the hall are built in *opus testaceum* with the employment of bipedal tiles and simple tiles (3.7 cm thick). The walls are externally covered with a thick layer of white plaster that features a decoration composed of engraved lines, probably an imitation of a covering with marble slabs.

The façade of the monumental hall is 10.80 m wide and is characterized by a big opening at the centre (6.60 m wide). This opening is embellished with a white marble doorstep, composed of four slabs (1.20 m long and 60 cm wide), with a raised internal margin (12 cm wide). The slabs present four square cavities located at regular distances, which were used to insert the iron pins necessary to secure the door wings.[72] The west façade is framed by a pair of large L-shaped composite pillars. These pillars are composed of a rectangular pilaster and three-quarters of a circular column joined together. The pillars are placed on a curvilinear base that is covered with light pink plaster. Both the pilaster and the column are covered with a thick white stucco layer that reproduces a fluted shaft. The pilasters are surmounted by corinthianizing capitals.[73]

Large windows (2.14 m wide) open in the lateral walls of the hall. These windows are framed by rectangular pillars marked by a pilaster on the external front. The pillars are constructed in *opus testaceum* (4.60 m high). They are crowned with architraves composed of two superimposed rows of three beams, which are enclosed within a row of bipedal tiles and surmounted by a flat arch with an *opus testaceum* relieving arch and an upper *opus reticulatum* face. The pillars were protected by wooden *antepagmenta* (16 cm thick). Part of a shutter belonging to one

71 It must be said that this room does not present the same orientation of the terrace on which it is located, as suggested at the time of the Infratecna Excavation (De Simone and Ruffo 2002, 333; 2003, 303), but it is slightly rotated in a north-west/south-east direction.

72 De Simone and Ruffo 2002, 335; 2003, 305.

73 One of these capitals is still visible on the north pillar that has collapsed on the terrace floor. At the time of the Infratecna Excavation, a wooden *antepagmentum* with the remains of a curtain was still attached to the capital.

of the lateral windows has been found near the south wall. It is decorated with a series of mouldings. The hall had a flat roof that featured a cocciopesto floor supported by wooden beams.[74] Some of the wooden beams were more than 6 m long.[75]

Taking into account the height of the pillars that framed the doors and the windows, the height of the wall faces placed above the architraves and the flat arches, as well as the thickness of the cocciopesto floor and of the parapet which may have protected the upper terrace, it is possible to calculate a maximum height of 7.60–8 m for the hall. This would mean that hall VPSO (a) was as high as the front of the entire *basis villae* of the atrium quarter.

The monumental character of the hall's architecture is matched by the wealth of the decorative display presented in the interior of the hall, which emphasizes the public character of the building. The pavement is in *opus sectile* with an extremely elegant decoration of coloured marbles, such as giallo antico and rosso antico. This pavement, which was cleaned of volcanic material during the present excavation, is generally missing. The removal of the slabs must have taken placed in antiquity, since no evidence of the passage of the Bourbon tunnels was found in this area.[76]

The decorative scheme of the pavement may be reconstructed on the basis of the surviving elements (fig. 36): a double slate fascia (thickness: 4.4 and 6.3 cm) runs along the walls of the hall and frames a marginal band composed of giallo antico lozenges (29 cm wide), arranged in three rows along the west wall and in six rows along the south wall and separated by rosso antico listels (8 mm thick); a second slate fascia (10 cm thick) framed by two other rosso antico listels separates the edge frill from the central area of the pavement, which is composed of square giallo antico tiles framed by rosso antico listels.[77]

74 De Simone and Ruffo 2002, 335; 2003, 305.

75 One of the beam is still *in situ* in the same position in which it collapsed and is 6.60 m long.

76 It is reported that during the Infratecna Excavation only "due frammentarie fasce parallele, in marmo bianco (ampie cm 10), poste a una distanza di cm 80, che delimitano una preparazione di malta al cui interno si evidenziano i segni della messa in opera di piastrelle di marmo quadrangolari, non rinvenute" were unearthed: cfr. *Diario di Scavo Infratecna*, 21-7-1997 and 29-7-1997; De Simone and Ruffo 2002, 336; 2003, 305.

77 The pavement of this room is still a mixed *opus sectile* floor, with the employment of both marble and non-marble elements. Typologically, the pavement of

The opulence of the pavement is matched by the marble *crustae* decoration along the lower part of the walls, up to a height of 1.10 m. A low plinth of African marble (12 cm high) runs along the walls and is crowned with a white marble moulding cornice, on which a covering of rectangular African and giallo antico marble slabs is placed (height of the slabs: 70 cm). A second moulding cornice runs above this row of slabs, on top of which a second row of rectangular slabs made of African, *bardiglio* and *cipollino* marbles (22 cm high) is placed.

The upper part of the pillars is decorated with white almost-beige plaster, framed by simple red fascias. Two masonry bases are located at the south-west and north-west corners of the hall. The bases are characterized by an irregular cavity and are covered with marble slabs and an African marble plinth. *Bardiglio* slabs framed above and below by white marble mouldings are located on the plinth. The two bases probably supported statues, such as the Peplophoros and the so-called Amazon discovered during the Infratecna Excavation (see De Simone in this volume, figs. 17–20).[78]

Outside terrace VPSO (b), a wall which was supposed to have delimited the terrace on the west side was discovered during the Infratecna Excavation. This wall was considered to be a small parapet (20 cm high; 30 cm wide) with an external "double step" masonry.[79] A small rectangular structure was also identified near the south-west corner of the terrace, which was interpreted as a pool due to the thick hydraulic mortar layer on its walls.[80] Three masonry steps were identified to the south of this structure, which were interpreted as part of a staircase leading to the beach.[81] On the basis of these elements, it was suggested that area VPSO may have been a landing place – a monumental access to the Villa from the coast.[82]

---

hall VPSO (a) is similar to the floor from Sacellum B of the Herculaneum Sacred Area, where the same marbles with the same decorative arrangement (central area with square slabs enclosed within a marginal fascia of lozenges) were adopted. It is probable that, due to the exceptional standard of both the complexes, the same workers built the two. For the typological description of the pavement see Guidobaldi and Olevano 1998, 233–234.

78 On the two sculptures see Moesch 2008, cat. no. 6–7, 249, with previous bibliography.

79 De Simone and Ruffo 2002, 332; 2003, 303.

80 *Ibidem.*

81 De Simone and Ruffo 2002, 333; 2003, 303.

82 De Simone and Ruffo 2002, 342–343; 2003, 309.

In order to verify these hypotheses, a first minor trench was excavated near the "double step" wall, which was almost immediately recognized as the border of a monumental swimming pool (width: 5 m, length: 18.30 m, depth: 2 m) (fig. 37).[83] The walls of the swimming pool are covered with a light pink hydraulic mortar layer (average thickness of 2.5–3 cm), on top of which a thin layer of limestone is placed. A moulding of hydraulic mortar with oblique profile is visible at the bottom of the swimming pool. A lead *fistula*, serving the water supply of the pool, was found on the south wall of the basin, and a drainage hole was found on the south-east corner. The first two steps of a masonry staircase, which were used to enter the swimming pool, were identified at the north-east corner of the pool, against the north wall.[84] Large fragments of collapsed walls including extensive portions of *opus testaceum* and *opus reticulatum* masonry were found near the staircase, where they must had been dragged by the violence of the surges. These fragments probably belong to the pilasters and the upper part of hall VPSO (a). Among the several collapsed walls, the fragment of an angular pillar stands out. The pillar is constructed in *opus testaceum* and furnished with marble *crustae* on the inside, with rectangular slabs of African marble, which are crowned with a cornice moulding surmounted by two horizontal fascias.[85] A layer of rubble and volcanic sand covering the bottom of the pool was identified under the collapsed walls.

After completing the excavation of the south area of swimming pool VSPO (c), the trench was enlarged to the south east of the terrace in order to clarify the nature and function of the so-called pool and of the small stonework staircase that was discovered during the Infratecna Excavation.

The staircase – VPSO (e) – could be reached through a very narrow opening, barely 50 cm wide, which is located at the south-west corner

83 A very small portion of the swimming pool has been excavated at the time of the present works. Unfortunately, it was partially cut by the ditch built to drain the water table at the time of the Infratecna Excavation.

84 Also this staircase was cut by the Infratecna ditch built to drain the water table.

85 The slabs were fixed to the wall through bronze cramps. Some of the cramps are still attached to the wall face and are located within a 3–4 cm thick mortar layer.

of terrace VPSO (b) (figs. 38–39).[86] The staircase is built in *opus caementicium* and is completely covered with hydraulic mortar.[87] After the fourth step, a ramp – VPSO (f) – begins, which is characterized by a very slight east-west slope,[88] and widens as it reaches the wall that delimits the south side of swimming pool VPSO (c). This latter extends toward the coast with an *opus reticulatum* wall. A 1.30 m long portion of the wall's ridge, characterized by a curved profile, was unearthed. The enlargement of the excavation in the area south of the ramp – VPSO (f) – revealed the presence of volcanic layer, which is characterized by an almost tufa-like texture and strongly adheres to the walls. Unfortunately, the vicinity of the ditch built to drain the ground water did not allow us to enlarge the excavation in this area. It has therefore been impossible to reach the ancient ground level in the area south of ramp VPSO (f).

The small structure VPSO (d), which was identified by the first excavators as a pool on the basis of the thick hydraulic mortar layer on its wall, is located north of staircase VPSO (e). The present excavation revealed that this structure is a small room (3 x 1,80 m). The walls, which have survived up to a height of no more than 1.20 m, are built in *opus reticulatum* with angular scarf-joints and door frames in *opus vittatum*. The entrance is located at the west side of the room towards ramp VPSO (e) and is barely 70 cm large. The remains of a decoration with very faint vegetal motifs and shrubs have survived on the external south wall. The inside of the room was not investigated during the present excavation for reasons of preservation. However, it was possible to identify a red monochrome frieze with a scene of *symplegma* between pygmies or dwarfs on the east wall (fig. 40). The presence of this frieze, which probably stretched out along the other walls of the room, demonstrates the residential use of this room – which was very small but prominently located on the ramp that allowed the Villa's inhabitants to reach the sea from terrace VPSO (b).

Domenico Esposito

---

86 During the excavation, the door was also found. Only one leaf of the door has survived, characterized by two bronze hinges with trapezoidal wings, which were still attached to the remains of the frame.

87 Width of the steps: 1 m; tread: 30 cm; riser: 30 cm.

88 Elevation found in the excavated area: max + 1.60 m above sea level.; min. + 1.37 m above sea level.

D.1. The wooden furniture lined with ivory

On the eastern side of room VPSO (a), very close to the limit of the excavation trench and in an area greatly affected by groundwater flooding, the remains of a few wooden pieces of furniture covered in ivory reliefs decorations were found. These pieces of furniture may have been left voluntarily in this spot, but it also possible that they came from some rooms behind room VPSO (a) and were dragged there by the might of the surge. The recovery of the furniture during the excavation and its restoration in the lab were extremely difficult. The entire layer containing the items was removed and transported to the restoration lab of Maria Labriola (Consorzio Pragma), which took care of the wooden finds discovered at the time of the present excavation and restored the ones recovered during the previous excavations by Infratecna.[89] The very first items found in autumn 2007 were restored and presented on December 4, 2007 in a press conference held by the Superintendency at the former Chiesa di S. Marta al Collegio Romano in Rome. There, it was hypothesized that the two big fragments that were available at that time[90] may have been part of the legs of a wooden throne (*solium*), a sort of a chair provided with a back rest and arms that, for the Roman period, has been known up to this point only through images.[91] Further analysis in the lab revealed information that did not fit well with the *solium* hypothesis. It is now clear that correct identification and reconstruction of the furniture will be possible only when all the isolated fragments are consolidated and studied together.[92] Above all,

89 We would like to thank Maria Labriola and her team for the exceptional work that they have conducted as well as the excellent analysis and documentation that they have produced, which forms as the basis for our brief discussion here.

90 These two fragments are now identified as element 1a of furniture piece 1 and element 1 of furniture piece 4.

91 Guidobaldi 2007. On the *solium* see De Carolis 2007, 114–120.

92 The need to carry out an analysis of the different fragments compatible with the precarious conditions of their conservation suggested the use of 3D analysis, which allows the restorer to minimize the manipulation of the finds. In fact, the only action required is the examination with a laser scanner. 3D analysis was carried out by the Ditta Tebec at Priverno through FARO ScanArm™ technology, which allows the researcher a resolution of 0,025 mm. The accuracy and the high resolution of the 3D analysis already carried out will be useful for creating 1:1 exact copies of each piece as well as containers for storing the originals, through systems of production assisted by computer (CAM) and ma-

it will be fundamental to complete a resin reproduction of the individual items together with their missing parts, which will be virtually reconstructed on the basis of an interpretative model.[93] This resin reproduction will be elaborated using the 3D analysis of the finds, which was already carried out at the beginning of the restoration process. The amount of work needed for the completion of the restoration and conservation of these items is still enormous; however, we can now present some certain facts due to the work already carried out by the team of the Consorzio Pragma lab which, as already mentioned, has conducted a preliminary investigation and 3D analysis of the finds.

First, the 3D reconstruction, which has demonstrated the compatibility of the single pieces, suggests that the objects under examination are indeed "legs," belonging to at least four different pieces of furniture of the same typology – probably tripods that were possibly already taken apart before the eruption (fig. 41).[94]

The wooden elements appear to be mineralized, partially burnt on their surface and characterized by a quite compact structure (especially in the case of supporting elements) and of major thickness. On the latter, marks of carving are still clearly visible. The thinner pieces appear to be broken and in some cases deformed because of their position in the deposit. In order to preserve these objects it is essential to maintain the

chines for the rapid production of the prototype. In this way the restorer will be able to manipulate the digital copies in order to reconstruct the object.

93 In spring 2009 the Superintendency was able to assign Ditta Tebec, which had already carried the 3D analysis, the task of producing a resin model of all the finds and of the missing parts. The production of the resin model, which is essential to understanding and rebuilding each item, is a fundamental part of the definitive restoration process. This project also includes the testing of the consolidation treatments, which have been assigned to Istituto per la valorizzazione del legno e delle specie arboree of the CNR-IVALSA.

94 The system of installation/fitting of the whole item has been understood on the basis of the position of element 1b of piece 2 as well as some of the adjacent elements. A wooden element characterized by a curved ending (C3) is the base of the furniture piece and rests directly upon the ground. Another wooden element characterized by a smooth horseshoe-shaped veneer (D3) is placed on C3. The ivory lion leg is located above these elements. It is equipped with a square cavity that allowed the user to insert the leg. Under the lion leg there is a wooden and ivory round frame (R). Very interesting too was the recovery of the ties (Z4) which probably converged towards the centre of the round furniture piece. An ivory knob is placed in the centre of these ties. A fragment of the knob was recognized by the restorers among the sporadic materials brought to the lab separated by layer (U4).

same conditions in which they were found at the moment of the excavation; for this reason they are constantly kept humid and in sealed chests, in an anaerobic environment and at present stored in a climatic room in the Deposito archeologico degli Scavi di Ercolano that has been provided by Consorzio Pragma. The anatomical analysis (xylotomia), carried out by Dr. Macchioni (Istituto per la valorizzazione del legno e delle specie arboree of the CNR-IVALSA), has demonstrated that the kind of wood used was mainly ash (*Fraxinus excelsior).*

The wooden structure of each piece is lined with an ivory veneer of variable thickness: between 1 and 3 mm at its plain surface, between 2 and 12 mm at the mouldings and between 1.5 and 8 mm at the bas-reliefs; while the lion-shaped legs reach a full volume and are made out of a single piece of wood. The trace of a thin silver layer has been identified on one of the lion-shaped legs.

The dark brown colour that the hard and compact ivory has assumed is probably due both to the move and absorption of the tannin of the wood as a result of the high temperature. The rear part of the thin layer of the veneer, which can be seen on the detached fragments, presents both regular and parallel marks of cutting and polishing, as well as more marked incisions against the direction of the wood-fibres, which probably served to ease the gluing of the two parts. The glue has been partly preserved and consists of rich protein material. The same parallel marks observed on the back of the thin layers of veneer are also present on their front surfaces, although they appear to have been smoothed subsequently. The marks left by the carving instruments on the parts formed in relief are also visible. Very rich and complex are the scenes represented on the upper part of the "legs" of the four pieces of furniture. The remaining parts of the legs are decorated with various types of grooves. The symbolism of the scenes is mainly related to the Dionysian sphere. This paper provides only a partial description of the decoration of the furniture. A more specialized study will follow after the completion of the restoration.

Piece of furniture no.1, fragment a (figs. 41 and 42). The decoration of the upper part of the leg of this piece of furniture features a female dancer wearing a short *chiton* and a tall headdress of woven reeds, the *kalathiskos,* on top of a metope embellished with a bucranium. The elements of the woman's outfit enable the identification of this woman as one of the *Lacaenae saltantes* (the Laconian dancers of Spartan rituals). This character is very well known from several Hellenistic and Roman representations, recurrent on Campanian terracotta reliefs and

Arretine pottery. These representations were inspired by models dating to the end of the fifth century B.C.E. attributed to the sculptor Callimachus (Plin. *HN* 34.92).[95]

Piece of furniture no. 1, fragment b. The lower part of the leg is decorated with grooves and ends with a lion foot in solid ivory; however, it is of smaller dimensions in comparison with fragment 1b that belongs to piece of furniture no. 2.

Piece of furniture no. 2, component 1a, side b (figs. 41 and 43). The decoration is preserved only on one side. It represents Attis, or rather a Cupid dressed up as Attis, near a pine tree – his sacred plant – picking up pinecones to use in offertory rituals, while another Cupid dressed as Attis is climbing a ladder placed against the pine tree. Immediately under the decorative element there is a rectangular slot with a fragment of a crossbar, probably a circular crossbar, as can be deduced by element 1b of the same piece of furniture.

Piece of furniture no. 2, fragment 1b (fig. 41). The lower part of this fragment, which joins with element 1a, culminates in a solid ivory lion's foot. Near the lower end of the leg, a curved bar lined with decorated ivory in bas-relief featuring floral elements is inserted through a rectangular slot. This bar is a part of the connecting ring between the legs.

Piece of furniture no. 2, fragment 2. The decoration is preserved on sides b and c. On side b, three naked Cupids are represented decorating the palm branch from which dates hang down (figs. 41 and 44). On side c, which surmounts sides a and b, a naked Dionysus leaning over a tall thyrsus with his left hand stands out. A short cloak hangs from his head onto his shoulders; rosettes within volutes frame the figure of the god (fig. 45).

Piece of furniture no. 3, fragment 1. On side a features a scene of offering to a statue of Priapus near a pine tree, from which hangs a *syrinx* or Pan-pipe. A Psyche carries a tray of pinecones to the small altar at the foot of the pine tree, while behind her, on a rock, a naked Cupid plays a double tibia (figs. 41 and 46). On side b features a scene of offering to a herm of a naked Priapus located in front of a tree, which could be either an oak or a pear tree, and from which hang a *tympanum* and some cymbals. In this case the figures of the offerer and the music player are inverted: a naked Cupid adds fruits (pinecones and apples), which he car-

95 Rizzo 1934; Bacchetta 2006, 276 with bibliography. See also Tortorella 1981, 70, and figs. 12–14 (for the motif on Campanian terracotta reliefs) and Pucci 1981, 107 and fig. 6 (for the motif on Arretine pottery).

ries on a tray, to the altar where apparently this kind of fruits is already burning. Meanwhile Psyche, sitting by the tree, plays a double flute with different pipes (*tibiae impares*) (fig. 47). On side c, which surmounts sides a and b, a high relief decoration displays a Satyr holding the infant Dionysus, and making him play with a tragic mask. The composition is clearly inspired, with variations, by the group of Praxiteles that represents Hermes with the infant Dionysus from Olympia (fig. 48). Two rectangular slots are preserved on this leg as well. The distance between them is more or less the same as the distance between the two rectangular slots on piece of furniture no. 2 (fragments 1 and 2, fig. 41). They were probably employed to insert the circular cross bars, as has also been observed in the case of piece of furniture no. 2.

Piece of furniture no. 4, fragment 1. Side a features a scene of offering by a Cupid to an ithyphallic Dionysus herm (fig. 49), while side b features the herm of a Satyr surrounded by a group of Cupids. One of them holds the mystical basket that contains the phallus, while another one has just uncovered this basket. In the top right of this representation feature two large cymbals (fig. 50). This entire scene seems to evoke the Dionysiac ritual of the *liknophoroi* which consisted in carrying in procession the mystical basket (*mystica vannus*) containing a dough-made phallus. Furthermore, this rite reminds one of the mystical formula pronounced by the initiates at the opening of the mysteries of Attis: "I have eaten from the tympanum, I have drunk from the cymbal, I have carried the *kernos*." This leg has analogous rectangular slots for bars to the ones identified in pieces no. 2 and no. 3.

Maria Paola Guidobaldi

Final remarks

The open-air excavation of the atrium quarter and the partial re-exof the Bourbon tunnels in the area of the two peristyles carried out during the Infratecna Excavation have provided us with fundamental information for the reconstruction of the architectural plan and volume of the Villa.

The data obtained from the recent archaeological investigation carried out by the Superintendency have enabled us to integrate and elaborate hypotheses on the typological classification and dating of the monument already made by De Simone and Ruffo.[96] The recent excavation of the lower levels of the Villa, particularly the *basis villae* and the VPSO area, have revealed considerable new data.

The structures that were unearthed during the Infratecna Excavation demonstrated the substantial unity of the plan of the Villa, the core of which gravitated towards the atrium quarter. The building techniques used for the walls – the *opus quasi reticulatum* and *opus vittatum* in tufa for the secondary walls and the *opus testaceum* for architectural elements subjected to major static pressure (doorposts and corners) – are constantly used in all the sectors of the Villa explored until now. This is also confirmed by the investigation of the structures visible in the tunnels in the areas of the square[97] and rectangular peristyles.[98] The traditional reconstruction of the architectural development of the Villa needs to be revised on the basis of these new elements, naturally bearing in mind the partiality of the exploration to date. According to earlier reconstructions, there was an original nucleus of the Villa of the Papyri built around the atrium and the square peristyle – dating to the first half of the first century B.C.E. – to which the rectangular peristyle would have been added by the end of the same century.[99]

The open-air excavation of the atrium quarter has demonstrated that this area was planned as a whole and that throughout its life it was slightly modified. Furthermore, the layout of this area of the Villa can be compared, both in its general arrangement and in some of its architectural peculiarities, to other contemporaneous buildings such as the Villa at Settefinestre,[100] as well as in slightly older buildings such as the Villa of the Mysteries in Pompeii,[101] the Villa A at Torre Annunziata[102] and the Villa Arianna in Stabiae.[103]

---

96 De Simone and Ruffo 2002, 341–344; 2003, 306–311; De Simone 2007b.

97 See *supra* section A2.

98 De Simone 1987, esp. 23–25.

99 Mustilli 1956, esp. 95, followed by *Wojcik,* 36. The same hypothesis also in Gros 2001, 297. On the basis of the architectural plan of the Villa doubts on this hypothesis – that the rectangular peristyle, the garden leading to the "Belvedere" were added to the Villa's original nucleus around the third quarter of the first century B.C.E. – were also expressed by M.P. Guidobaldi in Pesando and Guidobaldi 2006b, 257–270, esp. 261.

100 Carandini (ed.) 1985.

101 It has recently been demonstrated that the Villa of the Mysteries was characterized by an organic and coherent structure built around the first decades of the first century B.C.E. (and not earlier). Esposito 2007.

This interpretation is further supported by the coherent arrangement of the surviving decoration in the atrium quarter of the Villa. The pavements preserved in the area of the atrium are in *opus tesselatum* mosaic with insertions of limestone or coloured marble (rooms c, h), or of black and white mosaics (rooms a, d, e, l, m, n, q, r, t, u), that were often associated with polychrome *emblemata* (rooms f, i) or at least framed by polychrome fascias (room "o" in Weber's plan, fig. 3). The mosaic workshop which produced these pavements was inspired by a repertoire characteristic of the mature phase of the Second Style, and therefore dating to the second half of the first century B.C.E.

The chronology that derives from the stylistic analysis of the pavements[104] is further defined by the analysis of the surviving wall paintings, all dating, in our opinion, to the third quarter of the first century B.C.E. The Second Style wall paintings of the Villa of the Papyri are very close to those of the House of the Cryptoporticus in Pompeii[105] and of the House of Augustus in Rome.[106] Many similar details can be also found in other contemporary decorations such as those of the House VI 17 (*Ins. Occ.*), 41,[107] the House of Ceres,[108] the House of the Silver Wedding[109] and the House of the Epigrams[110] in Pompeii. The fragment of megalography found in room (i) can be compared with the megalography in Villa (6) of Terzigno,[111] or with the fragment of megalography recently found in Baia.[112]

All these wall paintings can be attributed to the Ic and IIa phases of the Second Style, according to Beyen's classification,[113] and therefore can be dated between 40 and 30 B.C.E. The chronology of the wall paintings dating to the first phase of the Villa agrees with the chronology of the statues. The recent study of V. Moesch has demonstrated that the

102 De Franciscis 1975; Fergola and Pagano 1998; Fergola and Guzzo 2000; Fergola 2004; Thomas and Clarke 2007 and 2008.
103 Camardo 2001; De Simone 2002.
104 De Simone and Ruffo 2002, 341; 2003, 306; 2005.
105 Spinazzola 1953, 454–538; I. Bragantini in *PPM* 1, 193–277, figs. 1–150.
106 Carettoni 1983; Iacopi 2008.
107 Strocka 1993; De Simone 2006.
108 De Vos 1976.
109 Ehrhardt 2005.
110 Strocka 1995.
111 Cicirelli 2003; Sampaolo 2005; Moormann 2005; Strocka 2007.
112 Cfr. C. Capaldi in Miniero and Zevi 2009, 76–77; Miniero and Capaldi (in press).
113 Beyen 1938–1960.

majority of the statues can be dated before the third quarter of the first century B.C.E., while "only in a few cases it is reasonable to suggest a lower chronology."[114]

On the basis of these observations, it would be appropriate to lower the chronology of the first phase of the monument to the third quarter of the first century B.C.E.[115]

The same chronology is also applicable to the room of the first lower level of the *basis villae.* As De Simone and Ruffo have already pointed out,[116] the rooms of this level were not simple service areas but seem to have been used as residential quarters since the first phase of the Villa. This is clearly demonstrated by the recent excavation of room (I) on the first lower level of the *basis villae.* The arrangement of these rooms is very similar to that of the terraced houses of *Insula Occidentalis* and *Insula* VIII 2 in Pompeii.

Furthermore, we need to address the arrangement of the Villa on three levels and its scenographic articulation in front of the atrium quarter. The uniformity of the atrium's front is broken at the north-west corner by an airy bow window, still largely buried. The roof of this bow window begins from the pavement level of the rooms located at the first lower of the *basis villae* and reaches down to the tufa bed on which the structure of the Villa is based. On the opposite side, a second construction characterised by a circular profile is placed against the front of the atrium.[117]

The second lower level of the *basis villae* seems to have been connected with the monumental structure (a) of area VPSO by means of a construction not yet unearthed. This structure has a coaxial orientation in respect to the other buildings of the Villa. The excavation of the south-west side of this complex and the new survey of the collapsed area on the north-east side of the terrace have shed some light on the nature of these structures. Terrace VPSO (b) rests mainly upon a natural

---

114 Moesch 2008, 79.

115 On the basis of the analysis of the frescoes and especially of the fragment of megalography recovered in room (i), De Simone and Ruffo had envisaged a wider chronological span – 60–40 B.C.E. – and suggested that the villa may have been erected around 60 B.C.E. De Simone and Ruffo 2002, 342, n. 30; 2003, 307 and n. 57.

116 De Simone and Ruffo 2003, 307–308.

117 As the exploration of these structures is impossible at the moment, we cannot propose a hypothesis concerning their function.

tufa bed, which, in this area of the coastline of Herculaneum, must have been the last drop in elevation before reaching the shore.

In front of the terrace there is a large swimming pool, to the south of which an artificial slope towards the shore had been formed. A short staircase of four steps and a ramp are built into the natural rock bed of this slope. In the middle of large terrace VPSO (b) there was room VPSO (a), an airy panoramic hall decorated with marbles and statues. The chronology of complex VPSO is slightly lower than that of the sector of the atrium. The *opus sectile* pavement of hall VPSO (a) could be dated between the late Augustan period and the first half of the Julio-Claudian period on the basis of the construction materials and possible comparisons. A dating to the Augustan period has been recently proposed for the Peplophoros statue and the Amazon head found in this area during the Infratecna Excavation.[118] This structure, therefore, must be considered as a coherent architectural and decorative ensemble, built a few decades after the construction of the Villa as a luxurious pavilion erected directly on the ancient seashore.[119] The marble *crustae* that embellished the lower section of the hall's walls bear evidence to a phase of decorative renovation taking place during the reign of Nero and the Flavians. However, signs that the room had fallen into disuse before the volcanic eruption can be seen in the partial dismantling of the pavement as well as in the removal of the cocciopesto lining of the terrace.

The recent investigation has also enabled us to confirm that a restoration of the upper floors of the Villa was taking place at the moment of the eruption in 79 C.E. Wall paintings of the Fourth Style had been already recovered during the 18th century exploration, which clearly indicate that a renovation of the decoration was taking place in some areas of the Villa.[120] Several restorations of the pavements in the areas of the atrium and the square peristyle have been noted, surely a sign of the wearing effect of time. However, the substitution of the pavements must have been also motivated by the damage caused by the phenomenon of bradyseism, which had affected the entire shoreline

118 V. Moesch in Guidobaldi (ed.) 2008, 249, cat. nos. 6–7, with previous bibliography.

119 It is a very similar situation to that identified under the southern wing of the House of the Relief of Telephus and the pavilion ISAH of *Insula* I in Ercolano. Similar architectural solutions are found in the case of the so-called "Terma Ginnasio" located at Ponte di Rivieccio in Torre del Greco. Pagano 1993–1994, 256–267 and fig. 64, 259.

120 This is clearly normal for such an exceptionally large and old building.

throughout the first century C.E.,[121] as well as after the 62 C.E. earthquake and the increasingly violent earthquake waves that preceded the eruption of the Vesuvius, especially in the last few months before the final explosion.[122]

The excavation of room (I) of the first lower level of the *basis villae* has confirmed all these hypotheses. This room, decorated originally in Second Style during the first phase of the Villa, had been furnished with a new wall painting decoration around the middle of the first century C.E. (phase IIb of the Third Style), preserving only the Second Style stuccoes of the original vaulted ceiling decoration. However, a group of painters were again engaged in the restoration of the wall paintings and stuccoes of this room in 79 C.E.

There is a final comment on the significance of the frieze featuring weapons room (I) of the *basis villae*, especially in relation to the rest of the decoration of the Villa of the Papyri. As stated earlier, the frieze does not make reference to any specific battle. The piling up of weapons is generally interpreted as indicating that the weapons had been laid down and were no longer in use, and therefore as a sign of peace.[123] This is also the impression given by the frieze in the Villa of the Papyri, rather than referring to specific military campaigns accomplished by the unknown *dominus* of the Villa, or his ancestors.[124] It is probable that the frieze carried a deeper symbolic meaning; one that was surely related to the self-reof the owner and was also linked to the rich sculptural collection found in the Villa.

After the fundamental work by Domenico Comparetti in the second half of the 19th century, studies concerning the meaning of the decorative apparatus of the Villa have flourished since the 1970 s – such as works by Pandermalis and Sauron. The former coupled the study of the Villa's decoration with the Epicurean doctrine, implicit in the library and in the figure of Philodemus, and proposed to understand the meaning of the sculptures on the basis of the contrast between *res publica* and *res privata*.[125] Sauron also considered essential the bond between the Epicurean doctrine embodied by the library, where Philodemus' works

121 Cinque and Irollo 2008.

122 On the earthquakes which preceded the 79 C.E. eruption see the proceedings of the *Archäologie und Seismologie* conference (1995).

123 Polito 1998, 37.

124 It must be noted, as already stated above, that the frieze included Western barbarian weapons, Eastern weapons and weapons of Hellenistic tradition.

125 Pandermalis 1980.

were found, and the decorative apparatus of the Villa. According to Sauron, the Villa reproduced in its planning and decoration the Greek gymnasium, with the purpose of recalling the lost world of Epicurus, which is identified with the garden of the blessed ones in the Orphic tradition.[126] Wojcik, also taking into account De Petra's interpretations, proposed a new reading of the decorative program as rearticulating the contrast of *otium* and *negotium*.[127]

More recently, Sheila Dillon[128] and Valeria Moesch[129] have offered two new interpretations of the sculptures of the Villa of Papyri, which undermine the connection between the Epicurean doctrine and the decorative apparatus of the Villa. Specifically, Dillon has pointed out that the majority of the statues of the Villa are portraits of Hellenistic sovereigns, rarely found in the portrait galleries of Greek personalities, which instead mainly included portraits of philosophers, poets and orators. The presence of portraits of Hellenistic kings and leaders could be explained as the wish of the owner of the Villa to be associated with the royal status of these characters – also suggesting, through the simultaneous presence of statues of Greek thinkers, the role of philosophers as advisors to the Hellenistic kings. According to V. Moesch "it is likely that the will of the owner of the Villa was to re-create the scenario of a Hellenistic court in his own house, while the reference to the Epicurean philosophy does not seem to be a distinguishing element."[130]

In the last decades of the Republic, it seems clear that the noblemen belonging to the aristocracy of the Roman Senate wanted to reproduce in their *domus* and villas a lifestyle inspired by the Hellenistic courts. The same characteristics are present in the Villa of the Papyri, which stands out among similar buildings for its exceptional dimensions[131] and the opulence of its decorative apparatus. The decoration is particularly rich in references to the environment of the Hellenistic courts but, at

126 Sauron 1980; 2007b, 176–185.

127 *Wojcik*, 259–284.

128 Dillon 2000; 2006, 48–49.

129 Moesch 2008.

130 Moesch 2008, 79; 2009.

131 The Villa covered a surface of at least 20.000 m^2, merely considering the level of the atrium and the two peristyles, without taking into account the two lower floors.

the same time, includes frequent and abundant motifs recalling the power of the new masters of the world.[132]

Domenico Esposito

132 Among the several allusions to this theme, beyond the frieze with weapons from room I on the *basis villae*, see the *Nikai tropaiophoroi* painted in the dado of the east wall of *oecus* (g).

Wall Paintings in the Villa of the Papyri. Old and New Finds

ERIC M. MOORMANN

My contribution on the painted decorations of the Villa of the Papyri to the Oxford meeting first of all urges me to return to an old essay written on the mural paintings from the Villa of the Papyri when I was at Naples in the early 1980s.[1] This paper has been relatively unknown to archaeologists working on the topic of this suburban complex, since it is hidden in the three-volume proceedings of an international congress on papyrology. Of course, the challenge is not to present that text again, whether or not including some new insights on the basis of the material known from the 18th century, but to attempt to integrate this study into the context of the new excavations.

Apart from Agnes Allroggen-Bedel and Rita Wojcik, whose work I did not know at the time, no colleague had ever studied the fragments of paintings cut out from the Villa complex during the campaigns of Karl Weber in the 1750 s.[2] I was able to identify 26 fragments that still existed (see table 1)[3] and could be attributed to two phases of the Villa: the middle of the first century B.C.E. and the later decades of the first century C.E., which means from the mid Second Style to the Fourth Style – to use the terminology developed around 1880 by

1 Moormann 1984. I thank Domenico Esposito for discussing this paper; he has completed a PhD on the wall decorations of Herculaneum and was kind enough to give me the part of his hitherto unpublished work on the Villa of the Papyri. Many thanks are also owed to Maria Paola Guidobaldi and Pier Giovanni Guzzo for their permission to study the new excavations and for discussion on the topic.

2 Allroggen-Bedel 1976; in Italian version Allroggen-Bedel 1983; *Wojcik*, 15–38. Stephan Mols was kind enough to make some photographs when we visited the site in September 2007 and discussed the situation.

3 Moormann 1984: 36 pieces in total. Comparetti and De Petra (*CDP*) have 33 pieces; Allroggen-Bedel (1976 and 1983) has 9 pieces, but does not aim at a complete discussion; Wojcik (*Wojcik*), lists 31 fragments; Pagano and Prisciandaro (2006) have 25, among which 2 pieces not mentioned in the other lists. See Table 1 for all references.

August Mau. The original location of the various fragments was partly reconstructed on the basis of Weber's excellent documentation, conveniently collected by Domenico Comparetti and Giulio De Petra in 1882 (fig. 1).[4]

When we now enter the Villa from portico (a) in front of the atrium quarter, we see that the 18th-century excavators stripped the walls of their wall paintings and left almost nothing but bare walls.[5] Evidently, the ruined state of all but the floor mosaics must have been caused by the fervid activities of the workers of the Bourbon kings.[6] In the following, I take up first some of the conclusions drawn in my 1984 paper, and then pass on to the murals that can be studied today in the part excavated by Antonio De Simone in the 1990s and more recently by Maria Paola Guidobaldi.[7]

Unfortunately, I cannot discuss the mosaics, although they belong to the interior decoration and are clearly contemporary with the paintings. It has been observed by the excavators that several *opus sectile* floors seem to have been removed by the Bourbon explorers.[8]

4 *CDP*, 278–284. See the distribution map in Moormann 1984, fig. 1.

5 I use the numbers applied in the excavation reports. See in this volume, De Simone, fig. 7, and Guidobaldi and Esposito, fig. 2.

6 See De Simone et al. 1998, 47. Everywhere fragments of paintings have been found in "terra di risulto:" De Simone 1987, 34, fig. 16; Guidobaldi and Esposito in this volume, 25, fig. 4.

7 De Simone 1987; De Simone et al. 1998; De Simone and Ruffo 2002 and 2003; De Simone in this volume. For the more recent excavations see Guidobaldi and Esposito in this volume.

8 The marble *impluvium* must have been taken out as well; the atrium floor has no indication whatsoever, being covered with modern concrete (De Simone and Ruffo 2003, 289). In the *triclinium* (c) they found "scaglie" (De Simone and Ruffo 2003, 291–292). Rooms (p), (i), (g) and (f) have black and white mosaics (De Simone and Ruffo 2003, 293; 293–295; 295). Room (l) has a beehive motif in black and white mosaic (De Simone et al. 1998, fig. 17). For room (f), see De Simone 1987, 23, fig. 10, and De Simone et al. 1998, fig. 18. A modest white mosaic with small black motifs is in (a) (De Simone et al. 1998, 32, 33). Room (b) has a braid motif (De Simone et al. 1998, 33). See De Simone in this volume, 9–11. It is clear that these publications are not sufficient for a careful study of the mosaics.

Second Style[9]

In my 1984 study, in so far as I could deduce from the 18th century excavation reports, I determined that the fragments of wall paintings belonging to the Second Style came from the atrium of the Villa and its adjacent rooms (see fig. 1) – without however being able to indicate from which rooms exactly.[10] Since this very part of the Villa has been reopened during De Simone's excavations we are able to assess the reliability of my 1984 reconstruction in light of the modern finds.[11]

Two significant large fragments of wall paintings coming from this area are well known and, as the Italians say, "pubblicatissimi." One is a monochrome landscape panel (NM 9423 in fig. 2; no. 15 in table 1) the other features a marble veneer imitation on which two deer are lying at the bottom, with three ducks hanging above them (fig. 6; no. 3 in table 1).

Alae (d) and (e)

In my 1984 reconstruction the fragment of a landscape monochrome panel (NM 9423 in fig. 2; no. 1 in table 1) was combined with a meander fragment (NM 8548 in fig. 2; no. 1 in table 1), which was found in the area of the Villa's atrium and was also partly reused in the panel with the animals.[12] This reconstructed panel could have been part of a series of imitations of reliefs like those in Villa A at Torre Annunziata, the so-called Villa of Poppaea at Oplontis, or in two fragments of wall paintings from Portici, now in the Naples Museum (fig. 2).[13]

9 De Simone and Ruffo (2002, 328) spotted Second Style in rooms (e), (f), (g), (i) and (q), whereas Fourth Style was found in room (r).

10 Moormann 1984, 638–644. I was not able then to distinguish between fragments from the atrium and the *alae*. De Simone and Ruffo hint at the old finds in a few occasions (2003, 292: 8548, 8759 and 9423 come from the atrium).

11 As De Simone and Ruffo (2003, 289) observe, the remains of murals *in situ* were scanty. They also found fragments in the debris (cf. note 6), but do not give any clue as to their nature and quantity. Apparently room (b) had nothing (290), room (l) fragments of a dado (293), rooms (n), (p) and (o) nothing.

12 There is also a second landscape panel but entirely faded away.

13 Allroggen-Bedel 1976, 88; 1983, 68 (NM 8594 and 9847). On the imitations of relief see also Moormann 1984, 645–649; 1988, 36–39.

The new excavations have revealed that the fragment of the monochrome landscape panel does not come from the atrium itself but from one of the *alae*, as remains of similar monochrome landscape panels with the same framing have been found on the north-east sidewall of *ala* (e) and on the north-west wall of *ala* (d).

The north-east sidewall of *ala* (e) (fig. 3)[14] shows on the higher part of its middle zone a panel decoration, where red panels with landscape representations are separated by columns depicting a palm tree surface.[15] The north-west wall of *ala* (d) has a better-preserved fragment of a red panel with landscape representation (fig. 4). No precise cuttings from the Bourbon activities can be observed, except for the lack of plaster from the upper part of the middle zone downwards, along a more or less regular horizontal line. On top of these red landscape panels, the lower parts of blue panels can be seen. There are two features that enable us to ascribe the fragment of the monochrome landscape panel found in the 18th century to these rooms: the dark-red band with the flower wreath and its adjacent moulding in light red-orange framing the sides of the landscape panels, which are also present in the monochrome landscape panel; and, of course, the landscape motif itself.

Whereas the monochrome landscape panel from the Villa is yellow, the landscape panels that remain on the walls of the Villa are red. However, this is in fact no oddity: the red is a discolouration of the yellow ochre caused by the hot temperature of the volcanic material that filled the room. In my 1984 article I had suggested this on the basis of observations by fellow *pompeianisti*, like Paul Herrmann and Agnes Allroggen-Bedel. After examining the wall paintings on the walls of the *alae* in the newly exposed part of the Villa I was doubtful, as there was a large amount of red in them and yellow was absent. The red colour of the central panel of the middle zone on the north-east wall of *ala* (e), however, is different to the red of the side panels. On the basis of recent ongoing investigations and discussions, it seems that the hottest volcanic stuff arrived in the central and higher sections of the walls and affected the murals in these areas more – therefore changing the yel-

14 *Ala* d has fewer remains than *ala* (e). In *ala* (d) a small part of a dado, with vertical elements, has been found (De Simone and Ruffo 2003, 295–296). On *ala* (e), see De Simone and Ruffo 2003, 298 (they locate here NM 9423).

15 As to the shrubby columns, I refer to the megalography from Terzigno, dating also to the middle of the first century B.C.E. (Moormann 2005; Strocka 2005–2006).

low ochre into red.[16] For this reason I am again of the opinion that the central panel must have been red and the lateral ones yellow.

When we consider the relocation of the monochrome landscape panel, the following conclusion can be drawn. We can reconstruct a system of panels adorned with monochrome landscape representations in both *alae*. The long walls of the *alae* had three panels, separated by shrubbed columns (fig. 5; see also Zarmakoupi in this volume, fig. 10b), and the short ones two juxtaposed panels, if we do not take into account the doors and/or windows. Unfortunately, too little data is available for the lower and upper zones of the walls.

A red band with flower wreath features along one side of the meander fragment, and at one point a tiny branch projects at a square angle, indicating that there was a perpendicular band attached. For this reason I placed the meander fragment on top of the monochrome landscape panel in my 1984 reconstruction (fig. 2). However, there is a difference I did not notice at the time, which proves to be crucial: the colour of the tiny band next to the red band in the meander fragment is yellow, whereas the one in the landscape panel is white. Therefore the meander fragment must now be excluded from the decoration system of the *alae*.

Atrium

In the 1980s I was not able to establish the exact location of the fragment of large still lifes (fig. 6, no. 3 in table 1), as well as five other fragments of still lifes cut from the atrium walls that belong to the same system of decoration (nos. 2, 26–27, 30–31 in table 1). The recent excavations have not shed light on this problem since the unearthed walls of the atrium have been found up to the height of the dado and do not

16 E.g. Allroggen-Bedel 1976, 85 no. 1; 1983, 65 no. 1. During a round table discussion at Bologna in January 2008, entitled "Vesuviana: Archeologia a confronto," organized by Daniela Scagliarini and Antonella Coralini, I proposed, as I did in Oxford, that the red had turned into yellow because of the dominance of the red on the walls of the *alae*, but chemists and archaeologists alike confirmed the change from yellow into red (e.g. the archaeologist mentioned, Agnes Allroggen-Bedel, and the chemists Paolo Baraldi, Paolo Zanini and Gian Antonio Mazzocchini). I thank these colleagues for their comments. To be sure about the process of discolouration, a chemical analysis of the pigments should be carried out. The proceedings of this meetings are now available: Coralini (ed.) 2010.

show any traces of painting. As a decoration system, it seems not to differ much from the panel paintings with the landscapes, although here there is a suggestion of depth in the form of the "bench" on which the animals are lying.

In the fragment of large still lifes (fig. 6, no. 3 in table 1), the ducks are hanging from a red orthostat. In this fragment as well as in two more (nos. 2, 27 in table 1) animals – deer, roosters and duck – have their legs tied and lie on a green bench-like structure. This "bench" is likely to be interpreted as part of the usually green podium that we encounter in the Terzigno painting and that features in many other paintings of the Second Style.[17] It suggests a protruding dado on which columns could be placed, like those on the *alae* paintings in the Villa of the Papyri, and like those surrounding a jutting *aedicula* on the one of the two famous fragments in Naples from the *Insula Occidentalis* at Pompeii – which may also serve as a parallel for the large still lifes from the Villa of the Papyri.[18] In the fragment of still life from the Villa of the Papyri (fig. 6), the deer lie on a slab of slate or a slate-like stone that rests on a red layer, the topside of the dado. The *aedicula* of the *Insula Occidentalis* also features a single slab, here of fake red porphyry, that covers the green top layer of the podium.

The fragment of still life (fig. 6) contains a small part of a meander and I believe, in contrast to my 1984 publication, that this indeed belonged to the same decoration system with the other five fragments of still lifes (nos. 2, 26–27, 30–31 in table 1). As mentioned earlier, the colour of the floral band is yellow; it has green vertical borders and cannot be placed in the monochrome landscape system of the *alae* (d) and (e) (fig. 5).[19]

Another piece found in the atrium shows a panther's head presented as an appliqué on a yellow ground (fig. 7; no. 24 in table 1). This fragment comes from the beam of a doorframe and served as its adornment. The new excavations revealed a shallow niche, unfortunately devoid of paintings, but furnished with a doorstep in marble that clearly stands for a fake door (fig. 8). This fragment might have adorned the doorframe of

17 Moormann 2005.

18 Naples, NM 8594 and 9847 from Pompeii, VI 17 (*Insula Occidentalis*) 41, room (17). So Allroggen-Bedel 1976, 87–88; 1983, 67–68. See now Strocka 1993 and *PPM* 6 (1996) 27–56.

19 Sauron 2007a, 181–182 sees in the panel with deer and ducks a reference to the allegorical warning of mankind not to neglect celestial matters. But see my review in *Gnomon* 71 (2009), 452–458, esp. 458.

this fake door. Such fake doors were popular in Roman painting from the late First Style onwards and enhanced the suggestion of richness in the sense of inaccessible rooms behind the real space, especially when architectonically enriched by features like the doorstep and reliefs. An example of the First Style in the vestibule of the House of C. Julius Polybius at Pompeii provides a good comparison for our case: the painting is applied in a shallow niche. In that case the knobs and beams are smoothly painted surfaces.[20]

Other rooms with Second Style paintings

In a few more rooms tiny fragments of Second Style decorations have been found in place, of which no pieces seem to have been cut out and transported to the museum in Portici by Karl Weber's excavators.[21] Room (g) has some remains of a dado with a red plinth, red and yellow panels on the side walls and, on the back wall, a red plinth, a yellow dado with the base of a column adorned with the suggestion of a relief showing a winged Victoria carrying a trophy on her hand (see Guidobaldi and Esposito in this volume, fig. 7).[22] The corners of the room are marked by pink pilasters.

Architectonically, room (s) stands isolated. The excavators found Second Style paintings in the shape of bases of columns and vertical bands.[23]

The probably large room (q) has been only partly unearthed and no longer displays its treasures. De Simone observes that it must have contained traces of a grand architectural scenography similar to those in Boscoreale and Torre Annunziata. Elements of the bases of columns

20 Tybout 1989, 153, pl. 87.2; *PPM* 10 (2003) 188–192. For painted fake doors of the Second Style see Tybout 1989, 153, 263,282, 285, pls. 1, 9, 16, 23, 27, 32, 42–48 (Villa A at Torre Annunziata, room [14], with "our" heads on the door panels). The latter examples always stand on a podium and cannot serve as immediate parallels for our situation.

21 As we have seen, De Simone's reports are very laconic on paintings (cf. notes 6 and 9). De Simone and Ruffo 2003 is the most extensive one but, like the other publications, lacks sufficient images.

22 De Simone and Ruffo 2003, 295; Guidobaldi and Esposito in this volume, 26–27, and fig. 8, for elements of the main and upper zones.

23 De Simone and Ruffo 2003, 299–301.

could be traced.[24] The scanty information available hints at a similar decoration in room (r), which might have formed a couple with room (q).[25] According to De Simone and Ruffo, the wall painting decoration of *oecus* (f) must have been similar to the one in *alae* (d) and (e), but no remains can be seen there any longer.[26]

To be singled out is a decoration system with a large woman standing in front of a red slab, some fragments of which have been found in room (i) (fig. 9). She wears a mantle blown by the wind and holds a green thin branch, possibly a *thyrsus*, with her left hand against her shoulder.[27] The height of almost one meter indicates a fragment of a megalography. I refer again to the example of Terzigno that is contemporary.[28] The decoration belongs to a luxurious *triclinium* looking onto the sea and brings the aspect of a learned pastime during a relaxed moment of *otium* into the Villa. More or less the same situation is that of the famous room (5) of the Villa of the Mysteries, from which the users could look onto the seascape through a portico. As to dating, the decade 50–40 B.C.E. seems the most likely era of application, taking into account the correspondence with the complexes mentioned. This matches the dating proposed by Guidobaldi and Esposito in this volume.

We may conclude that the scanty remains of Second Style decorations in the Villa of the Papyri are of a high level and do not differ from better-known contemporary ensembles like the Villa at Boscoreale and Villa A at Torre Annunziata, with their variety of motifs and themes. There is too little data available to conduct an analysis of the relationship between the functions of the rooms and the decoration, which has been

---

24 De Simone and Ruffo 2003, 297.

25 De Simone and Ruffo 2003, 298–299: columns and pilasters; probably a meander; panels with "finto bugnato." About the concept of couples or doubles and triples of rooms in the late Republic, see Dickmann 1999, 159–253 and (briefly) Moormann 2005. Black and white geometric mosaic in room (r): De Simone and Ruffo 2002, fig. 3.

26 De Simone and Ruffo 2003, 296–297.

27 This is one of the few items described in detail by De Simone and Ruffo (2003, 294): "figura femminile inquadrata a sinistra da una colonna, e tracce di architetture illusionistiche di cui si distinguono pochi elementi: una colonna con grossa base modanata di tipo attico e un pilastro angolare prospettico giallorosso che inquadra a sua volta un pilastro viola prospettico arretrato rispetto al piano." Moreover, it is almost the only painting illustrated in one of these reports (De Simone et al. 1998, 58, fig. 16).

28 Moormann 2005.

done in an exemplary way by Rolf A. Tybout for the aforementioned parallels.[29]

Patrizio Pesando and Maria Paola Guidobaldi conclude in their recent book on residences of the Roman elite at Pompeii and Herculaneum that the decorations of the Second Style in the Villa of the Papyri perfectly matched the architecture. I cannot but endorse this vision. It is an extra argument to assume that the paintings belong to the construction of the Villa, a conclusion I had drawn as well in my 1984 publication.[30] They were carefully respected for more than a hundred years and show how the venerable traditions were fostered in this gentleman's property in the old Roman manner.

Fourth Style paintings

Regarding the fragments of the Fourth Style found in the 18th century, it must be said that they are small and rather insignificant, showing small figural motifs cut out of larger wall systems that cannot be reconstructed at all.[31] I think that their original location might have been one of the porticos of the small and/or big peristyle, where a paratactic scheme of panels would do well. The small goat (no. 5 in table 1) could have adorned a dado, whereas the putto (no. 13 in table 1) might be reset as a vignette in a panel decoration. The small landscapes (nos. 14, 17–20, 25 in table 1) seem to have formed vignettes on panels, but we also know them as adornments in *aediculae* in the upper zones of walls or in small friezes between two horizontal layers of the wall systems. They are sketchy, which does not mean that their quality is poor, but it cannot be established whether they belong to high-quality wall decorations. We may recall the decorations in the peristyles of the House of the Dioscuri or the House of the Vettii at Pompeii or the Villa San Marco at Stabiae with similar decoration systems.[32]

29 Tybout 1993. See also Dickmann 1999 and Pesando and Guidobaldi 2006b.

30 Pesando and Guidobaldi 2006b, 261. In their section on the Villa (257–270) they amply discuss the question of the owner and seem to advocate Pagano's assumption of Gaius Memmius. On the Villa as a sort of *gymnasium* in possession of Calpurnius Piso: Sauron 2007a, 176–185. See on villas in this area also Moormann 2007.

31 Moormann 1984, 672.

32 *PPM* 4, 956–995 (Dioscuri, peristyle [53]); V, 508–525 (Vettii, peristyle [l]; Barbet and Miniero 1999, pl. I.2, 4–5 (Stabiae).

Unfortunately, I am not able – as no painting expert would be – either to propose a precise chronology or to ascribe the fragments of wall paintings to specific rooms of the Villa. The first question is more important, as we have the hypothesis that the Villa was out of use around 79 C.E., when the book scrolls, to mention one of the major finds only, were collected unsystematically on shelves and in crates in a room not far from the atrium and some of the garden statues were standing under the portico. Apparently, reconstruction works were going on, like those we know from other villas in the Vesuvian area, for example in the Villa A at Torre Annunziata.

The Fourth Style paintings found *in situ* seem to bring the solution in this chronological matter. It was a great surprise to see that the pilasters of the portico (a) in front of these rooms are adorned with a fantastic marble veneer (figs. 10a-b).[33] The manner of representation is typical for the Fourth Style. At Herculaneum, there are no other instances of marbling, whereas there are some real marble revetments in several buildings, like those in the House of the Relief of Telephos. It is a decoration custom introduced according to Pliny in the period of Claudius, but Nero set it as a trend with his Golden House. It is likely that marbles and marbling in Pompeii and Herculaneum were applied after Nero's death in 68 C.E. That might be a chronological indication for the fourth style in our complex.

As to the Fourth Style decorations in room (I) of the *basis villae* (see in this volume, De Simone, fig. 12, and Guidobaldi and Esposito, figs. 24–26), I think that they are a typical example of Herculanean Fourth Style, whereas Antonio De Simone and Fabrizio Ruffo have suggested an earlier date.[34] It has been observed by various scholars, but not worked out in detail, that the fourth style in Herculaneum dif-

---

33 Not recognized by De Simone and Ruffo (2003, 289–290). From north to south we see above a smooth double band in yellow and green or yellow and red two times *rosso antico*, two times *giallo antico* and two times, again, *rosso antico*. Above these plaques there is a green surface. Domenico Esposito informed me after the colloquium that a stratum with Second Style paintings was found under this layer, which makes it clear that the portico belongs to the building phase of the Villa.

34 De Simone and Ruffo 2002, 331–332, fig. 6 ("fase di transizione fra III e IV stile"); 2003, 301–302. See also Guidobaldi and Esposito in this volume, 34–42 with figs. 25–26. Domenico Esposito pointed out to me after the colloquium that this decoration has two phases: a late Third Style decoration and a Fourth Style restoration, for which my late dating should be changed to include a subdivision into two phases.

Table 1: Table of fragments found in the Villa of the Papyri in the 18th century.

	Inv. Naples (NM)	*CDP* (p. and date)	Allroggen-Bedel 1976; 1983	Moormann 1984	*Wojcik* 1986	Pagano and Prisciandaro 2006[a)]
1	8548 meander	283 no. 107 (10-03-1754)	86 n. 10; 66 n. 10	643–644, figs. 9–10	17 cat. 4, pl. V.A	211
2	8753 two roosters	282 no. 98 (24-03-1754)	87–88 n. 12; 67–68 n. 12	639, 642 fig. 4	22 cat. 10, pl. VII	211
3	8759 ducks and deer	282, no. 97 (10-06-1754; 30-0-1754: small elements to adjust)	87–88 n. 15, fig. 2; 67–68 n. 15 fig. 2	639–640, fig. 2	15–16 cat. 1, pl. IV	211
4	8779 panther	283 no. 103 (17-02-1754)		653, fig. 14 (erroneously: tiger)	21 cat. 8, pl. V.B	210
5	8806 goat	283 no. 101 (07-04-1754)		655–656, fig. 20	29 cat. 16, pl. XIII	211 [mistakenly inv. 8662]
6	8818 Medusa			671, fig. 29		
7	8820 Medusa			671, fig. 30		
8	8821 A Medusa	282 no. 96c (15-06-1755)		657, fig. 28	31–32 cat. 23, pl. XVIII	212
9	8821B Medusa	281 no. 92b (15-06-1755)		657 fig. 25	31 cat. 22, pl. XVII	212

Table 1: Table of fragments found in the Villa of the Papyri in the 18th century. *(Continued)*

	Inv. Naples (NM)	*CDP* (p. and date)	Allroggen-Bedel 1976; 1983	Moormann 1984	*Wojcik* 1986	Pagano and Prisciandaro 2006[a)]
10	8821C Medusa	281 no. 92 (15-06-1755)		657, fig. 24	30–31 cat. 21, pl. XVI	212
11	8821D Silen	282 no. 96c (22-06-1755)		657, fig. 27	34 cat. 30, pl. XXI	213
12	8821E Silen	281 no. 92b (15-06-1755)		657, fig. 26	34–35 cat. 31, pl. XXII	212
13	9319 putto	281 no. 90 (20-05-1753)		652, fig. 13	25–26 cat. 14, pl. X	210
14	9399 landscape	281 no. 95b (24-02-1754)		654, fig. 18	23 cat. 12, pl. IX	
15	9423 landscape	283 no. 106 [lost]	85–88, fig. 1; 65–68 fig. 1	643–644, figs. 8, 10	18–19 cat. 7, pl. VI	
16	9447					212, n. 225 (15-06-1755)
17	9458 landscape	282 no. 95 (17-02-1754)		654, fig. 17	21 cat. 9 [erroneously inv. 9439]	210
18	9465 landscape	282 no. 95e (15-06-1755)		656, fig. 21	32 cat. 24	

Table 1: Table of fragments found in the Villa of the Papyri in the 18th century. *(Continued)*

	Inv. Naples (NM)	*CDP* (p. and date)	Allroggen-Bedel 1976; 1983	Moormann 1984	*Wojcik* 1986	Pagano and Prisciandaro 2006[a)]
19	9467 landscape	281–282 no. 95d (15-06-1755)		656, fig. 22	33 cat. 26, pl. XIX	
20	9499 landscape	281 no. 95c (16-03-1755)		654, fig. 16	21–22 cat. 21, pl. XV	212 (15-06-1755)
21	9891 jug					212 (15-06-1754)
22	9902 goat	283 no. 102 (27-10-1754)		655, fig. 19	29 cat. 17, pl. XIV	212 [no inv.]
23	9944 still life	283 no. 105 (22-06-1755)		653, fig. 15	34 cat. 29, pl. XX	213
24	9951 feline's head	282 no. 96 (24-03-1754)	87–88 n. 12–14; 67–68 n. 12–14	642, fig. 7	22–23 cat. 11, pl. VIII	211, 213 (22-06-1755: two tiger heads)
25	S.n. 31[b)]			656, fig. 23		
26	Standing duck	282, no. 99 (23-06-1754)	88 n. 19; 63 n. 19	639, fig. 5	16 cat. 2.	
27	Duck and fowl suspended	282, no. 99b (23-06-1754)	88 n. 18; 68 n. 18	639, fig. 6	16–17 cat. 3.	211
28	Meander[c)]	283 no. 107b (17-03-1754)	1976, 66; 1983, 66	639–640, fig. 3	17–18 cat. 5	

Table 1: Table of fragments found in the Villa of the Papyri in the 18th century. *(Continued)*

	Inv. Naples (NM)	*CDP* (p. and date)	Allroggen-Bedel 1976; 1983	Moormann 1984	*Wojcik* 1986	Pagano and Prisciandaro 2006[a)]
29	Landscape – lost	173, 281 no. 94	86 n. 5; 66 n. 5	643	18 cat. 6	212
30	Still life, duck – lost	283 no. 100 (05-01-1755)		639	29–30 cat. 18	? 212 (12-01-1755)
31	Still life; duck – lost	283 no. 99c (12-01-1755)		639	30 cat. 19	? 212 (05-01-1755)
32	Still life; jug – lost	283 no. 104 (17-06-1755)		653	32 cat. 25	
33	Woman's head – lost	281 no. 93 (09-05-1753)		651	25 cat. 13	210
34	Seahorses – lost	281 no. 91 (20-06-1751)		650–651	27–28 cat. 15	
35	Bird – lost	(20-06-1751)		651		
36	Bird – lost	(20-06-1751)		651		
37	Panther – lost	283 no. 103b (22-06-1755)		653	33 cat. 27	213 [mistakenly inv. 9891; see above]

Table 1: Table of fragments found in the Villa of the Papyri in the 18th century. *(Continued)*

	Inv. Naples (NM)	*CDP* (p. and date)	Allroggen-Bedel 1976; 1983	Moormann 1984	*Wojcik* 1986	Pagano and Prisciandaro 2006[a)]
38	Panther – lost	283 no. 103c (22-06-1755)		653	33 cat. 28	213 [mistakenly inv. 9891; see above]

[a)]Pagano and Prisciando 2006, 206–217. I add the date, if it lacks in or differs from *CDP*.
[b)]S.n.: Senza numero d'inventario (without inventory number).
[c)]This has probably been inserted in NM 8759 (Allroggen-Bedel 1976, 87; 1983, 67; Moormann 1984, 639–640 n. 11).

fers considerably from that in Pompeii. There are far fewer figural scenes in the first place, and, if they are present, they are huge or small! There seems to exist a tendency for monochrome panels in the central zone and fantastic upper zones; often in different colours on a white ground, for example in the House of the Tuscan Colonnade. Here we might refer to the House of the Black Saloon and a house in front of the *palaestra*, the latter especially because of the great contrast between the heavily red main zone and the eerie upper zone. The early dating, therefore, is not compulsory and the decoration might be contemporary with the marbling in portico (a).

Conclusion

This exercise of bringing together old and new finds surely has brought new insights. First of all, we observe how the owners appreciated the Second Style decorations and kept them well preserved for almost 140 years in the traditionally most important part of the house, the rooms around the atrium. As far as the fragments and the pieces *in situ* can be good indications, the fashion of these decorations matches the one in Second Style decorations elsewhere in the Vesuvius area. They are considerable additions to the few examples of this period found hitherto in Herculaneum. The rooms have a great variety of decoration modes that follows the use of different decorative systems in opulent villas like the ones at Boscoreale and Torre Annunziata. The presence of a megalography corresponds with a fashion of which we unfortunately know few examples, but seems to be in high estimation in the middle of the first century B.C.E. – the Villa of Mysteries is the forerunner of this fashion.

The Fourth Style murals seem to come from the last decade of the Fourth Style and have a precious elegance, typical for Herculaneum. They show the new language of the introduction of real or fake marble decorations into the private sphere after the death of Nero and, at the same time, the application of compositions and colours typical for Herculaneum and rarely encountered at Pompeii.

Programming Sculpture? Collection and Display in the Villa of the Papyri

CAROL C. MATTUSCH

On July 2, 2007, an article appeared in the *New York Times* about a property that Christie's was offering for sale – the Hala Ranch, a ninety-five-acre estate near Aspen, Colorado, with a 56,000-square-foot main house.[1] According to the advertisement, "enormous windows throughout . . . frame the wraparound views of the Rocky Mountains." There are fifteen bedrooms, a barbershop, a massage room, and a beauty salon off the master bedroom, sixteen bathrooms, and space to entertain 450 people. Suites on the main level open onto a courtyard with a pool, flowers, and a waterfall. The children's wing has four bedroom suites and a sitting room. There is an indoor pool, as well as a steam room, an exercise room, a racquetball court, a tennis court, a fish-pond, ski trails, a fire pit, a heated stable, and a heated hay-barn. The "commercial" kitchen and the laundry are in the basement. Built in 1991, the house has had only one owner, a Saudi-Arabian prince who was for twenty-two years the ambassador to the United States.

The $135-million price tag does not include the paintings, but an American classic, a painting by Albert Bierstadt (1830–1902; Hudson River School), is said to be hanging over the main fireplace. Otherwise, "television screens dominate the décor." These provide the guests with entertainment, not quite like the live entertainment that Petronius's Trimalchio provided his dinner-guests, but at least lively, and available in every bedroom.

This was the most expensive home on the market in the United States in July 2007. One thousand people had asked to look at it by the time the *New York Times* ran its article, but the agent had evidently taken only eleven people through the property. He told the reporter from the *New York Times* that whoever buys this place will be the sort of person who will own two or three other homes as well. Most of the people who have so far shown an interest in the estate are

1 Johnson 2007.

"from old money," in other words, money that is at least one generation old.[2]

This modern villa, which the Christie's advertisement describes as "perhaps the most magnificent property ever offered for sale anywhere in the world, . . . elevating the standards of luxury and comfort to previously unimagined levels," serves as an appropriate introduction to the far grander Roman Villa of the Papyri at Herculaneum.

According to my calculations, the Villa of the Papyri covered about 65,000 sq. Ft. (20,000 m^2), taking into account that the excavations of the 1990s revealed a number of bedrooms, and made it clear that the Villa was a multi-storey structure, at least on the side descending the steep hillside to the shoreline of the Bay of Naples. Antonio De Simone has calculated that at least some parts of the Villa of the Papyri rose to a height of four storeys. My estimate of square-footage does not include the probably extensive service areas, which have not yet been located, and which are likely to have been on the ground floor of the complex, as is the case with the princely Hala villa outside Aspen. Nor have the family's private apartments yet been identified.

Ninety-five acres near Aspen, Colorado, may be more land than was available in Roman times for a waterfront estate right outside the town of Herculaneum. After all, from the second century B.C.E. onwards, there was building underway all along the coastline from Miseno to Naples, and from there on to Herculaneum, Sorrento and the island of Capri. Julius Caesar, the subsequent emperors and their families, consuls, senators, politicians, military leaders, and the idle rich had homes there. Strabo observed that the entire coastline from Miseno to Sorrento was packed with cities, houses, and plantations. And Horace complained about all the construction debris being thrown into the sea (*Epist.* 3.1.33–37).

Mark Antony's situation was an unusual one, because he was the third generation of his family to own the same villa at Miseno. It is easy to imagine the kind of décor that his family must have accumulated during those years. When a villa was sold, however, it was not unusual for the furnishings, the library, and the collections to be sold as part of the package.

Was it usual for there to be a program of sculptural decoration for a grand home in town or for a country villa? The large number of sculptures from the Villa of the Papyri suggests that this was not the case, be-

2 Johnson 2007.

cause they are of different styles, techniques, materials, and sizes, meaning that they must have come from different workshops at different times.

Modern scholars have attempted to figure out comprehensive programs for the sculptures adorning Greek and Roman temples and public monuments. Those subjects and themes were expected to be readable by the people who looked at them, to make some sense as a whole, and to make a religious or political point. Unfortunately, almost no ancient public monument comes with a written explanation of what its decoration is about. In the case of even so well-known a monument as the Parthenon in Athens, there are countless modern debates about the identities of individuals portrayed on the frieze, about the theme of the frieze, and about many other questions whose answers would have been obvious to fifth century B.C.E. viewers. Today we wonder whether the frieze represents an actual procession or a generic procession, who the participants are, and even whether the critical figure on the east side of the building is a boy or a girl.

When the Villa of the Papyri was unearthed between 1750 and 1761, there was, of course, great interest in making sense of what was being found. There were 85 freestanding sculptures, mostly bronzes, and many new characters to identify, all of them from one great suburban villa. The logical approach was to find a comprehensive program for the whole group of sculptures.

One by one, most of the sculptures were restored. Many of the statues were complete, but some of them needed to be reassembled. That was true of the bronze statue of a youthful seated Hermes (NM 5625) (fig. 1). When Johann Joachim Winckelmann saw it in the early 1760s, he was told that it had been "broken into more than one hundred pieces," but he surely did not notice that himself, because by the time he saw the statue it had been repaired, leaving almost no sign of what work had been done to hide the damages.[3] The head was in the worst condition, and it had been repaired and then painted (fig. 2). The eyes, which would originally have been inset in stone and bone, had been replaced with plaster and painted. Then or at a later date, the lips were also painted. Today both eyes and lips are reddish in colour.

It is difficult even now to tell that the dozing young satyr (NM 5624) has an 18th-century right arm and pieced-together stomach

3 Winckelmann 1762, 41 (transl. by the author).

(fig. 3). Many other bronze heads were broken off at the neck, perhaps from having been pulled out of the ground by eager diggers (their original mounts are mentioned in excavation notes). The heads were then restored as busts, so that today we cannot always be sure if the heads were originally attached to busts or to herm-posts. From the varying widths of the surviving ancient works, however, we know that both busts and herms were set up in the Villa.

Of course the surviving heads had to be mounted for display in the Royal Museum. Some bronze body-parts that could not be repaired were used as scrap and remelted to use for casting repairs. So, for example, a number of heads have plaster eyes that were painted to look like bronze. And some of the chests are repaired with screws and poured bronze at the join between the ancient Roman neck and the 18th-century chest. The cast restorations are much thicker and more irregular than the walls of the ancient bronzes.

The restorations have in effect programmed the way in which we look at these sculptures and interpret them. One might say that the opposite is true of ancient marbles, which were originally painted, but which are now mostly bare stone, and today's viewers tend to expect them to look that way. Very little paint survives on the group of Pan and a goat (NM 27709): there is some red-brown hair on Pan's neck; his beard and legs are dark brown; and the hapless goat has reddish hair and black hooves (fig. 4).

Those who acquired permits could visit the Royal Bourbon Museum and see the antiquities. They were arranged roughly according to types: bronze statues were together; marble busts were together; works regarded as pornographic were sequestered in a Secret Cabinet and required a special permit. Visitors to the Bourbon Museum were not allowed to take notes or to make drawings of objects in the rapidly growing collection, because the king's antiquities from Herculaneum and Pompeii – mainly bronzes and paintings – were being published officially by the king's team of 15 scholars.[4] The antiquities were studied in committee, one at a time, the focus being on their identification and on what was known from the literary testimonia about the gods and rulers that could be identified. Very little had been written down about precisely where they had been found, and that usually no more specific than, for instance, "Portici." Between 1757 and 1792 the king's scholars published eight volumes on the Antiquities. During that long time,

4 *Antichità 1757–1792.*

there were of course news reports, and publications that were not sanctioned by the royal family. For instance, Johann Joachim Winckelmann, with gleeful malice, published an illicit picture of a small bronze inscribed portrait of Demosthenes from the Villa of the Papyri and used it to identify other heads of Demosthenes that had previously been misidentified.

Karl Weber, a Swiss military engineer, was directly responsible for the excavation that was being done around the Bay of Naples for the Bourbon royal family. He systematized the excavations, he kept daily records, and he drew plans of the ancient buildings that were discovered (fig. 5). These plans included the tunnels that were being dug to explore the ancient foundations. He made notes all around the edges of his plan of the Villa of the Papyri, referring to numbers and letters that he marked on the plan itself.

Karl Weber finished working on his annotated plan of the Villa of the Papyri in 1758. It was eventually published in 1883, by Domenico Comparetti, a philologist, and Giulio De Petra, an archaeologist.[5] They reversed Weber's plan, putting north at the top. The burgeoning interest in the sculptures from the Villa of the Papyri had not been checked against Weber's plan, which had been virtually unknown for 130 years, and the number of publications had been growing apace without the help of Weber's contextual documentation. In effect, the modern lives of those sculptures were independent of their previous settings. The sculptures were studied individually, as in the case of the head of the Doryphoros by Polykleitos (NM 4885) (fig. 6), or in groups of, for example, Greek rulers and intellectuals, the focus being first on identifications, then on the possibility that they represented a single overarching theme.

There was, however, an exception to this practice. In the case of sculptures being found within a few days of each other in a single tunnel, some connection between them might sometimes be made at an early date. For example, the bust of a "kouros or Apollo" (NM 5608) (fig. 7) and a female head (NM 5592) (fig. 8) were found side by side on April 28 and 29, 1756. The fact that one head was archaic in style and the other was classical did not deter scholars from identifying the two heads as Apollo and Artemis.[6] This is not an unusual response, how-

5 *CDP*.

6 Even as recently as 1986, Maria Rita Wojcik identified the woman as Artemis because she was found beside the "Apollo:" *Wojcik*, 90–91. For discussion of these two heads, see *Mattusch*, 225–230, 236–242.

ever, to the problem raised by the Villa of the Papyri with its unbelievably large number of sculptures, of which only a few small busts of Greek intellectuals survived with their inscribed names.

Even today the scores of sculptures from the Villa remain for the most part unidentified. There are sculptures of literally every style that had been created from as early as the sixth century B.C.E. to as late as the 70 s C.E. Some of the sculptures are marble, but most of them are bronze. The latter were cheaper to produce but they could be melted down and re-used, making them less likely to have survived until today, and thus more highly prized in our world than are marbles. The types range from over life-size statues to small fountain figures to tabletop busts to heads of various sizes from herms that – we must not forget – were restored as busts during the 18th century. There are reproductions of famous Greek statues; portraits of historical and contemporary figures and of a few family members; and rustic subjects. There are Greek and Italic marbles, there are groups of bronzes that can be traced to a single foundry, and there is even one signed work – the head of the Doryphoros, made by Apollonios, an Athenian (NM 4885) (fig. 6).[7] It is clear that this collection of sculptures represents a broad range of collecting interests, rather than an all-inclusive program or theme.

The urge to find a program is linked to the question of identity: are a group of five young women likely to be dancers, nymphs, vestals, *kistophoroi* (basket-carriers), offering-bearers, priestesses, married women, women adorning themselves, actresses, *kanephoroi* (jar-carriers), *hydrophoroi* (water-carriers), or Danāids, the 49 or 50 daughters of King Danāus of Argos, who had to carry water in Hades in pots with holes in them (fig. 9)?[8] If they could be associated with water, then they might have fit neatly around the pool in the square courtyard of the Villa. This is where many scholars have placed them, and this is where reproductions of them were installed in the J. Paul Getty Museum's Villa. We might like to see them there, but Karl Weber's plan shows exactly where these sculptures were found: he made little drawings of four of them within the colonnade surrounding the large garden of the Villa of the Papyri. He drew the fifth one in the garden, between the colonnade and the pool.

---

7 *Mattusch*, 276–282.
8 *Mattusch*, 212–215.

In the atrium of the Villa, two niches on one wall held bronze over-lifesize busts of a Ptolemy with a diadem (NM 5600). We cannot be certain which Ptolemy he is, but he could well be Ptolemy II Philadelphus. That might suggest that the bust of a woman wearing a peplos (NM no number) is his powerful wife and sister, Arsinoe II. An opposite niche holds another Hellenistic ruler, again perhaps a Ptolemy (NM 5596). Portraits of important Ptolemies make sense in a Roman aristocrat's house, and there are two additional Hellenistic rulers' portraits in the Villa's garden, a marble Ptolemy II (NM 6158), and a bronze head, likely to be Seleucus II Nicator (NM 5590). Three of the bronze Hellenistic dynasts (NM 5590, 5596, and 5600) have the same alloy, meaning that they were cast from one batch of metal, all at one time. The busts are also the same size, type, and style. Surely this means that they were all ordered at once. We do not know when that was, and we cannot say why they did not all end up in one room of the house. Sculpture is movable, of course. And then there is the second Ptolemy II (?) in the garden, that one in marble (NM 6158). Why? There is no inventory, of course, except for Karl Weber's record of discovery. We can only imagine how a succession of home-owners might have added to the collections in the Villa of the Papyri.

Beyond the atrium, a large square courtyard surrounded by stuccoed brick columns contained numerous bronzes. In the colonnade, there were seven heads of important Greeks, all mounted on marble posts. There were three bronze herm-heads of bearded Greek intellectuals, usually identified today as philosophers or scholars: one may be Aristotle (NM 5602); a second, with a turban, is most often called Pythagoras (NM 5607); and a third is perhaps another Aristotle, or somebody else (NM 5623) (fig. 10). It is curious that we do not have a securely identified portrait of Aristotle.[9] Of course, the missing posts for these herm-heads would have had inscribed names. There is also a pudgy woman (NM 5598), who may be a Ptolemaic queen, though not everyone agrees that it is a 'she' despite the hairstyle and the soft features.[10] So far nobody has been able to identify the head of an unbearded male (NM 5588), whose draped bust was added in the 18th century. Finally, a pair of herm-heads from famous Greek "Polykleitan" statues face each

9 Gisela Richter identifies eighteen portraits of Aristotle on the basis of a lost 16th-century drawing but she includes neither of these heads on her list: Richter 1965, vol. 2, 171–172.

10 *Mattusch*, 230–233.

other. The pairing was certainly by design: the heads even have the same metal alloy. One is a woman whom we cannot identify (NM 4889) (fig. 11), though she is similar to "Polykleitan" Amazons, and the other is the head of the Doryphoros (NM 4885) (fig. 6), signed in Greek by the Greek artisan, no doubt to direct potential clients to the best company in the business of making reproductions.

From the square courtyard, between two columns leading to the *tablinum*, stood a 2 m tall marble archaistic Panathenaic Athena (NM 6007) (fig. 12). One can almost reconstruct the conversation in which the owner brags to a guest that this large Athena is made of Pentelic marble, just like the one that he bought and paid to have installed on the Athenian Acropolis.[11]

Inside the *tablinum* stands an even larger woman (NM 6240), in Carrara (?) marble, perhaps the well-born lady of the house? But this is a large room, at about 87 m^2, and there is space for much more sculpture, in different styles, genres, and sizes. One can imagine a huge table in the centre that would have held the three ancestral portrait-busts (NM 5634, 5586, 5587), two busts of Greek youths (NM 5633, 5614), and three small busts, maybe gifts – one of Livia or Agrippina (NM 5474), one of Demosthenes (NM 5469), and one of Epicurus (NM 11017).

A couple of nearby rooms contained only small busts – of Demosthenes, Epicurus, Hermarchus, and Zeno, with some repetitions, but never two portraits of the same individual in a single room. In another room stood a single marble statue, but only its feet were found, and those soon disappeared. Elsewhere, a magnificent bronze bust of Dionysus/Priapus (NM 5618) faced a marble Polykleitan youth (NM 6164) across a hallway.

But the huge colonnaded garden, over 90 m long, with an about 66 m long pool in the middle presented the most opportunities for sculpture during the Villa's lifetime of probably close to two hundred years. Was this garden known as the "Gymnasium" or perhaps the "Palaestra"? "Was it the "Academy"? Or was it just the garden (*viridarium*), with décor to fit every taste?

In the colonnade at the east end, one would have seen standing with over-life-size marble statues of Aischines (NM 6018), of another scholar or two whose identities have been lost (NM 6126), and of perhaps a Greek leader (NM 6210). Looking out into the *viridarium*, one would

11 *Mattusch*, 147–151.

have been a vast array of life-size sculptures. At the near end of the pool, there were nine bronzes: three young male deer (NM 4886, 4888), a female piglet (NM 4893), a dozing young satyr (NM 5624), all suitably bucolic, and with them traditional "Greek" busts, both Archaic (NM 5608) (fig. 7) and Classical (NM 5592, 5594) (fig. 8) in style.

Sometimes placement was carefully planned: pairs of marble herm-portraits of important Greeks were installed back-to-back along the north side of the pool (fig. 13), and probably on the south side too, but those were apparently displaced by the mud-flow and were not uncovered in the 18th century. Most of the marble herm-heads were intact when they were discovered.[12] Pan and his she-goat were there too (NM 27709) (fig. 4), alongside the marble herm-portraits. At the other end of the pool: on one side sat a pensive young Hermes (NM 5625) (fig. 1); on the other side a drunken satyr keeled over backwards, snapping his fingers (NM 5628); farther back a *puteal* separated two identical bronze runners (NM 5625, 5626). The alloys of these two youths are so different that they were surely not made at the same time. Were they bought at the same time, or was one added later when someone wanted to redecorate? And it goes on: there is a bronze head of a "Polykleitan" athlete (NM 5610) just like the marble one (NM 6164) in the house, and a very popular portrait, the so-called pseudo-Seneca (NM 5616). The Romans knew him well: there are 45 examples of this type, but today we have no idea who he is. The same is true for most of the portraits in the Villa. And, apart from this one, very few of the others are portraits of which there are multiple examples.

Karl Weber actually drew twenty of the sculptures on his plan (fig. 5), just where they had been dug out. These drawings and his notes have provided all we know about where the sculptures were placed in the Villa. As we look through that evidence, we see that the décor of the Villa does not suggest a unifying program, nor does it make only one point. The sculptures send many messages, addressing many different audiences. Once we abandon the notion that we need to identify everyone represented in the Villa's sculpture or that there must be a program linking all the sculptures in the Villa, we begin to see that there are many programs of which this heterogeneous collection is comprised.

---

12 NM 6147, 6148, 6149, 6150, 6151, 6152, 6153, 6154, 6155, 6156, 6158, 6162, 6188, 6322.

We still have no idea how big the Villa of the Papyri really is, but more than 85 sculptures have been found. It is a remarkable piece of good fortune that the locations of the first 85 were recorded – by the man who may well have been the first to approach excavation not as digging for collectibles but as a scientific undertaking, all of whose findings were important, and for which a record ought to be kept. There is still an opportunity to learn much more about this Roman villa, whose size, form, and contents will undoubtedly far surpass its distant modern parallel in Aspen, Colorado.

Who Lived in the Villa of the Papyri at Herculaneum – A Settled Question?

MARIO CAPASSO

A complex problem, *sui generis*

The problem of identifying the owner of the Villa of the Papyri at Herculaneum (or, better said, the owners) is one of the most complex Herculaneum papyrology has to offer, as is evident from the lively and at times heated discussions that have been underway for more than a century. It is also one of much more importance, since the various solutions adopted from time to time suggest different contexts for the Greek and Latin libraries. I may say straight away that we are dealing with a unique problem, *sui generis*. At first sight it appears a quite common, even normal sort of problem from an archaeological point of view, inasmuch as archaeology often has the task of identifying on the basis of often quite scanty materials discovered within it a particular public or private building in which no unequivocal evidence has been found (such as an inscription). Such is the case with the Villa of the Papyri, whose owner has often been identified on the basis of the books it contained. What is unusual is the fact that the evidence of these books, numbering several hundred – a quite extensive library, if one assigns the house to a single *gens* or extended family – has not always been accepted by the archaeologists, who have more than once sought to downplay it. In practice there has arisen an opposition, which has once again divided papyrology and archaeology, between written text and material evidence, confirming the not always easy rapport between these two disciplines at Herculaneum. In the present paper I will re-examine the question. Although I am a papyrologist, I will try to look objectively at the motives of the two parties and attempt in particular to find a way of narrowing or perhaps eliminating the gap between the two disciplines.

The terms of the problem: four questions

The problem of identifying the owner of the Villa of the Papyri may be expressed in the following four questions: 1. When was the Villa built? 2. Why was it built? 3. Who built it? 4. Who lived in it in the period between its construction and the eruption of 79 C.E.? Questions 3 and 4 are of particular interest, but in order to frame them in a better way I think it is appropriate to consider also the first two.

The first two questions: when and why was the Villa built?

The precise era in which the Villa was constructed has not yet been established with absolute certainty. For this to happen, it would be necessary to examine the stratigraphy of the entire complex, which will not be possible until it has been excavated. The theory with the greatest favour is mainly based on the building's plan as well as on its wall and floor decorations. These yield a date of construction of the first half of the first century B.C.E. Mustilli was the first to propose this chronology, observing that the plan of the Villa indicates an arrangement typical of aristocratic pseudo-urban villas in Campania, such as the Villa of the Mysteries or the Villa of Diomedes at Pompeii. The two most important parts of these villas were the atrium and the peristyle; and in the first years of the first century B.C.E. the peristyle (designed not for farming but for leisure) replaced the yard that would have been found in regular rural villas. According to Mustilli, the Villa of the Papyri underwent an important modification with the addition of the rectangular peristyle, a modification which in his view is a little later, dating to the middle of the first century B.C.E., inasmuch as it "still respects the basic idea of a four-sided portico enclosed by a boundary wall, with rich decoration concentrated inwards."[1] This scholar then posited a third and final phase of habitation of the Villa quite close to the catastrophe of 79 C.E., primarily on the basis of considerable quantities of grain found near the square peristyle and of numerous fishhooks found in another quarter, as well as on the basis of the scarcity of domestic furnishings in the building. In this phase the transformation of the building (probably under new owners) from aristocratic villa to farm dwelling would

1 Mustilli 1983 (reprint of 1956 article), 17.

have begun, in accordance with a tendency affecting many aristocratic villas in the course of the first century of the Empire.

The hypothesis of three phases of habitation of the Villa (original nucleus, with atrium, peristyle and various quarters built around it, built in the first half of the first century B.C.E.; addition of the rectangular peristyle around the middle of the century; final transformation into farm dwelling) is generally accepted. It has found some confirmation also from the dating of the Second Pompeian style paintings in the atrium, unearthed by the 18th-century excavations; according to Moormann, "they date to about 50–40 B.C.E., that is to the period of the construction of the villa itself."[2] Further evidence of the final transformation of the complex has been seen in the 60 or so lamps discovered near the atrium[3] and in the fact that not a few papyri, at least 161 by my count, were found in at least three carrying cases and heaped on the ground along the length of the two peristyles.[4] This has been considered "proof that they were being removed as preparation for a new use of the quarters and the new purpose of the villa,"[5] owing perhaps to "socio-economic consequences of the eruption of 62 C.E.,"[6] consequences which some have wished to see directly also in the interior of the villa, for example in the presence of a tub of lime near the pool, and in the fact that some of the statues were found far from their original location.[7]

According to results of the new excavations carried out between 2007–2008 the building was constructed in the third quarter of the first century B.C.E.[8] More uncertain are the date of the possible later addition of the rectangular peristyle and the change to rural domicile. Only the complete excavation of the building can provide more solid evidence of one or the other. Partial confirmation, in this sense, has come from the 1996–1998 excavations of the atrium area, whose wall and floor decoration according to De Simone and Ruffo fits exactly into "the circle of luxury residential villas built between 60 and 40 B.C.E., the period of the greatest expansion of the second Pompeian style of wall painting … in accordance with an obvious unity of archi-

2 Moormann 1984, 637–675, esp. 671.
3 Scatozza Höricht 1983, 137; *Wojcik*, 37 n. 173.
4 De Franciscis 1984, 630.
5 *Ibidem.*
6 De Franciscis 1984, 629.
7 Mustilli 1983, 18.
8 See Guidobaldi and Esposito in this volume.

tectural and decorative idiom in Campania, Latium and Etruria, in suburban, pseudo-urban and coastal contexts."[9] According to these two scholars, the pictorial fragments found in the atrium tend to support a dating of the atrium complex to around 60 B.C.E.[10] The same campaign of 1996–1998 brought to light in the atrium area one of the granaries of the Villa, probably in the loft of the building; the area is the same one where in the 18th century, as mentioned earlier, a large quantity of grain was found.[11] If, as seems probable, a granary was located on the upper floor of the quarters that opened on to the atrium, one of the indications that have led people to speak of a change to rural use becomes weaker.[12]

That the Villa was originally conceived as a luxury dwelling is beyond discussion. Cleverly placed, for climatic reasons, with the corners and not the sides oriented towards the cardinal points of the compass, it was a complex structure on five levels, with a monumental seafront façade. In the period of its greatest splendor it extended along a front of 250 meters, on a longitudinal northwest/southeast axis, in a wonderful location that permitted the enjoyment of a panorama in all directions, whether towards mountain or sea. The recent excavations have shown that it was not really detached from the city, but was in the immediate vicinity of the urban area, as De Franciscis had happily suspected.[13] Completely surrounded by cultivated gardens and vineyards, in its ample dimensions, the disposition of its parts, its rich library and splendid collection of art, the Villa fits the description of a dwelling meant for contemplation and repose.

The third and fourth questions: who built the Villa, and who lived in it?

In the course of more than a century, eight proposals altogether have been advanced for the attribution of the Villa: 1. Lucius Calpurnius Piso Caesoninus; 2. Marcus Octavius; 3. Lucius Calpurnius Piso Pontifex; 4. Appius Claudius Pulcher; 5. the Mammii; 6. the Balbi; 7. Lucius Marcius Philippus; 8. Caius Memmius. I will examine them

9 De Simone and Ruffo 2002, 341–342.
10 De Simone and Ruffo 2002, 342.
11 Mustilli 1983, 18.
12 De Simone and Ruffo 2003, 292 n. 28.
13 De Franciscis 1984, 622.

one after the other in chronological order, attempting at the end to draw possible conclusions.

The first proposal is certainly the oldest and most favoured. It was first advanced in English circles in the first decades of the 19th century; on this occasion it is pleasant to recall the complacency of W. Drummond and R. Walpole when they reflected in the preface of their volume *Herculanensia; or Archeological and Philological Dissertations* (London 1810) on "the extraordinary revolution of events" which had so arranged affairs that the remains of the library of one of the Pisones had come into the hands of an English prince, thus giving the descendants of the rude and unlettered Britons described in the pages of Caesar and Tacitus the opportunity to bring to light, by unrolling the papyri, the treasures of Greek and Latin literature.[14]

The merit of being the first to work out the hypothesis in a thoroughly scientific manner belongs to Domenico Comparetti. After an initial formulation in 1879 he published his argument more extensively in his famous book *La Villa ercolanese dei Pisoni. I suoi monumenti e la sua biblioteca*, written in collaboration with G. De Petra and published at Turin in 1883.[15] This first attempt to attribute ownership of the Villa was made by an excellent classical scholar and papyrologist who had a particular sensitivity for archaeology, and who had published various archaeological interpretations. Significantly, his effort was founded principally on the presence of Greek books in the building. Comparetti's argument proceeded as follows:

1. The massive presence in the Villa's Greek library (a library consisting of Epicurean texts) of works by Philodemus, an author on the whole little known in antiquity except for his epigrams, appreciated for their elegance by Cicero and preserved in the *Palatine Anthology*,[16] leads one to think that it was Philodemus himself who assembled the library. It accords with this basic point that among these same treatises of Philodemus are found works meant not for public circulation but for his own exclusive use, and others which have the form of preliminary drafts.[17]

14 Drummond and Walpole 1810, XIII-XIV; see also IX.
15 *CDP*.
16 Cic. *Pis*. 68–72; see Gigante 1983, 35–53.
17 *CDP*, 4.

2. Philodemus cannot be the owner of a "rich and luxurious"[18] villa like that of Herculaneum, since basically, according to what Cicero tells us and as we can infer from some of his own epigrams, he was a "Greekling" (*graeculus*) who flattered his patron and needed his protection.[19]
3. The Villa must have belonged to a rich and noble man, a contemporary and friend of Philodemus, who housed his *protégé*, or at least his books, in this dwelling; this can only be Piso Caesoninus, father-in-law of Julius Caesar and consul of 58 B.C.E., intimate friend and patron of Philodemus. Their close relationship, which was to last more than 30 years, comes through clearly in the venomous oration written by Cicero against Piso in 55 B.C.E.[20]
4. The contents of the Villa other than the library accord with the personality and career of Caesoninus: the scarcity of domestic furniture and of everyday objects of any value can be attributed to the avarice of Piso, whom Cicero accused of a sordid and shabby lifestyle, whereas the splendid marble and bronze sculptures which adorned the house were the fruit of the despoliations inflicted by Piso, according to Cicero, on Byzantium and many other Greek cities during the course of his proconsulship of Macedonia (57–55 B.C.E.).[21]
5. It is very probable that upon the death of Caesoninus after 43 B.C.E. the Villa passed into the hands of his son Lucius Calpurnius Piso Pontifex, consul in 15 B.C.E. and proconsul of Syria and Pamphylia in 13 B.C.E., confidant of Augustus and Tiberius, who died in 32 C.E. at the age of 80. Neither he nor his heirs appear to have occupied themselves much with the luxurious villa: they added little to the art collections; they left the walls in their antique condition, that is to say covered with paintings dating to the Republican period; they left untouched the integral library of Greek Epicurean texts "which reminded the Pisones of Caesoninus and his Philodemus," while adding a few score of Latin books, including the poem on the battle of Actium (*P.Herc.* 817), composed at a time when neither Caesoninus nor Philodemus could have been alive.[22]

18 *CDP*, 5.
19 Cic. *Pis*. 68.
20 *CDP*, 6.
21 *CDP*, 11–12.
22 *CDP*, 14.

6. The portrait of Caesoninus can be identified in the bust of the so-called pseudo-Seneca, in which we can recognize the careless personal appearance and the odd physiognomy, between stern and flabby, repeatedly ridiculed by Cicero.[23]
7. The name of the Piso *gens* can be identified in a fragmentary inscription (*CIL* X 8168) cut into the stand of a bust which, according to Comparetti, is that of Aulus Gabinius, colleague of Caesoninus in the consulship of 58 B.C.E.: *Te[ctor]es Pis | Figuliq*; the inscription would be a dedication to Piso by the plasterers and potters who worked in the Villa.[24]

The strongest points in Comparetti's argument are the relationship between Caesoninus and Philodemus and the presence among the writings of Philodemus of provisional drafts of his works. The other points, for example the absence of domestic furnishing in the Villa being considered "Pisonian," the identification of the bust of pseudo-Seneca as Caesoninus, or the "Pisonian" restoration of the inscription on the column, are no more than ingenuities. Nonetheless they do not impugn the exemplary collaboration between philology and archaeology that his contribution achieves, which characterizes not only the hypothesis of the ownership of the Villa but the entire volume written together with De Petra.

The Pisonian hypothesis (reaffirmed 30 years later by Comparetti when he sketched an outline of the chronology of the library of the Villa on the basis of progress in Herculaneum papyrology) was immediately contradicted, especially in Germany. Theodor Mommsen's view is well known; he contested Comparetti's interpretation of the bust of pseudo-Seneca and his restoration of the inscription, and noted the complete absence of archaeological and epigraphical evidence relevant to the *gens Calpurnia* at Herculaneum.[25] The Italian scholar reacted rather resentfully, defending his reasons and noting that "everybody knows that Theodor Mommsen is the biggest villain of our time."[26] Forty years later, in 1927, in a portrayal of Comparetti, Giorgio Pasquali said of this disagreement: "One of his conjectures, that the villa in which the papyri were discovered belonged to Caesar's father-in-law L. Piso, was much ridiculed abroad. I am sufficiently old-fashioned to

23 *CDP*, 15–20.
24 *CDP*, 28–32.
25 Mommsen 1880, 32–36.
26 *CDP*, 28.

consider it, if not certain, probable, against Mommsen and who knows how many others … The resolution of this uncertainty will come perhaps from the new excavations at Herculaneum, which it is the merit of the present government to have put in course."[27]

From a letter Hermann Diels wrote to Hermann Usener on 13 May 1880 we learn that not even he believed in the Pisonian theory.[28] It is to Diels that we owe the second of the theories of identification, Marcus Octavius. He advanced it in 1882 on the basis of the name Μάρκου Ὀκταουίου placed, as if an *ex libris*, beneath the penultimate column in *P.Herc.* 993/1149 (Epicurus, *On Nature* II) and *P.Herc.* 336/1150 (Polystratus, *On the irrational contempt for popular opinion*), arguing that this Marcus Octavius had owned these two rolls, which were later joined with the library of Philodemus, and was the owner of the Villa. According to Diels, the fact that in each roll the signature was written in a different hand from that of the text prevented one from thinking of a scribe. Basically for Diels attributing the ownership of the building to Octavius was no less adventurous than attributing it to Piso or to that Poseidonax whose name appears in the lower margin at the end of *P.Herc.* 1426 (Philodemus, *On Rhetoric* book III).[29] (Actually this Poseidonax was probably the scribe of the roll, as Bassi and Comparetti had thought, who signed his name and the number of columns copied for purposes of remuneration.)[30] Diels's theory, after a varying reception, has been reassessed several times since 1958; for example, B. Hemmerdinger argued that Marcus Octavius should be identified with the Roman politician of that name, *curule aedile* in 50 B.C.E.[31] I will not dwell on the very sound objections raised repeatedly on many sides against Hemmerdinger's arguments.[32] I will limit myself to noting the extreme fragility of the equation "Marcus Octavius owner of only two rolls = Marcus Octavius owner of the entire library = Marcus Octavius owner of the whole Villa." In my opinion the most sensible hypothesis is that Marcus Octavius was a reader, or more likely the previous owner of the rolls, which joined the stock of the Villa's library probably at the end of the first century B.C.E.

27 Pasquali 1927, 17–18.
28 The letter has been published in Capasso 1987, 116–117.
29 Diels 1882, 383–384.
30 Bassi 1909, 483–484; Comparetti 1910, 125.
31 Cf. Hemmerdinger 1959, 106.
32 Cf. Capasso 1991, 46–47.

Comparetti's theory found favourable reception especially in English-speaking regions, where as we said the possibility of Piso's ownership was regarded as a strong possibility quite early on. It was asserted several times by H. Bloch, among others, who in 1940 used an inscription of 56–55 B.C.E. in honour of Piso Caesoninus found at Samothrace as evidence of the politician's philhellenism, so that he could legitimately be considered the owner of the luxurious Campanian villa.[33] Subsequently in 1965 Nisbet expressed doubts that the library of the Villa was Philodemus', downplaying the preponderance of the Gadarene's writings there. Since he was the most famous Epicurean philosopher of his own day, "he would have been well represented in any Epicurean library."[34] Bloch replied that the library of Herculaneum was not just "any Epicurean library:" if in the course of more than a century, from the death of Philodemus to the eruption of 79 C.E., there were no new accessions, it meant that they wished to respect the integrity of the collection of Philodemus' books and papers, which can only be explained if the Villa remained in the possession of the Piso family to the end.[35] Bloch's two interventions strengthened Comparetti's theory to some extent, even if he admits the lack of objective proof that the Greek library of the Villa received no acquisitions after the death of Philodemus (conventionally placed at about 25 B.C.E. at the latest). In fact, as is known, and as we shall see in the following, according to Cavallo there were some acquisitions of Epicurean works, including some by Philodemus himself, between the end of the first century B.C.E. and 79 C.E.[36]

There remained, practically untouched, the old objection of Mommsen regarding the absence at Herculaneum of archaeological and epigraphic evidence.[37] In 1960 it was weakened to an extent by Lily Ross Taylor, who was convinced that the Villa belonged to the Pisones and noted that after the Social War the citizens of Herculaneum were assigned together with the citizens of Pompeii to the Menenian tribe, to which Caesoninus belonged. The close connections of the Pisones with Herculaneum, according to Taylor, were precisely what

33 Bloch 1940, 485–493.
34 Nisbet 1961, 186–188.
35 Bloch 1965, 561.
36 Cavallo 1983, 65.
37 Cf. Mommsen 1880, 32–36.

favoured this assignation.[38] Taylor's clarification was warmly welcomed by Bloch, who for his part stressed the importance of an inscription on a marble slab found at Herculaneum and published in 1959, which mentioned Lucius Marcius Philippus, one of the first two *duoviri* (magistrates) of Herculaneum. Consul in 56 B.C.E., owner of a villa in the region of Cumae (Cuma) or Puteoli (Pozzuoli), and colleague in 43 B.C.E. of Caesoninus himself on an embassy sent by the Senate to negotiate with Marc Antony, this Philippus, according to Bloch, was very probably chosen by the people of Herculaneum as a *duovir* because of his close ties to Naples.[39] Taylor's intervention was further emphasized in 1970 by John D'Arms: in an era when not a few Romans who were sympathetic to Epicureanism owned luxury villas in Campania, this one was built by Piso, in whose library his friend Philodemus could work.[40] For D'Arms, Mommsen's objection was overcome.

The following year, 1971, Pandermalis brought a new consideration to the debate which henceforth could not be ignored: the significance of the complex, coherent sculptural decoration of the building, its guiding principle and its relation to the library.[41] The possibility that the rich sculptural apparatus was organised by a single person according to a precise plan was already mooted in 1923 by G. Lippold,[42] but Pandermalis was the first to reconstruct a clear programme for the sculpture and to relate it directly to the inherited library of the house, in order to identify the owner. In the history of scholarship on the Villa Pandermalis marks the moment in which papyrology and philology on one side and archaeology on the other interact most closely. Pandermalis, an art historian and archaeologist, moves from the texts of Philodemus (including the epigrams) to the sculptures, after the reviewing of which he returns to the papyri – an exemplary itinerary, but which in my view, in its attempt to be totally comprehensive, finishes up being too ramified and ambitious and thus weakened in its final analysis. According to Pandermalis, the many writings of Philodemus found in the Villa make a valuable contribution both to the reconstruction of intellectual movements in Italy of the late Republic and to the characterization of the owner's cultural formation. There are, he urges, several points of con-

38 Cf. Taylor 1960, 200, 311.
39 Bloch 1965, 561–562.
40 D'Arms 1970, 56–60, 173–174.
41 Pandermalis 1971 (1983, Italian transl.).
42 Cf. Lippold 1923, 77.

tact between the Epicurean's writings and the ideology of his patron Piso Caesoninus, owner of the Villa in the common view:

1. The praise of the country life and disdain of personal labour on the farm, expressed by Philodemus in his treatise *On Household Management* (col. 33 Jensen), accord with a recommendation to live in luxurious rural villas.[43]
2. The *joie de vivre* exalted by the Gadarene in many of his epigrams is reflected in the presence of statues of fauns and silenes in the atrium of the Villa.[44]
3. Philodemus' assertion that democracy is the most obtuse political system (*On Rhetoric* I 375 col. 97 1–8 Sudhaus) accords with the Piso's conservative political orientation.[45]
4. The philhellenism of the Villa's master is demonstrated by the preponderance of Greek over Latin papyri, and of the ratio of Greek to Roman sculptures (15:1), while his sympathy for Epicureanism explains the presence in various parts of the house of busts of Epicurus and his followers Metrodorus and Hermarchus.[46]
5. The Epicurean circle of Siro and Philodemus was frequented also by Virgil, Horace, Atticus and for some time also Cicero, who often speaks of the galleries of statues that adorned his villas: the parallels between these and the Villa of the Papyri are certainly not accidental.[47]

According to Pandermalis the Villa's owner organized his sculptural decoration following a coherent scheme inspired by Philodemus and centred on the opposition between private and public, between the contemplative life and the active life. In his view Philodemus intended a comparison between two concepts of existence, on the one side that of the erudite scholar, the philosopher and Epicurean poet, who lives a secluded life, and on the other the politically active man, the orator and soldier, a conception rather close to contemporary Stoic ideas. The dualism that animates the Villa's decorative programme is explained by the necessity that Philodemus had to adapt Epicurean ideology to a Roman context, somewhat resistant to its cardinal rule that one should abstain completely from political life.

43 Pandermalis 1983, 19.
44 *Ibidem.*
45 *Ibidem.*
46 Pandermalis 1983, 19.
47 Pandermalis 1983, 19, 22.

Pandermalis' stylistic study of various finds and historical data lead him to place the decoration of the Villa in the last decades of the first century B.C.E. This is a very important conclusion, which has perhaps not been sufficiently considered by all parties. In fact, if this dating is accepted and one holds that the building complex belonged to the *gens Calpurnia*, one must conclude that Philodemus could not have suggested the decorative programme to Piso Caesoninus, who died probably about 42 B.C.E. In fact Pandermalis is of the opinion that, more probably, the owner was his son, the above-mentioned Lucius Calpurnius Piso Pontifex (48 B.C.E.–32 C.E.), friend and patron of the epigrammatist Antipater of Thessalonica and praised by Velleius Paterculus (2.98.3) for his rare ability to reconcile the love of leisure (*otium*) with the busy activity necessary for the performance of one's duties (*negotium*).

Pandermalis' theory received important support in 1990 from the archaeologist Adamo Muscettola, according to whom the bust from Herculaneum, that in all probability depicts Piso Pontifex, originally stood in the *tablinum* of the Villa, together with portraits of other members of the owners' family.[48] If he is right, the bust constitutes the unequivocal archaeological evidence for the relationship between the Villa and Herculaneum in general, on the one hand, and the Pisones on the other, which as we have seen Mommsen had demanded if one is to attribute the building to this family. For my part I note that if Philodemus conceived the programme for the galleries of statues and busts and suggested it to Pontifex, this could not have happened before 28 B.C.E., when the Roman nobleman was twenty years old. However, we do not know whether Philodemus was still alive then. In particular I pose the following question: can we systematically relate to a single decorative programme, as Pandermalis tends to do, all the sculptures of the Villa, from the biggest to the smallest, and from the first-rate to the lesser ones? To limit myself to just one example, the imposing statue of Panathenaic or Promachos Athena, located between the two columns which joined the *tablinum*, a room meant probably for reading the household books, with the square peristyle: could it really have symbolized, as Pandermalis would have it, the antithetical interrelationship of wisdom and power? Is it not strange to think that an Epicurean who, however much he tried to adapt to the mentality of a Roman – certainly did not love war – would have suggested putting in a crucial place – on

48 Adamo Muscettola 1990, 145–155.

an axis with the two openings of the *tablinum* and therefore quite visible also from the end of the rectangular peristyle – a statue which according to Pandermalis himself was a favourite of the hated Stoic rivals?

In 1980 Pandermalis' reconstruction was completely rejected by G. Sauron in an article which can count as the extreme limit of speculation in critical attempts at a comprehensive interpretation of the Villa.[49] Sauron starts from the datum, which he takes as incontrovertible, that the proprietor was an Epicurean adept, but he does not tackle the problem of the owner's identity. He regards Pandermalis' antithetical principle in the sculptural decoration as the result of a flawed methodology, which "combines the systematic exploitation of specifics extrapolated for the most part from their contexts with an *a priori* conception of the commissioning patron's intentions."[50] One needs rather to consider the details of the plan and the ornamentation holistically and compare them with all the literary evidence, Epicurean and other, which can help identify the guiding principle of the decoration. It is not possible to understand this decoration without first considering the frame of reference in which it is placed. "Cicero's letters," writes Sauron, "teach us that the decoration was chosen as an element of already constructed spaces, of their significance and the tricks of perspective which the subtleties of the layout permitted."[51] Sauron's main conclusions are:

1. The Villa to a great extent reproduced a late Hellenistic *gymnasium*.[52]
2. The owner of this type of structure wanted to represent the Garden of Epicurus, in keeping with a fashion of the mid-first century B.C.E., when people attempted to recall the philosophical schools of Athens by means of *gymnasia* dedicated to Athena, these schools being typically located in *gymnasia*.[53]
3. He identified this Garden of Epicurus with the Garden of the Blessed and populated it with the heroes of Greek politics and culture contemporary with Epicurus; he felt a close spiritual affinity with them. "Without doubt, the owner of the Villa of the Papyri

49 Sauron 1980.
50 Sauron 1980, 73.
51 Sauron 1980, 73.
52 Sauron 1980, 75–76.
53 Sauron 1980, 81.

> wanted to represented his own beatitude by recalling the world in which Epicurus lived."[54]

Sauron's reconstruction is at once evocative and questionable. Methodologically what makes it weak however is his point of departure, that is to say the study of the Villa's plan considered as evidence of the owner's intentions; relying on the plan of a building in order to advance a date or an interpretation is a procedure that can be hazardous. It has been justly observed that in the mid-first century B.C.E. the plan of the great suburban and pseudo-urban complexes spread throughout Latium and Campania, though starting from well-established models, varies appreciably from case to case, since it must necessarily be adapted to the landscape, take advantage of the vantage points and take into consideration the approach to the villas. How treacherous it can be to rely on the plan is shown, in my opinion, by an article of B. Frischer in 1995, who proposes, though admittedly "as a matter purely of speculation," to see in the villa of Herculaneum the source of inspiration for the plan of the Sabine Villa of Horace. Frischer relies on the presence, in both complexes, of a long rectangular peristyle, "an apparently unusual characteristic for the age." Since peristyles were usually square in the late Republican era, "it is possible that Horace, in constructing his villa, wanted to evoke at Licenza the memory of a place where he had certainly passed many happy hours in company with his friends and Epicurean teachers."[55] However, the dimensions of the two peristyles and the fact that Horace's Villa was probably a "luxurious complex like the Villa of the Papyri" and not a "humble, rustic farm" are the only elements in support of Frischer's theory.[56] Too little, I think. Returning to Sauron's theory, it is not impossible that the owner wanted to imitate a Greek *gymnasium* in some way, but to think that in practice he identified himself with Epicurus is surely too much.

In 1980 the problem of the commissioning of the sculptures and the related one of the Villa's proprietor were taken up by Wojcik in an essay[57] that anticipated a more extensive study of the Villa's finds published in 1986.[58] With Wojcik archaeology invades the field of research on the ownership of Villa completely, utterly banishing papyrology, or

54 Sauron 1980, 81.
55 Frischer 1995, 211–229.
56 Frischer 1995, 219.
57 Wojcik 1979–1980, 359–368.
58 *Wojcik*.

all but. For Wojcik, the separation between papyrological and archaeological examination results from separate treatment of the material on which these two research areas focus, which consequently leads to the predominance of the Epicurean and Philodemean content of the papyri in efforts to understand the Villa. Yet, she argues, the rolls that have so far come to light probably represent only the remnants of the Villa's library. For Wojcik, the art gallery was motivated less by aesthetic intentions or sympathy for Epicureanism than by eclectic cultural tensions of a kind rather widespread among the *nobilitas* of late Republican Rome, which tended by this time to transcend the opposition between *otium* and *negotium*, typical of the preceding era, in an effort of synthesis intended to reclaim *otium* as a value, as contemplation, which distinguished man from beast and was figured as "a necessary activity and useful precisely as a function of public life."[59] Consequently the Villa's Epicurean aspect is completely re-evaluated. Together with the old objection of Mommsen, this leads to the rejection of Comparetti's view, that the Villa belonged to Caesoninus, and of Pandermalis', that it belonged to Piso Pontifex. According to Wojcik the owner was Appius Claudius Pulcher, the consul of 54 B.C.E. and uncle of the homonymous patron of Herculaneum, consul in 38 B.C.E. This Pulcher's philhellenism was more profound than Piso's and his connections with Asia Minor were closer; he was a man of letters and an orator who took part in the political life of the late Republic; his profile is better suited than anyone else's to the image of the owner one derives from the Villa's sculptures and their cultural and ideological underpinnings (dating according to Wojcik to the same period as the building, from the middle to the end of the first century B.C.E.).[60] She accepts the possibility that at the time of the catastrophe a removal was underway or at any rate a change in use, as evidenced not only by the papyri in cases and by grain in one part of the master's quarters, but also by the change in the decoration of the *tablinum*.[61] As C. Gallavotti first realized,[62] this was originally used as a monumental entrance to the once adjacent library and subsequently used also for displaying the portraits of the new owner's family, different from the Appius Claudius Pulcher who

59 *Wojcik*, 260.
60 *Wojcik*, 272.
61 *Wojcik*, 168–170.
62 Gallavotti 1941, 129–145.

commissioned all the sculptures.[63] According to Wojcik the new owners were the family of the Mammii, which emerged in the Julio-Claudian era as the new patrons of Herculaneum, supplanting the Claudii Pulchri. Among its members were Lucius Annius Mammianus, *duovir quinquennalis*, who lived at the time of Augustus and built the theatre of Herculaneum, and the rich freedman Lucius Mammius Maximus, *augustalis* (priest of Augustus' cult) in the Claudian era, to whom the people of Herculaneum dedicated a bronze statue in the *summa cavea* of the same theatre.[64]

Some support for Wojcik's attempt to cancel the link between the Villa and the Pisones came in 1984 from Costabile. Two Latin papyri, *P.Herc.* 1067 and 1475, were identified as a political and a judicial oration respectively. In light of this, Costabile suggested that the Greek section of the library, which probably belonged to Philodemus, could have been combined with the general household library, consisting of several sections; one of these could have included the poem *On the Battle of Actium* and the two speeches. For Costabile these three texts fitted perfectly with the Republican ideology that Wojcik argued as the basis of the sculptural programme. He thinks the owner could have been an Epicurean, or an eclectic with Epicurean sympathies, at any rate a representative of senatorial ideology and tradition: alongside Appius Claudius Pulcher, Costabile thinks that Lucius Marcius Philippus, consul in 91 B.C.E., whose philhellenism is attested many times by Cicero, is a possible candidate.[65]

In 1987 Scatozza Höricht and Longo Auricchio subjected Wojcik's research to a justifiably severe assessment, in archaeological and papyrological matters respectively.[66] Scatozza Höricht pointed out among other things that about Wojcik's interpretations of individual pieces of sculpture are not always reliable, since they are often weak in the absence of copies of the various sculptures. Moreover Scatozza Höricht finds Wojcik's attempt to downplay the Epicurean presence in the Villa unconvincing. She does not exclude the attribution of the ownership to the Pisones; however, given the possibility that the portraits, commonly thought to have been found in the *tablinum*, more probably came from some other quarter of Herculaneum, she thinks that the attribution of

63 *Wojcik*, 279–284.

64 *Wojcik*, 278–279.

65 Costabile 1984, 591–606.

66 Scatozza Höricht and Longo Auricchio 1987.

the ownership to the Balbi has some likelihood – the proconsul Marcus Nonius Balbus, patron of Herculaneum, belonged to this family. Wojcik had excluded this family both because they came to prominence in a later era than the construction of the Villa, and because the portrait of Marcus Nonius Balbus, well known to us, does not match those found in the *tablinum*. For Scatozza Höricht, if the portraits do not come from the Villa, the Villa could also have belonged to the Balbi.[67] The attribution of the ownership to the Balbi had also been advanced by G. Guadagno in 1984, in an essay in which he expresses doubts about the attribution to the Claudii Pulchri and the Mammii.[68]

Longo Auricchio observed among other things that the approximately 1,000 papyri probably did not constitute, as Wojcik wrongly thought, the "remnants" of the original library, but a proper specialist library, which must have been Philodemus' personal library containing, as Cavallo showed,[69] rejects and provisional drafts of parts of *The History of Philosophy* and *On Rhetoric*. Longo Auricchio finds that Wojcik's attempt to loosen the link between Philodemus and Piso Caesoninus, by proposing, after Allen and De Lacy,[70] the existence of other patrons for the Gadarene, is weak. The close association of these patrons with Siro, Quintilius Varus, Varius Rufus, Plotius and Virgil does not by any means preclude a relation with Piso, who remains the most probable owner of the Villa.[71]

In 1987 Gigante intervened in the debate.[72] For him Wojcik's rejection of the Epicurean influence and multiplication of keys to reading the decoration gave rise only to a fragile hypothesis, and Piso Caesoninus remained the most probable owner of the building and commissioner of the sculpture. Philodemus to a greater or lesser extent could have designed this: his work substantially represents all of Hellenistic science and culture that we find reproduced in the Villa. The Hellenistic rulers Ptolemy II Philadelphus, Demetrius of Phaleron, Archidamus III of Sparta, Philetaerus of Pergamon, Pyrrhus king of Epirus, Demetrius Poliorcetes, Seleucus I Nicator, Antiochus IV Epiphanes, all portrayed in the house, "are not only those under whom the civilisation reviewed

67 In Scatozza Höricht and Longo Auricchio 1987, 158.
68 Guadagno 1984, 155 n. 63.
69 Cavallo 1983, 62–64.
70 Allen and De Lacy 1939, 64–65.
71 Scatozza Höricht and Longo Auricchio 1987, 166.
72 Cf. Gigante 1990.

by Philodemus was developed, but also a model of politics."[73] In fact in the treatise *The Good King according to Homer*, dedicated precisely to Caesoninus, great dynasts appear as negative exemplars, opposed to the Homeric heroes (Nicomedes III Euergetes, Cambyses, Demetrius Poliorcetes). According to Gigante, the presence of statues of Aeschines, Isocrates and Demosthenes is explained by the *Rhetoric* of Philodemus, while Sappho, Panyassis, and Antimachus represent the kind of poetry that the Gadarene wrote at considerable length; Pythagoras, Empedocles, Zeno of Citium recall in their turn the *History of Philosophy* at least; the images of divinities such as Athena, Hermes and Pan reflect, finally, the theology of the Garden, according to which, among other points, the gods were anthropomorphic.[74]

In 2005 thanks to a rich volume by Carol Mattusch a new discipline entered the discourse, even if it was only indirectly: archaeometry.[75] Mattusch, like Wojcik in 1986, thoroughly re-examined and re-catthe more than 80 sculptures, statues, herms and busts, in bronze and marble, found in the Villa. On each case Mattusch considered, among other things, the location and date of the find, the interpretations, ancient and modern restorations, and published the results of the archaeometric study of the materials, whether marble or bronze, and of the X-ray radiography conducted on some of the bronzes. The technical analysis and the radiography were done under the supervision of H. Lie, Director of the Straus Center for Conservation and Technical Studies at Harvard University Art Museums, with the aim of going back to the construction and original execution of the individual pieces, identifying the materials used, reconstructing the methods of the producing workshops, outlining the movements of the ancient art market, and establishing the ways in which these same pieces have been reworked in the modern period. These are the most relevant conclusions reached by Mattusch:

1. The selection of the statues and herms of the Villa illustrates "perhaps even more than the owner's tastes" the wide range of artworks that wealthy Romans living in luxury villas around the Bay of Naples between the first century B.C.E. and first century C.E. could order.[76]

73 Gigante 1990, 61.
74 Gigante 1990, 60–62.
75 *Mattusch*.
76 *Mattusch*, 184.

2. The old thesis (sustained for example by D. Mustilli) that all the sculptures, being made of Pentelic marble, are copies produced in Athens, and therefore imported, is no longer appropriate. The analysis of the marbles in the Villa showed that 14 are made of Pentelic marble, 4 of Carrara marble and 4 of marble of uncertain origin. Considering that copies of a certain number of marble or bronze sculptures were also found in other sites (for example the pseudo-Seneca, the Sciarra Amazon, the Doryphoros, the Polykleitan Herakles, Epicurus and Demosthenes), it is more probable that various kinds of marble were available in Campanian workshops (from Pentele, Carrara, or Paros), and that one could ask Greek artists, residing in Italy, to make reproductions of figures whose models were locally well known. One of these shops must have worked for the owners of the Villa. It is not however excluded that the sculptures in Pentelic marble came from Athens.[77]
3. In the garden of the Villa the majority of the sculptures were made of imported marble. The fact that the persons represented were Greek, combined with the high price of the material in which they were represented, no doubt increased the admiration of the guests for the owners, who subtly induced their guests to reflect on the great rulers, orators, writers, athletes, goddesses and women of Greece. The four sculptures made of Carrara marble (including the group of Pan and the goat, the herm of Athena with helmet and the statue of the young man some have seen as a portrait of Piso Pontifex) are of better quality. This marble of Italian provenience was less costly than that imported from Attica but it was evidently associated with sculptural productions of particular value.[78]
4. The small bronze busts of Epicurus (three examples), Hermarchus (two examples), Demosthenes (two examples) and Zeno of Citium found in the *tablinum*, in adjacent locations and in the library recall the Roman habit of adorning libraries with portraits of great writers, mentioned by Pliny the Elder (*NH* 35.2.9). They evidently came from a local shop "that produced small-scale bronze busts of famous literati from the Greek world." The owners of the Villa could have obtained them directly, "but it is easy to imagine guests stopping at the shop on the way to the Villa and buying the busts to take to their

77 *Mattusch*, 182–187.
78 *Mattusch*, 185.

hosts as gifts."[79] Such a circumstance would explain also the presence of duplicates. Also part of this group was the small bust of a woman found in the *tablinum* and representing a member of the Julio-Claudian family (probably Agrippina the younger, 15–59 C.E., wife and perhaps the assassin of emperor Claudius), which the owner of the house during the first century C.E. probably wanted to exhibit in order to demonstrate his close relations with the imperial family. Acquisitions of the imperial age include also the three bronze busts found in the *tablinum* that represent perhaps "three members of different generations of the same family,"[80] two of which probably date to Tiberius's reign.[81]

5. The technique of execution of the bronzes is similar but the analysis of the alloys, quality, forms, styles and subjects show that some pieces were probably acquired in groups, while others came into the collection at different times.[82]
6. The people who lived in the Villa between the first century B.C.E. and first century C.E. collected through purchase and gift all kinds of bronze and marble sculpture, really valuable artefacts in some cases, in others the result of true mass production. The variety and duplication of subjects show that they had different tastes.[83] Some sculptures show a certain complaisant imitation of the tastes of the imperial family. The sculptures came from at least four different local shops: the already mentioned one of the small busts, a second which produced marble herms of famous rulers and Greek writers, a third specializing in full-size marble copies of famous Greek statues, and a fourth which manufactured ornaments for fountains. The visitor to the house would easily recognize the wishes and tastes of the owner. He would know, for instance, that with the archaizing statue of Athena Promachos was intended to recall the owner's close connections to Athens (where there was a similar statue) and would recognize the other portraits whose identity escapes us today.[84]

79 *Mattusch*, 294.
80 *Mattusch*, 272.
81 *Mattusch*, 275.
82 *Mattusch*, 333–334.
83 *Mattusch*, 332–333.
84 *Mattusch*, 149, 182, 332.

7. Neither in the rectangular peristyle nor in any other part of the Villa does there seem to have been a single decorative programme, as one is led to think by the notable variety of forms, styles, types of production and subjects of the various pieces on display.[85]
8. The close tie between Philodemus and Piso Caesoninus remains fundamental for the attribution of the Villa to the latter. The most compelling proof that the building belonged to Piso is the vituperative portrait Cicero paints of him in his oration of 55 B.C.E. The candidacy of Piso Pontifex is weaker. It is however not possible to know which pieces formed part of the collection at the time of Caesoninus, who made additions to it and when, and whether the building changed ownership in the course of time. The fact that the writings of Philodemus were still in the Villa more than a century after his and Piso's death suggests in any case that it could have remained in the possession of the same family – even if it is more probable that in 79 C.E. the building and its contents, including sculptures and library, had been sold to others.[86]

The principal merit of Mattusch is to have applied sophisticated archaeometric analysis to a particularly varied and substantial collection of sculptures coming from a single location. These analyses do not always yield definite results, and Mattusch is well aware of the many questions relating to the individual works that remain unresolved. However, I regard as fundamentally important the perspective she has given to the collection, at once diachronic and dynamic, as it were – a collection organized in her opinion over a long period of time, and originally produced in many workshops.

The more recent theories on the Villa's ownership show that among archaeologists there is still considerable perplexity over the Pisonian hypothesis. Symptomatic in this regard is the change of opinion of M. Pagano, formerly director of the excavations at Herculaneum, who after many times expressing himself favourable to the attribution of the ownership to Appius Claudius Pulcher (a proposal by Wojcik that, it must be said, was met with little agreement) quite recently suggested in passing the candidacy of Gaius Memmius (praetor in 58 B.C.E., orator and man of letters, author of erotic poems and husband

85 *Mattusch*, 182–185, 332–335.
86 *Mattusch*, 20–23.

of Fausta, daughter of Sulla).[87] He is known especially as the dedicatee of Lucretius' *De rerum natura* (1.26). Pagano based his view on the presence of the Memmii *gens* at Herculaneum and on the fact that this Memmius in the course of his exile in Athens (where he was sent after being accused of electoral corruption) "restored the house of Epicurus." In reality, as Guidobaldi already observed rightly refuting this idea, Pagano misunderstood the episode of Epicurus' house, about which we are informed in a letter written by Cicero to this same Memmius at the end of June or in July 51 B.C.E.[88] From it we learn that Memmius had intended to demolish the house of Epicurus situated in the district of Melite, because it hindered some of his building projects in his property there. At the aggrieved and insistent request of Patro, head at that time of the Epicurean school in Athens, and also of his friend Pomponius Atticus, Cicero asked the Roman politician to support the abrogation of a decree of the Areopagus permitting the demolition of the illustrious abode. At the time of writing, however, Memmius had already given up his plans for rebuilding, although he still showed some resistance to complying with Patro's wish.

According to Guidobaldi, "if one really has to play the game of attributing a name to an archaeological structure … the path that leads to the Calpurnii Pisones" appears "very promising."[89] In her view however, Pagano has the merit of calling attention to the fate of the house of Epicurus, with which the Villa could actually have had some relationship. In the crumbling house in the district of Melite in the mid-first century B.C.E. the entire library of Epicurus could have been located, which, as Diogenes Laertius testifies, the philosopher had bequeathed to his successor Hermarchus together with the house itself (Diog. Laert. 10.17; 21). Once one accepts that it was Philodemus himself who brought the books of the founder and of other disciples of the Garden to Italy to constitute the founding core, as it were, of the Villa's library, it is possible, according to Guidobaldi, that it was the Gadarene himself who withdrew the books from the by now ruined house of Epicurus and put them in safekeeping in Italy.[90] This is a very suggestive hypothesis but it does not take into account that Philodemus moved to Italy from Athens, where he attended the lectures of the then head of

87 Pagano 2005, 8.
88 *Fam.* 8.1; cf. also *Q. fr.* 1.2.4; *Att.* V 11.6; 5.1.3.
89 Guidobaldi in Pesando and Guidobaldi 2006b, 269–270.
90 *Ibidem.*

school Zeno of Sidon, around 80–75 B.C.E., when the Garden still enjoyed the best of health.[91] Nor do we have any reason to think that Philodemus later, around the middle of the century, came into possession of Epicurus' library: the oldest Herculaneum rolls containing books from Epicurus' *On Nature* date from the third to the second centuries B.C.E.

Conclusion

These are the salient moments in a debate lasting about 130 years and involving papyrologists, ancient historians, archaeologists, art historians, and historians of ancient law. Among them there is a Nobel laureate for literature (T. Mommsen), a great representative of European philology and papyrology of the nineteenth century (D. Comparetti) and the greatest representative of Herculaneum papyrology of the twentieth (M. Gigante). The importance of identifying the owner is sufficiently clear, I think, as I indicated at the beginning of my paper. In my view we can make out the following firm points:

1. We do not have incontrovertible proof that the Villa belonged to a particular family.
2. This could come only from a complete excavation of the Villa, which will give us firm indications also on the phases of construction and habitation.
3. The Greek library, with its sketches and provisional drafts of writings of Philodemus, and also with second copies of his works, is an insurmountable obstacle to those who do not believe in the Pisonian hypothesis, which remains the most favoured and best grounded of all.
4. Lucius Calpurnius Piso Caesoninus is the most probable owner of the house during the first half of the first century B.C.E. and in the following years. There is nothing that would indicate that he did not also build it. He welcomed there his *protégé* Philodemus, and it is difficult to think that the Gadarene did not visit it on occasion in company with his friends, the Augustan intellectuals Plotius Tucca, Lucius Varus, Quintilius Varus and the great Virgil, to whom he frequently turns in his important ethical treatise *Vices*

91 Cf. Dorandi et al. 1979, 142.

and their Opposing Virtues, written probably about the middle of the first century B.C.E.

5. The three small busts of Epicurus, the two of Hermarchus and the bronze statue of a month-old piglet found at the eastern end of the rectangular peristyle are important elements augmenting, if possible, the Epicurean presence in the Villa. I am not sure if Mattusch is right that the piglet "adds a comical touch to the rural scene,"[92] which together with the statues of two deer located nearby greeted those who passed from the interior of the house into the great garden. It would be hard for them not to relate the animal more or less directly to the Epicurean atmosphere that pervaded the house.
6. The sculptural collection was multifarious and multipartite and was probably formed, as Lorenz and Mattusch maintain, over a fairly long period of time. Precisely because of its variety it is difficult to give it a unitary interpretation. Perhaps Philodemus made suggestions to Caesoninus about this or that piece, but I wonder if it is too easy to think that the sculpture reflects practically the whole of Philodemus' work or a good part of it. If that were true, would we not have found traces of Philodemean suggestion also in the wall decoration, even in its surviving part? It seems to me more prudent to consider the gallery of the Villa as the result of successive acquisitions, reflecting the tastes and requirements of the various masters of the house and the aesthetic fashions of their time.
7. There is no reason to think that at the death of Caesoninus (about 42 B.C.E.) the Villa did not pass into the hands of his son, Piso Pontifex, who could well have been involved in adding more Epicurean texts to the Villa's library – if Cavallo is right to date some of the papyri of Epicurus, Metrodorus, Colotes, Polystratus, Demetrius Laco and Philodemus himself to the end of the first century B.C.E. or the beginning of the first century C.E.
8. The Villa could have remained in the possession of the *gens Calpurnia* until the catastrophe of 79 C.E., like the villa of Caius Calpurnius Piso at Baiae, which belonged without interruption to the Calpurnii from the Augustan to the Neronian period.
9. In the present state of knowledge the supposed final transformation of the Villa into a farm dwelling remains only a vague hypothesis, as moreover the recent excavations also seem to indicate. This ques-

92 *Mattusch*, 329.

tion also will only be resolved by the complete excavation of the building.

The Books of the Villa of the Papyri

DAVID SIDER

Although ancient Herculaneum was rediscovered in 1709, it was not for almost another half-century that its papyri were recognized for what they were. This is hardly surprising: Prince d'Elbeuf of Austria, whose workers discovered and then excavated the town, was interested solely in decorative objects for his nearby palazzo in Portici, and of these Herculaneum supplied many superb examples, many among the best preserved art works from classical antiquity. Yet, the depths of Herculaneum also contained another sort of treasure, one of a unique type even if far less beautiful and certainly far less well preserved: a library.

Although it is true that other collections of papyrus rolls have been found in Egypt, these generally go by the more prosaic name of archives, to reflect their non-literary nature – official records of various kinds. Every library of literary texts mentioned in extant sources, however, has perished, such as that of Pisistratus the tyrant of Athens, containing the texts of the *Iliad* and the *Odyssey*; or that of Aristotle, containing not only his own works, as well as that of some of his students, but also many of the texts he had gathered to provide the basic facts upon which he could construct his ethical and political theories.[1] Although Egypt is the source for all but very few of our literary papyri, these texts have been found either dumped in dry wells or reused as mummy cartonnage (papier mâché; fig. 1). Some reasonable links can occasionally be inferred between isolated texts, but nothing close to the holdings of one library can be established.

Thus, to ignore for the moment the actual contents of the books, the mere existence of a library containing texts, most by authors whose names were previously known, was excitement enough. A library, though, consists of books, yet it was far from clear to the workers excavating the ancient town, all of whom were ignorant of the form taken by ancient books, that this is what was found underfoot. Nor

---

1 Platthy (1968) collects the ancient testimony on both private and public libraries, but since for the Villa of the Papyri there is no testimony other than its very existence, Platthy has nothing to say on it.

did it help that these rolls had been badly charred on the surface and looked like nothing more than blackened pieces of wood, some of which, it is suspected, were used as firewood, for which no blame can be assigned (see fig. 2). Many were found exposed on the floor of the villa, while others were placed in containers (*capsae*) that are, as it happens, not unlike the containers still used for holding fireplace logs. One wonders, though, why they thought that others had been placed on the shelves in wooden cabinets; see fig. 3). It also has to be acknowledged that many were "turn'd to a sort of charcoal, so brittle, that, being touched, it falls readily into ashes."[2]

Finally, on October 19,1752, when one of these rolls broke after falling to the ground, its exposed interior revealed that it contained writing, of however an illegible sort. News of this discovery was taken to the local Spanish court (the Austrians having been expelled in 1734) and then spread beyond the Alps. And excitement was quite naturally high, as Paderni, not the only person involved in the excavation of Herculaneum eager to gain personal advantage, exaggerated his own accomplishments. He also tellingly chose in this same letter, to describe the new texts in the most favourable way. Thus, although by far the great majority of them were Greek, he chose to announce to the world at large the discovery of a new Latin text: *The form of the characters, made with a very black tincture, that overcomes the darkness of the charcoal, I shall here, to oblige you, imitate two short lines; my fidelity to the king not permitting me to send you any more.*

N · ALTERIUS · DVLC

DEM · CVRIS · CRVDE

This is the size and shape of the characters. In this bit there are eight lines. There are other bits with many other words; which are all preserved in order for their

---

2 Camillo Paderni, in a letter translated and published in the (London) *Philosophical Transactions* 48.1 (1754) 71–73. Paderni, who became director of the Museum Herculanense in 1751, was instrumental in the initial stages of the discovery of the papyri, and his published reports in the *Philosophical Transactions* stirred great interest in England and are among our most important contemporary sources of information. He will be quoted again in this paper. They are conveniently reprinted in *CDP*, and are now also available on JSTOR. See Knight 1996.

publication.[3] This fragment can no longer be located, but it almost certainly comes from a Latin hexameter epic poem concerned with, at least in the fragments remaining, the battle that took place at Actium between Caesar and Antony, who was allied with Cleopatra – the stuff of legend, as told by Plutarch and Shakespeare,[4] especially the bit about Cleopatra's death: both Plutarch and the papyrus fragment contain the gruesome scene in which she orders slaves to kill themselves by various means to that she can decide which form of suicide she finds most satisfactory.[5]

Identifying, let alone reading, the new texts, however, was far from easy. With the outer part of the roll charred and highly friable (and no roll could escape this as the pyroclastic flow through Herculaneum guaranteed that every surface would be surrounded by hot ash and gases), any kind of normal handling was sure to crumble at least part of it. Attempts to open the books by simple unrolling produced more damage. But as the incident described above showed, there was often a central core of the roll where the papyrus, although still greyish in colour, allowed for some decent contrast between background and writing. How to get at this legible core (or *midollo*, the Italian term that is now universally used)? Our friend Paderni, who paints such a complimentary

3 Knight 1996. The raised dots (interpuncts) serve to separate words, which in many inscriptions are completely run together with neither spaces nor interpuncts between them.

4 Plutarch (*Vit. Ant.* 71) tells the story of the prisoners put to death, all by various poisons. In Shakespeare, *Antony and Cleopatra* V, ii, 241–79, 305–11, she calls directly for the snake. Incidentally, Cleopatra, acknowledged by all to be intelligent and learned, inveigled Antony to give her the entire library of Pergamum, the second largest Greek library in the world, at about 200,000 volumes, which she must have added to what was already the world's largest library of texts (mostly Greek, but also some in Hebrew and Carthaginian), the library of her capital city Alexandria (Plut. *Vit. Ant.* 58).

5 What little Paderni quotes is consistent with the hexameter rhythm (– u u – and – – –), and the extant fragments are usually eight lines in length. (The last word is either a form of *crudelis* or its adjective *crudeliter*, which would contrast nicely with some form of *dulcis* on the preceding line.) For a translation of the section where Cleopatra ponders the form of her suicide, see Sider 2005, 67–8. The fragments of this poem (*P.Herc.* 817) were first published in *Herculanensium Voluminum quae supersunt* 2 (Naples 1809) v-xxvi. Apart from some few papyri now elsewhere, all the papyri are identified by Papyri Herculanensis (*PHerc.*) numbers; see Gigante 1979, for a description, so far as it can be given, of each papyrus, along with a complete bibliography. This has been brought up to date in (i) Capasso1989; (ii) Del Mastro 2000.

picture of himself in his letters to London, had little patience and (if one reads between his lines) destroyed a few rolls in trying to open them.

In Italy, Paderni had few friends and fewer defenders. The famous student of ancient art, the Abbot J.J. Winkelmann, thought that he appeared "as distinguished an impostor as he was an ignorant dolt."[6] This, though, was mild compared with what was said of him by the man who was soon brought in to work on the papyri, Father Antonio Piaggio delle Scuole Pie, who had been working in the Vatican Library on their manuscript miniatures. He, if anyone is, is the hero of this story. Very soon after his arrival, he was horrified to learn how, even after the workers realized that it was not carbonized wood they found, they thought them burnt clothing or fishnets, and, then, "breaking them with their hands or their pick-axes, they threw the fragments back into the earth, where they were mixed together and reburied without any hope of being seen again!" Imagine his further horror as he describes Paderni's ruinous haste in showing off his discoveries: "He adds how he ran immediately to Their Majesties, even though it was inconvenient, and having opened one of the rolls (that is, he cut one with a knife) in their presence, made them conceive the value of the hidden treasure he had uncovered." In ancient Greece a knife that had been used in a murder could itself be brought up on charges and punished by being thrown into the sea. Such is the feeling some of us still have when we read Piaggio's words.

And yet, more gently to be sure, that was the method employed to get at the more legible interiors of many rolls: slice vertically down a roll to expose the *midollo*. One can readily imagine that any such slices would be excising a certain number of letters on every line of its path. Since a book was rolled so that one opened it to title/author information[7] and then to column one, there are relatively few initial col-

6 "Tanto insigne nell'impostura quanto sciocco e ignorante." Winckelmann (1961 edition by Zampa), 89. More famously, Winckelmann had said of the destructive engineer in charge of the excavations at Herculaneum, Roque Joachín de Alcubierre, that "This man, who (to use an Italian saying) had had as little to do with antiquities as the moon has with crabs, was through his inexperience guilty of much harm and of many losses of beautiful things" (transl. by C. Mattusch). Winckelmann (1771; originally published in 1762), 70. In England, however, where his letters were avidly awaited, he was named a Fellow of the Royal Society in 1756.

7 Thanks to multispectral imaging techniques, what looks like a totally black page can now be read, so that recent years have seen a marked increase in the num-

umns. Split a roll in two like this, though, and one can identify the work and its author from the colophon. Ideally one could now peel away this layer to read the next one, but more likely the layer would be destroyed in its removal, as was soon realized. Scribes were brought in to make drawings (*disegni*) while the visible layer was still in place. These were carefully numbered from one on until legibility failed. What was not so carefully numbered were the two halves of the original roll, with the result that wildly different *P.Herc.* inventory numbers may all belong to the same roll. And if it had been broken in two horizontally before each were split to the *midollo*, there can be four (or more) numbers for parts of the same roll. All papyrologists are masters of jigsaw puzzles, all the more so because they rarely have all the pieces; those who work on Herculaneum papyri have earned the papyrological equivalent of a black belt for their ability to join disparate fragments in both two and three dimensions, as they take even the curvature of the pieces into consideration.[8]

Other means of opening the rolls were sought. Since dryness was the main characteristic, some rolls were placed with some moisture in bell jars exposed to light, in the hope that the papyrus would absorb some of the water vapour and become more flexible. Unfortunately, the carbon-black ink on the outer layers suffered from the humidity. Letters lost shape, to the extent that the language was now taken to be Oscan, an Italic dialect related to Latin.

A less destructive method was devised by Piaggio: the exposed end of the roll was glued to a thin animal skin, which was pierced along its width so that strings could attach it from below to a pulley (fig. 4). The tension on the pulley was increased slowly so that significant lengths of the papyrus could be separated without breakage, or before it was necessary to break it in order to unroll more. As the illustration shows, the

---

ber of book beginnings. The colophon (*subscriptio*) at the end, in addition to author and title, could also include the number of columns, lines, and even *kollemata,* that is, the number of papyrus sheets pasted together to form the roll. All this information was to serve as a guarantee that a lazy or unscrupulous scribe had not short-changed the buyer. See Capasso 1995, 119–37, "I titoli dei papiri ercolanesi I: Un nuovo esempio di doppia soscrizione nel *PHerc.* 1675;" Essler 2007a and 2007b.

8 One could also add to their difficulties that it was soon forgotten that those pieces detached from the *midollo* were numbered from the end of the roll toward the beginning. Thus, scholarly editors, placing the fragments in numerical order, in fact printed them in reverse order. See Obbink (ed.) 1996.

first successful unrolling was of Philodemus' *Peri Mousikes* or *On Music*. The letter delta indicates that it is the fourth "book," which in the ancient world meant the fourth *biblion*, that is, volume; that is, roll. When a book number higher than one appears, it is safe to assume that the library contained all the previous books and maybe some later ones as well. If the number one appears, it means that the work comprised more than one book, and that they too were probably in the library. Some multi-book works were tied together by cords (made of thicker papyrus), but these were soon separated and the bundles dispersed.[9] In the case of Philodemus' *On Music*, Book one has also been found, but, so far as is known, nothing of books two or three. The final paragraph of book four seems to indicate, furthermore, that this was the very end of the work on music.[10] Notice, though, that the illustration takes liberties with the truth. Whether the artist wanted, as I think, to indicate that the title information was the first thing to be revealed – which is false –, or he knew that it was found in the subscription at the very end, the writing would have to be turned around, with the tops of the letters on the viewer's right. There is, however, a long tradition, beginning in the fifth century B.C.E., of artists misrepresenting the way scribes wrote papyrus rolls and the way people read them.

The work of opening and reading continued in fits and starts. Another important figure on the scene in Herculaneum was the Reverend John Hayter, whose *Second Letter* of 1811 remains a fascinating contemporary account.[11] The Prince of Wales (later King George IV), intrigued by the possibilities suggested by the unopened books, had sent Hayter to Naples, at royal expense, to give what aid he could. From 1800 to 1806 he supervised at the Officina dei Papiri the opening and transcribing of about two hundred rolls. Workers who knew no Greek drew these strange forms onto paper. The idea was that in their ignorance they would draw only what they saw, uninfluenced by knowledge that might lead them astray as their minds sought familiar forms. Of course there was supervision; more learned supervisors checked their work against the original. On the whole, though, there were far more failures

9 This was recorded by Winckelmann 1771 (orig. publ. in 1762), 81, who notes that in antiquity these wraps were called *emporetica*; see Plin. *HN* 13.76, where papyrus unfit for writing purposes is said to be used by merchants to protect (higher quality) papyrus and other merchandise. Only Pliny and another Latin passage (Isid. *Etym.* 6.10.5) attest to the existence of this Greek word.

10 So Delattre 2007, 279.

11 Hayter 1811.

than successes in the various attempts to open the rolls. Honourable mention, however, should be granted Sir Humphry Davy, who applied the most scientific means then known to analyze the chemistry and physical nature of the papyrus in order to mitigate any damage.[12]

As was mentioned above, one pressing reason for the sketching of these columns was because the originals would have to be destroyed in order to reach the layer below. It turned out that this would have been an excellent idea in any case, for, as Winckelmann observed not long afterwards, the brittle papyri soon lost bits and pieces no matter how carefully they were handled. Metal engravings were made for publication, which preserved the original readings as well as making them available to a wider audience outside of Naples.

Winckelmann was one of the first after Paderni to write about the papyri for a wider European audience, in his *Critical Account* of 1762, describing in especially great detail the workings of Piaggio's unwinding machine.[13] The results, however, disappointed. The first four rolls were all, as their subscriptions showed, by Philodemus: After *On Music* 4 (which Giaccomo Martorelli, one of the first to see these rolls, argued was actually "a public act concerning a law suit")[14] came this same author's *Rhetoric* book two, then his *Rhetoric* 1, and his *Virtues and Vices*. A newly discovered text then as now usually excites attention and these were no exception – scholarly work on them began very soon – but from the very beginning the wish was expressed that everybody would be even happier were the library to produce something other

12 See the third-person abstract of a paper Davy delivered before the Royal Society on March 15, 1821, "Some Observations and Experiments on the Papyri Found in the Ruins of Herculaneum," *Abstracts of the Papers Printed in the Philosophical Transactions of the Royal Society of London*, 2 (1815–1830), 145–146. The first sentence alone distinguishes Davy from the many amateurs before and after him: "Having in some preliminary experiments upon fragments of a roll of papyrus found at Herculaneum, the leaves of which adhered very strongly together, ascertained that it afforded, by exposure to heat, a considerable quantity of inflammable gaseous matter; that when digested in nitric and muriatic ether it coloured those fluids; and that, when immersed in an atmosphere of chlorine, it was evidently acted upon; – Sir Humphry Davy concluded that there yet remained in these papyri no inconsiderable portion of undecomposed vegetable matter."

13 For accounts of some contemporary French writers' description of the literary discoveries, see Grell 1982, 104–109.

14 Winckelmann (1771; orig. publ. in 1762), 95; see further Porter 2007, 103–104.

than the writings of a philosopher so minor that antiquity produced only about a dozen references to him.[15]

It is true that 23 of his rather elegant epigrams were available in the many editions of the popular anthology of Greek epigrams, but these were dispersed over seven books.[16] In any case, it was not Philodemus' – or anybody's – poetry that was found, nor was it, it seemed, what anybody wanted. People are such ingrates. Winckelmann was probably the first to compose a wish list of preferred texts. Being an art historian, he especially yearned for the lost "rules of symmetry composed by Pamphylius [Pamphilus] for the use of painters,"[17] but he also expressed a desire for the historians Diodorus Siculus and Theopompus, as well as lost plays of Sophocles, Euripides, and Menander. Wordsworth in 1819, by which time the nature of the collection was clear, expressed the wish that Herculaneum might yet disclose some Greek poetry, especially his own favourites among the lyric poets, Simonides and Pindar.[18] In our own century, by which I mean the 20th, Norman Douglas, a reprobate of sorts who spent many pleasant years on Capri, wanted to see the memoirs of Tiberius, who had enjoyed this island in much the same

15 They are collected in my *Epigrams of Philodemos* (Sider 1997, 227–34), to which add Acro on Horace's *Sat.* 1.2.119–22.

16 These editions essentially reprinted the manuscript in Venice written by Maximus Planudes. More epigrams, by Philodemus and others, are contained in another manuscript (split between Heidelberg and Paris), but these were not printed until F. Jacobs' 13-volume edition of 1794–1814.

17 The painter Pamphilus of Amphipolis (fl. 390–40 B.C.E.) was mentioned by Aristophanes (*Plut.* 385) and his mathematic theory of art was described by Pliny (*HN* 35.76). For all the ancient sources, see Overbeck 1868, 1746–51. For his possible influence on Plato's views on art, see Steven 1933, esp. 154.

18 William Wordsworth, "Upon the Same Occasion" (1819), the last two stanzas.
O ye who patiently explore
The wreck of Herculanean lore,
What rapture could ye seize
Some Theban fragment, or unroll
One precious, tender-hearted scroll
Of pure Simonides!
That were, indeed, a genuine birth
Of poesy; a bursting forth
Of genius from the dust:
What Horace gloried to behold,
What Maro loved, shall we enfold?
Can haughty Time be just!
See Porter 2005.

way as did Douglas. His remaining list contained some equally arcane texts: "the lost historical works of Pliny the Elder, Cremutius Corda, Paterculus, Seneca, and others."

The damp reception accorded the new texts can be explained. Although Gassendi had written an influential book on Epicurus in the preceding century,[19] there was little interest shown in him during the 18th century: a translation by John Digby in 1712 (London) and a French one by Charles Batteaux, and very little else.[20] All that was extant and complete in manuscripts and then printed books were the three philosophical letters preserved by Diogenes Laertius, who, being an Epicurean himself, devoted the 10th book of his history of Greek philosophy to Epicurus, the only figure to have a book all to himself. If only these letters spent more time on atomic theory, they would have been valued for the light they would shed on Lucretius, whose popular poem *On the Nature of Things* overlaps hardly at all with the three letters.

So much on Epicureanism. So much by Philodemus, some titles in duplicate copies.[21] That these books were found in or near Naples is not surprising, where there was a thriving community of Greeks (Posilipo, Naples, and Herculaneum were Greek before they were Roman). And Philodemus' name is linked by our texts with Virgil and his circle, all of whom were sympathetic in their early years with the Epicureans on the Bay of Naples. Nor was it altogether surprising that texts of this nature should appear in the wealthiest home in Herculaneum, for many Romans of the ruling class found comfort in the moral writings of this school, which taught that true pleasure and happiness were to be found in the company of friends. Still, the books of the Villa cover more than ethics, including severe technical treatises on literary theory and music, filled with detailed arguments with Stoics and even other Epicureans.

What Roman – and only a Roman could have been rich enough to own this Villa – would have purchased or otherwise come to own such

19 Gassendi 1647.

20 Batteux 1758.

21 A complete list of all the preserved titles, whether or not there is much text to go with the title information, can be found in Gigante 1979, 45–48. Many more works have been given conjectural titles; ibid. 49–52. A list of edited and published texts can be found on the web site of the Herculaneum Society: http://www.herculaneum.ox.ac.uk/. Follow the links to "papyri" and "The books from Herculaneum." An annual list of editions in progress can be found at the end of every issue of *Cronache Ercolanesi*.

a scholarly library? As it happened, an obvious candidate soon presented himself: Lucius Calpurnius Piso Caesoninus, a rich and powerful Roman politician who was Julius Caesar's father-in-law, and who would have ample opportunity while serving in Samothrace to acquire some of the statues that adorn the villa and the wealth to purchase others. Other names have been put forth over the years, but they have never won many supporters. Some of these had unassailable credentials in Herculaneum, such as Marcus Nonius Balbus, who was honoured by the citizens of Herculaneum in several inscriptions that were discovered there,[22] whereas no concrete link has ever been found between the Piso family (Calpurnius' sons would be expected to have taken over the Villa after his death ca. 43 B.CE.) and the bay of Naples in general, let alone the town of Herculaneum and its chief villa.

Nonetheless, Piso seemed so likely to be the owner that for many years the Villa was known by his family name: the Villa dei Pisoni. The links that tie him to the Villa all pass through Philodemus, the author found in greatest abundance in the library. First, and probably most significant, Philodemus actually addresses two of his works to him, a practice that usually signifies that the addressee is the patron of the author. One of these addresses occurs in an epigram in which Philodemus invites Piso to attend a philosophical gathering of friends who plan to celebrate Epicurus's birthday in Philodemus' "modest hut." As we know from other texts, such a gathering was the equivalent of a modern small philosophy group, during which the attendees would discuss the meaning of Epicurus' texts. The second text in which Piso is addressed is a prose treatise, *The Good King according to Homer*, which unusually, since Epicureans eschewed political activity, was a sort of Handbook for Princes.[23]

Second, when Cicero delivered a speech prosecuting Piso (*In Pisonem*), he spent time, as was, and remains, normal for political attacks, by attacking his associates as well. Cicero's point here was to paint a picture of Piso as an uncultured person who assumed the mere veneer of an Epicurean. The associate Cicero singles out is not named; he is identified

22 One of these, *CIL* 10.1426, was copied in the frontispiece of each of the large folio volumes of *Delle antichità di Ercolano*, as part of a group of objects, including papyrus rolls, associated with the discoveries. Usually obscured by the necessary shrinkage required to get the whole image onto a normal octavo page, it – this corner alone – is reproduced at near full scale in Sider 2005, 17, fig.17.

23 See Dorandi (ed.) 1982; Murray 1965. A new edition will be prepared by J. Fish.

merely by the insulting diminutive "little Greek," *Graeculus*, but since this person was an Epicurean who composed "elegant epigrams," there can be no doubt that Philodemus was meant. Cicero uses the phrase "lived with" to describe their relationship, but this clichéd term means only that Piso was Philodemus' patron, not that Philodemus lived within the Villa complex. Indeed, for all that Cicero tells us, this could very well have been in Rome, where all Romans of Piso's class were politically active, but the large number of Philodemus' books in the Villa, located where many Romans withdrew for a rest from politics and where Epicureans were thick on the ground, strongly suggests that Cicero was, without having to specify, placing Piso's dabbling with Epicurenism on the Bay of Naples.

A third link between Piso and Philodemus is less secure. Catullus' poem 47, an invective against one or another member of the Piso family, possibly Caesoninus but also possibly one of his sons, begins with an insulting address to two of his associates, one of whom is called Socration, which looks very much like a diminutive, "Little Socrates," which stood for a Greek philosopher of Piso's acquaintance. Since Socratics were thin on the ground in Italy, it was long ago suggested that this was a nickname for Philodemus, which gains further support from his epigrams, where a wife-like figure is given the same name as Socrates' wife, Xanthippe. These literary links have convinced scholars that Piso Caesoninus was the original owner of the Villa[24].

Without firm, or even relative, dates for the deaths of Philodemus and his patron, it is not sure how Philodemus' working library made its way from his smallish house to the Villa. One possibility is that Piso took possession of them after Philodemus' death, but even if poet outlived patron, Piso's learned sons, who served as addressees – i. e., dedicatees – of Horace's famous *Ars Poetica*, would not have been averse to receiving such a distinguished library into their father's capacious villa. Not being as interested in Epicureanism, however, they would not have added much to this particular part of the Villa's holdings – as in fact the palaeographical evidence suggests.[25] For them, however, this specialized library would have formed only one

24 See Capasso in this volume.

25 See Cavallo 1983, who shows that a small number of the Herculaneum papyri were written toward the end of the first century B.C.E.; the rest, however, date from Philodemus' lifetime and even before, volumes that Philodemus would have brought with him from Athens to Italy.

part of a much larger library of Greek and Latin literary texts. Surely the sons would have owned texts by Horace, who would have sent them a deluxe edition, to which the scribe would have paid extra attention.[26] Perhaps, as Martial writes later of one of his books he sent as a gift, Horace would have made some corrections in his own hand.

So far the finds of Latin texts in the Villa have been meagre: in addition to the fragmentary poem on the Battle of Actium, tiny scraps of Lucretius and Ennius have been recently announced, along with a as-yet unedited larger piece, containing parts of 400–500 lines, of a previously unknown Latin comedy by Caecilius Statius, *Obolostates* or *Faenarator*. Since both titles translate as *The Usurer*, we can be sure that Caecilius, as was normal among Latin Comedy writers, based his plot on a Greek original of, most likely, the fourth or third century B.C.E.[27] Other, tinier, scraps of Latin have long been known, but very little can be made of them.

Palaeographical considerations date them from the mid first century B.C.E. up to the eruption of Vesuvius in 79 C.E. Not for the first time, then, the question arises as to what happened to these later volumes, which classical scholars would very much love to see. Conceivably they were successfully removed from the Villa before it was covered by pyroclastic flow. The love of literature in Herculaneum and Pompeii is ably demonstrated by the many portraits of men and (more often) women reading and writing in wall paintings. Many small busts and other portable objects, however, were left behind. Were Piso's heirs (if indeed it was in fact they who held title at this late date) still so literary that books were removed to safety? Another, more tantalizing, possibility is that they are still there, waiting for further excavations to bring them to light. All the books were found very close to the northeast corner of the Villa as it was known to Weber, thanks to the tunnels driven through the volcanic rock surrounding and filling the Villa (see find spots in De Simone, ch. 1 in this volume, fig. 26). Note the peristyle, which had to have been enclosed by interior walls, which in turn would have fronted a number of rooms, any one or more of which can contain the Villa's Latin library.

26 See Kenyon 1951 (121–134), who collects a number of passages in Latin authors where the form of the book is described, all of which pertains equally to contemporary Greek books.

27 Caecilius' text is being edited by Knut Kleve. See his preliminary description of the papyrus and the plot: Kleve 1996.

As described above, all the Greek volumes opened by various means since the 18th century have suffered damage. There has been further loss as small pieces of already opened pieces break off and crumble. The future, however, promises new, non-invasive, techniques of reading, which will leave the fragile rolls untouched as computer tomography (CT) penetrates the solid mass of the roll in order to produce volumetric (i. e., three-dimensional) pixels (called voxels) of varying densities that can be assembled along the interiors surfaces, from which a two-dimensional image will be produced on which ink will be distinguished from papyrus surface in a continuous reading of the roll.[28] Still in the early stages, this process should eventually be able to print out an image of entire texts from the first column (which will probably not be the original first column as the author wrote it) to the last, and then the subscription information. If this were to be done on one long sheet of paper, it would have to be rolled up for ease of carrying and reading. In other words, students and scholars could be given exact photographic duplicates of the original roll. We will have come full circle in the history of book production.

---

28 See Lin and Seales 2005; Seales and Lin 2004. For a less technical account, see A.P. Gregory, "Digital exploration: unwrapping the secrets of damaged manuscripts," *University of Kentucky Odyssey* (Fall 2004), electronic document, http://www.research.uky.edu/odyssey/fall04/seales.html (accessed October 9, 2010).

The Getty Villa: Recreating the Villa of the Papyri in Malibu

KENNETH LAPATIN

The J. Paul Getty Villa in Malibu, California, reopened to almost universal acclaim in January, 2006, following a long closure for refurbishment. Despite on-going negative publicity relating to the provenance of some objects in the Museum's collection, the public flocked to the site, and reviews have been uniformly enthusiastic.[1] This positive response to the Villa is a far cry from the Villa's original reception, in 1974, when, at the height of modernism in architecture, the construction of a full-scale replica of an ancient Roman luxury villa was descried as a throwback, reactionary, a rich man's folly.[2]

J. Paul Getty, a reclusive oilman, who was outed in the late 1950s as the world's richest man, opened in 1954 a small private museum in his Malibu home, which he had purchased a decade earlier. He collected in three areas: classical antiquities (mostly statuary), Old Master Paintings, and French Decorative Arts.[3] He considered himself an "art addict," and in his autobiography wrote that "the difference between being a barbarian and full-fledged member of a cultivated society is the individual's attitude towards fine art. If he or she has a love of art, then he or she is not a barbarian. It's that simple." Getty rejected destruction in the name of progress, and in his autobiography wrote disparagingly of moderns "no less barbarians than those of the Dark Ages who dressed in animal skins and wore horned helmets. Twentieth century barbarians cannot be transformed into cultured, civilized human beings until they acquire an appreciation and love for art. The transformation cannot take place until they have had the opportunity to be exposed to fine art – to see, begin to understand and finally to savour and marvel. These,"

1 See, e.g., *The Los Angeles Times*, January 1, 2006; January 26, 2006; *USA Today*, January 26, 2006; *Art News*, January 2006; *Apollo*, February 2006; *The New Yorker*, February 27, 2006. For disputed objects, now returned to Italy, see, e.g., Godart and De Caro 2007.

2 E.g., Lapatin 2005, 13.

3 E.g., Walsh and Gribbon 1997, esp. 21–39; True and Silvetti 2005, 3–10.

Getty wrote, "were among the many reasons why the Getty collection 'went public.'"[4] Of course, there were also tax advantages.[5]

The museum, originally located in Getty's "Ranch House," was initially open a few afternoons a week. As the collection grew, Getty built an extension to the Spanish-style building to house ancient marbles. When, by the late 1960s, the enlarged Ranch House proved too small for his growing collection, Getty asked his architects to draw up plans for a new building altogether. Getty's 64-acre Malibu property, which filled the Cañon de Sentimiento and stretched, in a triangle, from the Santa Monica Mountains down to the Pacific Coast, housed not only the Ranch House and its museum, but also a small menagerie that included bears, bison, sheep, wolves, and lions. Getty was particularly fond of his lions, a cub called Teresa (fig. 1) and a male named Nero. Getty's on-site menagerie recalls the larger animal collection of his older contemporary and rival, William Randolph Hearst, who created a sprawling private retreat up the California coast at San Simeon. Though now a state museum, San Simeon, unlike the Getty property, was never intended for the public during its founder's lifetime.[6] When it came to his new museum, Getty must have had in mind San Simeon and other historically themed buildings, such as the Cloisters in New York and the Stoa of Attalos in Athens, both financed by the Rockefellers, as well as the Pompejanum in Aschaffenburg. Other examples of the sort of historicizing house museum he might have considered are the Frick and Wallace Collections.

Getty quickly rejected the proposed Spanish-style extension of the Ranch House and he didn't like the contemporary or Palladian designs either. He refused "to pay for one of those concrete-bunker-like structures that are the fad among museum architects – nor for some tinted-glass-and-stainless-steel monstrosity" – what he later described as "Penitentiary Modern."[7] Stephen Garrett, his architectural advisor and the first director of the Getty Villa recalls that the decision to recreate an

4 Getty 1976, 276–277.

5 Getty denied that he profited from the Museum and shortly before his death calculated that operating the Museum cost him $3 million annually. Getty 1976, 279–288.

6 For Getty's zoo see Walsh and Gribbon 1997, 31; Lapatin 2005, 10–11. For San Simeon see Kastner 2000. For Hearst's zoo see Belozerskaya 2006, 307–373.

7 Quotes from Getty 1976, 278, 283; for rejected plans see True and Silvetti 2005, 10–11; Walsh and Gribbon 1997, 42.

ancient Roman luxury villa seemed entirely unanticipated: "Getty suddenly said, on a November evening in 1968, in his rather deep voice, 'I want you to recreate the Villa dei Papiri.' I had absolutely no idea what he was talking about, and I think that very few people except for a few scholars of antiquity would have known what he was talking about."[8]

This was no mere whim of the moment, however. The genesis of the idea in Getty's mind must go back several years. As a young man he visited ancient sites throughout the Mediterranean: Herculaneum in 1912 at age 19; Baalbek in Lebanon sometime later; and he owned homes at Palo, near Rome, and in the Posiluppo neighbourhood of Naples. He knew well the collections of the Naples Archaeological Museum, including the spectacular bronzes and marbles recovered from the Villa of the Papyri in the mid-18th century, even if he could not have seen the Villa itself. He was not only well-travelled, but also well-read. He had studied at various universities, including Oxford. He was admitted to Magdalen after an interview with college president Herbert Warren to whom he presented a letter of introduction from U.S. president William Howard Taft, a family friend, and he graduated in 1913 with a non-collegiate diploma in Economics and Political Science.[9]

It is not necessary, in this context, to rehearse the history of the exploration and interpretation of the Villa of the Papyri itself or its association with Lucius Calpurnius Piso, but the fact that the building was widely considered to have belonged to Julius Caesar's father-in-law must have appealed greatly to Getty, who constantly strove to associate himself with the great figures of history. He eventually explained that his decision to build a replica of the Villa of the Papyri to house his museum principally stemmed from his desire to contextualize his collection of Greek and Roman art: "What," he asked, "could be more logical to display it in a classical building where it might originally have been seen?"[10]

But Getty's fascination with the Villa of the Papyri can be traced back long before the late 1960s. In 1955, a year after he opened the Ranch House to the public, he published a novella called *A Journey from Corinth*, in which the ancient Villa and its gardens figure promi-

8 Video interview conducted in summer 2005, prior to the reopening of the Villa.

9 Getty 1976, 61.

10 See True and Silvetti 2005, 17.

nently.[11] The protagonist of this anachronistic tale is Glaucus, a Greek landscape architect, who emigrates from Corinth to Naples in 147 B.C.E., the year before the Romans conquer Greece. Glaucus is hired by Piso, who was, in Getty's fantasy, just then building his great luxury Villa outside Herculaneum. Although Piso's contemporary Cicero paints a very unflattering picture of the ancient Roman millionaire,[12] Getty's description of him has more than a little of the self-portrait about it: "...a pleasant looking Roman in his late-thirties, although a trifle pompous in manner... Piso was born in Rome, the only child of a very rich father who was now Consul. He had hoped to make a career for himself in politics, but after a brief experience decided that he possessed little political ability; and since he was a man of great wealth, would be better out of political life than in it. Subsequently he left Rome, bought some two hundred acres of land on the Bay of Naples – adjoining the little village of Herculaneum – and in recent years occupied his time building this great Villa. The work had progressed well. Only some of the gardens remained to be completed."[13]

When Getty's Piso interviews Glaucus, he warns him "You seem to have a flexible mind. If you understand that I mean to have my own way in landscaping, and you wish to act as my assistant and to further my efforts, instead of trying to thwart them, you and I shall get along very well"[14] – a warning, perhaps, to Getty's future collaborators. Glaucus, in any case, gets the job; and then, when his hometown is sacked by the Romans, he encourages his patron to attend an action of the booty at Rome (an ancient parallel for Getty's own early purchases of art at bargain prices during the Depression). And Glaucus advises Piso to buy his own favourite work from Corinth, a statue of Herakles, which is duly installed, in Getty's fiction, in the Villa of the Papyri. Actually, Getty had bought this statue, which was carved about half a century after the eruption of Vesuvius, in 1951, from the Marquess of Lansdowne, and for some time it was housed in the garden of the Ranch House.[15] The idea that it had formed part of the Villa of the Papyri collection was pure whimsy, yet when Getty decided to build a replica of the Villa some 15 years later, the statue was given pride of place:

11 In Le Vane and Getty 1955, 286–329.
12 Cicero *Red. Sen.* 6.13–14.
13 In Le Vane and Getty 1955, 311, 312.
14 In Le Vane and Getty 1955, 312.
15 JPGM 70.AA.109: Lapatin 2005, 17, cf. p. 10.

its own circular gallery on the Villa's main axis, the "Temple of Herakles," complete with a replica of the stunning, *tromp l'oeil* marble floor first discovered by well-diggers outside Herculaneum in 1750 in the belvedere of the Villa of the Papyri (fig. 2).[16]

The Herakles Lansdowne was one of Getty's favourite works. He valued it not only for its beauty, but also for its provenance. He prized works with illustrious previous owners, and his decorative arts collection includes objects that belonged to Augustus the Strong, the elector of Saxony, Frederick Augustus III, King of Poland, Czar Paul I of Russia, the Dukes of Argyll, Buckingham, Marlborough, Newcastle, and Northumberland, the Earl of Caledon, the Marquess of Exeter, not to mention Marie Antoinette, and various Kings of France; he had also acquired antiquities from the Elgin, Hope, and Mattei collections.[17] The Herakles, however, had belonged not just to the illustrious Lansdownes: it was said to have been recovered in 1790 in the ruins of Hadrian's Villa. In fact, Getty once remarked that his two great rivals as collectors were William Randolph Hearst and the emperor Hadrian. He later revised that: deeming Hearst undiscerning, he declared that only Hadrian could rival his taste and his means.[18]

When it came to reconstructing the Villa, there were various problems to be solved. The Malibu coast offered a charming climatic analogue for the Bay of Naples, but although the ground plan of the ancient Villa of the Papyri was known from Karl Weber's plan, the elevations were not preserved. Thus Getty turned to architectural historian Norman Neuerburg, who painstakingly researched and assembled, through various recombinations, the diverse large and small architectural elements that make up the pastiche that is the Getty Villa.

First, to fit the topography of the narrow Malibu canyon site, the building, which in Italy ran parallel to the coast, was turned 90 degrees and situated perpendicular to it. Second, apparently due to topography as well, the arrangement of atrium and inner peristyle was reversed. Third, various outbuildings, including the site of the ancient Villa's library where most of the papyri discovered,[19] were omitted. And, of course, modern materials were used, and modern conveniences, such

16 Lapatin 2005, 42, 80–81; *Mattusch*, figs. 1.21, 2.9; True and Silvetti 2005, 38–39; Walsh and Gribbon 1997, 56–57; Neuerburg 1975.

17 Wilson and Hess 2001, 264–272; Getty 1965, 18–19.

18 See True and Silvetti 2005, 16.

19 Sider 2005, 16–23 and 62, fig. 64.

as parking lots, elevators, etc., were included, but were largely hidden. A Roman road was constructed of modern asphalt. Reinforced concrete was used for the core construction (fig. 3). Ionic and Corinthian column capitals were mass-produced. Some floors and walls were covered with mosaics and marble veneer derived from ancient spolia and/or Mediterranean quarries. Walls were also painted in Pompeian style by Garth Benton. The Villa A at Torre Annunziata had recently been discovered and provided a model for some of these paintings, as did the House of the Labyrinth at Pompeii and a vignette depicting ducks and antelope removed from the Villa of the Papyri (fig. 4; cf. Moormann in this volume, fig. 6).

As the elevations of the Villa of the Papyri were not preserved, the Malibu Villa itself combined architectural elements of various structures – from Pompeii, Herculaneum, other sites on the Bay of Naples, and the city of Rome. There are too many of these to give a comprehensive account here, but a few examples will suffice: The arches of the south facade are modelled on those of the House of Aristides at Herculaneum; the *opus reticulatum* imitated that of Pompeii's central baths with decorative medallions after those of a house in *Insula* IV; and the stone grills were copied from a tomb at the Porta Romana necropolis at Ostia. The north porch of the Malibu Villa, meanwhile, has spiral columns modelled on those of the Villa San Marco at Stabiae and lamps copied from Pompeii. The atrium is a copy, largely, of the Samnite House at Herculaneum while its *compluvium* combines elements from the House of the Vettii at Pompeii and the Temple of Apollo at Metaponton. The illusionistic marble "tumbling block" floor pattern at the entrance of the Villa copies that of the House of the Faun, and the first style walls of the Inner Peristyle also imitate the walls of that same house. The so-called "Basilica" of the Malibu Villa (fig. 5) is quite eclectic, with a floor copied from the Villa of the Papyri, stucco ceiling from the Forum Baths, lunettes from the House of Menander, and polychrome marble capitals from the House of the Deer.[20]

Gardens were an important part of Getty's vision: Glaucus, after all, was a landscape architect. In addition to the Getty Villa's frequently reproduced inner and outer peristyle Gardens, copied from the Villa of the Papyri, the east garden is modelled on that of the House of the Large Fountain at Pompeii, complete with an exact copy of its water-

20 For the "Basilica" see Lapatin 2005, 74–77; True and Silvetti 2005, 37; Neuerburg 1975. Other borrowings are addressed elsewhere in these volumes.

works. The Malibu Villa also has an extensive kitchen garden, in which the plants are all Mediterranean species, many brought from Italian hothouses.

The result was extreme opulence. When the museum opened late in 1974, long before the days of virtual reality, there was little that was virtual about the site. Visitors experience not only the sights and spaces of an ancient Roman luxury villa, but also the cool breezes off the nearby water and, on hot days, the fragrance of Mediterranean herbs. (It is, however, worth noting that the great pool in the outer peristyle [fig. 6] is only 18 inches deep, not only to accommodate the parking garage underneath, but also because if it were any deeper, the City of Los Angeles would require a life-guard.) As Mr. Getty had hoped, his Villa provided the public the opportunity to experience an opulent ancient Roman home.

But the Getty Villa was also a strange place, for it originally housed all of the Getty Museum's collections. Thus, from the ancient galleries below, visitors would ascend to more traditional upper galleries, passing from ancient Rome to an ersatz Versailles, with parquet floors and velvet walls in galleries exhibiting Old Master paintings and French decorative arts. As the collections grew after Mr. Getty's death in 1976 (ironically, he never saw the completed Villa, although he was eventually buried on the property), illuminated manuscripts, photographs, prints and drawings were added to the second floor galleries. And there were other problems with the site as well: it lacked proper conservation facilities, loading dock and freight elevator. Thus a decision was taken to build the new, Getty Center in Brentwood, five miles inland, and refurbish the Villa to focus exclusively on antiquity.

Archaeologists, like Julius Caesar, tend to divide things into threes, and we can look at the Getty Museum in Malibu, too, in three principal phases: the Ranch House; the "original" Villa of the 1970 s, described above; and the new, refurbished Villa, which is largely the brainchild of Venezuelan-born architects Rudolfo Machado and Jorge Silvetti, who, working closely with former curator Marion True, reconceptualised the entire site.[21]

Being situated in Los Angeles, the Villa always had a severe parking problem, and providing space for more cars, as well as better circulation for visitors, were primary tasks for Machado and Silvetti. In the past, visitors drove up from the Pacific Coast and parked underneath the outer

21 True and Silvetti 2005.

peristyle garden – hence the shallow pool. They then either entered the museum through the basement, or ascended to the outer peristyle, entering the building, essentially, through the back garden. The architects were charged with creating not only more parking, but a new entry sequence that would bring visitors to the front door of the Villa – so that they would enter through the Atrium. The Getty also desired more room for conservation labs, offices for staff and visiting scholars, a café and gift shop, lecture hall, and an outdoor classical theatre for the performance of ancient drama.

There were many ups and downs with the planning and construction, including lengthy lawsuits brought by a few wealthy neighbours, who tried to block the entire programme. In an early plan, Machado and Silvetti not only added parking in the northeast part of the site, but also placed the theatre up on the hill, where it would have been serviced by a funicular and commanded a stunning view of the Villa and the ocean beyond. This, however, was deemed impractical.[22]

In the end (figs. 7–8), new visitor parking was built to the south, and the theatre and other public amenities were placed to the west, and non-public buildings expanded or built to the north. Today visitors enter through an entry pavilion, walk alongside the Villa, and descend through the theatre to enter the museum. Machado and Silvetti always intended to contextualize the Villa, and by framing a '70s-era replica with post-modern architecture, they have given it age and no little grandeur.[23]

Machado and Silvetti's entry pavilion introduces their vocabulary of unabashedly modern, yet earthen materials: various conglomerates, board-formed concrete, a few rough stones, including limestone as a nod to Richard Meier's Getty Center. Visitors enter, take stairs or an elevator up through a horizontal portal framed with translucent onyx, and emerge with a commanding view of the Pacific (which, owing to curvature of the coast is south, rather than west of the Villa).

Turning north, visitors walk along an Entry Path, looking down at the Villa just as modern visitors to Herculaneum enter that site from above. The winding path ends with a panoramic view (fig. 9), whence visitors see the museum entrance on the right, opposite the theatre, to the left, which doubles as a gathering place. The theatre, a pastiche of ancient theatres, currently hosts an annual outdoor production in Sep-

22 True and Silvetti 2005, 110–111.

23 Lapatin 2005 and especially True and Silvetti 2005.

tember. The museum façade serves as the *scenae frons*, and actors who are accustomed to the dingy backstage space of fictive palaces have been amazed upon entering the marble-clad Villa interior.

Beyond the theatre plaza the new café (fig. 10) refers to – but does not quote – the Villa's architecture. Its tall columns, with onyx shims as capitals, uneven intercolumniations, and a wooden shed roof supported by stone I-beams all make a post-modern reference to the Villa as an archaeological site, but also alludes to California architecture of Richard Neutra and others, with its long glass walls.

The excavation trope is continued below the café level, where the various materials are layered as if archaeological strata (fig. 11). These layers extend across the site. In fact, as a playful exercise, the architects created a series of drawings hypothetically burying and excavating the Malibu Villa. They also added an *opus reticulatum* facing to newly exposed parts of the Villa's foundations.

Inside the Villa there have also been several changes, too many to enumerate here. The most significant, however, is the opening up of windows and skylights and the fact that the upper storey no longer evokes Versailles, but is an integrated, light-filled, space for the display of antiquities.

The Ranch House, too, has been remodelled, and now houses state-of-the-art conservation labs, as well as offices for curators and visiting scholars, and a small library. New buildings in the north accommodate additional conservation facilities, the UCLA/Getty Program in Archaeological and Ethnographic Conservation, and a business centre for conferences and other events. And there is even a proper loading dock and freight elevator.

While all this was being achieved in Malibu, new excavations were taking place in Herculaneum, as described elsewhere in this volume. Only a small corner of the ancient Villa was brought to light: part of the atrium was exposed, and some wall paintings were revealed. Significantly, the ancient Villa was shown to have been built on multiple stories, rather than just the one shown on Weber's plan. This seems to justify Neuerburg's two-storey plan for the Malibu Villa, though that decision made not so much for archaeological reasons as for functional ones. The new discoveries did not inform the renovations that took place at the Getty Villa. Rather, it can be argued that the Getty Villa and not any archaeological evidence has inspired other reconstructions of the ancient Villa of the Papyri, like the virtual reality model of Gaetano Capasso and his colleagues, which seems to draw on the Malibu

Villa rather than what was found on the ancient site. For example, Capasso's rendering of the inner peristyle, with the so-called "Danāids" around the small pool seems to draw directly on the decoration of the Getty Villa, with its bronze replicas from the Chiurazzi foundry in Naples (fig. 12).[24] The original find spots of the figures in the Villa in Herculaneum, however, are well known, and were even referenced as early as the 19th-century reconstruction published by Giacomo Castrucci in his *Tesoro letterario di Ercolano* in 1852 that places the women in the rectangular peristyle colonnades not far from where they were found (fig. 13).[25]

As for the continuing influence of the Getty Villa, which played such an important role in the self-fashioning of its founder,[26] whether it has also inspired its modern visitors to be a little less barbarous, as Mr. Getty hoped, remains an open question.

24 *Mattusch*, 342–349.

25 Capasso 2002, Herculaneum, 10–13; cf. Castrucci 1852.

26 See Lapatin 2011.

En Foüllant à l'Aveugle: Discovering the Villa of the Papyri in the 18th century

DANA ARNOLD

In this paper I want to interrogate the process of excavating the Villa of the Papyri and how this related to ways of imaging and imagining it. The question that this allows me to explore is the ways in which knowledge can be made visible. In the 18th century the past became a knowable place partly through the discovery of textual accounts and partly though the unearthing of its physical remains by antiquarians and archaeologists. I am interested in how these two strands of knowledge combine and the Villa of the Papyri offers a unique opportunity to consider this. Cultural and psychoanalytic theory, albeit used anachronistically, helps me to think about this and elucidates the way in which thought is visualised. In other words how the images in the imagination become something we can see and how in the case of the Villa of the Papyri this worked to make the past visible. My discussion is informed firstly by the Derridean idea of a kind of blindness that is implicit in every act of drawing. This refers to the act of looking at that which is to be drawn and the moment when the image retained in the imagination is transferred to paper. The process of transcribing the thought in to an image results in an absence of sight – blindness. The object is no longer in view, it is held instead in the thought/imagination of the beholder; it becomes knowledge that needs to be made visible.[1] This enables me to think about the role of the imagination in the production of images, which is germane to the way knowledge of the past was able to be seen at this time. I also consider the subterranean process of emptying and filling – the making of solid and void – using Freud's concept of archaeology as a means of exploring how the Villa plays on the subconscious, conscious and indeed the preconscious mind. In this way the discovery of the Villa of the Papyri offers an opportunity to question the ways in which we interpret objects according to their space-time location. We are used to thinking about the past as a

1 Derrida 1993.

continuous sequence that we encounter and then order in a linear way. In the 18th century the past, or rather history, was a newly discovered place and its physical remains were an important part of its identity.

The eruption of Mount Vesuvius in 79 C.E. buried the history of its surrounding area. As the remains of Pompeii were unearthed so the image and history of the site became intelligible and imaginable. In contrast to its neighbour Herculaneum, the type of volcanic ash that covered Pompeii made excavation possible. Whereas although the mud that had engulfed Herculaneum had preserved the city its removal would have meant the destruction of the buildings, so the city remained underground. What, then, of the past that could not be seen? Here the overlaps and asynchronies of historical sequence and archaeological superposition are important factors in helping us think about how this invisible past was imagined in a different way. Moreover, the specific circumstances of the Villa of the Papyri prompt questions about the nature of archives – in other words what we need to see in order for an archive to exist. I use "archive" here in the broadest sense to mean the body of knowledge we have about a given subject. The physical location of the Villa, hidden underground invites the question if in fact a physical space or place is a necessary predicate for an archive? It is at this moment that the two theoretical frames I am using in this essay cohere in Derrida's critique of Freud in his essay *Archive fever.*[2] Here for Derrida the theory of psychoanalysis becomes the theory of the archive and not only a theory of memory.[3]

The Villa of the Papyri

It is first of all important to remind ourselves of the way in which the Villa of the Papyri was discovered and explored. In the 18th century the Villa was known only through a series of subterranean excavations and contemporary accounts speak of the discovery of the architectural form and contents of the villa through the process of mining. Whilst the contents of the Villa were brought to the earth's surface, its spaces remained underground. Despite the intense activity surrounding the re-discovery of the Villa at this time, the building remained unseen. Its spaces were explored through a series of vertical access shafts and hor-

2 Derrida 1996.
3 Derrida 1996, 19.

izontal tunnels that serviced temporary chambers. These chambers were excavated sequentially, as the rubble was cleared from one room it was placed in the previously hollowed out space. Unlike most other archaeological sites the Villa was experienced principally by touch rather than by sight. When the Villa was seen it was in fragmentary glimpses of its spaces and architectural details revealed by the subterranean excavations, which were carefully recorded by Karl Weber.[4] The notion of blindness is common to many of the contemporary descriptions of this method of exploration and I discuss these later on in this essay.

The middle years of the 18th century saw the discovery of several ancient sites in southern Italy and an active programme of excavation overseen by the Kingdom of Naples. The temples at Paestum, together with the ancient cities of Pompeii, Herculaneum and Stabiae, all burst on to the architectural scene within a few years of each other attracting much attention from Grand Tourists and antiquarians. Access to all these sites required permission and any recording of the buildings or artefacts was restricted.[5] But it is likely that all these sites were known of in the centuries prior to their re-rediscovery but received attention due to the increased interest in the ancient past during the 18th century. There is no doubt that their remote location and inaccessible condition, either from overgrown vegetation or volcanic activity, coupled with their antiquity excited the imagination. And this was especially the case at Pompeii and Herculaneum where the growing interest antiquarians had in archaeological excavation came to the fore. The circumstances of the discovery of these sites were the subject of many narratives. In this regard the finding of the Villa of the Papyri was no exception and what follows is a typical example.

> As some workmen were digging at the foot of this mountain (Vesuvius) about two miles from the sea; having come to a pretty great depth, they observed some strata of earth, which appeared to be regularly disposed, as tho' they were floorings or pavements, horizontally placed, one above the other.
>
> The owner of the ground, being thereby invited to search further, continued the digging, and under the fourth layer, finding some stones

4 The process of excavation and recording of the villa by Karl Weber a Swiss military engineer who supervised the excavations Herculaneum, Pompeii, and Stabiae is discussed at length in Parslow 1995, esp. 85–103.

5 The discovery of these sites and the restricted access to them has been extensively covered in numerous publications. See for instance Parslow 1995 and Serra 1986.

with inscriptions on them, he ordered them to continue their search, till the water coming in should prevent them. Whereupon they dug till they came to above a hundred palms depth, and found various flooring, alternatively one under another; one of cultivable earth, another of black vitrified stone. [...][6]

The way in which the Villa appeared in fragments which were brought out of the earth is striking in this account. The treasures and precious materials rendered by the digging caught the attention of the Prince d'Elbeuf who was in Naples in 1711 in order to build himself a pleasant house on the sea-side.

[...] He knew that some persons at Resina, attempting to build a well, had found in that place some pieces of yellow antique an other coloured Grecian marble. Whereupon he ordered that they should continue to dig, on a level with the water in the well, and search out for a sufficient quantity of that marble.[7]

The way in which the excavators twisted their way through the space under the earth's surface – literally digging in the dark – is evoked in the following description of their activities:

[...] Scarce had they begun to dig sideways, before they found some beautiful statues, among which was a marble one of Hercules, and another one which was imagined to represent Cleopatra. Then proceeding on towards the farm of don Antonio Brancaccio, the diggers met with several wrought columns of alabaster, which appeared to them to be a temple of round form, ornamented on the outside with twenty-four of those columns.[8]

This helps us think about the discovery of the Villa of the Papyri in the 18th century as we have the material culture such as the statues and fragments of pavements, as well as the charred remains of the library that gave the Villa its name. These artefacts were exhumed out of their subterranean surroundings by the teams of excavators working on the site. However, they did not have the spatial context in which to situate these items. This remained invisible to 18th-century visitors and excavators. As a consequence, the underground location of the Villa had an influence on its interpretation.

In an attempt to tease out the ways in which the Villa was imaged and imagined I aim first to attempt to understand the idea of underground both as a metaphor and as an actual space or place. I then

6 Venuti 1750, 47.
7 Venuti 1750, 49–50.
8 Venuti 1750, 50.

move on to look at how the association between the discovery of the idea of history and the discovery of the physical remains of the past worked together in the 18th century. Thirdly, I consider the actual process of excavation of the Villa as described in contemporary accounts. The visualisation of the Villa in the plan produced by Karl Weber (c. 1758) is then discussed as a means of understanding the spaces of the Villa and is placed in the context of the ways in which architecture in all its complexities was represented through contemporary graphic conventions. Finally, I try to tie together these various threads to see what we might learn about the ways in which the Villa was imaged and imagined at this time.

The idea of "underground"

Underground is both a metaphor and an actual space. The spiritual or literary connotations enrich our experience of the real place beneath the earth's surface and it is the simultaneous existence and intersection of the actuality and the abstract notion of underground that is at play here. The idea of underground varies across time and depends on individual responses whether they be literary in terms of author and reader or visual in terms of draftsman and viewer. In the classical world underground was associated with Hades – an imaginary space beneath the earth that is at once the locus of death and of rebirth where dead souls are washed of their memories and returned to life on earth. The Christian idea of hell changed this perspective associating underground with the idea of suffering, punishment and of evil. More recently underground has had a subversive connotation which implies a space that works to undermine the status quo whether that be social, political or cultural.[9] Importantly here underground is also a metaphor for the relationship of the individual and history as the discovery of the physical past is often achieved through excavation. This intersection of past and present operates differently at different times. But I would argue that the 18th century, and especially the latter half, is a key point in this relationship. It is at precisely the moment before the emergence of Archaeology and Geology as "sciences" that underground takes on a special significance, which the excavations of the Villa of the Papyri

9 For a broader discussion of the literary and historical idea of underground is discussed in Lesser 1987.

allow me to explore. Before the fragmentation of knowledge in to disciplinary divides the earth's stratigraphy remained layers through which the past is discovered. This is achieved through the simultaneous exploration of historical narratives, archaeological artefacts and the physicality of geological formations.

Literary constructions of the underworld can be found aplenty. Here I will mention only Virgil and Dante, both of whom gave structure to underground in order to present us with an underworld that exists in tandem with the world above it. For Virgil in the *Aeneid* the underworld exists not only as a spiritual location of the afterlife but also as a physical place.[10] Virgil's underworld, as discovered through the eyes of Aeneas, was accessed via Lake Avernus situated in the crater of a volcano beneath which lay the River Styx. The underground river had to be crossed in order to enter Hades and the bottomless pit of hell.[11] All these locations provide physical geographical co-ordinates to this imagined space under the earth's surface. Our notion of time is subverted in this subterranean world as when Aeneas comes across his father Anchises the latter is looking in to the future at his descendants who are yet to be born. These are in fact the cleansed souls of the already dead that are waiting to re-enter human bodies. My interest is not in the spiritual dimension that Virgil adds to our understanding of the underworld. Instead, I am more concerned with the idea that past, present and future can be juxtaposed in this place. How far can this space-time relationship help inform the discovery of the physical spaces of the classical past in the 18th century?

The underworld discovered by Aeneas is the product of Virgil's imagination and his descriptive powers become more active when the author himself becomes an interlocutor or cicerone. Virgil acts as one of Dante's guides in his journey through the three realms of the dead as described in his *Divine Comedy* (c. 1308–1321). There are of course similarities between the underworlds of Virgil and Dante. The pair enters through the gates of hell and thence reach the ferry that will take them across the River Acheron to hell proper. But for Dante hell comprises nine concentric circles that burrow into the earth, each containing different kinds of sinners. The deeper the circle the greater the wicked-

10 Verg. *Aen* 6.

11 Lake Avernus is taken to be Lago d'Averno situated about two miles northwest of Pozzuoli near the volcanic field known as the Campi Flegrei in the Campagna region of southern Italy.

ness, with this sequence ending at the centre of the earth where Satan is trapped. Once again, as in Virgil's *Aeneid,* the cast of characters is achronological comprising a mixture of figures from Italian history, classical mythology and the Bible. Dante's topography of the underworld gave it a structure and depth, a stratigraphy if you will. In Virgil, as in Dante, poetry resembles archaeology as it digs into the past unearthing its histories and meaning whilst at the same time providing a topographical description of "underground." Conversely, poetry was also an inspiration to archaeologists, or more accurately in the 18th century antiquarians, as its evocative descriptions of antiquity inspired them to excavate for its physical remains. The past, then, existed underground and the pen equals the spade in terms of digging through its layers.

The metaphor and actuality of digging into the past can be juxtaposed with the way in which underground or the subterranean was important for Freud's idea of the subconscious. The link of course is Freud's well-documented interest in archaeology and photographs of archaeological excavations as a metaphor for the human mind.[12] Here rather than re-visiting the well trodden ground of the influence of archaeology on the development of psychoanalysis, I want to think about how Freud's theories of the subconscious may help us to understand how the past was imagined in the 18th century – that is before the advent of archaeology as a "science." The Villa of the Papyri and more generally the nature of the excavations at Herculaneum provide apposite case studies, as the idea of retrieval is important here. This again brings us back to Freud for whom the story of Psyche was attractive as she had to enter the underworld so that she could retrieve the box of beauty from Persephone, so allowing her to achieve her own apotheosis when she fell into unconsciousness.[13] For Freud the idea of underground and retrieval became a kind of metaphor for psychoanalysis.

12 See for instance: O'Donoghue 2004.

13 When Psyche returned from hell, to the light of the world, she was ravished with great desire, saying: "Am not I a fool that knowing that I carry here the divine beauty, will not take a little thereof to garnish my face, to please my love with all? And by and by she opened the box where she could perceive no beauty nor any thing else, save only an infernal and deadly sleep, which immediately invaded all her members as soon as the box was uncovered, in such sort that she fell down upon the ground, and lay there as a sleeping corps." Apuleius, *The Golden Asse,* Book 5 (Adlington's 1566 translation), edited by M. Guy, 1996, electronic document, http://books.eserver.org/fiction/apuleius/ (accessed June 22, 2009).

When he first published *Interpretation of Dreams* his epigraph to the book was a line from Virgil:

> *Flectere si nequeo superos, Acheronta movebo.*
>
> If I cannot stir up the gods then I will move the powers of the underworld (Verg. *Aen* 7.312).[14]

The connection between the underworld and discovery continues in Goethe's Faust which also fascinated Freud. Here the search for answers about the nature of the human soul leads to a pact with devil – a link with the underworld to enable discovery. The combination, then, of underground – the depths of the human soul and knowledge – made possible through travel and through the stratigraphy of the earth is both powerful and deeply rooted in western culture. The literary and metaphorical explorations of underground cohere in archaeological excavations where physical sites were located on the basis of verbal descriptions. For Freud the link made between psychoanalysis and archaeology relies on the interaction of the physical and the metaphorical as it unearths deeply buried remnants of the past combining them with other fragments that are more accessible. In this way Freud structured the mind as a series of layers with the subconscious lying beneath the conscious mind and the id, or the unconscious, located even further down. It is the part of ourselves that we cannot normally see. And the rediscovery of these layers ruptures our linear understanding of ourselves and of how our past and present interact. This helps us to comprehend how the past was rediscovered at the Villa of the Papyri as it is a metaphor for its presence in underground layers as well as in the fragments brought to the earth's surface. In addition to the physical discovery of the site as evoked in the opening descriptive passages in this essay, and the a-temporal nature of the Villa by virtue of its underground location, Derrida confirms the addition of another layer of meaning:

> These blind men explore – and seek to foresee where they do not see, *no longer* see, or do *not yet* see. The space of the blind always conjugates these three tenses and times of memory. But simultaneously.[15]

14 My thanks to Professor Robin Osborne for this translation.
15 Derrida 1993, 5–6

Freud and Archaeology

The impact of Austrian archaeological projects on Freud's thinking about the workings of the mind is substantial and well documented.[16] The expanse of the ruins of the ancient world discovered by archaeologists also offered a metaphorical topography through which to explore the mind. This newly revealed landscape prompted an evocative visual record made possible through the medium of photography. Like the prints that described the excavations at Pompeii these images provided a romantic vision. But they were also quasi-scientific documentation as seen for instance in the photographic record of Heinrich Schliemann's excavations of Troy. The archaeological metaphor in Freud has occasioned an impressive bibliography and a range of interpretative possibilities.[17] Its use as a metaphor is important as it is at once the act of unearthing, of bringing to the surface that which is hidden, and a symbol of destruction and rebuilding. But here I want to turn the metaphor on its head, so to speak, to see what Freud can offer in terms of understanding archaeological excavations.

Saxa loquuntur, "let the stones talk," is a phrase used by Freud to bridge the gap between the narrative of unearthing and the process of ordering and understanding the human mind. To this end archaeology and psychoanalysis share a common goal of trying to decipher and reconstruct a lost history. Perhaps one way of exploring this is to discuss the physical processes of archaeology as if they were a metaphor for psychoanalysis.[18] Archaeology is the rupturing of an existing terrain making visible that which lies beneath it to recall what has been hidden from sight. In other words it enables us to see what is beyond perceptible limits. In this sense archaeology created a new discourse of surface in which the representation of antiquity emerged from the negotiation of topography and stratigraphy. This can be mapped on to our understanding of the subconscious as this is also not immediately perceptible, but hidden in the depths of the mind. The land's capacity to conceal was an essential aspect of archaeology as it worked to disrupt this overlay

16 See O'Donoghue 2004.

17 Freud's own collection of antiquities and their influence on his work together with that of contemporary archaeology is discussed in for instance: Barker (ed.) 1996; Cassirer Bernfeld, 1951; D'Agata 1994; Gamwell and Wells (eds.) 1989; Kuspit 1989; O'Donoghue 2004; Spence 1987.

18 Here I am extending and reversing the argument put forward by O'Donoghue (2004).

enabling the recognition of spatial and temporal layers that were stratigraphically distinguishable but unified as they were part of the same site. In this way excavations were in fact the location of a complex notion of place and stratum whose relationship required the reconstruction of the distant past. Psychoanalysis worked in a similar way to reveal the strata of the conscious, subconscious and preconscious mind. The representation of disrupted surfaces is a hallmark of the images of archaeology. This is seen not only in 18th-century prints that described excavations but also in the photographic record that had influenced Freud.

But it is important to remember that in the case of the Villa of the Papyri the surface was not disrupted. In this way the role of sight – the making visible and seeing remnants of the past – was part of a different process that relied on the imagination and memory. How could, then, the Villa be "reconstructed" when it was not encountered as a three-dimensional object in the same way as other archaeological sites, such as the excavated remains of Pompeii or the nearby ruins at Paestum? And it is here that we find the connection between the invisible layerings of the mind and the reconstruction of architecture using the imagination.

Access rights and techniques of archaeological investigation in later 18th century

The royal excavations at both Pompeii and Herculaneum and the king's museum at Portici, where all the finds were housed, were carried out under the aegis of the Kingdom of Naples. Perhaps as a consequence of the restricted access to the sites imposed by the Kingdom, the execution of the works received a very bad press. For instance Goethe remarked:

> It is a thousand pities that the site was not excavated methodically by German miners, instead of being casually ransacked as if by brigands, for many noble works of antiquity must have been thereby lost or ruined.[19]

This view may not have been an accurate assessment of damage done by the excavations but it expressed the commonly held opinion of the way the work was being carried out. Sir William Hamilton, the English ambassador and friend of King Ferdinand IV as well as of the Bourbon

---

19 Goethe 1962, 202.

court at Naples, was also critical of the excavations remarking on "the dilatory and slovenly manner in which they proceed in the researches at Herculaneum and Pompeii."[20] Indeed, criticisms of excavation method and techniques were also vigorously expressed by J.J. Winckelmann, who was Antiquarian to the Pope.[21] This included his observation that excavators at both Pompeii and Herculaneum went about their work with "beaucoup d'indolence & de lenteur."[22] But Winckelmann believed that the fact that the site required excavation was a good thing. In his *Sendschreiben,* published in 1762,[23] Winckelmann remarked that the advantage of Herculaneum being secluded from public view for nearly 1700 years had some merits as it meant that it was saved from the "ravages of Goths and Vandals, who destroyed most of the vestiges they found of the arts, and were preserved through a long series of barbarous ages for the improvement of very distant times."[24] In common with the emerging 18th-century view of the sense of the past, the value of the discoveries was not called in to question as he went on to note that the "study of antiquities ... [was] of greatest consequence in elucidating history." And Herculaneum was "as if reserved by the Omnipotent Disposer of all things, for the instruction and improvement of the present century."[25] Winckelmann goes on to give this erudite description that brings us back to the metaphors of Freud and the underworlds of Dante and Virgil:

> There have appeared, on opening the earth, manifest traces of discoveries, or rather searches, having been made prior to those lately undertaken at

20 Letter 5 May 1767 from William Hamilton to Rev. Dr. William Robertson, National Library of Scotland, 3942, fol. 58.

21 These are discussed in Ramage 1992.

22 As quoted in Ramage 1992, 654, n. 7.

23 Winckelmann 1762 was translated in to French in 1764: *Lettre de M. L'Abbé Winckelmann à M. Le Comte de Brühl sur les découvertes d'Herculanum* (Paris). This finally appeared in English as: *A Critical Account of the Situation and Destruction by the first eruption of Mount Vesuvius of Herculaneum, Pompeii, and Stabiae* (London 1771). All quotations are from the English translation.

24 Winckelmann 1771, ii.

25 Winckelmann 1771, ii. The use of images including artefacts in the discovery of the past is discussed for instance by Francis Haskell in his wide-ranging book *History and its Images: Art and the interpretation of the past* (New Haven and London: Yale University Press, 1995). Haskell outlines the many ways that historians have used images and how they became available or were discovered through excavation, the creation of private collections and public museums, as well as the increased popularity and ease of travel.

> Herculaneum. These ancient searches are laid down in the map of subterraneous cities, drawn up by the King's orders, and which I have had an opportunity to examine.[26]

The searches consisted of galleries scooped out with much labour but they also made it apparent that there were "no hopes of moderns ever being able to discover all, that the mountain has overwhelmed."[27] Winckelmann goes on to describe the process of excavation in more detail. This included the digging of a principal trench on either side of which chambers were hollowed out – six palmi in length, breadth and height – removing the rubbish as they proceeded from every chamber to the chamber opposite it that was left hollowed out. This process reduced expense and helped to support the earth above.[28] The effect of this method of excavation was to allow visitors only fleeting glimpses of the "Immoveable Discoveries"[29] as the rubbish was not completely removed so it was not possible to see the inside of the whole subterranean city of Herculaneum. And it was not without its critics, for instance William Hamilton felt that this method of excavation denied the possibility of any further discoveries which he was convinced were possible:

> At Herculaneum they have in a manner given over searching tho' it is very certain farther discoveries might be made, and they have filled up every part which they had cleared, except the Theatre.[30]

Yet Winckelmann saw no point in removing the "crust" that covers the site as "the laying bare of a parcel of old ruinous walls, merely to satisfy the curiosity of some virtuosi at the expense of a well built and populous city."[31] And in Winckelmann's opinion Pompeii, which was far easier to excavate and more fully on view, was enough to satisfy the curiosity of the visitor.

It is also important to remember that the "real" or "actual" spaces of the Villa of the Papyri were not known or experienced. Instead the spaces of the Villa were explored through the rooms carved out by the excavators as they groped blindly through the earth and the disorientating network of tunnels that zig-zagged down into the

---

26 Winckelmann 1771, part III, 18–19.
27 Winckelmann 1771, 19.
28 Winckelmann 1771, 24.
29 Winckelmann 1771, 27.
30 Letter 5 May 1767 from William Hamilton to Revd Dr William Robertson, National Library of Scotland, 3942, fol. 58.
31 Winckelmann 1771, 26.

earth. Indeed, these tunnels and "rooms" sometimes cut through the actual walls of the Villa itself. The darkness in which these discoveries were made and the concomitant lack of archaeological method is vividly evoked by Charles de Brosses in a letter dated 1 June 1749 describing the process of excavations:

> Tout ce qu'on y a trouvé dans ce genre, en foüillant à l'aveugle, peut faire juger de ce que produiroit une recherché méthodique.[32]

In a subsequent letter 10 June 1749:

> Après être sorti du souterrain, mon plus grand étonnment fut d'avoir vû qu'Hercluée & le Bourg, qu'on avoit postérieurement rebâti par-dessus avoient été purement couverts & enterrés.[33]

These techniques did improve and become less damaging to the site. Thomas Hollis writing in June 1755 remarked on the increasing skill of the miners as they become more experienced at excavating:

> particularly in digging at Herculaneum, where they never see the light, but at the hours set apart for rest … .[34]

But the archaeologists and miners remained in the dark…

The Weber Plan

This brings me finally to the plan of the Villa of the Papyri produced by Karl Weber for the Kingdom of Naples. This "image" of the Villa combines the memory of the experience of its subterranean spaces and the literary descriptions of villas found in writers such as Pliny, which helped to provide some kind of orientation to the architecture buried in the darkness underground. The Villa is represented in plan only, so its spaces are flattened in to two dimensions. In addition to the spaces that had never been seen in their entirety, the access tunnels used by those who explored the subterranean spaces of the Villa are shown, providing some kind of spatial/tangible reality to the image. We see something that we know is there but defined only by the spaces made to access

32 Charles de Brosses, Lettres sur L'état actuel de la ville Souterraine d'Herculée, 1750, p. 11, letter dated "1 juin 1749."

33 Charles de Brosses, Lettres sur L'état actuel de la ville Souterraine d'Herculée, 1750, p. 27, letter dated "10 juin 1749."

34 Letter from Camillo Paderni to Thomas Hollis 28 June 1755 translated in Philosophical Transactions of the Royal Society of London vol. 49, (1755–1756).

it. This calls in to question what we are looking at when we view the plan of the Villa produced by Weber. Here I suggest that the combination of memory and blindness produces an archiving of the Villa through the graphic techniques or in other words the recording and mimesis of it.[35] And this helps us to understand how forms of knowledge become visible.

This brings me back to the "gap" between the subject and the way in which it is represented, specifically here about the way in which representation makes us blind to its subject. The distance in the act of drawing or recording can be explained in Derridean terms as the kind of blindness that is implicit in every act of drawing since the process of looking at that which is to be drawn results in an absence of sight – blindness.[36] It is here in the gap – the moment of blindness – between looking at and recording images, and seeing images and interpreting, where the imagination comes in to play. My question here is what the Weber plan can tell us about how knowledge about architecture is made visible. The fact that the Villa was never seen is significant here as it elucidates how graphic conventions help make images from the imagined.

The system of architectural drawings using perspective views, orthogonal elevation, details and working drawings is not merely imitative. Instead buildings are disembodied and dissected, as if order is imposed on chaos – marks on paper evoke the built fabric. But the act of drawing is blind – the building is not in the sightline of the draftsman when it is being recorded. Instead, an image is held in his/her imagination and it is the rhetorical devices of architectural draftsmanship that determine how it is drawn.[37] Weber used some of these conventions of drawing as he depicted the building in plan he also included the notion of a symmetrical design to help with a notional spatial arrangement. Although Weber had seen parts of the Villa as he was excavating it, he never saw it in its entirety. Nevertheless, he was able to produce a plausible image of it that has endured to the present day and still informs our thoughts and knowledge of the Villa.[38] As with

35 Derrida 1996, 16.

36 Derrida 1993.

37 On this point see my recent essays Arnold 2003 and 2008. See also for instance Blau and Kaufman (eds.) 1989.

38 Indeed Antonio de Simone's recent excavations of the villa confirm that Weber's plan of it is basically correct, albeit with minor adjustments. See De Simone in this volume.

any architectural drawing it is not merely a representation of the building, instead the graphic conventions make the spaces intelligible. It is not a realistic representation, but as with orthogonal perspective, architectural details, and so forth we accept it as real. Weber makes knowledge visible using a set of graphic conventions that allow thought to be transformed into image. The significance here of the Weber plan, or perhaps drawing, of the Villa is that it operates like part of the layering of the Freudian mind; it is the ego that negotiates between the id and the superego using recognised "societal" graphic conventions. By this I mean that the invisible, subterranean Villa can in some ways be seen as the id and that is negotiated in to a "socially acceptable" presence (superego) by means of the graphic conventions of architectural drawing, which here perform the function of the ego.

The relationship between knowledge and images held in the mind and the ways in which this was made visible is not unique to the Weber plan or indeed the subterranean site of the Villa of the Papyri. As with other sites being excavated under the aegis of the Kingdom of Naples, sketching in situ was difficult if not forbidden and this was remarked on for instance by Goethe[39] and by the French visitors Cochin and Bellicard. This restriction did not, however, prevent the latter two from publishing a book that included illustrations of object found at Herculaneum, albeit that in the frontispiece it was noted the images were drawn from memory.

> The plates that he has added to his explanation, in order to increase their clarity, have been engraved after designs made from memory.[40]

In a pre-Freudian world imag(in)ing architecture becomes a juxtaposition of word and image where time and space, narrative and description stand side by side. The superposition of space and time, to which Freud alludes, helps us to explore, albeit anachronistically, how image and imagination combine and repel each other in the conscious and subconscious mind. Returning finally to the Villa, its spatial location determines its interpretation here as a superposition of space and time and an abstract pattern. But Weber's plan and the details of his tunnels are as much imaginary images as "scientific" orthogonal reconstructions or more pictorial narrative interpretations of ancient architecture.[41]

39 Goethe 1962, 203.
40 Cochin and Bellicard 1754 (repr. in 1972), 30.
41 On this point see Arnold 2002 and 2008.

These images in fact combine to show the impossibility of imag(in)ing architecture.

And, to bring full circle the theory and archive that have been at play in this essay we must remember that *Archive fever* ends on top of a volcano!

From pleasure, to "guilty pleasure," to simulation: rebirthing the Villa of the Papyri

DIANE FAVRO

Investigations of the Villa of the Papyri have emphasized the provocative eponymous scrolls, challenging excavation history, and persistent questions about ownership and architectural form. The everyday occupants of the building remain silent, buried beneath the mudflow of time. At the Herculanean Villa of the Papyri, the carbonized papyrus rolls reveal the literary and philosophical preferences of the occupants, but little about their reactions to the feel of the material, the sound made unfurling the texts, or the smell of the plants in the courts near the library.[1] The preserved wall paintings from the site depict neither the Villa nor its surroundings. Recent excavations are providing more information about the structure in three-dimensions, clarifying its placement on four terraces that rose 16 meters above the ancient coastline. Yet the evidence is incomplete about wall heights, upper floors, roofing, plantings; large segments of the building remain unexcavated (see Guidobaldi and Esposito in this volume, figs. 1 and 23). The technical difficulties of uncovering the site have resulted in new circulation pathways with reprogrammed sequences of sunlight and shade under modern protective roofs. Thus, while one can walk through parts of the Villa of the Papyri today the experience, as well as the human operatives, are much altered from antiquity. To occupy the lost spaces of this sprawling complex, to embody it with the ghosts of the original occupants requires not only an understanding of the architectural forms, but also of the sensory stimuli encountered.

The Villa of the Papyri, like all elite Italian Roman villas, was built as a physical container for reflective leisure and enjoyment. While reflection is cerebral, other activities of the Roman villa relied on positive sensory stimulation. After the natural birth of the Villa of the Papyri in the first century C.E., the sprawling Herculaneum complex was reborn

1 Attempts to link some of Philodemos' descriptions to the villa are unconvincing. Porter 2007, 100.

nearly two thousand years later in Malibu, California (see Lapatin in this volume, fig. 6). In this iteration the villa functions as a museum, but still evokes the positive, pleasurable experiential responses of the original. In the 21st century, the Villa of the Papyri is being reborn again, responding to new excavations and new digital technologies. The high-tech media employed in modelling contemporary reconstructions not only simulate architectural spaces, but also actively stimulate multiple senses.

The rebirths of the Villa of the Papyri – one physical, one digital – present notable case-studies in reconstruction history.[2] In contrast to traditional academic reconstructions these, following the example of the original complex, highlight sensorial embodiment. The Villa's physical situation was a generating factor. The solid volcanic overburden at Herculaneum impeded excavations for centuries. Knowledge about the site was based primarily on the impressive two-dimensional plan by the Swiss engineer Karl Weber derived from the infamous tunnelling explorations of the 18th century (see De Simone in this volume, fig 1). The inaccessible physical remains and minimal three-dimensional data forestalled the creation of comprehensive reconstructions, while the rich finds, especially the numerous texts discovered, begged for contextualization. Weber's magisterial plan stood for years as the iconic symbol of the Villa, a tantalizingly whisper of memory about lives once lived, and spaces once occupied. The impossibility of human engagement with the physical environment where the scrolls were read and the artworks appreciated only heightened the desire to experience the Villa's original spaces, smelling the plantings, hearing the fountains, touching the smooth marbles.

For any ancient site the evaluation of historic haptic responses, sightlines, movement, acoustics, smellscapes, and other sensorial factors requires a simulated holistic environment. Since no ancient site remains complete in three-dimensions hypothetical elements must be included in the quest for architectural completeness.[3] The surrounding physical context and ancient ecology are not readily recreated. Equally problematic is the evaluation of ancient sensory reception; personal responses

2 Each architectural reconstruction is irrevocably mired in its own period of creation, reacting to different knowledge, concerns, and sensibilities as well as different representational tools and techniques. This reality was made abundantly clear in the collection of reconstructions of Pliny's villas gathered by Helen Tanzer (1924).

3 Vacharopoulou 2005.

cannot be easily calibrated scientifically or readily compared. As a result, immersive reconstructions are controversial. Questions about accuracy and authenticity are enduring and legitimate. Also at play are deep-seated concerns about original intentionality and the validity of physiological uniformitarianism, the assumption that processes observed today also occurred in the past.[4] The debates are further complicated by enduring academic disciplinary preferences and prejudices regarding sensorial research and its means of analysis.[5]

Archaeology has had a love/hate relationship with immersive, sensory-rich three-dimensional reconstructions.[6] As the field began to professionalize in the early 20th century, scholars distanced themselves from populist visualizations with enticing sensory clues such as fragrant planting, cool shadows, eye-catching colours, and carefully rendered textures.[7] Such imagery was characterized as subjective, unverifiable, sensual and emotional ("feminine"), and thus removed from academic consideration. Researchers distinguished their own reconstructions as scholarly products illustrating knowledge and data acquired following rigorous scientific protocols. They did employ reconstructions, but distinguished them both functionally and graphically. Academic reconstructions were generally conceptualized as post-excavation illustrations, not as operative tools in knowledge formation.[8] The images were embedded in printed textual arguments or directly suffused with written information as with the inventories bracketing Weber's plan. Represen-

4 Chris Scarre (2006) proposes intentionality can be evaluated by considering patterned repetition and closeness of fit. Ruth Tringham explores how intentionality can be made explicit at a historical site: "Putting vision in its place: the interweaving of senses to create a sense of place at Çatalhöyük," electronic document, http://traumwerk.stanford.edu:3455/31/admin/download.html?attachid=157977 (accessed May 14, 2008).

5 The lack of concern with experiential, multi-sensory issues in art and architectural history aspects has often been noted. Hancock 1982, 30; Favro 2006.

6 Houston and Taube 2000.

7 Terminology in this field is notoriously ill-defined, with the four R's (recreation, reconstruction, replication, restoration) often conflated or confused with other terms (*anastylosis*, reassembly, simulation, evocation). Jean-Claude Golvin, "Signification et problèmes de definition," in: *De la restitution en archéologie, Archaeological restitution* (Paris 2008), 1–4, electronic document, http://editions.monuments-nationaux.fr/fr/les-ouvrages-en-ligne/bdd/livre/9 (accessed June 7, 2008).

8 The scientific reconstruction drawings by archaeologists had most often occurred in the post-processing phase, to borrow a term from film. This situation maintained the marginalization of experiential issues.

tational strategies highlighted the scientific nature of the inquiry. The plan of the Villa of the Papyri is an early representation of the emerging scientific approach to field work emphasizing rigorous measurement and data collection, and the analytical categorization of finds. In the majority of academic reconstruction drawings crisp lines project a clinical air, often presenting historical structures as abstracted objects floating in space, freed from the messiness of human occupation and the demands of environmental positioning as with the famous renderings by archaeologist, architectural historian, and engineer Auguste Choisy (fig. 1).[9] Three-dimensions were presented in axonometric drawings which maintain true measurements, but distort the experience of the human eye and omit sensory clues. Sensorily-rich visualizations were deemed appropriate only in educational contexts. Lacking expertise, non-expert audiences could only understand complex archaeological information when presented in an empathetic manner, replete with engaged human actors, colours, textures, allusions to sounds and smells.[10]

Today, several dynamic forces are colluding to encourage the valuation and assessment of physiological responses to past architecture. Shifts within the discipline during the 20th century have created a perfect storm to stimulate experiential analysis. Around mid-century the development of the so-called "New Archaeology" in the United States redirected scientific interest from history and the artefact to anthropology and the study of human behaviour, opening the door to hypothesis testing.[11] The phenomenological research of French philosopher Maurice Merleau-Ponty and parallel endeavours by others challenged Cartesian dualism and validated the scientific consideration of perception as an active and constitutive dimension of cultural production.[12] Architect Christian Noberg-Schulz's phenomenological analyses of architecture, and in particular Roman ideas and projects, encouraged experiential developments in archaeology. In most cases, however, these phenomenological investigations focused on Bronze Age cultures as with Christopher Tilley's work on landscape studies.[13] In the 1980s, the postmodern movement in Britain questioned archaeology's appeal to scientific positivism and impartiality, resulting in more self-critical theoretical reflex-

9 Choisy 1873.
10 James 1997.
11 Willey and Phillips 1958.
12 Maurice Merleau-Ponty 1962 (originally published in French in 1945).
13 Norberg-Schulz 1980; Tilley 1994.

ivity and interdisciplinarity. Place studies in anthropology, geography, and architecture, among other fields, localized and grounded sensorial investigations at various scales, leading to the formulation of an "archaeology of place."[14] In recent decades, researchers in history, art history, film, as well as the arts, architecture, and humanities have also engaged directly with the senses, further legitimizing archaeologists' consideration of the body as operative within space.[15]

Outside the discipline, the digital revolution has generated increased overall interest in experiential responses. As people interact with smaller digital screens, the longing for expansive sensory reactions has increased.[16] Simultaneously, the proliferation of profitable and complex immersive digital environments – from gaming to Second Life to pervasive computing – have sparked creative competition to develop richer and more diverse environmental experiences in digital realms, including historical reconstructions.[17] Modern designers are creating hyper-realis-

---

14 Particularly influential was work by the geographer Yi-Fu Tuan (1974 and 1977). See also Rodaway 1994 and Bowser 2004.

15 The bibliography for sensorial studies is rapidly expanding, ranging from multi-sensorial inquiries (Ackerman 1991; Smith 2007) to sense-specific works (Scarre and Lawson 2006, Classen, Howes and Synnott 1994). Sensorial analyses in archaeology have centred in select fields, especially New World and Bronze Age studies: Houston and Taube 2000; Ruth Tringham, Michael Ashley, and Steve Mills, "Senses of places: remediations from text to digital performance," electronic document, http://chimeraspider.files.wordpress.com/2007/09/bet_ret_ma_sm_0907_web.pdf (accessed June 8, 2008). Classical studies have remained largely resistant to research on the senses other than sight. This is changing as evidenced by the recent conference organized by Shane Butler, "Synesthesia: Classics beyond the visual paradigm," http://www.classics.ucla.edu/people/faculty/butler/Synesthesia/ (accessed April 30, 2010).

16 Given the mediation of the screen, it is not surprising that much important work on sensorial and mobility issues comes from film studies: Bruno 2002; Vivian Sobchack, "Real phantoms/phantom realities: on the phenomenology of bodily imagination," in: *Phantom Limb* (2004), electronic document, http://www.artbrain.org/real-phantomsphantom-realities-on-the-phenomenology-of-bodily-imagination/ (accessed June 8, 2008). Enactments of historical events, often in original environments, remain popular and have potential for expanding experiential research, but the characterization as hobby pursuits has limited rigorous documentation as well as analysis and will not be discussed here.

17 Representative of such projects is the Digital Roman Forum Project begun at UCLA over ten years ago which continues to evolve with the addition of localized sound, expanding historical coverage, and links to Google Earth: http://dlib.etc.ucla.edu/projects/Forum.

tic alternative worlds whose assessment is based largely upon the perceived authenticity of users' experiential engagement, that is, with the range and sophistication of replicated sensorial stimuli.[18] The scientific gloss imparted by the technology and the sheer computing power required to integrate sound, movement, and vision endorses perceptual issues as worthy subjects of academic interest. Distributable computing is facilitating embodied environmental analyses as with Christian Nold's bio-mapping project which geo-temporally documents emotional and sensory arousal.[19] Simultaneously, reconstructions have been theorized in the influential work of cultural theorists, sociologists, and philosophers who contemplate media reproductions. Notably, Jean Baudrillard blurred the distinction between replication and reality, arguing that simulations have their own reality as simulacra that provide unique experiences.[20]

Scholars today are examining experientially-rich recreated spaces embodied by kinetic contemporary observers who react to smells, sounds, textures, temperatures, and tastes. Sensory interests were integrated into the original design of the Villa of the Papyri. The architectural environments modulated the experiences, activities and responses of ancient occupants; conversely, sensory issues shaped design imperatives. After the eruption of Vesuvius, the dazzling art and intriguing texts carried up through the tunnels evoked great longing to breathe life into the spaces illusively represented on Weber's plan. As the building was born and reborn in reconstructions the descriptors reflect the trajectory of sensory research, moving sequentially from pleasure, to "guilty pleasure," to simulation.

---

18 Renewed concern for experiential design is also evident among contemporary architects: Pallasmaa 2005; Zumthor 1998; Barbara and Perliss 2006; Blesser and Salter 2007. The numerous attempts to spatialize sensorial experience are evident in the prevalent use of the term "scape" in contemporary discourse: visionscapes, smellscapes, noisescapes, soundscapes, etc.

19 Christian Nold, "Bio Mapping," electronic document, http://www.biomapping.net/index.htm (accessed June 5, 2008).

20 Baudrillard 1981.

Natural birth

James Ackerman perceptively identified the unique attraction of the villa as a building type explaining, "The villa accommodates a fantasy impervious to reality."[21] This definition succinctly explains the perseverance of the form in its essentials over the centuries, filling and representing an unending human desire for escape, return to nature, leisure, contemplation, dining, strolling, and, simply, pleasure. The Romans juxtaposed the country villa as a place of leisure (*otium*), with the city where business (*negotium*) dominated.[22] Of course this dialectic reflects an inherent elitism; the villa is and was always a status symbol indicting the owner's standing through its size, location, and ornamentation, and the activities it sheltered and promoted. While privileged Roman writers such as Cicero and Pliny emphasized reflective leisure at their villas, they also referred repeatedly to sensory delights, from viewing to sumptuous dining, from strolling to literally smelling the roses.[23] In a metropolis such as Rome wealthy patricians were bombarded by unpleasant experiences: the press of unwashed humanity; the odours of rotting garbage; the rough textures of unkempt plaster walls; the glare off polished marble surfaces; the clouds of dust and smoke; reverberating noises in the narrow streets; and so on. Once at a seaside retreat, a villa owner slowed down to enjoy carefully modulated sensorial stimuli, moving from the quiet cool shadows of the *atrium*, to a sunlit peristyle with fragrant rustling plants and chirping birds and natural vistas framed by strategically placed windows; passing to a cosy belvedere he was lulled by the sound of waves languorously fondling the shore.

To study Roman life scholars have plumbed texts and secondary imagery in paintings and other artwork to glean evidence about emotional responses.[24] These sources, however, are problematic for experiential research. Not only do most address the elite, the majority excludes references to sensorial experiences as too obvious to require mention.[25] Thus while Pliny's letter describing his Laurentine villa is filled with references to sounds, lighting, temperatures, aromatic stimuli, and tempera-

---

21 Ackerman 1986, 11.

22 D'Arms 1970; Ackerman 1990.

23 Ackerman 1986, 11; du Prey 1994, 3–39; Wojcik 1986.

24 For a recent example see Clarke 2007. Within the field of classical studies, the enduring segregation of "text specialists" from "object specialists" further complicates sensorial studies: Laurence 2004.

25 For the elite viewpoint in the Roman world see Clarke 2003.

tures, these have not been fully considered collectively as forming a choreographed sensorial experience (Plin. *Ep*. 2.17). In art, Roman representational conventions minimize or confuse physiological responses. For example, the artist of the famous reliefs from the Tomb of the Haterii privileged the iconography, patronage, and identification of the buildings depicted, and selected a reverential frontal viewing point, thereby conflating space and sightlines (fig. 2).[26]

The texts found at the Villa of the Papyri emphasize Epicureanism, a philosophy avowing that the criterion of good existence is pleasure. Alexander McKay described the Herculanean complex with its marble and bronze sculptures as providing "a perfect complement to reflective leisure and to the Epicurean tenor of life."[27] Yet a Roman did not have to be an Epicurean to enjoy the Villa's delights. Appreciation of perceptual pleasures can arguably be defined as an innate human trait, but it also had specific meaning for the Romans. An environment created to titillate the bodily senses implied the owner had disposable income for musicians, soft fabrics, warm braziers, sweet perfumes, tasty food, colourful paintings, and other stimuli. Simultaneously, enjoyable sensorial engagement also signalled sophistication and elite status to the Romans. The consumers of the carefully choreographed bodily experiences offered in ancient villas were privileged consumers who had not only the money and time, but also, the "sensibility" for sophisticated appreciation. Education and cultural training prepared them intelligently and perceptually to discern the differences in value and meaning between a wall of costly imported marble and a painted *trompe l'oeil*; a sophisticated flute composition and a simple ditty; aromatic haute cuisine from smelly peasant cuisine. In his famous letters Pliny the Younger describes with care the sensorial diversions offered by his villas not merely to entice his readers to visit, but also to affirm his own sophistication and discrimination (*Ep*. 2.17; 5.6). Such enjoyment extended beyond connoisseurship to imply the owner had *dignitas*. Pliny's uncle wrote, "the pleasure of perfume is among the most elegant and also the most honourable enjoyments in life" (Plin. *HN* 13.1).

Visual representations affirm the sensorial richness of Roman villas. Wall paintings are replete with experiential clues: lush plantings, splashing waves, singing birds, soft materials, aromatic fruits, enticing promenades, and so on (see in this volume, De Simone, fig. 12, Guidobaldi

26 Favro 2007.
27 McKay 1998, 111.

and Esposito, figs. 8 and 25, and Moormann, figs. 5 and 9). Many wall paintings from the residences in the Bay of Naples are self-reflective, depicting other villas, in some cases perhaps site-specific views of neighbouring structures, allowing for consideration of viewsheds to and from the complexes, as well as topographical and ecological explorations. To date few scholars have considered the sensorial implications of such villa imagery and decoration either in depth or holistically. Thus, while scholars have analyzed the comprehensive visual programming of Campanian residences, similar studies have not been conducted for other sensorial stimuli.[28] Roman soundscapes and other archaeoacoustical features remain resolutely the domain of ancient theatres.[29] The primary haptic studies have privileged quantified data such as the temperatures of Roman baths rather than more subjective experiential receptions.[30] While the rich smells of villa and *domus* gardens have been discussed, the examination of olfactory stimuli within built spaces remains largely generalized.[31]

For all the pages and pages of published research on the Villa of the Papyri, despite the informative and extensive recent excavations the complex projects an abandoned, impersonal air. Scholarly studies have compromised an essential aspect of the Villa's original *raison d'être*. The perfumes sprinkled in a *cubiculum* along with other sensorial delights that once informed and shaped the meaning and enjoyment of the Villa of the Papyri have long since dissipated. For centuries it seems as if their memory, their existence, their value had also evaporated until revived on a distant shore.

---

28 Bergmann 1994; Clarke 1999, 1–29. For a historiography of research on Roman domestic architecture see Metraux 1999.

29 To my knowledge no one had plumbed the iconic meaning associated with Roman sounds as has been attempted for those of Mesoamerica; Houston and Taube (2000) provide informative examples of how pictorial clues at Mesoamerican sites indicated the approach of specific sensorial stimuli. The concept of audial icons (wittily described as "earcons") explored in contemporary architecture may provide some insights into the soundscapes of Roman residences; Blesser and Salter 2007, 87.

30 Yegül with Couch 2003.

31 The most cited text remains the children's book *Smelly Old History, Scratch 'n' Sniff your way through History: Roman Aromas* (Dobson 1997).

Rebirth

In 1968 oil baron J. Paul Getty initiated plans for a new museum near his residence in Malibu, California, to house his burgeoning art collection including many antiquities (see Lapatin in this volume, fig. 6). Much to the disappointment of contemporary architects, he decided against a modern design, arguing that for Greco-Roman art, "what could be more logical than to display it in a classical building where it might originally have been seen?"[32] Getty chose to recreate a Roman villa, believing that the emulation of an ancient domestic structure was most appropriate, and that the form would distinguish his museum from others based on historical public buildings.[33] The decision was also timely. In overt rejection of sterile modernist designs in architecture, the short-lived Postmodern movement was beginning to advocate a return to historical (especially classical) precedent as more engaging.[34] During the 1960s and 70s experimental archaeology was receiving recognition and grudging scholarly acceptance. Adopting the model of scientific testing, this branch of the discipline called for the meticulous, full-scale recreation of historic structures using ancient building techniques to test structural aspects and other hypotheses.[35] Publications such as the influential book *Experiencing Architecture* by Steen Eiler Rasmussen

32 Gebhard 1974, 57.

33 Goldberger 1974; Gebhard 1974, 58. The model of Pliny's Laurentine Villa by Clifford Pember on display at the Ashmolean Museum may have been one of the many inspirations for Getty's choice of a Roman villa for his museum: *Illustrated London News*, 5653, Aug. 23, 1947, 220–1. The direct association of the building with famous texts and individuals was also a factor. Herbert Bloch described the Villa of the Papyri thus, "More than any of the ruins of villas in Tibur, Tusculum, Velitrae or Praeneste, the Herculanian villa gives us an idea of how one of the villas of Cicero really looked." Bloch 1940, 493.

34 John Greenwood noted that post-modern architects Rob and Leon Krier described urban space as "experiential and sensual rather than rationalized and functional." Greenwood 1990, 54.

35 John Coles championed the movement with two major publications in 1973 and 1979. Among examples receiving notoriety at this time was the Buster Iron Age farm, began in 1972; the Discovery Channel funded the construction of an adjacent Roman villa in 2002. A major concern for proponents of experimental archaeology was to distinguish themselves from hobbyists who attempted to live in the past or re-enact past events. Behavioral archaeology also developed in the 1970s and, like experimental archaeology, was interested in the making of material culture, but primarily in relation to human behavior.

attempted to rekindle interest in colour, hearing, lighting and other sensory factors.[36]

From all the hundreds of Roman villa remains Getty personally selected the Villa of the Papyri as the model for his new museum. The building was well known and the admired art works from the site were on public display in Naples.[37] The problem of how to read the celebrated scrolls continued to perplex scholars and attract the efforts of scientists. Weber's revered plan and accompanying inventory affirmed that the residence was large and well furnished as befitting a wealthy and sophisticated owner.[38] The elusiveness of the Villa's three-dimensional form may have been another potent reason for its selection. The extant documentation provided only fragmentary information about the walls, roof, and such features as windows and lighting. The uncertainties of the original plan allowed a certain interpretive leeway. Furthermore, unlike Pliny's retreats, the Villa of the Papyri had not been reconstructed repeatedly, allowing Getty to stake a proprietary claim.[39]

Programmatic, legal, and topographic restraints, as well as the patron's preferences, dictated significant changes in the original Villa's DNA. The architects Langdon and Wilson adjusted the plan to fit the new site on the Pacific shore, and meet the requirements of a modern museum and local building codes.[40] The layout of the original Villa was flipped along the horizontal axis, and the orientation to the sea rotated by 90 degrees (fig. 3; see also Lapatin in this volume, fig. 8).[41] The entire building was elevated on an artificial terrace that sheltered a car-park

36 Rasmussen 1959 (originally published in Danish in 1957). Architects gained further insights into perceptual studies through the popular work of psychologist James Gibson (1950 and 1966).

37 Even though there was little to be seen of the villa's remains, Amedeo Maiuri published a guidebook in several languages entitled *Herculaneum and the Villa of the Papyri* (1962).

38 The plan and related images appeared in the magisterial publication *Delle Antichità di Ercolano* (Naples 1757–1792).

39 This attitude is evident in the full title of the first guidebook by Norman Neuerburg (1975).

40 The Getty Villa recently underwent extensive seismic retrofitting and expansion, reopening in 2005. The discussion here focuses on the museum in its original incarnation: Filler 2006. See also Lapatin in this volume.

41 In the natural born Villa, the long axis of the peristyle was oriented to the north-west, with the body of the building to the south; in the reborn version the peristyle is oriented north-east with the body of building to the north.

and other service areas and an upper story added to expand exhibition space even though the existence of a second floor had not yet been confirmed at the Villa of the Papyri. Some original features were omitted, and other special rooms added such as the so-called "Temple of Herakles" to house the Lansdowne sculpture of the hero. Construction was of steel and concrete, with surface materials reproducing those of antiquity as much as possible. Art History professor Norman Neuerburg served as the mid-wife for the rebirth, described in the New York Times as Getty's "authenticity" expert.[42] Aiming to create a holistic, fully functioning building, he drew upon analogs from numerous other Roman villas in the Bay of Naples to "fill in the blanks."[43] For example, the attractive shell-embellished fountain constructed in the east garden was a literal copy of that in the House of the Large Fountain at Pompeii (fig. 4). Such borrowings allowed the patron to further extend his appropriation of the past. Neuerburg himself called the structure, "a recreation rather than a reproduction," justifying the ancient pedigree of each component borrowed from another Campanian building in mind-numbing detail at on-site lectures.[44] Public reception dictated other a-historical adjustments. Neurerburg noted that the colours of the recreated wall paintings were subdued from the garishness of the Roman originals to address contemporary taste.[45]

When the J. Paul Getty Museum opened in 1974 reactions were strong. At one extreme, architects bemoaned the historicist design, archaeologists criticized the melding of different sources into a bricolage of ancient components, and art critics labelled the results "kitschy" and inappropriate for housing art.[46] At the other extreme, the lay public praised the results, ecstatically thronging to the site in such droves that it initially had to be closed on weekends.[47] Almost all visitors commented on the pleasurable experience of moving through the various spaces of the recreated Villa, passing from sparkling marble-clad rooms to sunlit outdoor spaces with splashing fountains and lush gardens. For many,

---

42 Special to The New York Times. "Roman villa is recreated on coast to house Getty Art Collection," *The New York Times,* Jan. 17, 1974, 41.

43 Neuerburg 1975.

44 Filler 2006; Banham 1977.

45 See n. 42.

46 Goldberger 1975. Architecture critic Reyner Banham wrongly said the original Villa stood on agricultural land with no view of sea; to describe the reliance on analogs he invented a new verb, "bricolate;" Banham 1977.

47 Glueck 1974.

the sculptures gained new meaning when experienced in the recreated ancient domestic environment, though few acknowledged the discrepancy between the completeness of the architectural simulation and the incompleteness of the unpainted, fragmented original ancient sculptures.[48] Comments extended beyond the art objects to the sequencing of spaces, the tactile sensuousness of the finely crafted inlaid marble surfaces, the light-hearted sound of water, the golden light penetrating the spaces, the pungent aromas of the plantings, and the views of the glistening sea. Even the most venomous of academic critics adopted words similar to those used by the Romans when describing their villas. Paul Goldberger called the experience "relaxed" and "joyous." Reyner Banham exclaimed, "Delicious! You look from the vestibule down the long colonnaded water through a cleft in the wooded cliffs to the Pacific Ocean beyond, and it's as adorable and sybaritic as the sites where the Romans built... around the Bay of Naples" (fig. 5).[49] Martin Filler described the Getty Villa as a, "seductive, and undeniably entrancing environment, the guiltiest pleasure in the modern museum world."[50]

In this last statement lingers the academic dichotomy between scientific/conceptual (good) approaches and sensorial (bad) responses to environments. Yet sensuous pleasure was precisely what the original Roman villa owners sought and the modern patron J. Paul Getty wanted to evoke with his museum.[51] For Getty the project was more personal than academic or archaeological; he stated, "...the public should know that what they will finally see wasn't done on a mere whim or chosen by a committee delegated for such a task; it will simply be what I felt a good museum should be, and it will have the character of a building I should like to visit myself."[52] The emphasis on the character and "feel" of the building precluded, or at least minimized, the need to follow the strict tenets of experimental archaeology or international guidelines for reconstructions. By overtly aiming to recreate the positive bodily experiences of being in the Villa of the Papyri, Getty

48 Without the original paint, the sculptures stand in lifeless contrast to the colourful recreated wall surfaces; Eco 1990, 34. In some of the outdoor areas restored bronze sculptures matched the completed state of the building.

49 Banham 1977, 238.

50 Filler 2006; see also Goldberger 1975.

51 Getty argued, "Why not show Californians what an especially attractive Roman building would have looked like, with its gardens and fountains – even details such as the lamps and appropriate flowers?" Gebhard 1974, 60.

52 Gebhard 1974, 57.

equated himself with the patrician connoisseurs of the past and simultaneously garnered broad public praise. The lay visitors flocking to Malibu readily identified the building as an ancient Roman villa occupied in their minds, if not fact, by a contemporary equivalent to the original wealthy owner; architecture critic Martin Filler called the Getty a, "house museum offering a glimpse into the private life of modern-day Midas."[53] The recreated domestic context focused attention on sensorial, personal response to the building rather than on the building as a museum object. After all, good manners dictated that visitors to a private home enjoy the pleasures offered, not analyze the architecture.

The sensorial delights of the Getty Museum are immediate, but generalized and a-historical. While lay observers can readily connect the building's sensory stimuli with those of other villas, the specific association with the Roman era is blurred. Naturally the Museum lacks a real sense of habitation. The sterility of the interiors and their use for the display for art, while evoking the original Villa, inaccurately represent Roman villa life. Banham bemoaned the fact that the Getty Villa,

> doesn't even have the distant echoes of imperial sadism that lend nasty life to some of the other villa sites around Naples. No blood was spilled here, nor sperm, nor wine, nor other vital juice. No one even puked in the pool nor pissed in the fountains. Nor will they – the custodians hover, like thought-police, between the ancient marble and the ever-new stucco ornamentation.[54]

While I can personally attest to the spilling of wine at the site, the disjunction between the recreated architecture and the activities of the building both merit consideration. After helping to rebuild the Imperial Bath Gymnasium complex *in situ* at Sardis, Professor Fikret Yegül distinguished between reconstructing an institution and reconstructing a building. A recreated structure can allow observers to evaluate space, lighting, sequencing, acoustics, temperature, and so on, but it does not replicate the ancient activities or the human responses. Yegül noted, "Institutions of a past culture are meaningful to us only as embodiments of the human spirit and ideal within their full cultural context; they cannot be cut out, isolated, and transferred up and down the historical scale."[55]

53 Filler 2006. Umberto Eco compared J. Paul Getty with patrician Romans who attempted to show sophistication by emulating the Greeks; Eco 1990, 35.

54 Banham 1977, 238.

55 Yegül 1976, 172.

On a practical level, a full-scale reconstructed structure needs a purpose or it becomes a lifeless hull; historical embodiments are difficult to sustain. The Getty Museum recreated the sensorial stimuli of a Roman villa, but not the life. Anthropologist George E. Marcus succinctly observed, "The Getty lives the dialectic of fake and authenticity, but it does not reflect upon it."[56] While two-dimensional reconstructions and small-scale models are removed and objectified, a building is real and lasting and therefore difficult to footnote, or consider as a hypothesis.[57] Visitors who read the didactic labels at the Getty villa before its reworking in the 21st century, or perused the original guidebook learned the structure was based on the Villa of the Papyri, but were not fully educated about what parts derived from hard archaeological evidence and what from reasoned conjecture. The same was true for the generalized sensorial experiences. While the attempts to incorporate plants similar to those found in ancient Campania were proudly touted, the ancient meanings and impact of their colours and fragrances were not explored. The replication of ancient sensorial sequencing, day-lighting effects, and sounds were implied, but not analyzed. Geo-temporal interpretations were especially skewed. The Museum is constantly maintained in pristine condition, negating the reality of an aging residential structure with peeling stucco and cracking marbles, and sequential alterations.[58] Similarly, the reorientation and flipping of the plan (not to mention the use of electric illumination) significantly changed the natural lighting of the original, shifting the meaning and use of various rooms between the original Villa and its progeny. The power of place also contrasts significantly with the original. Though the climate and alleged hedonism of Malibu have led to its characterization as "Pompeii on the Pacific," the smog, ambience, sounds, interior regulated temperatures, and viewers remain distinctly different from those on the Bay of Naples in the first century C.E.

Nevertheless, the experience of the Getty Villa comes close in many ways. What distinguishes this rebirth is its overt effort to engage the senses without shame. J. Paul Getty, like Roman villa owners, sought

56 Marcus 1990, 329.
57 Yegül, 1976, 173.
58 The meticulous maintenance of the Getty Villa reflects not only the resources of the institution, but also the belief that a work of architecture is best represented at its moment of conception, and not as it ages and changes; see Brand 1994.

to impress visitors with a lush, pleasurable panoply of sensory stimuli. These brought positive responses and distinguished the patron as a member of the wealthy and educated elite. Unencumbered by academic prejudices, Getty and his public guests revelled in the experiential richness of his recreation. Academics responded to this rebirthing rationally and critically, having lost touch (and smell, and taste, and sound, and sight) with the intangible, unquantifiable perceptual pleasures of the original Roman inspiration.

Born digital

In the 21st century interest in sensorial stimuli is being rehabilitated by digital technologies. Virtual worlds and other immersive simulations employ movement, sounds, haptic clues, and temporality to approximate reality.[59] Today, numerous reconstructions of historic environments are "born digital," created on the computer with four-dimensional, sensory rich capabilities. Digital technologies incubated in the gaming and entertainment industry have pursued realism and immersion, enriching their simulations with multiple physiological stimuli. While full bodily immersion is unattainable, the quest both popularizes and legitimizes sensory issues as worthy of discussion, evaluation, and research. At least two detailed, (re)born-digital versions of the Villa of the Papyri have been created to date, each with specific agendas. That by Gaetano Capasso with Capware first released in 1997 draws upon archaeological data to address general audiences in museum displays.[60] The model created by Mantha Zarmakoupi presented in this volume meticulously incorporates new archaeological data and research as an operative tool for scholarly architectural history analysis (see Zarmakoupi in this volume, figs. 1, 5 and 6).[61] To complement her work,

---

59 Barceló et al. 2000. For a critical historiography of digital modelling in archaeology see Frischer 2008.

60 Digital video: *Viaggio a Pompei* (Naples 1997; 2002 2nd ed.); book: Gaetano Capasso, *Journey to Pompeii, Virtual tours around the lost cities* (Naples 2002 1st ed.; 2004 2nd ed.; 2005 3rd ed.).

61 See Zarmakoupi in this volume. An obvious advantage of digital reconstructing ancient buildings models is the minimization of disruption of the original material. At the villa site in Herculaneum excavators are also exploiting digital technologies for digging simulations and hypothesis testing in preparation for the next phase of exploration; Rossella Lorenzi, "Ancient villa rescued from

the discussion that follows considers how immersive simulations in general are affecting sensorial aspects of reconstructions and knowledge production.

Digital technologies are changing the interface between scholar and reconstruction fabricator, to the benefit of experiential concerns as the example of Dr. Zarmakoupi affirms. For the many pre-digital reconstructions, the illustrator did not have historical architectural expertise and thus did not understand the cultural factors shaping the design and experience of the structures they represented. Conversely, academic researchers had scant training in the spatial, structural, or experiential aspects of design and thus did not advocate representational strategies to make these aspects transparent.[62] Furthermore, fabricators were too frequently considered hired consultants who passively illustrated findings and interpretations generated by scholars. This hierarchical distinction deterred reconstruction illustrators from sharing their experiential expertise. With digital reconstruction the paradigm has gradually shifted. At the advent of the digital revolution a number of historical modelling projects were undertaken by computer scientists and commercial companies who wanted recognizable content to test their technology. Even the engaging model of the Villa of the Papyri by Capware (1997) seems to have been created to showcase the firm's computer-generated imagery technology, as well as to address the cultural heritage market in a touristic movie and book. Though popular, these "edutainment" products were largely disregarded by the academic community.[63]

Dissatisfaction with populist digital reconstructions encouraged scholars to become more directly engaged with digital reconstruction

---

Vesuvius' mud," electronic document, http://dienekes.awardspace.com/blog/archives/000040.html (accessed June 8, 2008).

62 Archaeologist Barry Cunliffe expressed admiration and a hint of envy that reconstructor Alan Sorrell could visualize in three dimensions (Cunliffe in Sorrell 1981, 7). See article by Alan Sorrell, "The artist and reconstruction," in the same volume (Sorrell 1981, 20–26).

63 Charles C. Kolb. Review of Forte, Maurizio and Alberto Siliotti (eds.), *Virtual Archaeology: Re-creating Ancient Worlds* (London: Thames and Hudson, 1997), *H-Net Reviews*, August 1997, online review, http://www.h-net.org/reviews/showrev.cgi?path=2068874530446 (accessed July 2008). The status of edutainment projects is further devalued for scholars by repurposing such as the incorporation of Capware's digital Pompeii model in a 2002 Director's Cut DVD of a Pink Floyd concert at the site in 1972. Such associations maintain the belief that reconstructions are best used to address non-expert audiences; cf. Kolb 1997.

production. In fact, the demands of digital modelling necessitate close collaboration. The amount of data required and the innumerable questions raised during the creation process ensure that researchers and modellers work closely together thereby promoting expertise exchange. The intensity of the partnership has redefined the positioning of visualizations in the process of knowledge production. Models are not solely visualizations of knowledge, they are operational in its formation, prompting new interpretations, hypotheses testing, and field work. Increasingly the new generation of scholars as exemplified by Dr. Zarmakoupi boasts historical, archaeological, architectural and digital modelling expertise. Familiarity with the digital programs allows researchers to exploit the tools' experiential capabilities as, for example, the evaluation of viewsheds, spatial sequencing, and kinetic pathways. Simply, scholars adept at modelling find inspiration in both the historical data and in the medium of representation.

Creation of a four-dimensional digital reconstruction is time consuming and demanding. Drawings and other two-dimensional reconstructions can be selective, with views carefully framed to present extant or verifiable data. Three-dimensional *in situ* rebuildings (*anastylosis*) centre on the presentation of extant original components with only minimal additions for stability not holistic representation.[64] In contrast, the digital reconstruction of a historic building such as the Villa of the Papyri requires almost the same comprehensive architectural information as to construct a physical structure, from data on wall thicknesses, materials, and precise measurements. Unlike the Getty Villa which was compromised by modern construction codes and functional requirements, a digital reconstruction model can incorporate period-specific materials, building techniques, and ancient aspects of construction knowledge (fig. 6).[65] The simulation of the construction process during modelling provides researchers with an intimate knowledge of the reconstructed structure in the round, as well as a sense of ownership not unlike that

64 Vacharopoulou 2005.

65 In each modelling project representational strategies must be carefully assessed; hyperrealism commonly familiar from films may not serve the research agenda: Emele 1998, 253. For the Digital Roman Forum Project researchers at UCLA adopted the operational premise that the models are "knowledge representations," a concept borrowed from the sciences, that depict what scholars today know about the environments; undocumented features such as colour, graffiti, statues, and landscaping are thus not represented.

of J. Paul Getty's, a "sense" that promotes immersion and thus sensory analysis.

Though born in a virtual realm, digital reconstructions are precisely positioned. The Cartesian grid associated with modelling programs and the facile incorporation of GPS coordinates for the archaeological remains promote exactitude in measuring and placement (fig. 7).[66] Significantly, this precision stands in marked contrast to earlier two-dimensional reconstructions which often generalized topographical positioning, especially along the z axis. The locational specificity grounds the building in place, thereby facilitating consideration of the diverse environmental factors that impact physiological reactions. Notably, these can be analyzed at multiple scales. Digital technologies allow researchers to transition seamlessly from the micro to the macro level as with digital reconstructions uploaded to geo-browsers such as Google Earth (fig. 8).[67] From a sensorial perspective, such telescoping broadens the inquiry, compelling scholars to consider environmental factors within a regional global context of weather patterns, geological shifts, plant distributions, floods, and seismic events.

Digital technology's inherent emphases on "space, time, and architecture" (*pace* Giedion) as well as sound and movement, compel the integration and valuation of experiential factors downplayed in earlier academic reconstructions.[68] Observers can move in and through the recreated environments in real time simulating changing viewsheds and the sequential experience of various spaces. Ideally such interaction should be at a human pace and human viewing level. The ability to move at an accelerated pace, or to fly over a building has obvious attractions and advantages, such as the ability to see an entire complex in a glance and to experience a large area in a short amount of time. Such enticements, however, should be resisted when exploring sensory responses

66 Before the digital revolution, acquisition of precise locational data was extremely difficult. Today accurate positioning along the x, y, and z axes is available both as GPS (Global Positioning System) and UTM (Universal Transverse Mercator) coordinates.

67 For an example upload the KML file of the Digital Roman Forum; http://www.etc.ucla.edu/research/projects/ancientRome.htm.

68 The issues raised by Sigfried Giedion in his influential book *Space, Time and Architecture: the Growth of a New Tradition* (1941; 5th edition in 1967) parallel those debated in digital modelling: the rapprochement between art and science, the confluence of contemporary and historic architectural ideas, and the organization of space.

since they distort the experience of the original occupants (fig. 9). Study of space and time is facilitated by the incorporation of aural stimuli. Period-appropriate sounds can be situated at selected positions, getting louder as the observer approaches and fading as one moves away. Unlike syrupy soundtracks associated with many edutainment models, such localized sound increases spatial understanding.[69] A colleague had often "moved through" the Digital Roman Forum model created at UCLA; after Latin speakers and other sounds were added at in specific locations he declared, "Ah. Now I see it better."[70] The extant digital models of the Villa of the Papyri can be programmed with appropriate environmental wave and bird sounds, the oral reading of Epicurean texts, and the soft white noise of slaves padding around in the background to inform the study of space, environmental factors, and that most elusive of feelings, mood.[71] Lighting studies based on site- and period-specific astronomical data can clarify the functional programming of areas at different times of day or year for ancient occupants who relied on natural illumination (fig. 10). Lighting simulations can show which areas would be best for reading the eponymous scrolls at a particular time of day.

Digital technology encourages temporal exploration. Duration can be shown in many increments, from the length of a stroll to the shade patterns evolving in a single day or the aging of wall materials (fig. 11).[72] In particular, digital representations allow scholars to address time's impact on memory by evaluating developments over broad temporal ranges. The Villa of the Papyri, like all architectural works, did not have a static existence, but underwent continuous alterations to meet the owners' changing needs and wishes. Constructed as a luxury villa in the second half of the first century B.C.E., the complex was repeat-

69 Despite the much touted spatial realism of immersive digital simulations, observers often have difficulty navigating through even familiar spaces in digital form; this problem can be addressed by the inclusion of plan-based navigators as popup windows.

70 Among sounds included in the Digital Roman Forum are the singing of birds known to have existed in the period, Latin speakers holding forum-appropriate conversations, and the noise of hobnail sandals on marble.

71 On the non-ecological "atmosphere of place" see Emele 1998.

72 The periodization of historical representations is being broken down by technological developments such as time sliders which promote nuanced evolutionary representations. Discussions about temporality in GIS are provoking consideration of phenomenological notions of time; Thomas 1996, 33.

edly reworked and expanded, ending its life in 79 C.E. as expansive luxury estate boasting numerous painted rooms, an extensive garden peristyle, *piscinae*, and a belvedere at the end of a long promenade overlooking the sea (see Zarmakoupi in this volume, figs. 4 and 18).[73] The digital depiction of this progression can clarify both changes in architectural form and the priorities accorded different sensory concerns as architectural, decorative, and landscaping alterations reprogrammed the experience of sounds, smells, and temperatures in various spaces. Time is a critical factor in the overall characterization of digital models. While pictorial and physical reconstructions are generally fixed, digital examples live, evolving as new information is added and the area modelled is expanded to neighbourhood and urban levels (fig. 12). This open-endedness further stimulates evolutionary thinking and promotes continuous reassessment.

A positive outcome of adopting digital media is the strengthened association with scientific concepts and approaches. Computer simulations can operate like scientific labs where scholars conduct a wide range of experiments (fig. 13). Here researchers can test hypotheses using analytic software that provided quantified results. For example, researchers can measure the refraction of light on painted surfaces or the decibel distribution of ambient sounds in a villa model; algorithms can be applied to represent the aging of materials. Collaboration with various experts, including lighting, acoustical, and heating engineers and architects, fosters interdisciplinarity and greater criticality.[74] In particular, the ease of distribution prompts experiment replication, at last giving historical reconstructions a means of evaluative verification. Though the scholarly vetting of historical digital models initially lagged behind their production, today many scholarly journals review digital reconstructions. This is notable not only for reinforcing methodological rigor, but also for promoting the reassessment of earlier non-digital reconstructions. The proliferation of digital reconstructions of the same structure also breaks down the iconic status of singular representations,

---

73 Prior to the recent excavations, the residence was thought to have followed a familiar developmental sequence evolving from a simple atrium-style country residence to a luxury estate: Wojcik 1986. Based on the complex excavation data, Antonio De Simone determined that the major part of the villa was an essentially unitary undertaking dated of the first century B.C.E. See De Simone, and Guidobaldi and Esposito in this volume.

74 The establishment and continual review of guidelines for model creation, standards of metadata, and overall evaluation remain in progress. Frischer 2008, vii.

weakening the iconic status of much publicized non-digital examples such as the Getty Villa. The open-ended nature of digital models reifies the characterization of research as a process not a product.

On a methodological level, digital multiplicity and accessibility is increasing humanities-based researchers' comfort with the indeterminacy of reconstructions. Experiments with "fuzzy logic" and "soft measurements" help scholars to deal with the multiple uncertain variables inherent in historical sensorial research.[75] The transparency of the evidence trail in digital reconstructions facilitates refutability, breaking down the negative associations of unitary or fixed reconstructions. Unlike pictorial or physical reconstructions, digital models can be directly linked with diverse data ranging from archaeological reports to rationales for reconstruction decisions, photographic archives, and textual references. Such digital footnoting and the direct associating of expansive cultural data provide a richer data set for assessing the complexities of past experiences. For example, a prescribed path through a digital Villa of the Papyri could be informed by links to Roman texts describing reactions to residential smells, sights, temperature, and haptic stimuli, as well as to recreations of Roman music or to economic information about the costs of sensory-rich elements.

As digital reconstruction models increase the credibility of sensory research, they spawn new concerns. Experientially rich digital experiences become accepted as fact simply because they are generated by computers. The continuous advances in simulation tools establish the false belief that authenticity and exactitude are ultimately possible. Though such recreations add movement, temporal aspects and sounds, they are not complete. For all the talk of "moving through" digital models, modern observers interact vicariously and are always prevented from true sensorial engagement by the fourth wall of the projection screen.[76] The senses presented are domesticated, orchestrated, and incomplete; most research centres on positive sensory stimuli, omitting negative smells, blocked views, and cramped spatial configurations. The critical

75 Koller 2008. Algorithms have been successfully applied to the modelling of urban infill buildings in a digital version of the famous plaster physical model of Constantinian Rome: Guidi, Frischer, De Simone et al. 2005.

76 Even with large immersive theaters the recreated digital environments are frequently experienced by seated observers. Yet to be ascertained are the research applications of digital attempts to simulate bodily engagement through the employment of avatars, combined real figures and simulated environments, or full-scale projection in so-called caves.

interaction between various senses and embodiment are rarely discussed in relation to digital models, leading to distortion of interpretation.[77] Ocularcentrism still dominates, minimizing consideration of olfaction, and haptic responses, as well as proprioception.[78] Scholarly analyses to date have tended to be sense-specific, not comprehensive syntheses of the full sensory array. The historical operant is largely absent or substituted for with stiff distracting avatars or with modern observers. We should all ask, as did Karen Franck, "When I enter virtual reality, what body will I leave behind?" "Are my bodily reactions the same as those of the past?"[79] Just how loud was too loud for a Roman attempting to sleep during villa revelries?[80]

All historical sensorial research has to be grounded in a specific period and place, and specific categories of human receptors. No amount of refinement can recreate the experience of being in a physical space feeling the temperatures, smelling the materials, hearing the ambient sounds, textures with the receptors of ancient occupants, but sensations can be explored relationally in context. Despite strong critiques of physiological uniformitarianism, too often the evaluation of digital experiential sensory simulations is based on modern sensory criteria. Reactions to stimuli are in large part culturally constituted. Researchers frequently portray sensory digital simulations as abstractions without cultural valuation as good or bad or indifferent. Building upon Michael Baxadall's concept of the "period eye" Roman scholars have explored visuality considering the social aspects of the gaze, reciprocity of viewing, and the meaning associated with angle of sight among other aspects.[81] Similar research and theorization is necessary about the period ear, period

77 Rodaway 1994, 177.

78 Tringham argues, 'The ability of digital media to focus on the intimate scale of sensing, close proximity, and immense detail has always been present, it is their creators who have lacked patience or motivation to take advantage of this potential;' "Putting vision in its place: the interweaving of senses to create a sense of place at Çatalhöyük," electronic document, http://traumwerk.stanford.edu:3455/31/admin/download.html?attachid=157977 (accessed May 14, 2008). The omission of the tactile-kinesthetic evaluations is especially damaging as it is important in the structuring of space: Porteous 1990, 6. Bernard Frischer presciently calls for the development of future sensorial tools to promote and evaluate haptic responses: Frischer 2008, xiii.

79 Franck 1995.

80 Pliny the Younger felt it necessity to include a sensory deprived room in his villa where he could be isolated from sounds and other sensory stimuli (*Ep.* 23).

81 Favro 2006; Favro 2007; Bergmann 1994; Zanker 1997.

foot, period time-sense, and period kinesthetic response. All sensory reactions must be evaluated not as quantified measurements, but as encompassing ranges reflecting human individual subjectivity and differences imposed by class, age, gender, health, and frame of mind.

In 1995 Martin Schmidt gave a paper entitled, "Are dull reconstructions more scientific?"[82] Over a decade researchers employing digital media can respond with a resounding "no." Engaging interactive digital recreations follow rigorous research practices and assessment; they are increasingly accepted as valuable scholarly tools which play a dynamic role in the creation of knowledge. In particular, the capabilities of simulation media forefront sensorial aspects. We can now simulate the experience of moving through the digital Villa of the Papyri assessing sight-lines to paintings, viewsheds to the countryside, the acoustics of the *cyptoporticus*, the sequencing of spaces, and diurnal changes in lighting. Yet in some ways the media subverts experiential assessment. Too often modern observers of digital environments forget they are engaging with a simulation; the tool becomes the reality evaluated.[83] Digital sensory explorations can become as addictive as Second Life, drawing users farther and farther away from the actual historical remains and places; conceptually they have the potential to be like the one-to-one scaled map described by Jorge Luis Borges laying on top of and obscuring the actual region depicted.[84] In addition, the theorization and quantification of sensorial data can diminish the empathetic connection between the researcher and the original occupants of the historic spaces simulated. After moving through a multi-sensory digital recreation of the Villa of the Papyri are we more in tune with the Roman experience of the first-century residents? Can we distinguish between positive and negative associations with each experiential response? Real-time digital reconstructions aggregate information and facilitate measured analysis, but they cannot replicate the rich, evocative bodily sensations experienced moving through the Getty Museum, running one's hand in the cool water of the pool or breathing in the perfume wafting from a nearby *cubiculum*.

82 Schmidt 1994.

83 Baudrillard 1981, 6. Digital technologies have helped to rehabilitate the word "simulation" which has been transformed from "an attempt to fool" into "an experiment."

84 Borges 1975, "Of Exactitude in Science," 141.

Conclusion

Recently professors Ruth Tringham and Michael Ashley wrote, "we [archaeologists] are not practiced in thinking about the role of non-visual senses and do not take pleasure in recording them."[85] Immersive three-dimensional reconstructions help to reverse this imbalance by engaging multiple sensory receptors. The DNA of the Villa of the Papyri was imprinted with potent sensory genes. When cloned in the 20th century, these remained operational. The Getty Villa revelled in a vibrant presentation of sensorial delights in defiance of scholarly denigration. The overwhelming popular response to the museum's rich experiences preserved a positive sensorial heritage. Today digital progeny are revitalizing this embedded trait by both referencing the Villa's ancestors and by utilizing new technologies and scientific methodologies.[86] The rebirthings of the Herculanean villa provide a clear historiography of scholarly reactions to sensorial issues. At the same time they affirm the enduring empathetic attraction of sensory-rich experiences. While all occupants' reactions are mediated by their cultures, the familiarity of bodily mediation forms a bond across the generations and centuries. We will never know what the Villa of the Papyri originally looked like, or how it was experienced by the ancient Romans. Yet we can still value the heritage of the sensorial features that formed the Villa's identity, meaning, and valuation of the Villa of the Papyri.[87] If a picture is worth a thousand words, how much is a sound worth? Or a smell? Or a texture? Or a movement? Or a feeling? Or a space? For me, the human reactions to time, space, and architecture are worth 1000 rebirthings.

---

85 "Senses of places: remediations from text to digital performance, Draft 1 March 1, 2007," electronic document, http://chimeraspider.wordpress.com/2007/03/01/beyond-etext-remediated-places-draft-1/ (accessed May 5, 2008).

86 The familial connection between reconstructions of reconstructions is evident with the Capware model which in many scenes replicate the Getty Villa. See Lapatin in this volume, 136–137.

87 The Getty rebirthing brought villa experiences to the forefront, simultaneously distinguishing the separation of lay and scholarly audiences. Digital models have given sensory issues a scientific legitimization, but distanced us from bodily engagement. In these two rebirthings, as in all reconstructions, care should be taken to assess not only the archaeological accuracy, but also what is being simulated, and stimulated, and for whom.

The virtual reality digital model of the Villa of the Papyri project

MANTHA ZARMAKOUPI

The virtual reality digital model of the Villa of the Papyri project has been developed over the past four years at the UCLA Cultural Virtual Reality Laboratory (CVRLab).[1] It demonstrates how virtual reality models may be employed to document and investigate archaeological sites as well as to present hypothetical reconstructions that may serve as virtual restoration proposals of architectural monuments. The aim of the project is threefold: 1) to create a digital architectural model of the Villa of the Papyri that incorporates both the architectural structures known from the 18th century as well as those found in recent excavations, 2) to present a virtual reality reconstruction of the architecture of the Villa that distinguishes between the structures known from Weber's plan (1758) and still lay underground, the structures that have been recently unearthed (1994–1998, 2007–), and proposed restorations, and 3) to reincorporate the surviving known fragments of the finds from the Villa, such as wall paintings, mosaics, sculptures and papyri.[2] In addressing these aims, the project will provide an invaluable research and teaching tool for the Villa of the Papyri. This paper presents the evidence, methodology and tools used for the construction of the virtual reality digital model of the Villa of the Papyri.

---

1 The project has been created with the support of the UCLA Experiential Technologies Center, the Friends of Herculaneum Society, University College London and the Excellence Cluster TOPOI.

2 The photographs of the Villa of the Papyri that are included in the digital model were taken by the author and are published here with the permission of the Ministero per i Beni e le Attività Culturali and the Soprintendenza Speciale per i beni Archeologici di Napoli e Pompei. I would like to thank Antonio De Simone, Maria Paola Guidobaldi and Domenico Esposito for discussing the most recent excavations at the Villa (see De Simone and Guidobaldi and Esposito in this volume). I am especially grateful to Domenico Esposito for discussing the reconstruction of the Villa of the Papyri.

The Villa of the Papyri and its reconstructions

Discovered and explored through a series of tunnels in the 18th century, the Villa of the Papyri remained effectively unseen until the beginning of the "New Excavations" by Infratecna in the 1990s.[3] The Villa lies beneath about 30 m of consolidated mud, the result of the 79 C.E. eruption, the deposition of material over time and several subsequent eruptions.[4] The original excavations at the Villa started in May 1750 and continued for eleven years until 1761; they were resumed briefly between 1764 and 1765. The 18th-century excavations were conducted by Karl Jakob Weber, the Swiss military engineer in the service of Charles of Bourbon, King of the Two Sicilies.[5] During this period, the Villa was accessed by wells and was excavated systematically through a series of tunnels, which led to the extraordinary finds of the large papyri and sculptural ensembles. On the basis of the tunnels that gave access to the spaces of the Villa, Weber produced a plan in 1758, now in the Archaeological Museum of Naples (see Mattusch in this volume, fig. 5), which was redrawn with annotations of the findings by Comparetti and de Petra in 1883 (see De Simone in this volume, fig. 1).[6] Weber's plan was our only guide to the Villa until the Infratecna excavation. This period of excavation from 1994–1998 and the most recent excavations by the Archaeological Superintendency of Pompeii (2007–) gave access to the atrium quarter, known from Weber's plan, as well as areas that were unexplored by the Bourbons – the first and second lower level of the *basis villae*, just below the atrium quarter, and the lower terrace structures to the south of the atrium quarter – but the entirety of the Villa still remains underground.[7]

The inability to access the Villa of the Papyri combined with the unique character of the finds from the Villa, the papyri and the sculptures, have led to its idealization as the Roman luxury villa par excellence. Scholarship has analyzed the ownership of the Villa, the philosophical affiliations of the owner as well as the ideological connotations

3 See De Simone in this volume, 1–8.
4 See De Simone in this volume, 6.
5 Parslow 1995, 85–106.
6 *CDP*, pl. XXIV.
7 See De Simone, and Guidobaldi and Esposito in this volume.

of the sculptural collection.[8] Due to the lack of available information, attempts to reconstruct the architecture of the Villa have been far less numerous. In fact, there have been only two: the Getty Villa by Langdon and Wilson with the advice of Norman Neuerburg (1974) and the Capware reconstruction by Gaetano Capasso (1997). The first one was produced before and the second one after the Infratecna excavations.

The Getty Villa first opened to the public in 1974 (see Lapatin in this volume, fig. 6).[9] It is not surprising that of all the available Roman luxury villas, J. Paul Getty chose to construct a full-scale reconstruction of the Villa of the Papyri in order to house his art collection in Malibu. The possible association with Julius Caesar's father-in-law, Piso, as well as the spectacular finds of this elusive site appealed greatly to Getty.[10] Furthermore, the fragmented character of the material remains of the Villa of the Papyri allowed for some flexibility in the adaptation of Weber's plan for the purposes of the Getty Villa as a museum. Without the architectural details, wall paintings or mosaics of the Villa of the Papyri, Norman Neuerburg, the academic advisor to the Getty Villa architects Langdon and Wilson, compiled a list from the pristine examples of Roman art and architecture that were used to fabricate the museum's environment.[11] The decoration of the Getty is a product of an eclectic selection of the most impressive surviving decoration from houses and public buildings around the Bay of Naples as well as the city of Rome,[12] which in some cases were adjusted to accommodate modern American taste, for example the colour of the wall paintings.[13] Getty's goal was not to produce an accurate reconstruction of the Villa of the Papyri, but rather to house his collection in what he "felt a good museum should be."[14] In the case of the Getty Villa, the lack of infor-

8 For example, on the ideological programme underlying the sculptural display: Pandermalis 1971, Sauron 1980, *Wojcik*, Neudecker 1988, 113, and Dillon 2000, 27–28.

9 For the construction history of the Getty Villa see True and Silvetti 2005.

10 See Lapatin in this volume. On the ownership of the Villa see Capasso in this volume.

11 Neuerburg's research notes on the design of the Getty Villa show this bricolage of ancient components: Neuerburg 1966–1987, "Series IV. Drawings and Designs, 1966–1976, 1979–1980, (bulk 1971–1973)," Box 7 and 8.

12 See Lapatin in this volume, 134–135.

13 See Favro in this volume, 166.

14 Gebhard 1974, 57; See in this volume, Lapatin, 130–131, and Favro, 167.

mation on the architecture of the Villa of the Papyri gave an interpretative leeway that was necessary for the adaptation of the Villa into a museum.

The Capware reconstruction of the Villa of the Papyri by Gaetano Capasso and his team was first released in 1997.[15] This digital reconstruction is based on Weber's plan as well as on the information from the Infratecna excavations and fills in the "blanks" of the unknown areas, such as wall paintings and mosaics, on the basis of the decoration of houses in Pompeii and Herculaneum – like the Getty Villa does. Capasso also drew on the Getty Villa itself as is evident from the similarity of the two reconstructions – especially in the appearance of the second floor.[16] Gaetano Capasso created this, as well as other reconstructions of sites around the bay of Naples, in order to appeal to general audiences. To this end, all the Capware reconstructions feature in a touristic movie and book and are presented in real time in the Museo Archeologico Virtuale in Ercolano, a museum designed for their display.[17] In order to satisfy the purposes of "edutainment," the Capware reconstruction of the Villa of the Papyri presents a homogenous three-dimensional environment with no differentiation between the existing elements and those added hypothetically.

The virtual reality digital model of the Villa of the Papyri project presented here has a different scope from either the Getty Villa or the Capware reconstruction. The project was created in order to visualize the information that we have about the Villa and provide a virtual reality reconstruction that distinguishes the material remains of the Villa from hypothetical additions. The model incorporates the results from new excavations into Weber's plan and puts forward one or more restoration proposals of the Villa's architecture. Hypotheses are necessary in the restoration proposals that are incorporated in three-dimensional reconstructions of archaeological sites,[18] and by putting forward several this project aims at facilitating further research on the Villa. Part of the flex-

15 Digital video: *Viaggio a Pompei* (Naples 1997 1st ed., 2002 2nd ed.); book: G. Capasso, *Journey to Pompeii, Virtual tours around the lost cities* (Naples 2002 1st ed.; 2004 2nd ed.; 2005 3rd ed.).

16 See also Lapatin in this volume, 137–138.

17 The Museo Archeologico Virtuale in Ercolano which opened on July 8th 2008 presents the reconstruction of the Villa of the Papyri, together with other Capware reconstructions of buildings from Herculaneum and Pompeii (www.museomav.it).

18 Vacharopoulou 2005.

ibility of this virtual reality reconstruction is the ability to select among existing state and different restoration proposals. Whereas the previous reconstructions put forth restoration proposals for the missing parts of the decoration in the style of the original, adopting the approach of Viollet-le-Duc,[19] the restoration proposals in this reconstruction do not imitate the missing decoration and feature a uniform colour. Furthermore, two different colours were used to differentiate the parts of the Villa that are known from Weber's plan and still lie underground from the recently excavated parts of the Villa. In this way, the colour-coding of the model enables one to distinguish between the kind of information that is visualized (fig. 1).

Methodology of the virtual reality digital model of the Villa of the Papyri project

A virtual reconstruction of an archaeological site is based on excavation data, historical sources, comparative studies as well as the modeller's informed hypotheses (fig. 2).[20] The virtual reality model of the Villa of the Papyri uses the data from the 18th-century excavations,[21] the Infratecna excavation[22] and the recent excavations of the Archaeological Superintentency of Pompeii.[23] The project used MultiGen Creator for the three-dimensional modelling and Adobe Photoshop for two-dimensional image processing of the textures applied to the surfaces of the model, including the images of the fragments of wall painting and mosaic decoration.

The 1883 publication of Weber's plan by Comparetti and De Petra was used as a basis for the model (fig. 3; See De Simone in this volume, fig. 1). Information provided by the new excavations allowed this plan to be adjusted and enriched. Specifically, the new plan of the atrium quarter was used to correct Weber's plan (see in this volume, De Simone, fig. 7, and Guidobaldi and Esposito, figs. 1 and 2), and the

19 Viollet-le-Duc 1854, vol. 8, 14–34; see Melucco Vaccaro 1996.
20 Hermon 2008, esp. 40–41.
21 *CDP*.
22 See De Simone et al. 1998; De Simone and Ruffo 2002, 2003, 2005; De Simone 2007b and in this volume.
23 See Guidobaldi and Esposito 2009 and in this volume; and Guidobaldi et al. 2009.

first and second levels of the *basis villae* structures as well as the lower terrace structures (VPSO area) were added (see in this volume, De Simone, figs. 15 and 16, and Guidobaldi and Esposito, figs. 1 and 34). The dimensions of Weber's plan, which were accurate overall,[24] were put into scale in relation to the measurements of the new plan of the atrium quarter. In addition, the pathway to the belvedere was given a more westward orientation according to the Infratecna excavation (see De Simone in this volume, cf. figs. 1 and 2). Finally, the information on the heights of the Villa from the Infratecna excavation (see De Simone in this volume, figs. 14 and 25) was used for the heights of the model (fig. 4).

Weber's excavation notes and annotations to his plan, published in the 1883 publication by Comparetti and De Petra, were used in order to clarify the difficulties of the plan resulting from the simultaneous graphic representation of structures and tunnels. They also allowed allocating the find-spots of the fragments of wall paintings and mosaics that were found and removed in the 18th century.[25] For the New Excavations of Infratecna the publications of Antonio De Simone and Fabrizio Ruffo were used.[26] Since the publication of results from the most recent excavations undertaken by the Archaeological Superintendency of Pompeii only appeared at the end of 2009, personal communications with Maria Paola Guidobaldi and Domenico Esposito, as well as their article in this volume, provided information on their findings.[27] Visits to the site were conducted in summer 2005 with the permission of the Archaeological Superintendency of Pompeii. Photographs of the mosaics and wall painting fragments taken during these visits were used in the model and are published here with the permission of the Ministry of Culture and the Archaeological Superentindency of Pompeii.[28] For the restoration proposals of the second floor above the atrium quarter as well as of the substructures of the rectangular peristyle facing the seaside, comparisons were made with other luxury houses and villas in Herculaneum, such as the House of the Relief of Telephus, and around the Bay of Naples, Villa Arianna A in Stabiae and Villa A at Torre Annunziata.

---

24 De Simone and Ruffo 1998.

25 *CDP*, 147–294, esp. 225–236.

26 See note 22.

27 See note 23.

28 See note 2.

As there is currently a terminological confusion in the field of visualizations,[29] a definition of the terms used in the virtual reality digital model of the Villa of the Papyri project is necessary. I use the term virtual reality reconstruction to refer to the model of the Villa of the Papyri model as a whole. This term does not differentiate the visualization of the existing structures and wall paintings of the Villa from their hypothetical reconstructions. The term virtual restoration designates the hypothetical reconstructions of the architecture and wall paintings, where restoration is defined as reconstitution of what is proposed to be the original state of the ancient building or decoration.[30] The term virtual restoration is used for the virtually created restoration of objects or structures that are either presented in virtual reality or projected in real-time on real-world objects.[31] The virtual realm of the model enables us to put forth several such restoration proposals, as none of them is invasive to the monument itself, and as such they are non-committal.

Presentation of the model

The model reconstructs and distinguishes the following areas of the Villa of the Papyri: (1) areas known from the 18th-century plan, (2) areas revealed during the new excavations by Infratecna and the Archaelogical Superintendency of Pompeii that are accessible today and (3) restoration proposals (fig. 1). The areas known from the 18th-century plan are indicated by a yellow-beige colour, (a) in the index of figure 1. A brown-beige colour is used for the areas revealed during the new exca-

---

29 Golvin, J.-C. "Signification et problèmes de définition," in: *De la restitution en archéologie, Archaeological restitution* (Paris 2008), 12–25, electronic document, http://editions.monuments-nationaux.fr/fr/les-ouvrages-en-ligne/bdd/livree/9 (accessed June 30, 2009).

30 Stubbs 2009, 23–24.

31 This term is used for the virtually created restoration of objects or structures whether these are presented in virtual reality or projected in real-time on real-world objects: Law et al., "Projecting restorations in real-time for real-world objects," in: *Museums and the Web 2009: proceedings*, edited by J. Trant and D. Bearman (Toronto 2009), electronic document, http://www.archimuse.com/mw2009/papers/law/law.html (accessed June 30, 2010); Peral et al., "Virtual restoration of cultural heritage through real-time 3D models projection," electronic document, http://public-repository.epoch-net.org/publications/VAST2005/shortpapers/short2002.pdf (accessed June 30, 2009).

vations, (b) in the index of figure 1. For the restoration proposals of the atrium quarter and the rectangular peristyle a gray colour is used, (c) in the index of figure 1. For the restoration proposals of the second floors above the atrium quarter and above the rooms in between the square and rectangular peristyles the yellow-beige colour of the 18th-century plan was used. As this latter restoration proposal does not feature in the main view of the model but is only shown as one option of the reconstruction of the Villa in the fly-through of the model, this colour was chosen for reasons of homogeneity and readability of the model. For similar reasons, the gray colour used for the restoration proposals of the substructures is also used for the floors in the areas of the square and rectangular peristyles. The aforementioned colour-coding choices were made in order to satisfy two goals: on the one hand, to create a reconstruction that makes as clear as possible what is reconstructed from the archaeological evidence and what is projected from the evidence in the form of restoration proposal and, on the other, to offer a reconstruction that is comprehensible as a three-dimensional building and it is not overly schematic. Finally, coloured walls occur only in two cases in which archaeological evidence indicates their existence: first, the inner walls of the *natatio* of the lower terrace and, second, the short wall of the long promenade that is adjacent to the southwest side of the rectangular peristyle.

The model gathers all the surviving fragments of wall painting and mosaic decoration from the Villa, both the ones found in the 18th century and in the recent excavations by Infratecna and the Archaelogical Superintendency of Pompeii (figs. 5 and 6). The mosaics and wall paintings found during the new excavations as well as those found during the 18th-century have been placed in their original locations, for example the mosaic and fragment of megalography in room (i) (fig. 7; see also Moormann in this volume, fig. 9) and the mosaic in room "XVI" in Weber's plan (fig. 8).[32] The fragments of wall paintings found in the 18th-century excavations were only schematically noted on Weber's plan. The Latin numbers and letters on Weber's plan indicate commentaries in his excavation notes where he lists the finds (sculptures, papyri, mosaics and fragments of wall paintings) of a given area over time.[33] For example, in the atrium area, "XIII" was used to indicate the location of

32 *CDP*, 224, "XVI."
33 *CDP*, 221–224.

the fragment of wall painting NM 8759 found on 16 June 1754[34] as well as two other fragments of wall paintings found on 23 June 1754 that have no inventory numbers,[35] and "XI" was used to indicate the location of the fragment of wall painting NM 8548 found on 10 March 1754.[36] These annotations do not indicate the exact find-spots of the fragments of wall paintings. The fragments of wall paintings have been placed in the model at the points where their corresponding annotations occur on Weber's plan, since these are the approximate "find-spots" for which we have evidence (fig. 9; cf. fig. 6).

The placing of the surviving fragments of wall paintings and mosaics on their exact or approximate locations aims at facilitating research on the Villa's wall painting and mosaic decoration. One of the options of the model is to switch between existing state and restoration proposals, such as the one of the wall paintings of *ala* (e) by Moormann (fig. 10; see Moormann in this volume, fig. 5). The reversibility and easiness of switching between proposals during navigation in the virtual reality model facilitates the presentation of several hypothetical reconstructions of such a nature.

Very little is known about the architectural details of the Villa. In order to reconstruct the Villa's architecture, comparative material from other luxury villas on the bay of Naples was used as well as architectural details surviving from other buildings of Herculaneum. There is no evidence for the order of the columns of porticoes (a), (u) and (m) of the atrium quarter (see in this volume, De Simone, figs. 7 and 8, Guidobaldi and Esposito, fig. 2). Plain Tuscan columns, similar to the tufa columns incorporated in the south and west façades of the House of the Relief of Telephus in Herculaneum, were produced for these porticoes. The surviving footprints of the columns (fig. 11) were used to adjust the intercolumniations indicated in Weber's plan. These suggest that a fence or a thin wall – such as the thin walls placed between the columns of porticus 13 and 24 in Villa A at Torre Annunziata – was placed in between the columns, both of which were reconstructed as options in the model (fig. 12).

---

34 *CDP*, 224, V. Explic. "XIII;" *CDP*, 282, no. 97; see Moormann in this volume, 73, table 1, no. 3.

35 *CDP*, 224, V. Explic. "XIII;" *CDP*, 287, nos. 99 and 99b; see Moormann in this volume, 75, table 1, nos. 26 and 27.

36 *CDP*, 224, V. Explic. "XI;" see Moormann in this volume, 73, table 1, no. 1.

The recent investigations by Maria Paola Guidobaldi and Domenico Esposito have given information about the columns of the square peristyle.[37] Their shafts were built in *opus testaceum* and were coated with white stucco that rendered their fluting. The capitals and bases were made of tufa; the capitals were Ionic and the bases were characterised by the Attic profile. A photograph of the base of a column in the north portico of the square peristyle (see Guidobaldi and Esposito in this volume, fig. 14) was used for the reconstructed bases and shafts of the columns of the square peristyle in the model. The Ionic capitals of the square peristyle are not fully visible. As they bear a strong similarity to the Ionic capitals from the recently re-excavated Basilica in Herculaneum, a photograph of one of the latter was used to reconstruct the capitals of the columns in the square peristyle (fig. 13).[38]

The area of the rectangular peristyle is known only from 18th-excavations. Weber's notes indicate that the columns of the rectangular peristyle were stuccoed.[39] Photographs of two different kinds of stuccoed columns with stuccoed Tuscan capitals from Villa A at Torre Annunziata (*porticus* 40, 33 and 34) were used to reproduce alternative solutions for the columns of the rectangular peristyle in the model, one with with incised flattened flutes (*porticus* 33 and 34) and one that is plain up to 1.20 m and then fluted (*porticus* 40) (fig. 14).

The reconstruction of the *basis villae* presents the openings of the rooms of the first lower level, which were exposed during the new excavations (fig. 15; cf. figs. 1, 4 and 12; see in this volume, De Simone, figs. 9–11, Guidobaldi and Esposito, figs. 23, 32 and 33). The first lower level of the *basis villae* is presented in brown-beige colour in the model. Below this first lower level the façade continues for another level presented in gray colour in the model, to indicate the second lower level of the *basis villae* whose existence is documented by Guidobaldi and Esposito but is not yet excavated.[40] Two rows of large windows found at the west end of the façade (see in this volume, De Simone, fig. 13, Guidobaldi and Esposito, fig. 32) indicate a 5.50 m high flat roof structure in front of the *basis villae*. The roof of this structure was at level +6.211 (see De Simone in this volume, fig. 14). The slight

37 See Guidobaldi and Esposito in this volume, 30.

38 I would like to thank Domenico Esposito for providing images and advising on the reconstruction of the columns of the square peristyle.

39 *CDP*, 294.

40 See Guidobaldi and Esposito in this volume, 42–44.

inclination of the structure suggests an apsidal or curvilinear *avant-corps*. The excavators propose that the two windows indicate a series arranged on two levels that continue around this curvilinear structure.[41] The model visualizes this restoration proposal (figs. 1, 4, 12 and 15).

The reconstruction of the structures of the lower terrace (level +2.30) incorporates the restoration proposal by Guidobaldi and Esposito that the terrace reached the front of the *basis villae*. The remains of the large monumental hall on the lower terrace allow for the front part of the hall to be reconstructed. Guidobaldi and Esposito estimate that the structure was as high as the *basis villae*, reaching the level of the atrium (+11.34). The model proposes that the roof of this hall reached back to a hypothetical terrace in front of the rooms at the south-east of the atrium quarter (fig. 4). Here again the existing structures are presented in brown-beige colour and the hypothetical reconstructed structures in gray.

Two restoration proposals have been created for the façade of the substructures of the rectangular peristyle that forms the continuation of the façade of the *basis villae* (first and second lower levels) to the north-west, for which there is no archaeological evidence. One restoration proposal was formed by comparison to the south-east façade of a projecting structure of the north-west *Insula* of Herculaneum that features two rows of a series of niches (fig. 16; see De Simone in this volume, fig. 5). This projecting structure is part of a large house, comparable to the House of the Relief of Telephus, and is part of the new excavations area to the south-east of the Villa of the Papyri (see De Simone in this volume, fig. 4). A second restoration proposal was formed by comparison to the vaulted substructures of Villa Arianna A and Villa Arianna B in Stabia presenting the façade of the substructures of the rectangular peristyle with two series of vaults (fig. 17).

A restoration proposal has been produced for the second storey above the areas of the atrium quarter and in between the square and rectangular peristyles. Like all the other restoration proposals of the Villa, it can be "switched" on and off during the fly-through the model (fig. 18). No restoration has been proposed for the second storey above the area of the library, room "IV" in Weber's plan, as the full extent of this area towards the north-east is not known.

41 See Guidobaldi and Esposito in this volume, 43.

Conclusion

By differentiating between the kind of information visualized in the model as well as by providing the option to switch between several architectural and wall painting restoration proposals and their existing state, the virtual reality digital model of the Villa of the Papyri project aims at providing a flexible and adaptable research and teaching tool. In the next stage of the project, the find-spots of the papyri and three-dimensional scans of the sculptures will be added. When this stage is completed a Google Earth KML file of the model, which will enable the three-dimensional model to be launched in Google Earth, will be available through the website of the UCLA Experiential Technologies Center (http://www.etc.ucla.edu/research/projects/projects.htm). This access will allow for a wider audience, of scholars and students at all levels, to use the model for research and to increase information available about the Villa of the Papyri. In the meantime, information on the virtual reality digital model of the Villa of the Papyri project is available online through the same website.

The abundant production of virtual reconstructions in the field of archaeology over the past three decades has led to arguments over the scientific qualities of these reconstructions and their instrumentality in academic research.[42] However, it is by now widely accepted that virtual reality reconstructions can be both accurate as well as instrumental in research.[43] The virtual reality digital model of the Villa of the Papyri project is an example for the application of virtual reconstructions both in the visualization of existing architectural remains as well as in virtual restorations. Restoration, that is an intervention that goes beyond the consolidation and preservation of an architectural structure to propose its original state, has two major disadvantages; first, it is a permanent intervention and, second, it has an impact on the existing architectural remains. In the virtual realm both these physical problems are superseded as several non-invasive restoration proposals can be put forth at the same time. The virtual restorations of the architecture of the Villa of the Papyri supersede an additional obstacle posed by the physical inac-

42 Favro 2006.

43 Favro 2006; Wulf and Riedel 2006; Frischer and Dakouri-Hild (eds.) 2008, especially Frischer, v-xxiv; Barcelò, Forte and Sanders (eds.) 2000. See also the proceedings of the annual CAA (Computer Applications in Archeology) conference: http://www.leidenuniv.nl/caa/.

cessibility of large part of the Villa. The virtual restorations serve as a mental link between the two kinds of architectural remains of the Villa, those still underground and those unearthed during the recent excavations, that enable us to understand them better. Furthermore, the visual differentiation of the restorations from the existing remains of the Villa as well as the multiple restoration proposals invite us to engage critically with the reconstruction of the Villa. In doing so the reconstruction presented in the virtual reality digital model of the Villa of the Papyri project not only deepens our understanding of the Villa's existing architectural structures but also sharpens our visual thinking and encourages a critical approach to reconstructions.

List of Contributors

Dana Arnold
University of Southampton
School of Humanities
Southampton, S017 1BJ
d.r.arnold@soton.ac.uk

Mario Capasso
Università di Lecce
Centro di Studi Papirologici
Via V.M. Stampacchia, 73100 Lecce
mario.capasso@unile.it

Antonio De Simone
Università degli Studi Suor Orsola Benincasa
via Suor Orsola 10, 80135 Naples (Na)
antonio.desimone@unisob.na.it

Domenico Esposito
Via Fiuggi 32, 80038 Pomigliano d'Arco (Na)
archeomimmo@hotmail.com

Diane Favro
University of California, Los Angeles
Department of Architecture and Urban Design
1317 Perloff Hall
Los Angeles, CA 90095
diane.favro@aud.ucla.edu

Maria Paola Guidobaldi
Scavi Ercolano
Corso Resina, 80056 Ercolano (Na)
mpguidobaldi@archeologicapompei.it

Kenneth Lapatin
The J. Paul Getty Museum
1200 Getty Center Drive
Los Angeles, CA 90049–1687
KLapatin@getty.edu

Carol Mattusch
George Mason University
Department of History and Art History
Fairfax, VA 22030
mattusch@gmu.edu

Eric Moorman
Radboud Universiteit Nijmegen
Faculteit der Letteren
Postbus 9103, 6500 HD Nijmegen
e.moormann@let.ru.nl

David Sider
New York University
Department of Classics
Silver Center, 100 Washington Square East
New York, NY 10003
david.sider@nyu.edu

Mantha Zarmakoupi
New York University
Institute for the Study of the Ancient World
15 East 84th Street
New York, NY 10028
mzarmakoupi@post.harvard.edu

Bibliography

Abbreviations for titles of journals follow those of the *American Journal of Archaeology* 104 (2000), 3–24. References to Classical authorities follow the standard abbreviations for authors and books in the *Oxford Classical Dictionary* (Oxford 1996, third edition), xxix-liv.

Abbreviations

Antichità 1757–1792
Delle antichità di Ercolano (Naples 1757–1792).

CDP
Comparetti, D. and G. De Petra. *La villa ercolanese dei Pisoni: i suoi monumenti e la sua biblioteca* (Turin 1883; reprint Naples 1972).

Diario di scavo Infratecna
Ufficio Scavi in Ercolano. *Diario di scavo Infratecna.*

Fonti Ercolano Stabia
Archivio di Stato di Napoli. *Fonti documentarie per la storia degli scavi di Ercolano e Stabia* (Naples 1979).

Mattusch
Mattusch, C.C. *The Villa dei Papiri at Herculaneum: life and afterlife of a sculpture collection* (Los Angeles 2005).

NM
National Archaeological Museum, Naples; used with inventory numbers.

Noticia
Alcubierre, R.J. *Noticia de las alajas antiguas que se han descubierto en las escavationes de Resina, y otras en los diez y ocho años, que han corrido desde 22. de octubre de 1738, en que empezaron, hasta 22. de octubre de 1756, que se van continuando* (Naples 1757). Manuscript preserved in the Library of Società Napoletana di Storia Patria, Naples.

PPM 1–10
Baldassarre, I. (ed.). *Pompei pitture e mosaici*, 10 vols. (Rome 1990–2003).

Pompei Ercolano Stabiae Oplontis
Biblioteca Universitaria di Napoli, *Pompei Ercolano Stabiae Oplontis, LXXIX – MCMLXXIX,* Mostra Bibliografica (Naples 1984).

Progetto Pompei
Progetto Pompei: primo stralcio. Un bilancio, Soprintendenza archeologica di Pompei (Naples 1988).

Wojcik
Wojcik, M.R. *La Villa dei Papiri ad Ercolano: contributo alla ricostruzione dell'ideologia della nobilitas tardorepubblicana* (Rome 1986).

Bibliography

Ackerman, D. *A natural history of the senses* (New York 1991).

Ackerman, J.S. The villa as paradigm, *Perspecta* 22 (1986), 11–31.

Ackerman, J.S. *The villa: form and ideology of country houses* (Princeton 1990).

Adamo Muscettola, S. Il ritratto di Lucio Calpurnio Pisone Pontefice da Ercolano, *CronErcol* 20 (1990), 145–155.

Allen, W., Jr. and P.H. De Lacy, The patrons of Philodemus, *CP* 34 (1939), 59–65.

Allroggen-Bedel, A. Ein Malerei-Fragment aus der Villa dei Papiri, *CronErcol* 6 (1976), 85–88.

Allroggen-Bedel, A. Un frammento di dipinto, in: *La Villa dei Papiri*, Second Supplement to *CronErcol* 13 (Naples 1983), 65–68.

Allrogen-Bedel, A. and H. Kammerer-Grothaus, Il museo ercolanese di Portici, in: *La Villa dei Papiri*, First Supplement to *CronErcol* 13 (Naples 1983), 83–128.

Archäologie und Seismologie: la regione vesuviana dal 62 al 79 D.C.: problemi archeologici e sismologici, Colloquium, Boscoreale, 26.–27. November 1993 (Munich 1995).

Arnold, D. Unlearning the images of archaeology in: *Envisioning the past: archaeology and the image*, edited by S. Moser and S. Smiles (Oxford 2003), 92–144.

Arnold, D. Facts or fragments? Visual histories in the age of mechanical reproduction, *Art History* 25:4 (2002), 30–48.

Arnold, D. Ima(gin)ing architecture in: *Ima(gin)ing architecture*, edited by L. Verpoest and Z. Borocz (Leuven 2008), 15–29.

Bacchetta, A. *Oscilla. Rilievi sospesi di età romana*, Il Filarete 243 (Milan 2006).

Banham, R. Lair of the looter, *New Society* 40:761 (1977), 238.

Barbara, A. and A. Perliss. *Invisible Architecture: experiencing places through the sense of smell* (Milan 2006).

Barceló, J.A., M. Forte and D.H. Sanders (eds.). *Virtual reality in archaeology*, BAR International Series 843 (Oxford 2000).

Barker, S. (ed.). *Excavations and their objects. Freud's collection of antiquity* (Albany 1996).

Bassi, D. La sticometria nei papiri ercolanesi, *RivFil* 37 (1909), 321–515.

Bastet, F.L. Villa rustica in contrada Pisanella, *CronPomp* 2 (1976), 112–143.

Bastet, F.L. and M. de Vos (eds.). *Proposta per una classificazione del Terzo Stile pompeiano*, Archeologische Studiën van het Nederlands Instituut te Rome 4 ('s-Gravenhage 1979).

Batteux, C. *La morale d'Epicure, tirée de ses propres écrits* (Paris 1758).

Baudrillard, J. *Simulacres et simulation* (Paris 1981).

Belozerskaya, M. *The Medici giraffe and other tales of exotic animals and power* (New York 2006).

Bergmann, B. The Roman house as memory theater: the House of the Tragic Poet in Pompeii, *ArtB* 76 (1994), 225–256.

Beyen, H.G. *Die pompejanische Wanddekoration von zweiten bis zum vierten Stil*, 2 vols. (Haag 1938–1960).

Blau, E. and E. Kaufman (eds.), *Architecture and its image: four centuries of architectural representation* (Cambridge 1989).

Blesser, B. and L.-R. Salter. *Spaces speak, are you listening? Experiencing aural architecture* (Cambridge 2007).

Bloch, H. L. Calpurnius Piso Caesoninus in Samothrace and Herculaneum, *AJA* 44:4 (1940), 485–493.

Bloch, H. Review of: *M. Tulli Ciceronis "In L. Calpurnium Pisonem" oratio*, edited with introduction and commentary by R.G.M. Nisbet (Oxford 1961), *Gnomon* 37 (1965), 561–562.

Borges, J.L. *A universal history of infamy*, transl. N.T. de Giovanni (London 1975).

Bowser, B.J. Prologue: toward an archaeology of place, *Journal of Archaeological Method and Theory* 11:1 (2004), 1–3.

Brand, S. *How buildings learn: what happens after they're built* (New York 1994).

Bruno, G. *Atlas of emotion: journeys in art, architecture and film* (New York 2002).

Budetta, T. L'esplorazione della Villa dei Papiri, *RStPomp* 2 (1988), 234–236.

Camardo, D. La Villa di Arianna a *Stabiae*, in: Stabiae *dai Borbone alle ultime scoperte*, edited by D. Camardo and A. Ferrara (Castellammare di Stabia 2001), 75–84.

Capasso, G. *Journey to Pompeii: virtual tours around the lost cities* (Ottaviano 2002).

Capasso, M. Gli studi ercolanesi di Hermann Usener nel suo carteggio inedito con Hermann Diels, in: *Momenti della storia degli studi classici fra Ottocento e Novecento*, edited by M. Capasso, S. Cerasuolo, M.L. Chirico, G. Giannantoni, M. Gigante, F. Giordano, E. Paratore and A. Salvatore (Naples 1987), 116–117.

Capasso, M. Primo supplemento al *Catalogo dei papiri ercolanesi*, *CronErcol* 19 (1989), 193–264.

Capasso, M. *Manuale di papirologia ercolanese*, Università di Lecce, Dipartimento di filologia classica e medioevale, Testi e studi 3 (Galatina 1991).

Capasso, M. *Volumen: aspetti della tipologia del rotolo librario antico* (Naples 1995).

Carandini, A. (ed.). *Settefinestre: una villa schiavistica nell'Etruria romana* (Modena 1985).

Carettoni, G. La decorazione pittorica della Casa di Augusto, *RM* 90 (1983), 373–419.

Cassirer Bernfeld, S. Freud and archaeology, *American Imago* 8 (1951), 107–128.

Castrucci, G. *Tesoro letterario di Ercolano, ossia, la reale officina dei papiri ercolanesi* (Napoli 1852).

Cavallo, G. *Libri scritture scribi a Ercolano: introduzione allo studio dei materiali greci*, First Supplement to *CronErcol* 13 (Naples 1983).

Cerulli Irelli, G. Il ritratto romano ad Ercolano, in: *La regione sotterrata dal Vesuvio. Studi e prospettive. Atti del Convegno Internazionale*, 11–15 November 1979 (Naples 1982), 697–700.

Choisy, A. *L'art de bâtir chez les Romains* (Paris 1873).

Ciardiello, R. (ed.). *La villa romana* (Naples 2007).

Cicirelli, C. Comune di Terzigno-Località Boccia al Mauro, *RStPomp* 8 (1997), 175–179.

Cicirelli, C. La Villa 6, in: *Storie da un'eruzione. Pompei, Ercolano, Oplontis*, exhibition catalogue, Museo archeologico nazionale, Naples, March 20-Aug. 31 2003, edited by A. d'Ambrosio, P.G. Guzzo and M. Mastroroberto (Milan 2003), 214–220.

Cinque, A. and G. Irollo. La paleografia dell'antica *Herculaneum* e le fluttuazioni, di orgine bradisismica, della sua linea di costa, in: *Nuove ricerche archeologiche nell'area vesuviana (scavi 2003–2006)*, Studi della Soprintendenza Archeologica di Pompei 25, edited by P.G. Guzzo and M.P. Guidobaldi (Rome 2008), 425–437.

Cioffi, U. Prodotti vulcanici anteriori al 79 nell'area archeologica di Ercolano, in: *Ercolano 1738–1988, 250 anni di ricerca archeologica*, edited by L. Franchi dell'Orto (Rome 1993), 655–658.

Classen, C., D. Howes, and A. Synnott. *Aroma: the cultural history of smell* (London and New York 1994).

Clarke, J.R. *Looking at laughter: humor, power, and transgression in Roman visual culture, 100 B.C.-A.D. 250* (Berkeley 2007).

Clarke, J.R. *Art in the lives of ordinary Romans: visual representation and non-elite viewers in Italy, 100 B.C.-A.D. 315* (Berkeley 2003).

Clarke, J.R. *The houses of Roman Italy 100 B.C.-A.D. 250: ritual, space, and decoration* (Berkeley 1999).

Cochin, C.N. and J.C. Bellicard, *Observations sur les antiquités de la ville d'Herculanum* (Paris 1754; reprint Geneva 1972).

Coles, J.M. *Archaeology by experiment* (London 1973)

Coles, J.M. *Experimental archaeology* (London and New York 1979).

Comparetti, D. La bibliothèque de Philodème, in: *Mélanges offerts à E. Chatelain*, Paris 1910, 118–129.

Conticello, B. Dopo 221 anni si rientra nella Villa dei Papiri, *CronErcol* 17 (1987), 9–13.

Conticello, B. and U. Cioffi. Il "rientro" nella Villa dei Papiri, in: *Restaurare Pompei*, edited by L. Franchi dell'Orto (Milan 1990), 173–190.

Coralini, A. (ed.), *Vesuviana. Archeologia a confronto, Atti del Convegno Internazionale, Bologna, 14–16 gennaio 2008* (Bologna 2010).

Costabile, F. Opere di oratoria politica e giudiziaria nella biblioteca della Villa dei Papiri, in: *Atti XVII Congresso Internazionale di Papirologia*, Naples 1983, 3 vols. (Naples 1984), vol. 2, 591–606.

D'Agata, A.L. Sigmund Freud and Aegean Archaeology. Mycenaean and Cypriote material from his collection of antiquities. *Studi micenei ed egeo-anatolici* 34 (1994), 7–41.

D'Arms, J.H. *Romans on the Bay of Naples. A social and cultural study of the villas and their owners from 150 B.C. to A.D. 400* (Cambridge 1970).

D'Arms, J.H. *Commerce and social standing in ancient Rome* (Cambridge 1981).

De Carolis, E. *Il mobile a Pompei ed Ercolano. Letti, tavoli, sedie e armadi*, Studia Archaeologica 155 (Rome 2007).

De Franciscis, A. *La villa romana di Oplontis*, in: *Neue Forschungen in Pompeji*, edited by B. Andreae and H. Kyrieleis (Recklinghausen 1975), 9–38.

De Franciscis, A. Considerazioni sulla Villa Ercolanese dei Pisoni, in: *Atti XVII Congresso Internazionale di Papirologia*, Naples 1983, 3 vols. (Naples 1984), vol. 2, 621–635.

Delattre, D. (ed.). *Philodème de Gadara: sur la musique. Livre IV* (Paris 2007).

Del Mastro, G. Secondo supplemento al *Catalogo dei papiri ercolanesi*, *CronErcol* 30 (2000), 157–241.

Derrida, J. *Memoirs of the blind*, transl. Pascal-Anne Brault and Michael Naas (Chicago 1993).

Derrida, J. *Archive fever: a Freudian impression*, transl. E. Prenowitz (Chicago and London 1996).

De Seta, C. *Cartografia della città di Napoli*, 3 vols. (Naples 1975).

De Simone, A. La Villa dei Papiri. Rapporto preliminare: gennaio 1986-marzo 1987, *CronErcol* 17 (1987), 15–36.

De Simone, A. Il progetto di scavo di Ercolano e della Villa dei Papiri, in: *Il Vesuvio e le città vesuviane 1730–1860. In ricordo di Georges Vallet. Atti del Convegno "Il Vesuvio e le città vesuviane 1730–1860," 28–30 marzo*, edited by G. Cafasso (Naples 1998), 75–100.

De Simone, A. Rilievo con satiri e ninfa. Testa di Amazzone, in: *Gli antichi ercolanesi: antropologia, società, economia: guida alla mostra*, edited by M. Pagano (Naples 2000), 22–23.

De Simone, A. Villa Arianna: configurazione delle strutture della basis villae, in: *Stabiae: storia e Architettura. 250° anniversario degli scavi di Stabiae 1749–1999*, *Convegno internazionale Castellammare di Stabia, 25–27 marzo 2000*, Studi della Soprintendenza archeologica di Pompei 7, edited by G. Bonifacio and A. M. Sodo (Rome 2002), 41–52.

De Simone, A. Presenze archeologiche e riqualificazione dei centri urbani nell'area vesuviana, in: *Archeologia, città, paesaggio. Atti del Convegno per il 40° anniversario ICOMOS. 16–17 dicembre 2005*, edited by R.A. Genovese (Naples 2007a), 71–83.

De Simone, A. La villa dei Papiri ad Ercolano, in: *La Villa romana*, edited by M.R. Ciardiello (Naples 2007b), 167–193.

De Simone, A. and F. Ruffo. Ercolano 1996–1998. Lo scavo della Villa dei Papiri, *CronErcol* 32 (2002), 325–344.

De Simone, A. and F. Ruffo. Ercolano e la Villa dei Papiri alla luce dei nuovi scavi, *CronErcol* 33 (2003), 279–311.

De Simone, A. and F. Ruffo. I mosaici della Villa dei Papiri ad Ercolano (Na). Il quartiere dell'atrio, in: *Atti del X colloquio dell'Associazione italiana per lo studio e la conservazione del mosaico: Lecce, 18–21 febbraio 2004*, edited by C. Angelleli (Tivoli 2005), 161–182.

De Simone, A., F. Ruffo, M. Tuccinardi and U. Cioffi. Ercolano 1992–1997. La Villa dei Papiri e lo scavo della città, *CronErcol* 28 (1998), 7–59.

De Simone, F. G. VI 17 Insula Occidentalis 41, in: *Pompei (Regiones VI–VII): Insula Occidentalis*, edited by M. Aoyagi and U. Pappalardo (Naples 2006), 43–68.

de Vos, M. Scavi nuovi sconosciuti (I,9,13) pitture e pavimenti della Casa di Cerere, *Meded* 38 (1976), 37–75.

Dickmann, J.A. *Domus frequentata. Anspruchsvolles Wohnen im pompejanischen Wohnhaus* (Munich 1999).

Diels, H. Stichometrisches, *Hermes* 17 (1882), 383–384.

Dillon, S. Subject selection and viewer reception of Greek portraits from Herculaneum and Tivoli, *JRA* 13 (2000), 21–40, figs. 1–8.

Dillon, S. *Ancient Greek Portrait Sculpture. Context, subjects and styles* (Cambridge 2006).

Dobson, M.J. *Smelly old history, scratch 'n' sniff your way through history: Roman aromas* (Oxford 1997).

Dorandi, T. (ed.). *Filodemo: Il buon re secondo Omero* (Naples 1982).

Dorandi T., G. Indelli and A. Tepedino Guerra, Per la cronologia degli scolarchi epicurei, *CronErcol* 9 (1979), 141–142.

Drummond, W. and R. Walpole, *Herculanensia; or archeological and philological dissertations, containing a manuscript found among the ruins of Herculaneum* (London 1810)

du Prey, P. *The villas of Pliny from antiquity to posterity* (Chicago 1994).

Eco, U. *Travels in hyperreality: essays*, transl. W. Weaver (San Diego 1990).

Ehrhardt, W. *Stilgeschichtliche Untersuchungen an römischen Wandmalereien von der späten Republik bis Nero* (Mainz am Rhein 1987).

Ehrhardt, W. *Casa delle Nozze d'Argento, (V 2, i)*, Häuser in Pompeji 12 (Munich 2005).

Emele, M. The assault of computer-generated worlds on the rest of time, in: *Cinema futures: Cain, Abel, or cable? The screen arts in the digital age*, edited by K. Hoffmann and T. Elsaesser (Amsterdam 1998), 251–299.

Esposito, D. *La pittura di Ercolano*, Ph.D. diss., Università degli Studi di Napoli "Federico II" (Naples 2005). Accessible at: http://www.fedoa.unina.it/1085/01/Tesi_Esposito_Domenico.pdf ; forthcoming in series: Studi della Soprintendenza Archeologica di Pompei.

Esposito, D. Pompei, Silla e la villa dei Misteri, in: *Villas, maisons, sanctuaires et tombeaux tardo-républicains: découvertes et relectures récentes*, Actes du colloque international de Saint-Romain-en-Gal en l'honneur d'Anna Gallina Zevi, Vienne, Saint-Roman-en-Gal, 8–10 février 2007, edited by B. Perrier (Rome 2007), 441–465.

Essler, H. What's in a name: Why were the books from Herculaneum given their titles? *Herculaneum Archaeology* 7 (2007a), 6.

Essler, H. Zu den Werktiteln Philodems, *CronErcol* 37 (2007b), 125–34.

Favro, D. Ancient Rome through the veil of sight, in: *Sites unseen: landscape and vision*, edited by D. Harris and D.F. Ruggles (Pittsburgh PA 2007), 111–130.

Favro, D. In the eyes of the beholder: virtual reality re-creations and academia, in: *Imaging ancient Rome: documentation, visualization, imagination, Proceedings of the Third Williams Symposium on Classical Architecture, held at the American Academy in Rome, the British School at Rome, and the Deutsches Archäologisches Institut, Rome, on May 20–23, 2004*, JRA Supplementary Series 61, edited by L. Haselberger and J. Humphrey (Portsmouth, R.I. 2006), 321–334.

Favro, D. The digital disciplinary divide: reactions to historical virtual reality models, in: *Rethinking architectural historiography*, edited by D. Arnold, E.A. Ergut and B. Turan Özkaya (New York 2006), 200–14.

Fergola, L. *Oplontis e le sue ville* (Pompei 2004).

Fergola, L. and M. Pagano (eds.). *Oplontis. Le splendide ville romane di Torre Annunziata. Itinerario archeologico ragionato* (Naples 1998).

Fergola, L. and P.G. Guzzo (eds.). *Oplontis. La villa di Poppea* (Milan 2000).

Filler, M. The Getty: for better and worse, *The New York Review of Books* 53:18, November 16, 2006 (2006), 47.

Fiorelli, G. *Documenti inediti per servire alla storia dei Musei d'Italia*, (Florence and Rome 1878–80).

Forte, M. and A. Siliotti (eds.). *Virtual archaeology: re-creating ancient worlds* (New York 1997).

Franchi dell'Orto, L. (ed.). *Restaurare Pompei* (Milan 1990).

Franck, K. When I enter virtual reality, what body will I leave behind?, *Architectural Design*, 65:11–12 (1995), 20–23.

Frischer, B. Fu la Villa Ercolanese dei Pisoni un modello per la Villa Sabina di Orazio?, *CronErcol* 25 (1995), 211–229.

Frischer, B. From digital illustration to digital heuristics, in: *Beyond illustration: 2D and 3D digital technologies as tools for discovery in archaeology*, edited by B. Frischer and A. Dakouri-Hild (Oxford 2008), v-xxiv.

Frischer, B. and A. Dakouri-Hild (eds.). *Beyond illustration: 2D and 3D digital technologies as tools for discovery in archaeology*, edited by B. Frischer and A. Dakouri-Hild (Oxford 2008).

Gallavotti, C. Nuovo contributo alla storia degli scavi borbonici di Ercolano (nella Villa dei Papiri), *RendNap* 40 (1940), 269–306.

Gallavotti, C. La libreria di una villa romana ercolanese (nella Casa dei papiri), *Bollettino dell'Istituto di Patologia del Libro* 3 (1941), 129–145.

Gamwell, L. and R. Wells (eds.). *Sigmund Freud and art: his personal collection of antiquities* (London 1989).

Gasparri, C. Due nuove sculture da Ercolano, in: *Storie da un'eruzione. In margina alla mostra*, edited by P.G. Guzzo (Pompei 2005), 51–74.

Gassendi, P. *De vita et moribus Epicuri libri octo* (Leiden 1647).

Gebhard, D. Getty's Museum. Is it 'disgusting' and 'downright outrageous?' *Architecture Plus* 2:5 (1974), 56–70.

Getty, J.P. et al., *The joys of collecting* (New York 1965).

Getty, J.P., *As I See It: The autobiography of J. Paul Getty* (Englewood Cliffs 1976; reprint Los Angeles 2003).

Getty, J.P. *My life and fortunes* (New York 1963).

Gibson, J. *The senses considered as perceptual systems* (Boston 1966).

Gibson, J. *The perception of the visual world* (Boston 1950).

Giedion, S. *Space, time and architecture; the growth of a new tradition*, Charles Eliot Norton Lectures 1938–1939 (Cambridge MA and London 1941; 5th revised and enlarged edition in 1967).

Gigante, M. Permessa, *CronErcol* 1 (1971), 5–6.

Gigante, M. *Catalogo dei papiri ercolanesi* (Naples 1979).

Gigante, M. *Ricerche Filodemee* (Naples 1983).

Gigante, M. *La bibliothèque de Philodème et l'épicurisme romain* (Paris 1987).
Gigante, M. (ed.). *Filodemo, Epigrammi scelti*, 2nd ed. (Naples 1988).
Gigante, M. *Filodemo in Italia* (Florence 1990). Italian edition of Gigante 1987 with additions.
Gigante, M. *Philodemus in Italy*, transl. D. Obbink (Ann Arbor 1995). English translation of Gigante 1990.
Glueck, G. Getty Museum is a hit with visitors, *The New York Times,* May 28 1974, 34.
Godart, L. and S. De Caro (eds.). *Nostoi: Capolavori ritrovati*, exhibition catalogue, Rome, Palazzo del Quirinale, Galleria di Alessandro VII, 21 dicembre 2007–2 marzo 2008 (Rome 2007).
Goethe, J.W. von. *Italian journey, 1786–1788*, transl. W.H. Auden and E. Mayer (London 1962).
Goldberger, P. Getty Museum's Roman styling once criticized, draws crowds, *The New York Times*, Aug. 6, 1975, 38.
Goldberger, P. The architecture of choice, *The New York Times*, July 28, 1974, 263.
Greenwood, J. Review essay, *Journal of Architectural Education* 43:4 (1990), 53–59.
Grell, C. *Herculanum et Pompéi dans les récits des voyageurs français du XVIIIe siècle* (Naples 1982).
Gros, P. *L'architecture romaine du début du IIIe siècle av. J.-C. à la fin du Haut-Empire*, vol. 2. *Maisons, palais, villas et tombeaux* (Paris 2001).
Guadagno, G. Note prosopografiche ercolanesi: i Mammii e L. Mammius Maximus, *CronErcol* 14 (1984), 149–156.
Guadagno, G. Nuovi documenti del XVIII secolo per la storia degli scavi di Ercolano, *CronErcol* 16 (1986), 135–147.
Guadagno, G. Ercolano. Eredità di cultura e nuovi dati, in: *Ercolano, 1738–1988: 250 anni di ricerca archeologica. Atti del Convegno internazionale Ravello-Ercolano-Napoli-Pompei, 30 ottobre-5 novembre, 1988*, edited by L. Franchi dell'Orto (Rome 1993), 73–98.
Guidi, G., B. Frischer, M. De Simone, et al. Virtualizing ancient Rome: 3D acquisition and modeling of a large Plaster-of-Paris model of Imperial Rome, in: *Videometrics VIII: 18–20 January 2005, San Jose, California, USA*, Proceedings of Electronic Imaging Science and Technology, SPIE 5665, edited by J.-A. Beraldin, S.F. El-Hakim, A. Gruen and J.S. Waltonet (Bellingham WA and Springfield VA 2005), 119–133.
Guidobaldi, M.P. (ed.). *Ercolano. Tre secoli di scoperte*, exhibition catalogue, Napoli, 16 october 2008–13 april 2009 (Milan 2008).
Guidobaldi, M.P. and D. Esposito, Le nuove ricerche archeologiche nella Villa dei Papiri di Ercolano, *CronErcol* 39 (2009), 331–370.
Guidobaldi, M.P., D. Esposito and E. Formisano, L'*Insula* I, l'*Insula* nord-occidentale e la Villa dei Papiri di Ercolano: una sintesi delle conoscenze alla luce delle recenti indagini archeologiche, *Vesuviana* 1 (2009), 43–180.
Guidobaldi, F. and F. Olevano. *Sectilia pavimenta* dell'area vesuviana, *StMisc* 31, 223–240, tabl. 1–18.

Gullini, G. Il progetto di esplorazione della Villa dei Papiri, *CronErcol* 14 (1985), 7–8.
Guzzo, P.G. Considerazioni sugli scavi di Ercolano, *CronErcol* 28 (1998), 61–67.
Guzzo, P.G. La Villa dei Papiri: fasti passati, novità recenti, *CronErcol* 29 (1999), 39–51.
Hancock, J.E. Architecture and its history: past futures and future pasts, *Journal of Architectural Education*, 36:1 (1982), 26–33.
Hayter, J. *A report upon the Herculaneum manuscripts in a second letter … to His Royal Highness the Prince Regent* (London 1811).
Hemmerdinger, B. Deux notes papyrologiques I: L'origine des Papyrus d'Herculanum, *Revue des études grecques* 72 (1959), 106.
Hermon, S. Reasoning in 3D: a critical appraisal of the role of 3D modelling and virtual reconstructions in archaeology, in: *Beyond illustration: 2D and 3D digital technologies as tools for discovery in archaeology*, edited by B. Frischer and A. Dakouri-Hild (Oxford 2008), 36–45.
Houston, S. and K. Taube. An archaeology of the senses: perception and cultural expression in ancient Mesoamerica, *CAJ* 10:2 (2000), 261–94.
Iacopi, I. *La Casa di Augusto. Le pitture* (Milan 2008).
James, S. Drawing inferences, in: *The cultural life of images: visual representation in archaeology*, edited by B.L. Molyneaux (London and New York 1997), 22–48.
Johnson, K. A $135 million home, but if you have to ask … , *The New York Times*, July 2, 2007 (2007), A1.
Kastner, V. *Hearst Castle: the biography of a country house* (New York 2000).
Kenyon, F.G. *Books and readers in ancient Greece and Rome* (Oxford 1951).
Kleve, K. How to read an illegible papyrus: towards an edition of *PHerc.* 78, Caecilius Statius, *Obolostates sive Faenerator*, *CronErcol* 26 (1996), 5–14.
Knight, C. Le lettere di Camillo Paderni alla Royal Society di Londra sulle scoperte di Ercolano (1739–1758), *RendNap* 66 (1996), 13–55.
Knight, C. and A. Jorio. L'ubicazione della Villa Ercolanese dei Papiri, *RendNap* 55 (1980), 51–65.
Koller, D.R. Virtual archaeology and computer-aided reconstruction of the Severan Marble Plan, in: *Beyond illustration: 2D and 3D digital technologies as tools for discovery in archaeology*, edited by B. Frischer and A. Dakouri-Hild (Oxford 2008), 125–134.
Kuspit, D. A mighty metaphor: the analogy of archaeology and psychoanalysis, in: *Sigmund Freud and art: his personal collection of antiquities*, edited by L. Gamwell and R. Wells (London 1989), 133–151.
Lapatin, K. *Guide to the Getty Villa and its gardens* (Los Angeles 2005).
Lapatin, K. The Getty Villa: art, architecture, and aristocratic self-fashioning in the mid-twentieth century, in: *Pompeii in the public imagination from its rediscovery to today*, edited by S. Hales and J. Paul (Oxford 2011).
Laurence, R. The uneasy dialogue between ancient history and archaeology, in: *Archaeology and ancient history: breaking down the boundaries*, edited by E.W. Sauer (London and New York 2004), 99–113.

Lesser, W. *The life below the ground; a study of the subterranean in literature and history* (Boston 1987).

Le Vane, E. and Getty, J.P., *Collector's choice: the chronicle of an artistic Odyssey through Europe* (London 1955).

Lin Y. and W.B. Seales. Opaque document imaging: building images of inaccessible texts, *International Conference on Computer Vision* 1 (2005), 662–9.

Lippold, G. *Kopien und Umbildungen griechischer Statuen*, München 1923.

Longo Auricchio, F. and M. Capasso. I rotoli della villa ercolanese: dislocazione e ritrovamento, *CronErcol* 17 (1987), 37–47.

McIlwaine, I.C. *Herculaneum: a guide to printed sources* (Naples 1988).

McKay, A.G. *Houses, villas, and palaces in the Roman world* (Baltimore 1998).

Manni, M. Per la storia della pittura ercolanese, *CronErcol* 20 (1990), 129–143.

Maiuri, A. *Gli scavi di Ercolano: storia delle scoperte e programma dei lavori* (Resina 1958).

Maiuri, A. *Herculaneum and the Villa of the Papyri* (Novara 1973).

Marcus, G.E., The Production of European high culture in Los Angeles: The J. Paul Getty Trust as artificial curiosity, *Cultural Anthropology*, 5:3 (1990), 314–330.

Marturano, A., S.C. Nappo and A. Varone. Trasformazioni territoriali legate all'eruzione del Vesuvio del 79 A.D., in: *Proceedings of the 2nd International Conference "Archaeology, volcanism and remote sensing,"* Sorrento 20–22 juin 2001), edited by F. Vitiello (Rome 2006), 89–107.

Marzi, M.G. (ed.), *Domenico Comparetti tra antichità e archeologia. Individualità di una biblioteca* (Florence 1999).

Melucco Vaccaro, A. Restoration and anti-restoration, in: *Historical and philosophical issues in the conservation of cultural heritage*, edited by N. Stanley-Price, M.K. Talley Jr and A. Melucco Vaccaro (Los Angeles 1996), 308–313.

Merleau-Ponty, M. *Phenomenology of perception*, transl. C. Smith (London and New York 1962).

Metraux, G.P.R. Ancient housing: 'oikos' and 'domus' in Greece and Rome, *JSAH* 58:3 (1999), 392–405.

Mielsch, H. *Die römische Villa: Architektur und Lebensform* (München 1987).

Mielsch, H. *La villa romana con guida archeologica alle ville romane*, transl. A.M. Esposito (Florence 1999). Italian translation of Mielsch 1987.

Miniero, P. La villa romana tardo-repubblicana nel Castello Aragonese di Baia, in: *Villas, maisons, sanctuaires et tombeaux tardo-républicains: découvertes et relectures récentes*, Actes du colloque international de Saint-Romain-en-Gal en l'honneur d'Anna Gallina Zevi, Vienne, Saint-Roman-en-Gal, 8–10 février 2007, edited by B. Perrier (Rome 2007), 157–176.

Miniero, P. and C. Capaldi. *Un nuovo contesto pittorico da Baia,* Associazione internazionale sulla pittura muraria antica, X Congresso Internazionale, Napoli 17–21 settembre 2007 (in press).

Miniero, P. and F. Zevi (eds.). *Museo Archeologico dei Campi Flegrei*, vol. 3. *Liternum, Baia, Miseno* (Naples 2008).

Moesch, V. La Villa dei Papiri, in: *Ercolano, tre secoli di scoperte*, exhibition catalogue, Napoli, Museo Archeologico Nazionale, 16 ottobre 2008–13 aprile 2009, edited by M.P. Guidobaldi (Milan 2008), 70–79.

Moesch, V. *Sculture in marmo dalla Villa dei Papiri ad Ercolano. Contributo alla conoscenza delle botteghe di scultori di età romana in Campania*, Ph.D. diss., Università degli Studi di Napoli "Federico II" (Naples 2009).

Mommsen, T. Inschriftbüsten. I: Aus Herculaneum, *AZ* 38 (1880), 32–36.

Moormann, E.M. Le pitture della Villa dei papiri ad Ercolano, in: *Atti del XVII Congresso internazionale di papirologia*, edited by M. Gigante, 3 vols. (Naples 1984), vol. 2, 637–674.

Moormann, E.M. *La pittura parietale romana come fonte di conoscenza per la scultura romana* (Assen 1988).

Moormann, E.M. Der römische Freskenzyklus mit großen Figuren in der Villa 6 in Terzigno, in: *Otium. Festschrift für Volker Michael Strocka*, edited by T. Ganschow and M. Steinhart (Remshalden 2005), 257–266.

Moormann, E.M. Villas surrounding Pompeii and Herculaneum, in: *The World of Pompeii*, edited by J.J. Dobbins and P.W. Foss (London and New York 2007), 435–454.

Murray, O. Philodemus on the good king according to Homer, *JRS* 55 (1965), 161–182.

Mustilli, D. La villa pseudorurbana ercolanese, *RendNap* 31 (1956), 77–97, reprinted in: *La Villa dei Papiri*, Second Supplement to *CronErcol* 13 (Naples 1983), 7–18.

Napoli, M. Il capitello ionico a quattro facce a Pompei, in: *Pompeiana. Raccolta di studi per il secondo centenario degli scavi di Pompei*, edited by A. Maiuri (Naples 1950), 230–265.

Neudecker, R. *Die Skulpturenausstattung römischer Villen in Italien* (Mainz am Rhein 1988).

Neuerburg, N. Norman Neuerburg papers regarding Getty Villa design and construction, 1966–1987, bulk 1970–1975 (19 boxes, 22 flat file folders, 3 rolls), Getty Special Collections (Malibu, CA 1966–1987).

Neuerburg, N. *Herculaneum to Malibu: a companion to the visit of the J. Paul Getty Museum building: a descriptive and explanatory guide to the re-created ancient Roman Villa of the Papyri built at the wishes of J. Paul Getty in Malibu, California, 1970–1974* (Malibu 1975).

Nisbet, R.G.M. (ed.). *M. Tulli Ciceronis "In L. Calpurnium Pisonem" oratio*, with introduction and commentary (Oxford 1961).

Norberg-Schulz, C. *Genius loci: towards a phenomenology of architecture* (New York 1980).

Obbink, D. (ed.). *Philodemus: On Piety. Part 1: Critical text with commentary* (Oxford 1996).

O'Donoghue, D. Negotiations of surface: archaeology within the early strata of psychoanalysis, *Journal of the American Psychoanalytic Association* 52:3 (2004), 653–671.

Overbeck, J.A. *Die antiken Schriftquellen zur Geschichte der bildenden Künste bei den Griechen* (Leipzig 1868).

Pagano, M. La villa romana di Contrada Sora a Torre del Greco, *CronErcol* 21 (1991), 149–186.

Pagano, M. Il teatro di Ercolano, *CronErcol* 23 (1993), 121–156.

Pagano, M. Torre del Greco. Scavi e restauri in località Ponte di Rivieccio (villa marittima romana detta Terma-Ginnasio), *RStPomp* 6 (1993–94), 256–267.

Pagano, M. La nuova pianta della città e di alcuni edifici pubblici di Ercolano, *CronErcol* 26 (1996), 229–262.

Pagano, M. *Ercolano. Itinerario archeologico ragionato* (Torre del Greco 1997).

Pagano, M. Mosaici romani nella reggia di Portici, in: *Atti del VII Colloquio dell'Associazione italiana per lo studio e la conservazione del mosaico*, Pompei, 22–25 marzo 2000, edited by A. Paribeni (Ravenna 2001), 335–342.

Pagano, M. *Gli scavi di Ercolano* (Naples 2003).

Pagano, M. Herculaneum. Eine Kleinstadt am Golf von Neapel, in: *Verschüttet vom Vesuv. Die letzten Stunden von Herculaneum*, edited by J. Mühlenbrock-D. Richter (Mainz am Rhein 2005), 3–12.

Pagano, M. Osservazioni storiche sul Castello, in: *Il Porto del corallo. Analisi storica del Porto di Torre del Greco*, edited by G. Troina and F. Russo (Torre del Greco 2007), 83–99.

Pagano, M. and R. Prisciandaro. *Studio sulle provenienze degli oggetti rinvenuti negli scavi borbonici del Regno di Napoli*, 2 vols. (Naples 2006).

Pallasmaa, J. *The eyes of the skin: architecture and the senses*, new revised and extended edition (Chichester and Hoboken N.J. 2005).

Pandermalis, D. Zum Programm der Statuenausstattung in der Villa dei Papiri, *AM* 86 (1971), 173–209.

Pandermalis, D. Sul programma della decorazione scultorea, transl. L.A. Scatozza Höricht, in: *La Villa dei Papiri*, Second Supplement to *CronErcol* 13 (1983), 19–50. Italian translation of Pandermalis 1971.

Pannuti, U. Il 'Giornale degli scavi' di Ercolano (1738–1756), *MemLinc* Serie 8, 26, 3, (1983), 163–410.

Pappalardo, U. *Le ville romane nel golfo di Napoli* (Naples 2000).

Parslow, C.C. *Rediscovering antiquity: Karl Weber and the excavation of Herculaneum, Pompeii, and Stabiae* (Cambridge 1995).

Pasquali, G. Domenico Comparetti, *Aegyptus* 8 (1927), 129–130, reprinted in: Pasquali, G. *Pagine stravaganti* (Firenze 1968), vol. I, 17–18.

Pesando, F. *Domus. Edilizia privata e società pompeiana fra III e I secolo a. C.* (Rome 1997).

Pesando, F. and M.P. Guidobaldi. *Pompei, Oplontis, Ercolano, Stabiae*, Guide Archeologiche Laterza 14 (Rome 2006a).

Pesando, F. and M.P. Guidobaldi. *Gli 'ozi' di Ercole. Residenze di lusso a Pompei ed Ercolano*, Studia Archaeologica 143 (Rome 2006b).

Platthy, J. *Sources on the earliest Greek libraries with the testimonia* (Amsterdam 1968).

Polito, E. Fulgentibus Armis. *Introduzione allo studio dei fregi d'armi antichi* (Rome 1998).

Porteous, J.D. *Landscapes of the mind: worlds of sense and metaphor* (Toronto and Boson 1990).

Porter, J.I. Herculaneum and the history of art criticism, *Herculaneum Archaeology* 3 (2005), 6–7.
Porter, J.I. Hearing Voices: The Herculaneum papyri and classical scholarship, in: *Antiquity recovered, the legacy of Pompeii and Herculaneum,* edited by V.C. Gardner Coates and J.L. Seydl (Los Angeles 2007), 95–113.
Pucci, G. La ceramica aretina: "imagerie" e correnti artistiche, in : *L'Art décoratif à Rome à la fin de la République et au début du Principat*, Table ronde organisée par l'Ecole française de Rome, Rome 10–11 May 1979, Collection de l'Ecole française de Rome 55 (Rome 1981), 101–119.
Purcell, N. Town in country and country in town, in: *Ancient Roman villa gardens,* Dumbarton Oaks Colloquium on the History of Landscape Architecture 10, edited by E.B. MacDougall (Washington D.C. 1987), 187–203.
Quilici, V. and G. Longobardi (eds.). *Ercolano e la Villa dei Papiri: archeologia, città e paesaggio* (Florence 2007).
Ramage, N.H. Goods, graves, and scholars: 18th-century archaeologists in Britain and Italy, *AJA* 96:4 (1992), 653–661.
Rasmussen, S.E. *Experiencing architecture*, transl. E. Wendt (Cambridge 1959).
Richter, G.M.A. *The portraits of the Greeks*, 3 vols. (London 1965).
Riemenschneider, U. *Pompejanische Stuckgesimse des dritten und vierten Stils* (Frankfurt am Main 1986).
Rizzo, G.E. *Thiasos. Bassorilievi greci di soggetto dionisiaco* (Rome 1934).
Rodaway, P. *Sensuous geographies: body, sense, and place* (London and New York 1994).
Rosini, C.M. *Dissertationis isagogicae ad Herculanensium voluminum explicationem, pars prima* (Naples 1797).
Ruggiero, M. *Storia degli scavi di Ercolano ricomposta su' documenti superstiti* (Naples 1885).
Ruggiero. M. *Degli scavi di antichità nelle provincie di terraferma dell'antico regno di Napoli dal 1743 al 1876* (Naples 1888).
Sampaolo, V. In margine alle pitture del salone 13 della Villa di Terzigno, in: *Storie da un'eruzione. In margine alla mostra*, edited by P.G. Guzzo (Pompei 2005), 113–126.
Sauron, G. Templa Serena. À propos de la "Villa des Papyri" d'Herulaneum: contribution à l'étude des comportements aristocratiques romains à la fin de la République, *MÉFRA* 92 (1980), 277–301. Italian translation by L.A Scatozza Höricht, in: *La Villa dei Papiri*, Second Supplement to *CronErcol* 13 (Naples 1983), 69–82.
Sauron, G. *La peinture allégorique à Pompéi: le regard de Cicéron* (Paris 2007a).
Sauron, G., *La pittura allegorica a Pompei. Lo sguardo di Cicerone*, transl. M. Castracane (Milan 2007b). Italian translation of Sauron 2007a.
Scarre, C. Sound, place and space: towards an archaeology of acoustics, in: *Archaeoacoustics*, McDonald Institute monographs, edited by C. Scarre and G. Lawson (Cambridge 2006), 1–10.
Scarre, C. and G. Lawson (eds.). *Archaeoacoustics*, McDonald Institute monographs (Cambridge 2006).
Scatozza Höricht, L.A. Nota bibliografica, in: *La Villa dei Papiri*, Second Supplement to *CronErcol* 13 (Naples 1983), 135–142.

Scatozza Höricht, L.A. and F. Longo Auricchio, Dopo il Comparetti-De Petra, *CronErcol* 17 (1987), 157–167.

Schmidt, M. Are dull reconstructions more scientific? in: *Les sites de reconstitutions archéologiques, actes du colloque d'Aubechies, 2–5 Septembre 1993*, edited by N. Barrois and L. Demarez (Aubechies 1994), 27–30.

Seales, W.B. and Y. Lin, Digital restoration using volumetric scanning, *Joint Conference on Digital Libraries* (2004), 117–24.

Serra, J.R. (ed.). *Paestum and the Doric Revival* (Florence 1986).

Sider, D. (ed.). *The Epigrams of Philodemos*, with introduction and commentary (New York and Oxford 1997).

Sider, D. *The library of the Villa dei Papiri at Herculaneum* (Los Angeles 2005).

Smith, M.M. *Sensing the past: seeing, hearing, smelling, tasting, and touching in history* (Berkeley 2007).

Sorrell, A. *Reconstructing the past*, edited by M. Sorrell (London 1981).

Spence, D. *The Freudian metaphor: towards paradigm change in psychoanalysis* (New York 1987).

Spinazzola, V. *Pompei alla luce degli scavi nuovi di via dell'Abbondanza (anni 1910–1923)*, 2 vols. (Rome 1953).

Steven, R.G. Plato and the art of his time, *CQ* 27 (1933), 149–155.

Strocka, V.M. VI 17, 41: Ein Haus mit Privatbibliothek, *RM* 100 (1993), 320–351.

Strocka, V.M. Das Bildprogramm des Epigrammzimmers in Pompeji, *RM* 102 (1995), 269–290.

Strocka, V.M. Troja – Karthago – Rom. Ein vorvergilisches Bildprogramm in Terzigno bei Pompeji, *RM* 112 (2005–06), 79–120.

Tanzer, H.H. *The villas of Pliny the Younger* (New York 1924).

Taylor, L.R. *The voting districts of the Roman Republic* (Rome 1960).

Thomas, J. *Time, culture and identity: an interpretative archaeology* (London and New York 1996).

Thomas, M.L. and J.R. Clarke. The Oplontis Project 2005–6: Observations on the Construction History of Villa A at Torre Annunziata, *JRA* 20 (2007), 223–232.

Thomas, M.L. and J.R. Clarke. The Oplontis Project 2005–2006: new evidence for the building history and decorative programs at Villa A, Torre Annunziata, in: Nuove *ricerche archeologiche nell'area vesuviana* (scavi 2003–2006), Studi della Soprintendenza Archeologica di Pompei 25, edited by P.G. Guzzo and M.P. Guidobaldi (Rome 2008), 465–471.

Tilley, C. *A Phenomenology of landscape: places, paths and monuments* (Oxford and Providence R.I. 1994).

Tortorella S., Le lastre Campana. Problemi di produzione e di iconografia, in: *L'Art décoratif à Rome à la fin de la République et au début du Principat*, Table ronde organiste par l'Ecole française de Rome, Rome 10–11 mai 1979, Collection de l'École française de Rome 55 (Rome 1981), 61–100.

True, M. and J. Silvetti. *The Getty Villa* (Los Angeles 2005).

Tuan, Y.-F. *Topophilia: a study of environmental perception, attitudes, and values* (Englewood Cliffs N.J. 1974).

Tuan, Y.-F. *Space and place: the perspective of experience* (Minneapolis 1977).

Tybout, R.A. *Aedificiorum figurae. Untersuchungen zu den Architekturdarstellungen des frühen zweiten Stils* (Amsterdam 1989).

Tybout, R.A. Malerei und Raumfunktion im zweiten Stil, in: *Functional and spatial analysis of wall painting,* Proceedings of the Fifth International Congress on Ancient Wall Painting, Amsterdam 1992, edited by E.M. Moormann (Leiden 1993), 38–50.

Vacharopoulou, K. Monument conservation in the Mediterranean: issues and aspects of anastylosis, in: *SOMA 2003: Symposium on Mediterranean Archaeology*, BAR International Series 1391, edited by C. Briault, J. Green, A. Kaldelis, A. Stellatou (Oxford 2005), 161–166.

Venuti, N.M. *Descrizione delle prime scoperte dell'antica città di Ercolano, ritrovata vicino a Portici, villa della Maestà del Re delle Due Sicilie* (Rome 1748).

Venuti, N.M. *A description of the first discoveries of the antient city of Heraclea, found near Portici, a country palace belonging to the king of the Two Sicilies. In two parts... Done into English from the original Italian of the Marquis Don Marcello di Venuti. By Wickes Skurray. To which are added some letters that passed between the learned Jo. Matthia Gesner..., Cardinal Quirini, and Hermannus Samuel Reimarus... concerning these discoveries* (London 1750).

Viollet-le-Duc, E.-E. *Dictionnaire raisonné de l'architecture française du XIe au XVIe siècle* (Paris 1854).

Walsh, J. and D.A. Gribbon. *The J. Paul Getty Museum and its collections: a museum for the new century* (Los Angeles 1997).

Willey, G.R. and P. Phillips. *Method and theory in American archaeology* (Chicago 1958).

Wilson, G. and C. Hess. *Summary Catalogue of European Decorative Arts in the J. Paul Getty Museum* (Los Angeles 2001).

Winckelmann, J.J. *Sendschreiben von den herculanischen Entdeckungen: an den hochgebohrnen Herrn Heinrich Reichsgrafen von Brühl* (Dresden 1762).

Winckelmann, J.J. *Lettre de M. L'Abbé Winckelmann à M. Le Comte de Brühl sur les découvertes d'Herculanum* (Paris 1764). French translation of Winckelmann 1762.

Winckelmann, J.J. *Critical account of the situation and destruction by the first eruptions of Mount Vesuvius of Herculaneum, Pompeii, and Stabia* (London 1771). English translation of Winckelmann 1764.

Winckelmann, J.J. *Lettere Italiane,* edited by Giorgio Zampa (Milan 1961).

Wojcik, M.R. La "Villa dei Papiri" di Ercolano. Programma decorativo e problemi di committenza, *AnnPerugia* 17 (1979–1980), 359–368.

Wulf, U. and A. Riedel, Investigating buildings three-dimensionally: the 'Domus Severiana' on the Palatine, in: *Imaging ancient Rome: documentation, visualization, imagination: proceedings of the Third Williams Symposium on Classical Architecture, held at the American Academy in Rome, the British School at Rome, and the Deutsches Archäologisches Institut, Rome, on May 20–23, 2004*, edited by L. Hasselberger, J. H. Humphrey and D. Abernathy (Portsmouth R.I. 2006), 220–234.

Yegül, F. The Marble Court of Sardis and historical reconstruction, *JFA* 32 (1976), 169–194.

Yegül, F. with T. Couch. Building a Roman bath for the cameras, *JRA* 16 (2003), 153–177.

Zanker, P. In search of the Roman viewer, in: *The interpretation of architectural sculpture in Greece and Rome,* Studies in the History of Art 49, edited by D. Buitron-Oliver (Washington D.C. 1997), 179–192.

Zumthor, P. *Architektur denken* (Baden 1998).

List of Electronic Bibliography

Apuleius, *The Golden Asse,* (Adlington's 1566 translation), edited by M. Guy, 1996, electronic document, http://books.eserver.org/fiction/apuleius/ (accessed June 22, 2009).

Golvin, J.-C. "Signification et problèmes de définition," in: *De la restitution en archéologie, Archaeological restitutior* (Paris 2008), 1–4, electronic document, http://editions.monuments-nationaux.fr/fr/les-ouvrages-en-ligne/bdd/livree/9 (accessed June 30, 2009).

Gregory, A.P. "Digital exploration: unwrapping the secrets of damaged manuscripts," *University of Kentucky Odyssey* (Fall 2004), electronic document, http://www.research.uky.edu/odyssey/fall04/seales.html (accessed October 9, 2010).

Law, A., et al., "Projecting restorations in real-time for real-world objects," in: *Museums and the web 2009: proceedings*, edited by J. Trant and D. Bearman (Toronto 2009), electronic document, http://www.archimuse.com/mw2009/papers/law/law.html (accessed June 30, 2010).

Lorenzi, R. "Ancient villa rescued from Vesuvius' mud," electronic document, http://dienekes.awardspace.com/blog/archives/000040.html (accessed June 8, 2008).

Nold, C. "Bio mapping," electronic document, http://www.biomapping.net/index.htm (accessed June 5, 2008).

Peral, R., D. Sagasti and S. Sillaurren, "Virtual restoration of cultural heritage through real-time 3D models projection," electronic document, http://public-repository.epoch-net.org/publications/VAST2005/shortpapers/short2002.pdf (accessed June 30, 2009).

Sobchack, V. "Real phantoms/phantom realities: on the phenomenology of bodily imagination," in: *Phantom Limb* (2004), electronic document, http://www.artbrain.org/real-phantomsphantom-realities-on-the-phenomenology-of-bodily-imagination/ (accessed June 8, 2008).

Tringham, R., "Senses of Places: remediations from text to digital performance, Draft 1 March 1, 2007," electronic document, http://chimeraspider.wordpress.com/2007/03/01/beyond-etext-remediated-places-draft-1/ (accessed May 5, 2008).

Tringham, R. "Putting vision in its place: the interweaving of senses to create a sense of place at Çatalhöyük," electronic document, http://traumwerk.stanford.edu:3455/31/admin/download.html?attachid=157977 (accessed May 14, 2008).

Tringham, R., M. Ashley and S. Mills, "Senses of places: remediations from text to digital performance", electronic document, http://chimeraspider.-files.wordpress.com/2007/09/bet_ret_ma_sm_0907_web.pdf (accessed June 8, 2008).

General Index

Plates

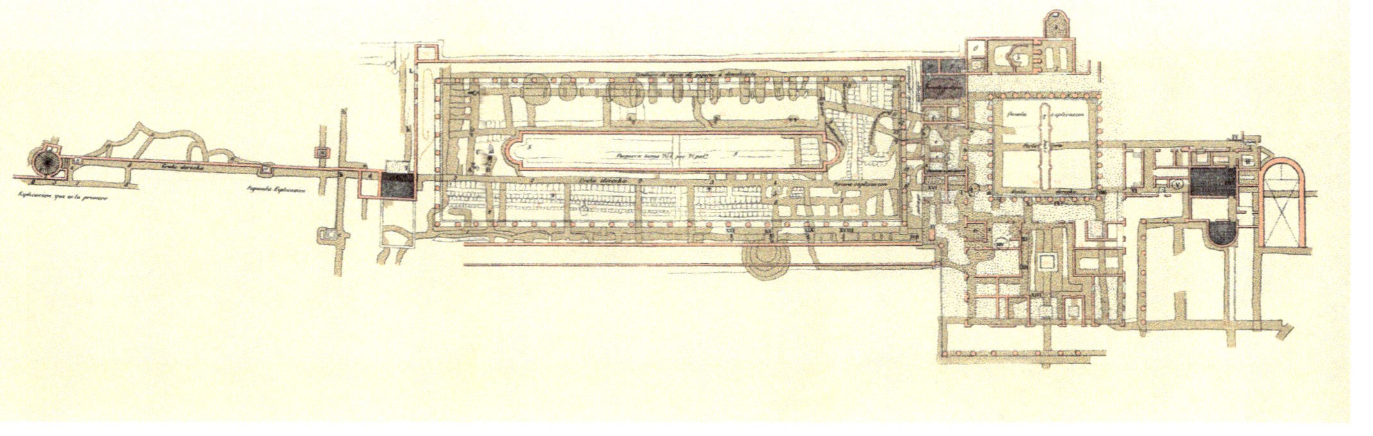

Fig. 1. Plan of the Villa of the Papyri by Karl Weber (1752) redrawn by Comparetti and De Petra in 1883 (source: CDP, pl. XXIV).

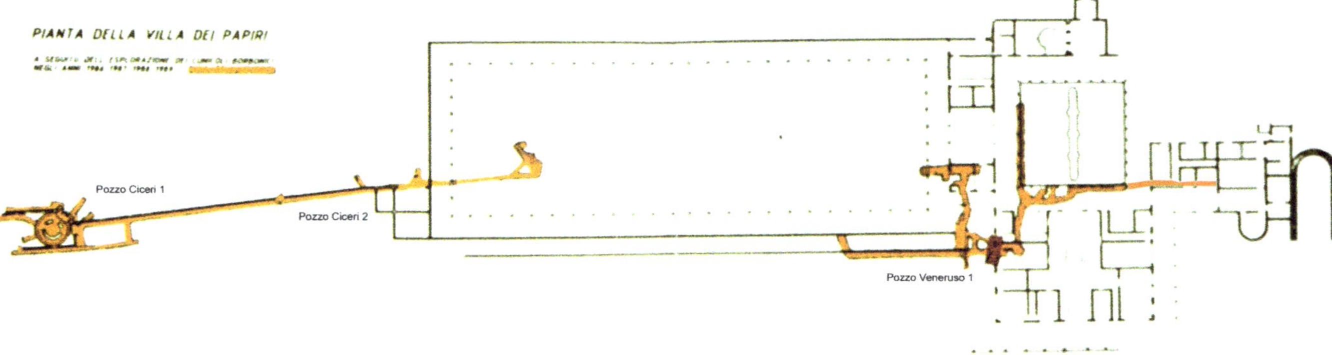

Fig. 2. Map of the Villa of the Papyri with the identification of the re-explored tunnels.

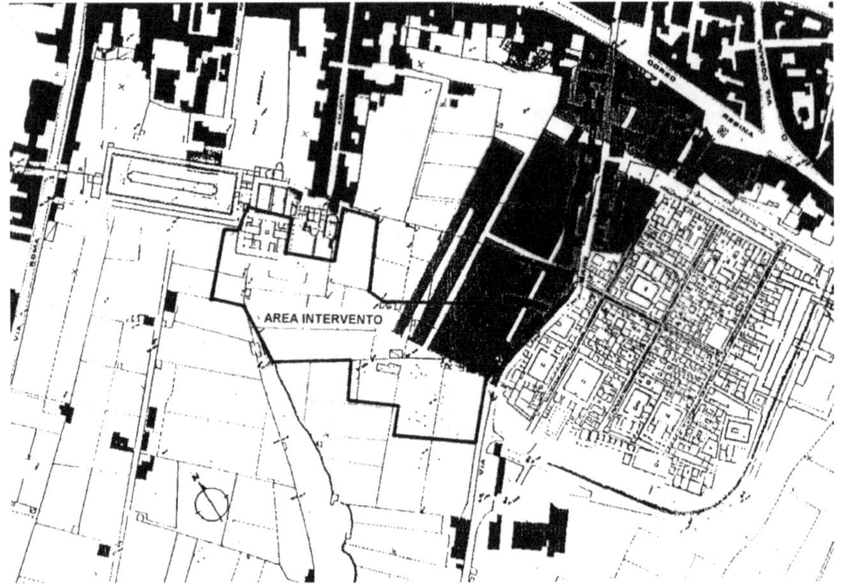

Fig. 3. Herculaneum, map of the excavation project.

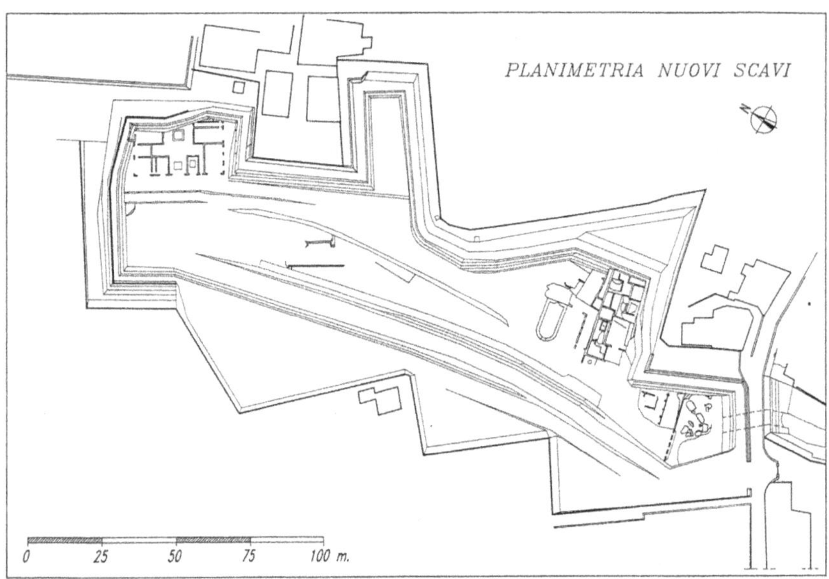

Fig. 4. Herculaneum, map of the New Excavations.

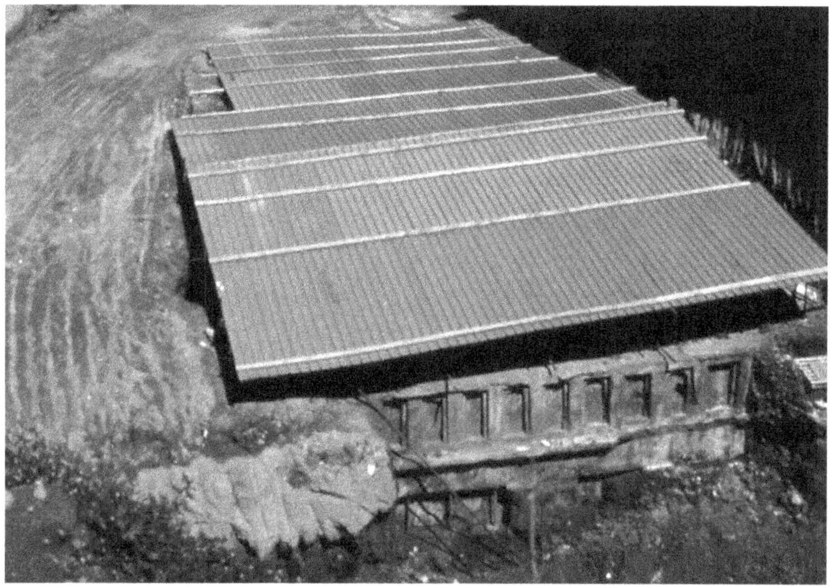

Fig. 5. Herculaneum, view of the late Republican building near the House of Aristides during the New Excavations.

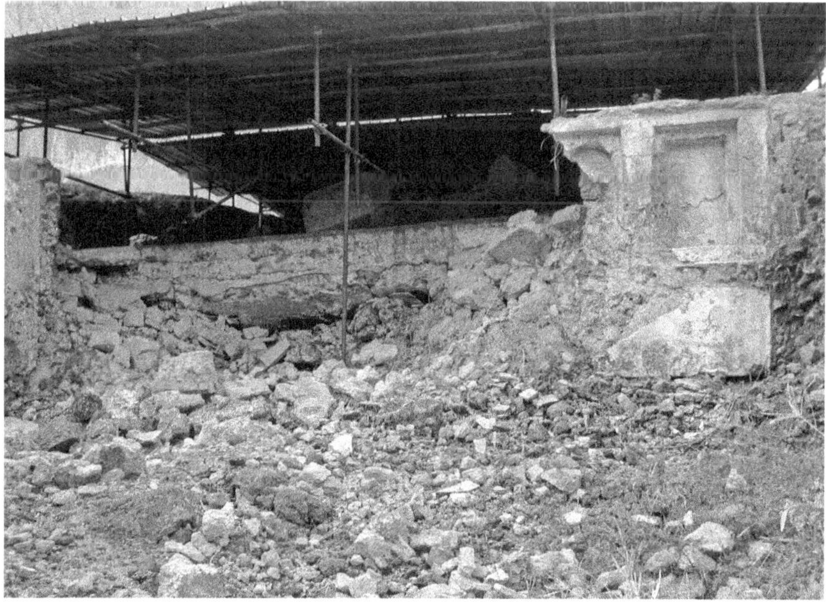

Fig. 6. Herculaneum, view of the late Republican building near the House of Aristides, after the end of the New Excavations, in 2000.

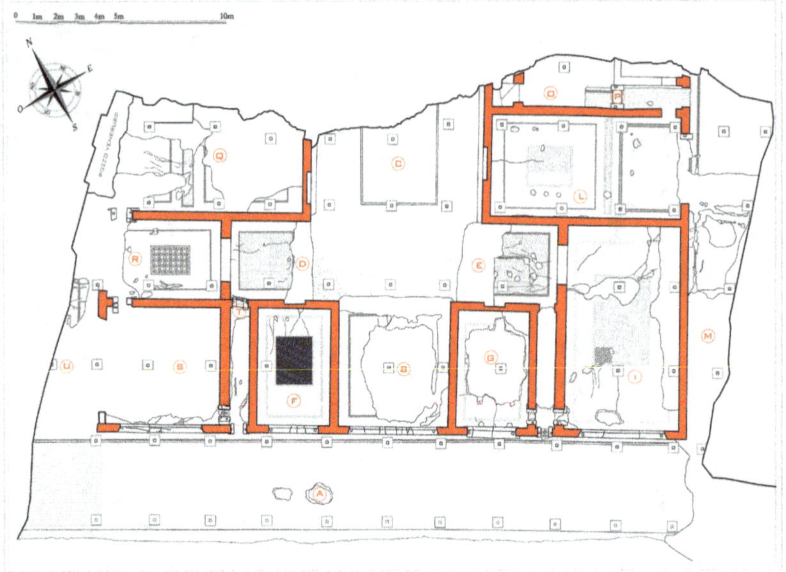

Fig. 7. Villa of the Papyri, atrium quarter: plan.

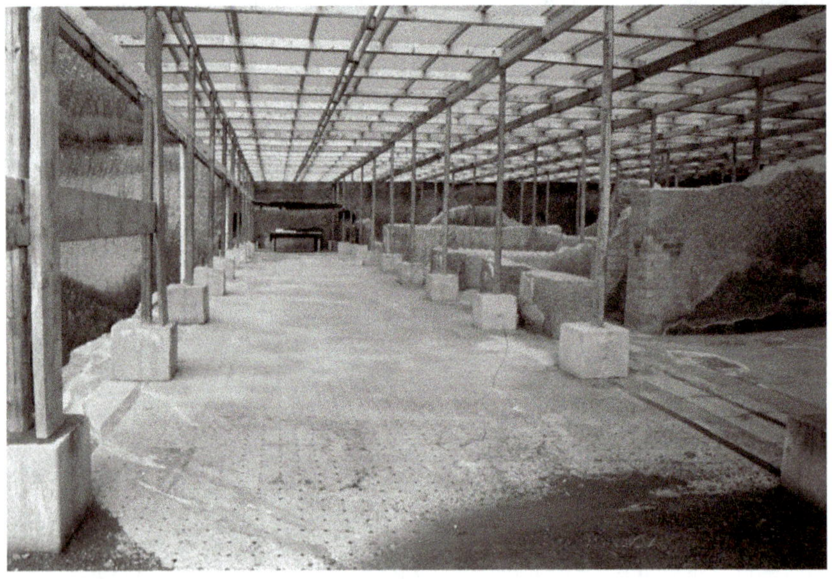

Fig. 8. Villa of the Papyri, atrium quarter: view inside portico (a).

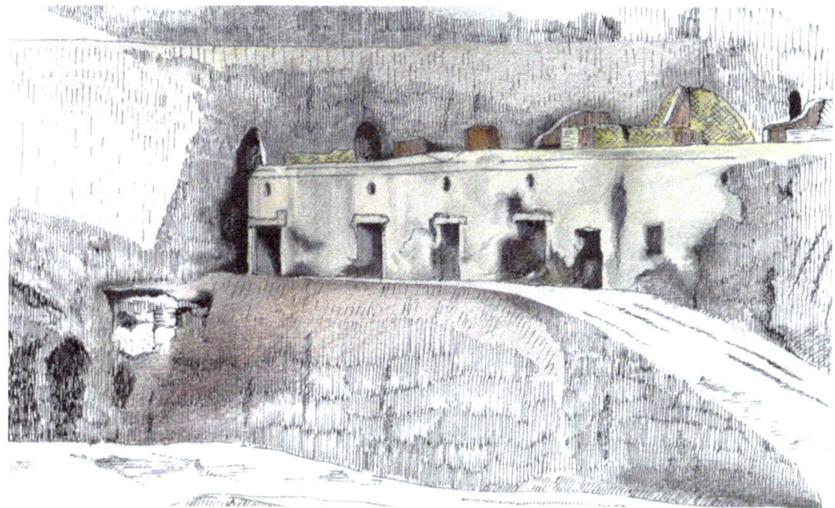

Fig. 9. Villa of the Papyri, drawing of the south-west prospect of the *basis villae* and portico (a) of the atrium quarter.

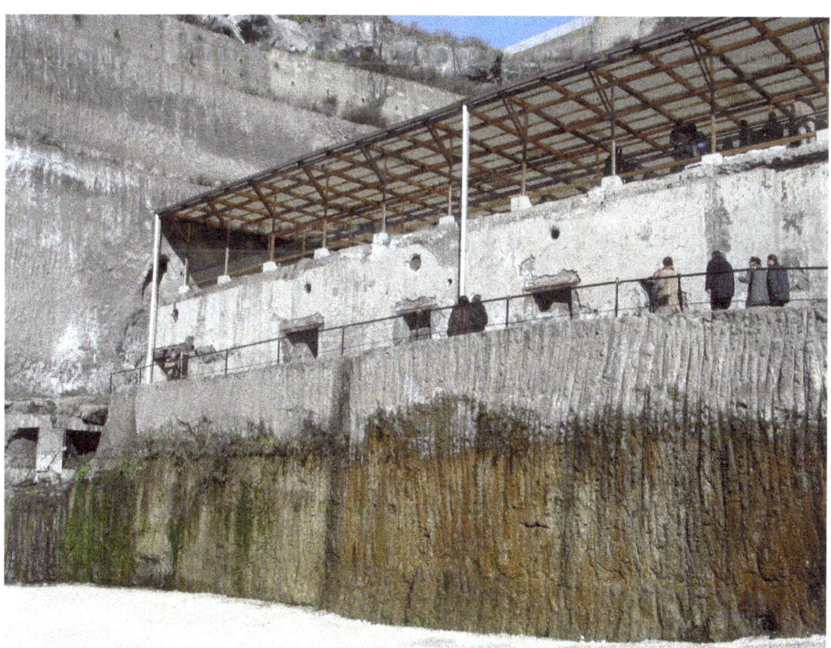

Fig. 10. Villa of the Papyri, view of the *basis villae* and portico (a) of the atrium quarter from the south.

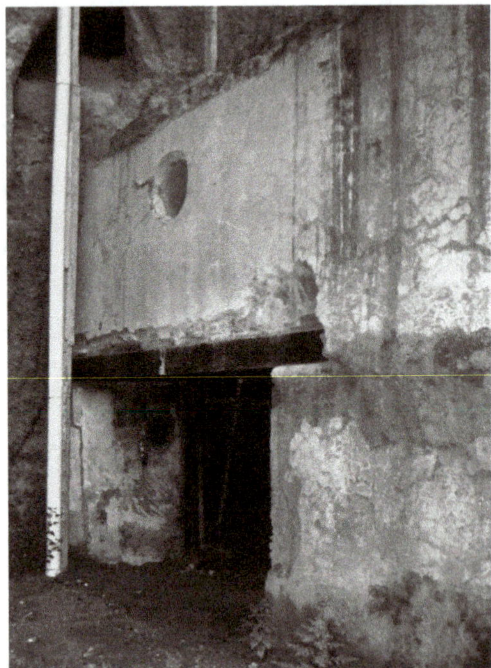

Fig. 11. Villa of the Papyri, first lower level of the *basis villae*: room (I), view from the outside.

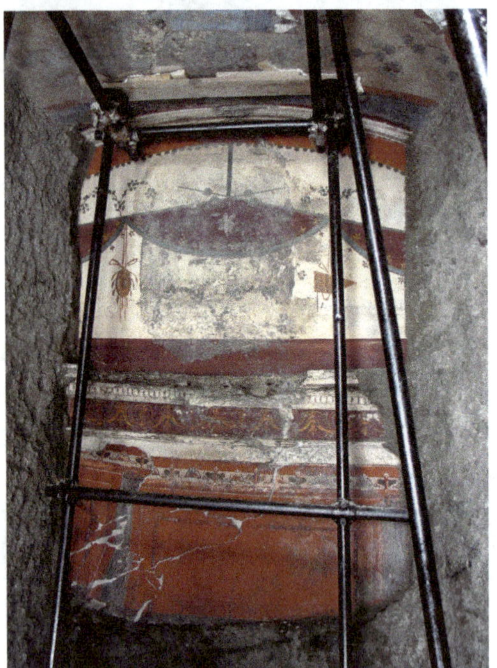

Fig. 12. Villa of the Papyri, first lower level of the *basis villae*: room (I), view from the inside.

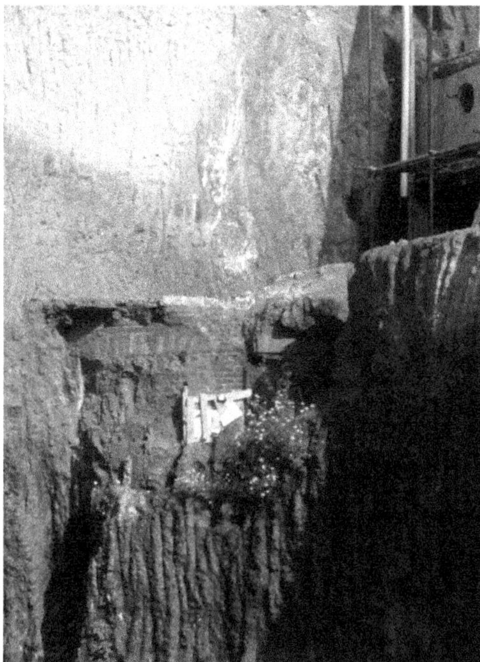

Fig. 13. Villa of the Papyri, second lower level of the basis villae: curved structure at the north-west edge of the *basis villae*.

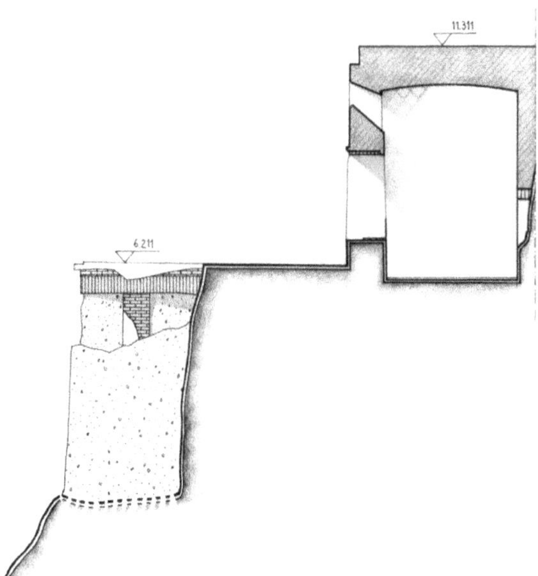

Fig. 14. Villa of the Papyri, first and second lower level of the *basis villae*: section.

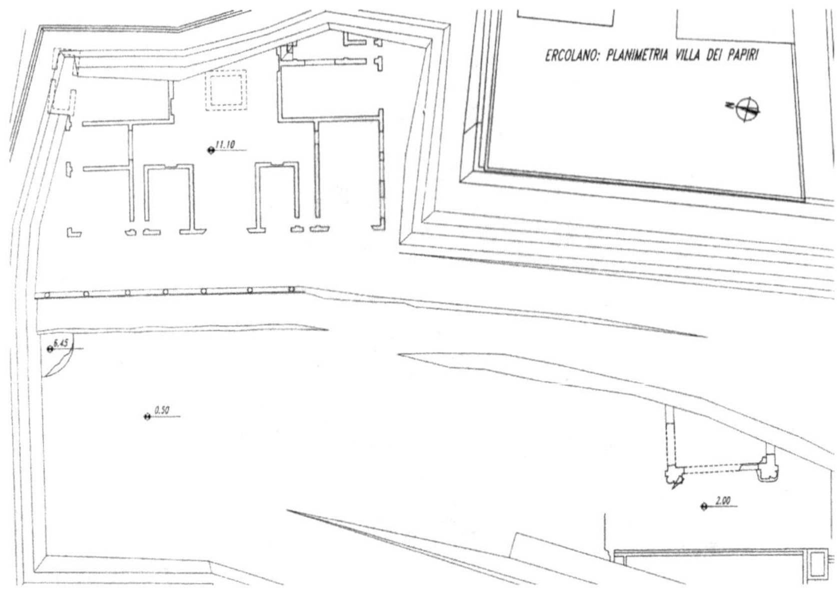

Fig. 15. Villa of the Papyri, plan of atrium quarter and lower terrace (VPSO area).

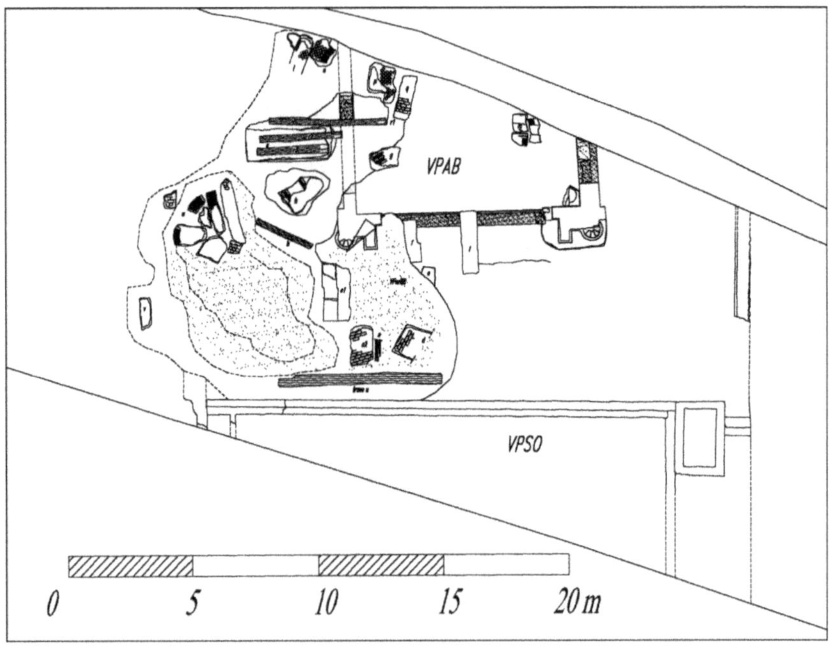

Fig. 16. Villa of the Papyri, VPSO area: plan.

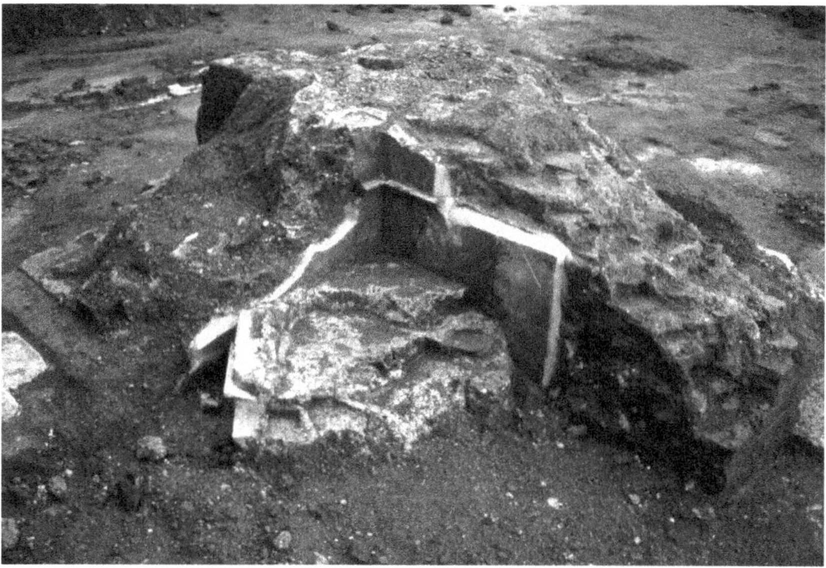

Fig. 17. Villa of the Papyri, VPSO area: the basement of the Amazon on the lower terrace.

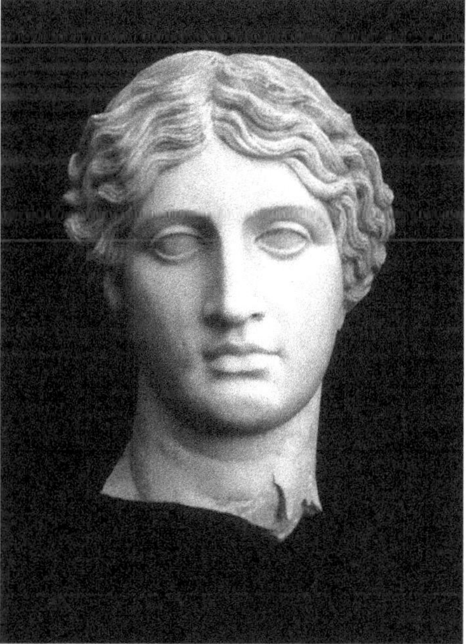

Fig. 18. Villa of the Papyri, VPSO area: the Amazon head.

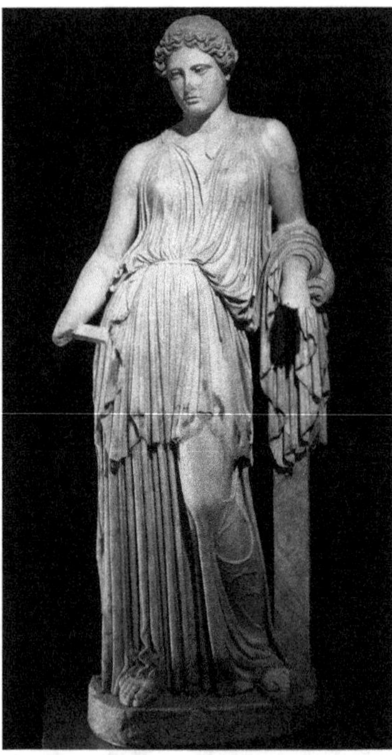

Fig. 19. Villa of the Papyri, VPSO area: the Hera statue.

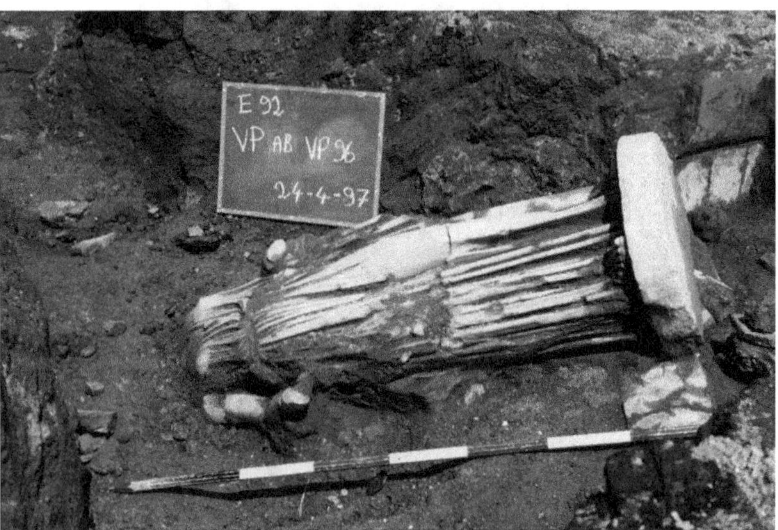

Fig. 20. Villa of the Papyri, VPSO area: the uncovering of the Hera statue.

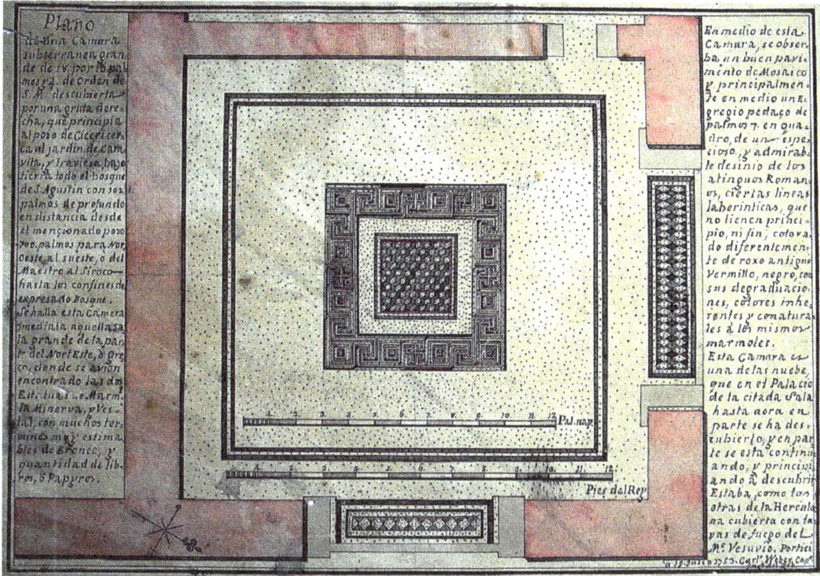

Fig. 21. Villa of the Papyri, room "XVI" in Weber's plan: the pavement from the drawings by Karl Weber (source: Ruggiero 1885, pl. X, 1).

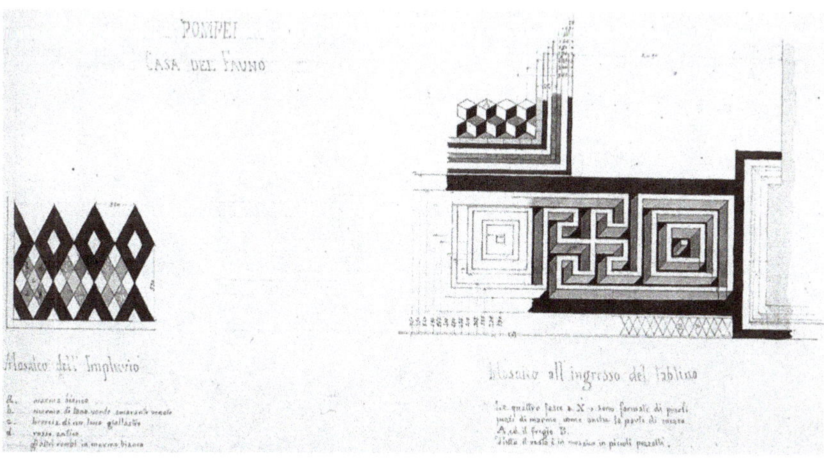

Fig. 22. Pompeii, House of the Faun: tablinum 33, the decorative elements of the pavement in an 18th-century drawing source (*PPM* 1-10, vol. 5, 109, fig. 32).

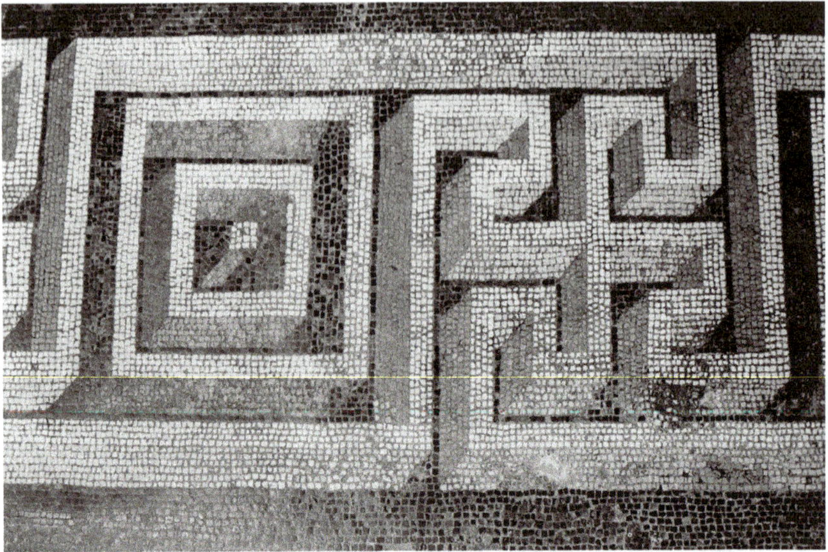

Fig. 23. Pompeii, House of the Faun: *tablinum* 33, meander with labyrinthic motif (PPM 1-10, vol. 5, 110, figs. 33).

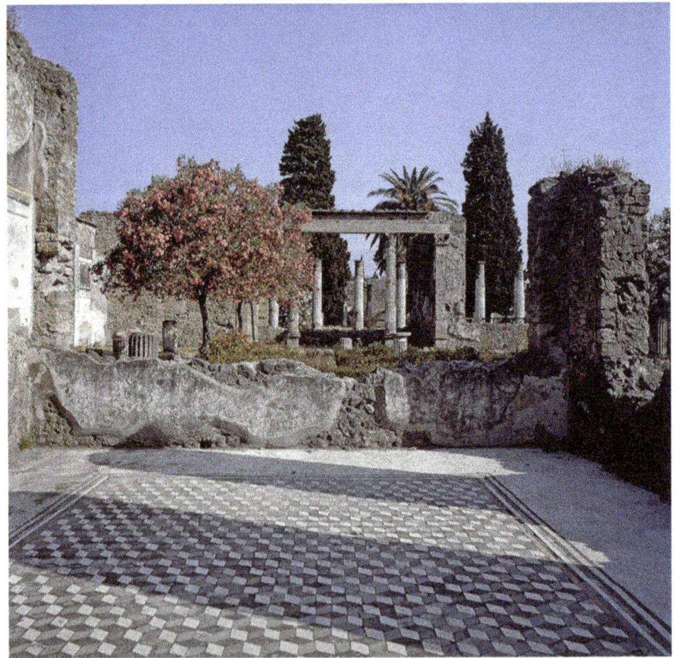

Fig. 24. Pompeii, House of the Faun: view of *tablinum* 33.

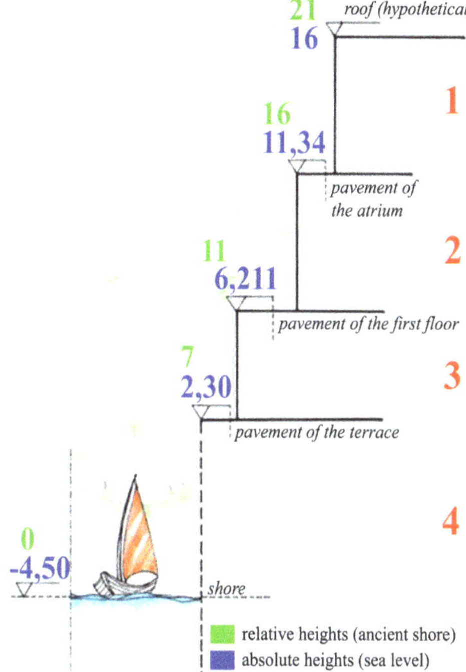

Fig. 25. Schematic section of the levels of the Villa of the Papyri.

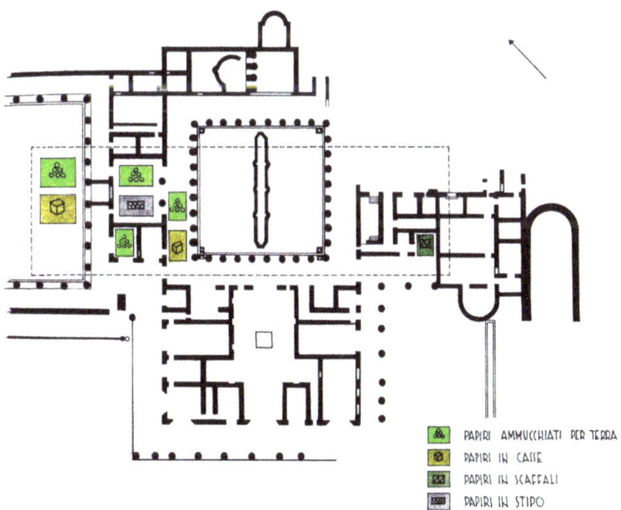

Fig. 26. Plan indicating the dislocation of the papyri found during the 18th-century survey (source: Capasso 1991).

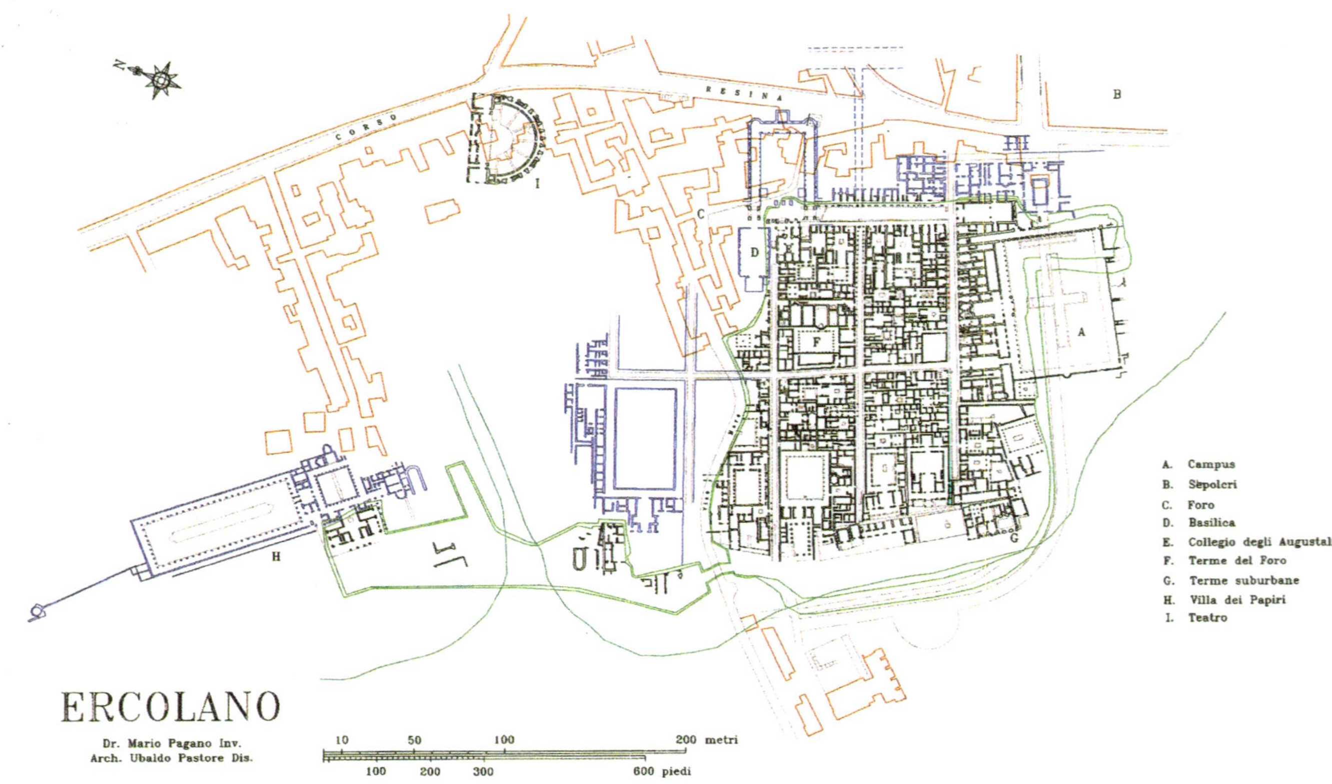

Fig. 27. Herculaneum, plan of the city including the area of the New Excavations (M. Pagano and U. Pastore).

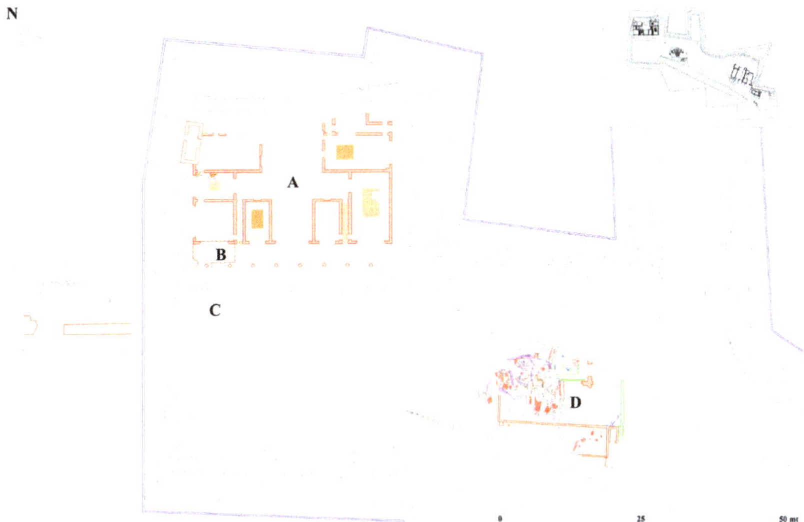

Fig. 1. Plan of the excavation area of the Villa of the Papyri with indications of the areas of intervention (A, B, C, D).

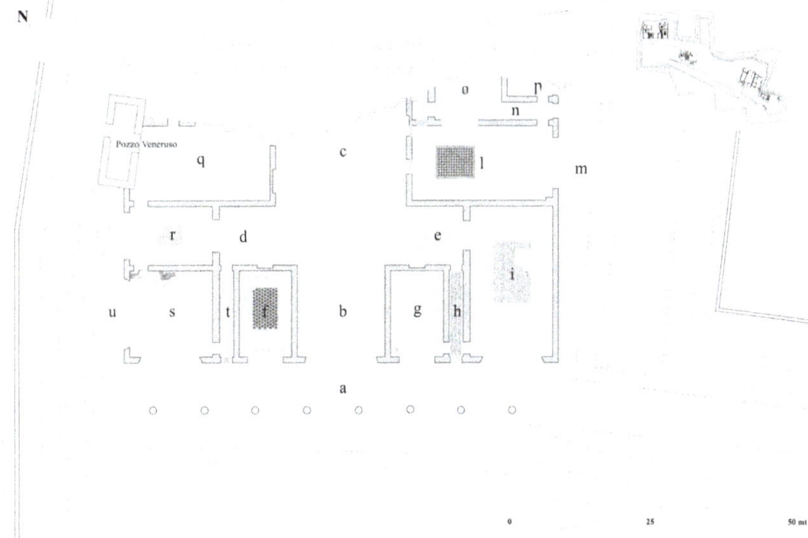

Fig. 2. Plan of the atrium quarter of the Villa of the Papyri.

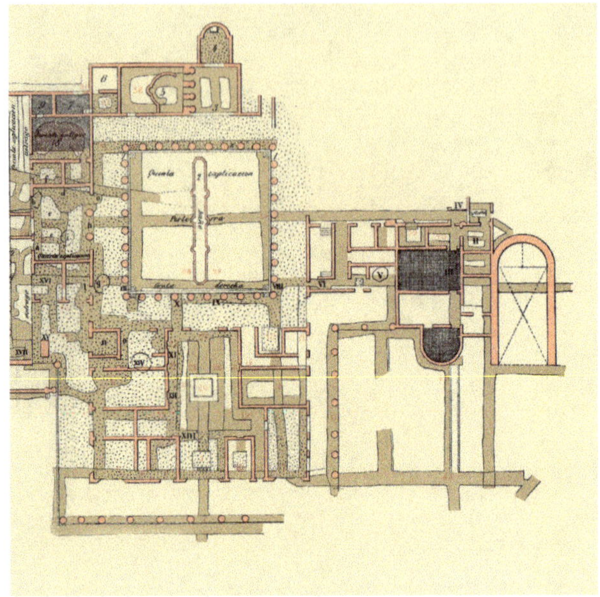

Fig. 3. Detail of Weber's plan of the Villa of the Papyri: the atrium quarter (source: CDP, pl. XXIV).

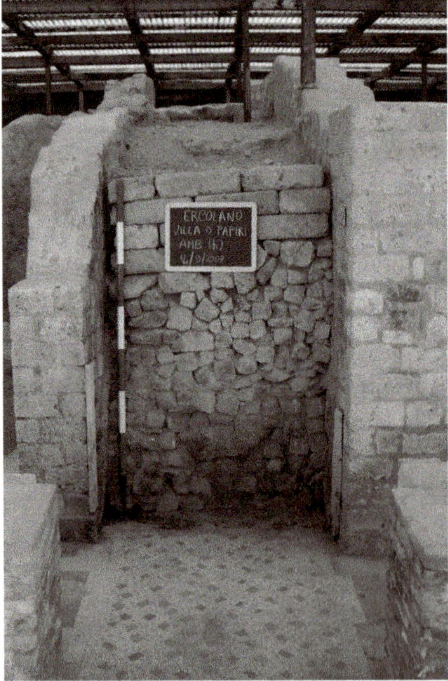

Fig. 4. Villa of the Papyri, atrium quarter: corridor (h) before excavation.

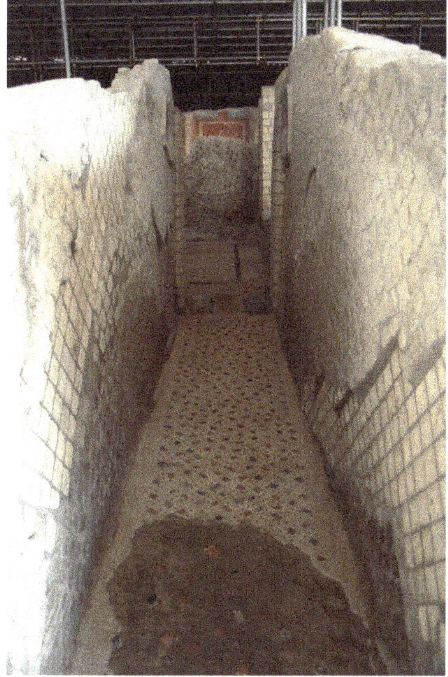

Fig. 5. Villa of the Papyri, atrium quarter: corridor (h) after completion of excavation and restoration operations.

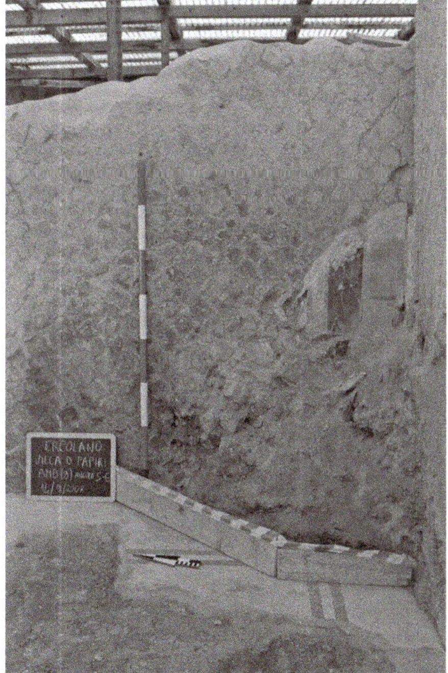

Fig. 6. Villa of the Papyri, atrium quarter: the south-east corner of room (g) before excavation.

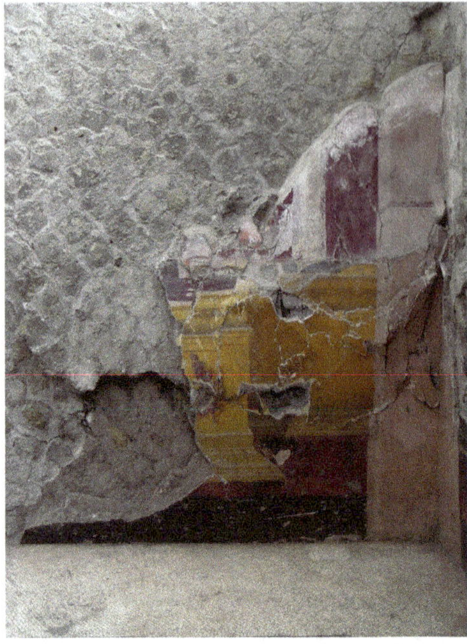

Fig. 7. Villa of the Papyri, atrium quarter: the south-east corner of room (g) after completion of excavation and restoration operations.

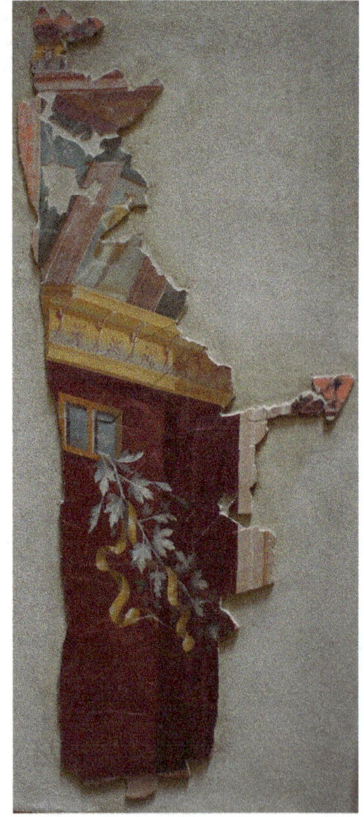

Fig. 8. Villa of the Papyri, atrium quarter: remains of the Second Style decoration on the south wall of room (g) after restoration operations.

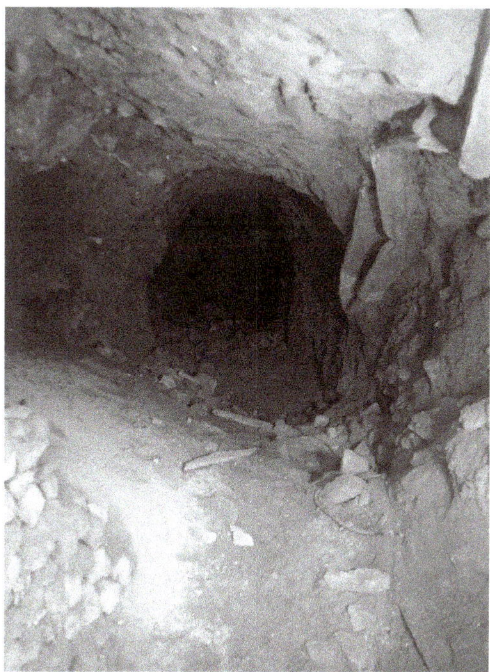

Fig. 9. Villa of the Papyri, atrium quarter: tunnel of room "o" in Weber's plan after the Infratecna Excavation and before cleaning operations.

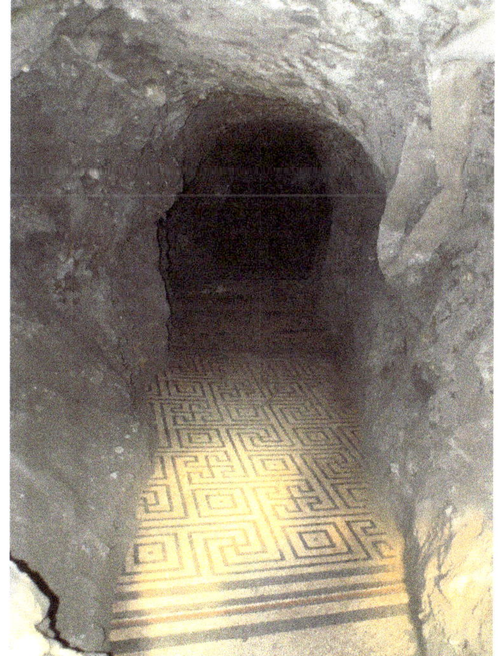

Fig. 10. Villa of the Papyri, atrium quarter: tunnel of room "o" in Weber's plan after cleaning operations.

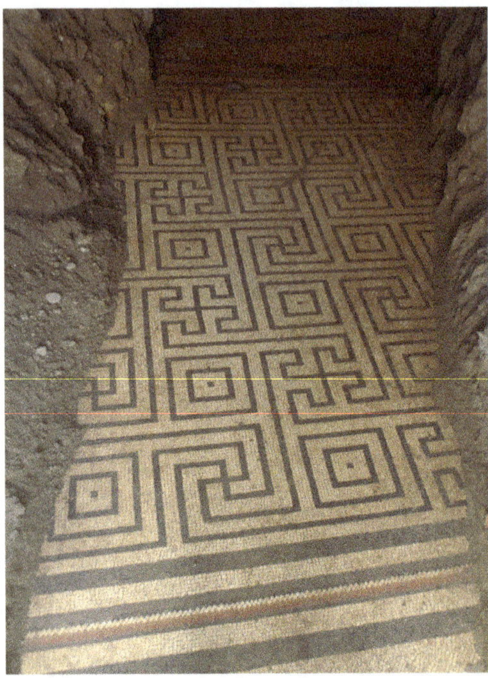

Fig. 11. Villa of the Papyri, atrium quarter: flooring in room "o" in Weber's plan. Emblema in black and white tessellatum reproducing a net of meanders, swastikas and inscribed squares.

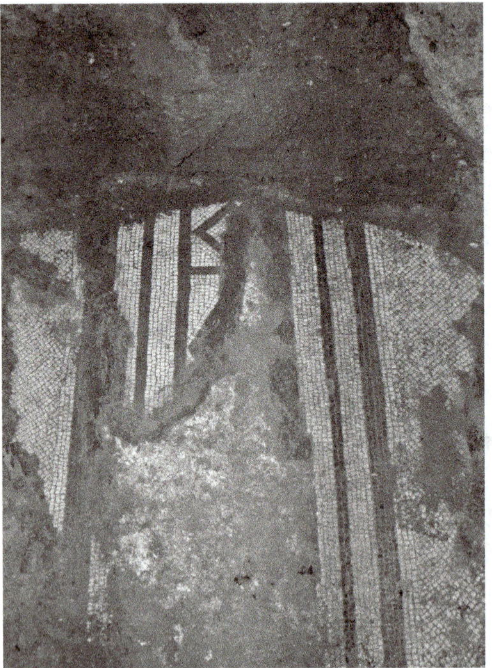

Fig. 12. Villa of the Papyri, atrium quarter: tunnel of room "o" in Weber's plan. Threshold of the opening leading towards the square peristyle.

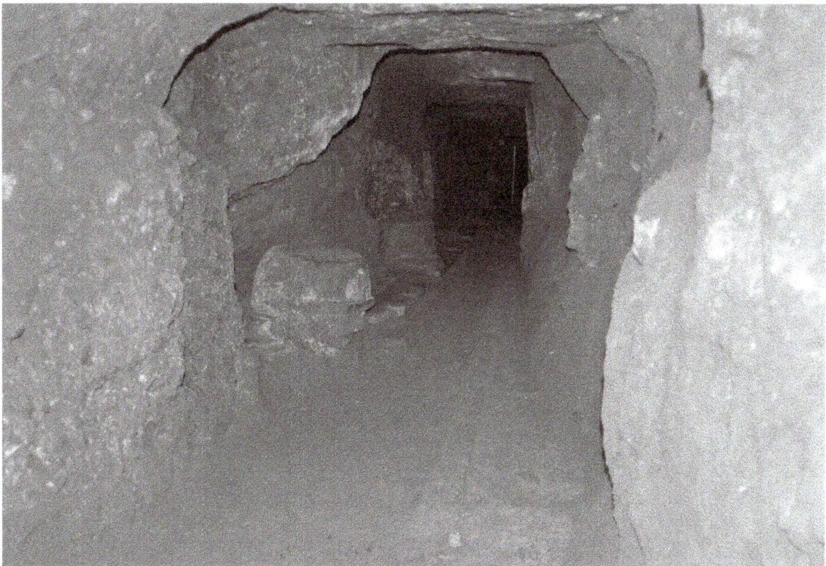

Fig. 13. Villa of the Papyri, atrium quarter: view of the north portico of the square peristyle after cleaning operations.

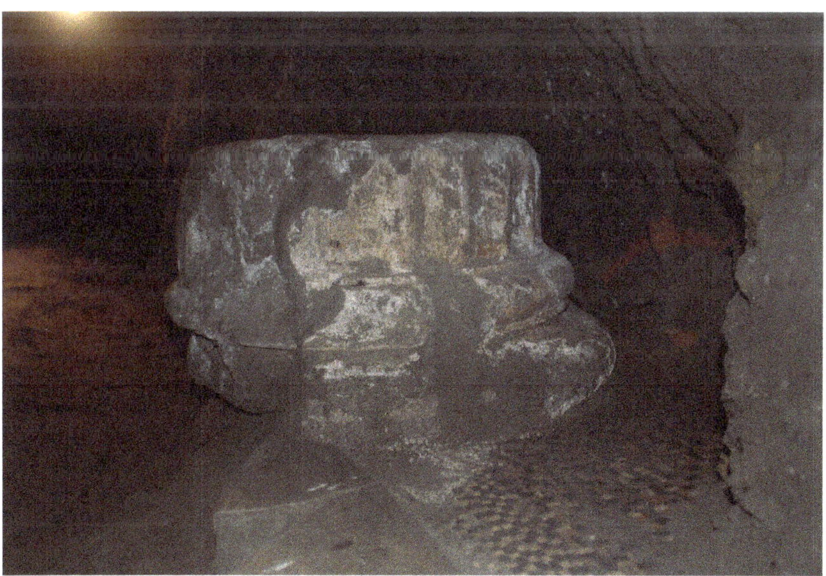

Fig. 14. Villa of the Papyri, atrium quarter: detail of the tufa base of a column in the north portico of the square peristyle.

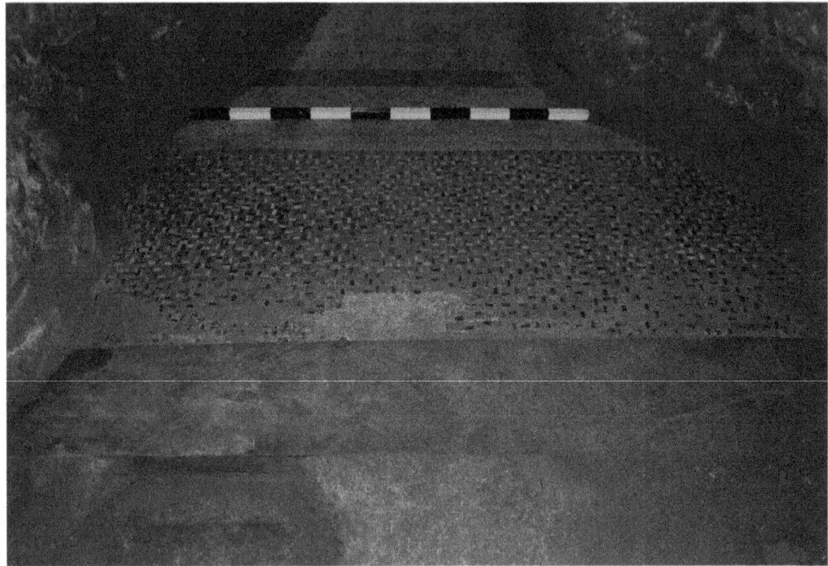

Fig. 15. Villa of the Papyri, atrium quarter: square peristyle, an intercolumniation of the west portico. Pavement of polychrome tessellatum with white, red, orange, black, grey/green limestone rectangular tesserae placed on a basket weave pattern.

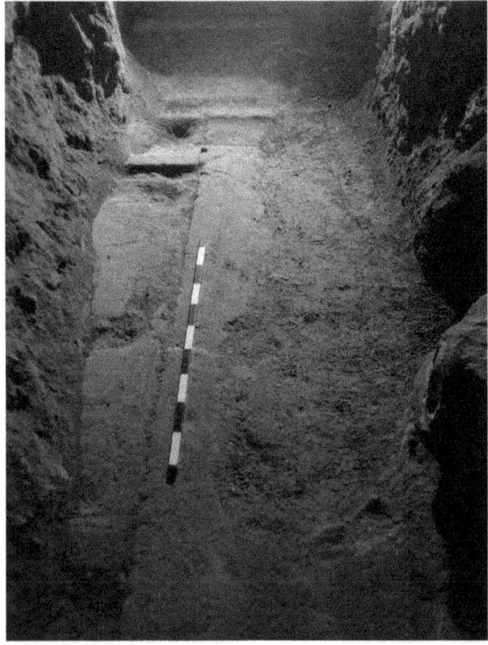

Fig. 16. Villa of the Papyri, atrium quarter: north-west corner of the square peristyle with the border of the watercourse.

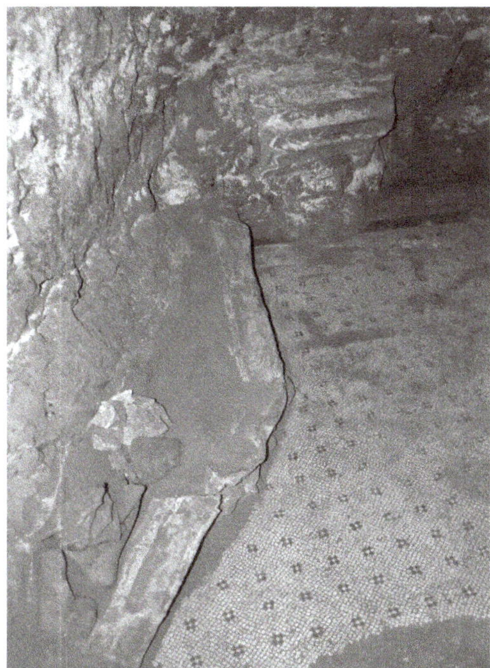

Fig. 17. Villa of the Papyri, atrium quarter: square peristyle, west portico. Detail of the pavement in black and white tesselatum with the remains of a lead fistula.

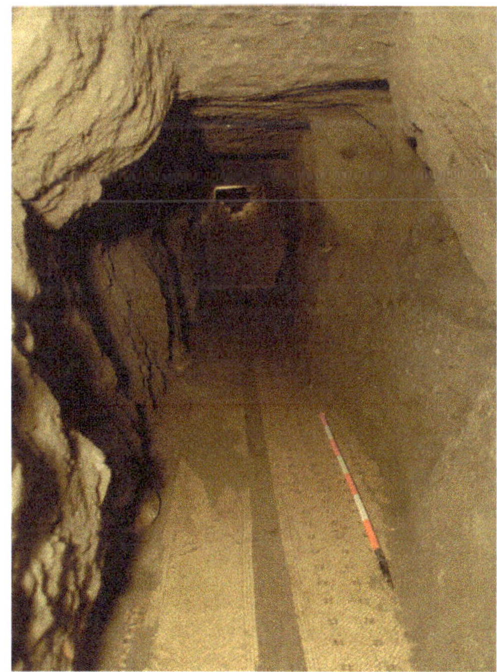

Fig. 18. Villa of the Papyri, atrium quarter: square peristyle, west portico, south part. Pavement of the ambulatory in black and white tessellatum with intercolumniations in polychrome tessellatum.

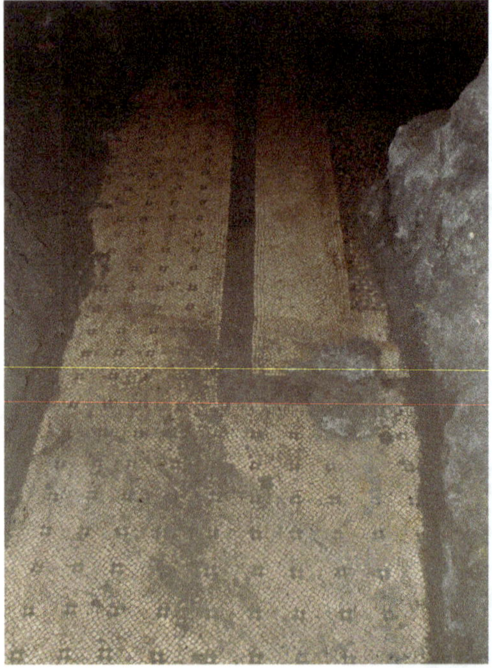

Fig. 19. Villa of the Papyri, atrium quarter: square peristyle, south-east corner. Detail of the pavement.

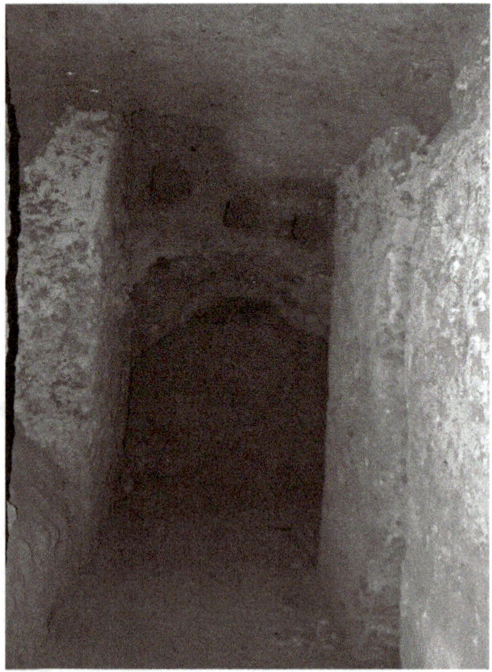

Fig. 20. Villa of the Papyri, atrium quarter: the so-called library (room "V" in Weber's plan). Supporting pilasters and retaining walls that were erected at the time of the Bourbon excavation.

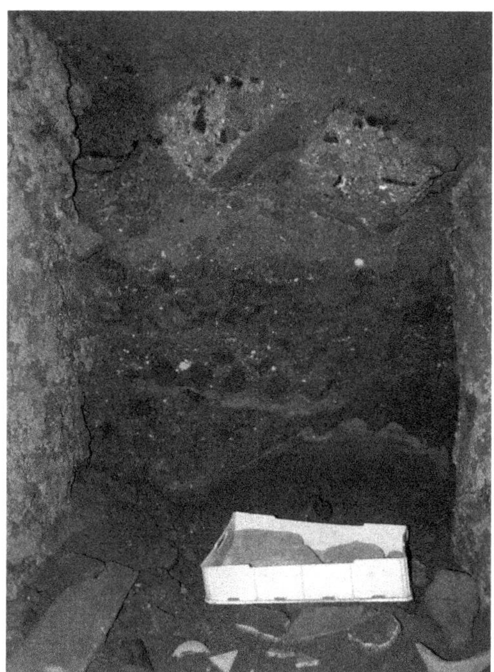

Fig. 21. Villa of the Papyri, atrium quarter: the so-called library (room "V" in Weber's plan). East wall with large fragments belonging to a collapsed upper-level floor. Fragments of wall paintings and pottery of unknown provenance were left here during the Infratecna excavation.

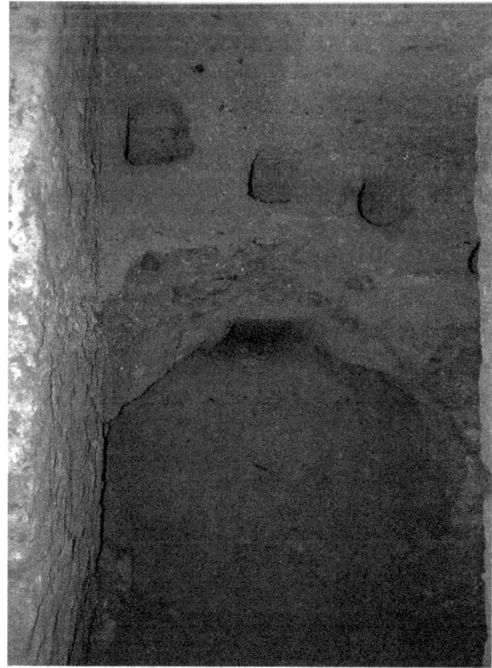

Fig. 22. Villa of the Papyri, atrium quarter: the so-called library (room "V" in Weber's plan). The south wall cut by a tunnel and a series of small round holes (the so-called pruebas) were excavated in the volcanic deposit to search for other materials.

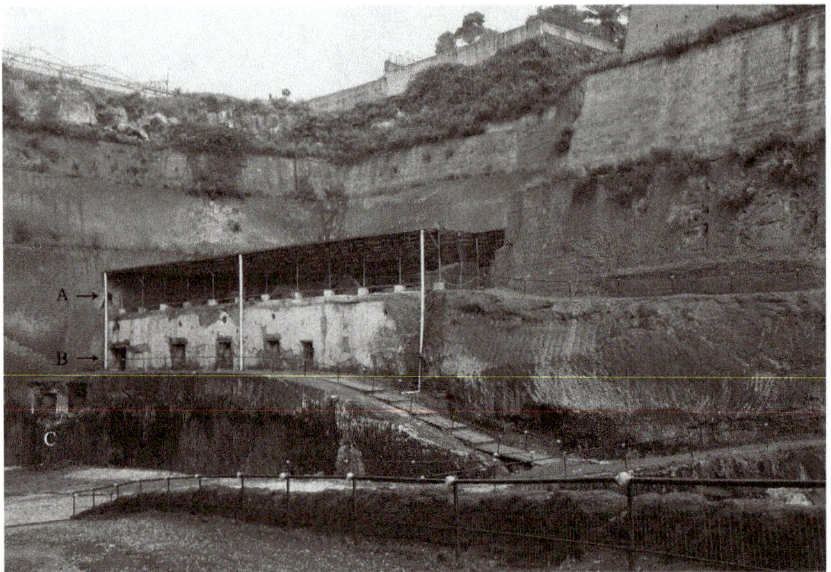

Fig. 23. View of the *basis villae* of the Villa of the Papyri (without the new protective shelter).

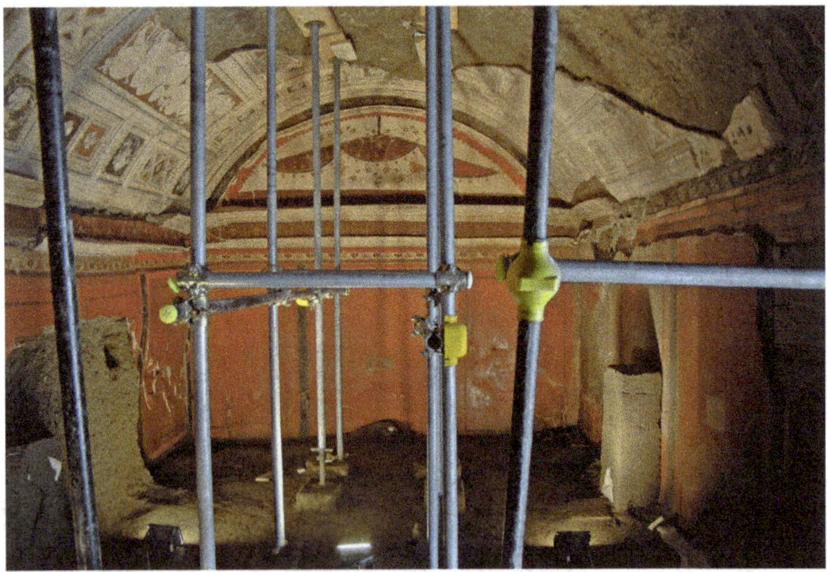

Fig. 24. Villa of the Papyri, first lower level of the *basis villae:* room (I) at the end of the new excavations by the Archaeological Superintendency of Pompeii. View of the south-east part of the room.

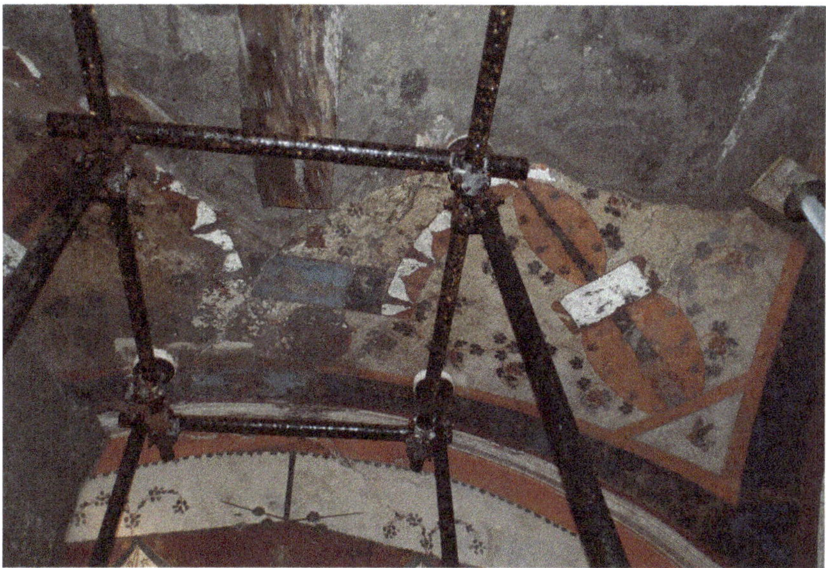

Fig. 25. Villa of the Papyri, first lower level of the *basis villae:* room (I), vault decoration of the antechamber dated to a transition phase between the Third and Fourth Style.

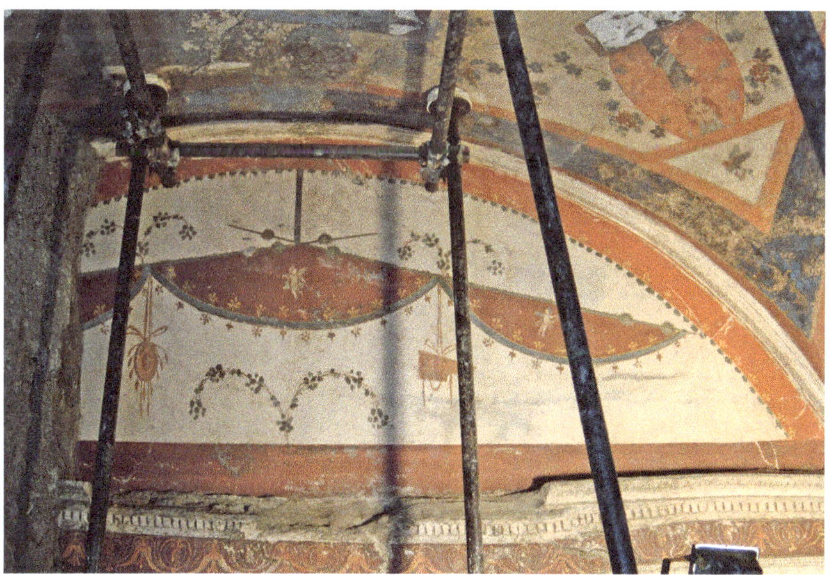

Fig. 26. Villa of the Papyri, first lower level of the *basis villae:* room (I), lunette decoration in Fourth Style on the antechamber's east wall.

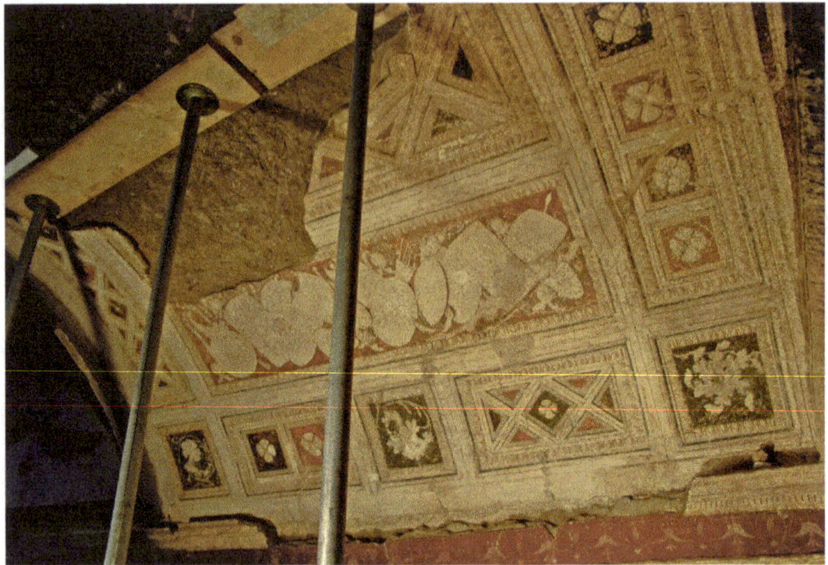

Fig. 27. Villa of the Papyri, first lower level of the *basis villae:* room (I), vaulted stucco ceiling of the room in Second Style.

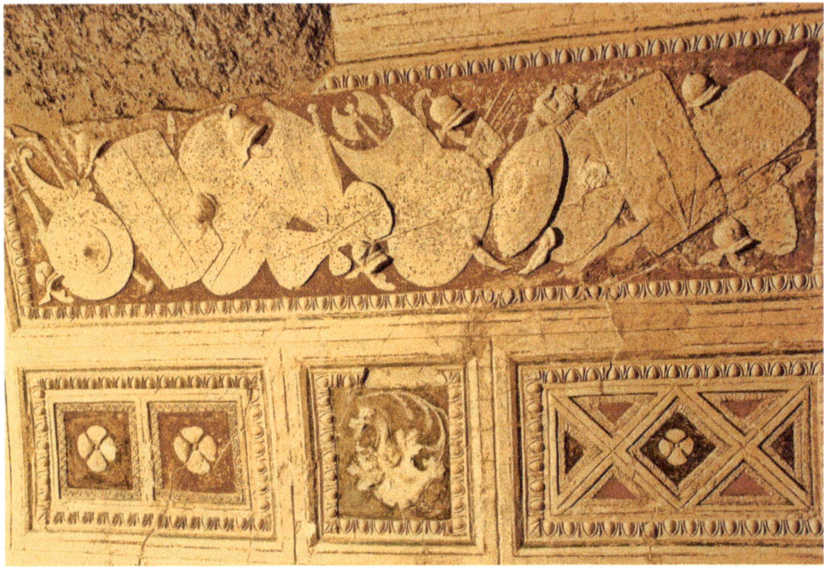

Fig. 28. Villa of the Papyri, first lower level of the *basis villae:* room (I), detail of the vaulted stucco ceiling of the room in Second Style; frieze with a pile of weapons.

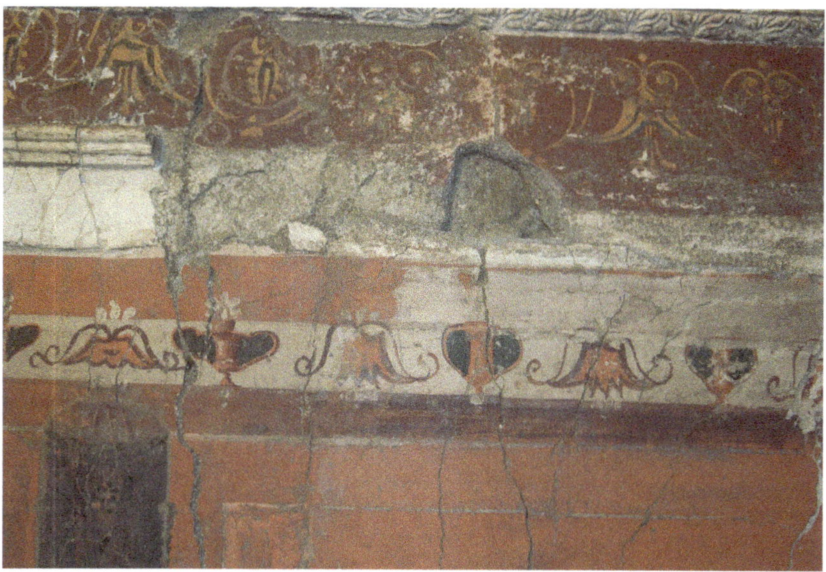

Fig. 29. Villa of the Papyri, first lower level of the *basis villae:* room (I), redecoration of the east wall.

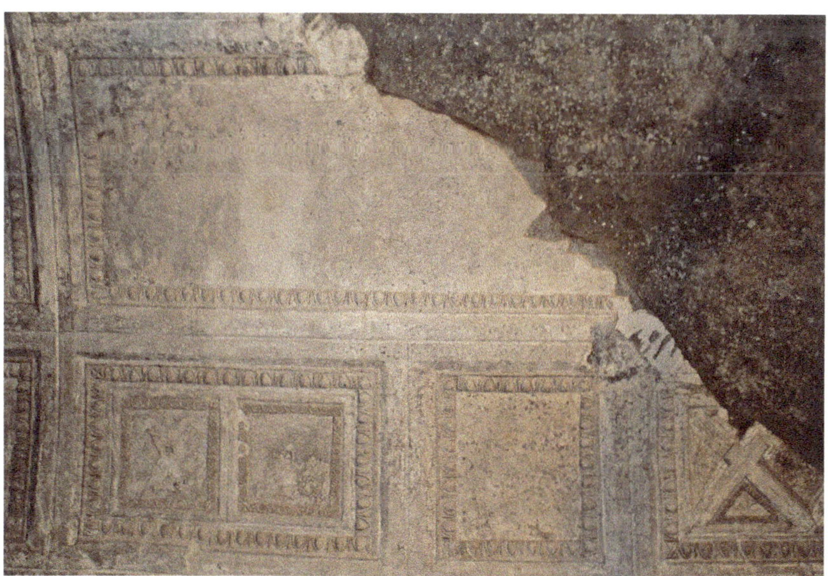

Fig. 30. Villa of the Papyri, first lower level of the *basis villae:* room (I), unfinished redecoration of the west half of the rooms's vaulted stucco ceiling.

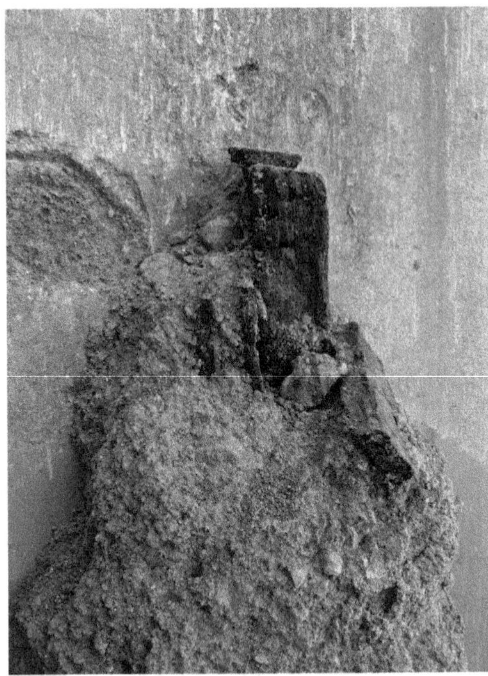

Fig. 31. Villa of the Papyri, first lower level of the *basis villae:* room (I), remains of a wooden structure at the base of the east wall.

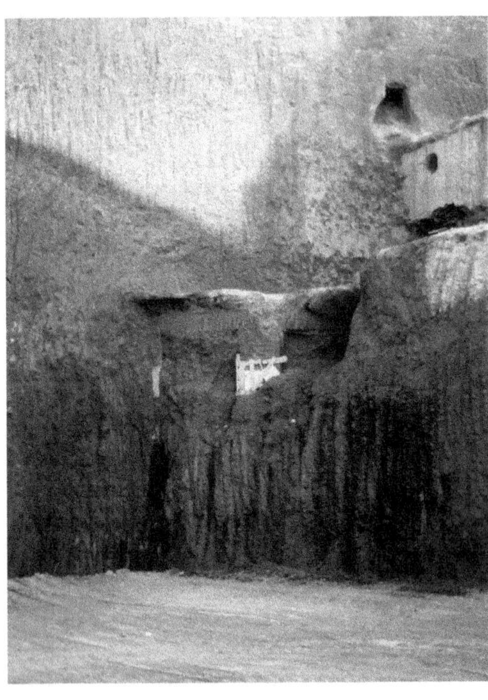

Fig. 32. Villa of the Papyri, second lower level of the *basis villae:* bow window.

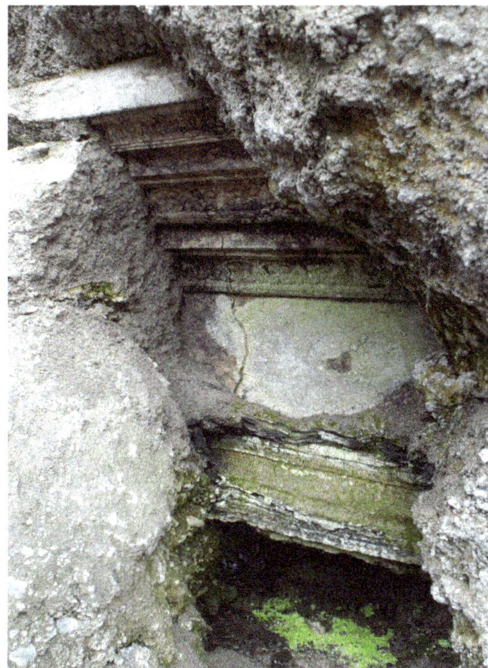

Fig. 33. Villa of the Papyri, second lower level of the *basis villae:* part of window opening with entablature and stucco cornices opening at the façade's south-east segment.

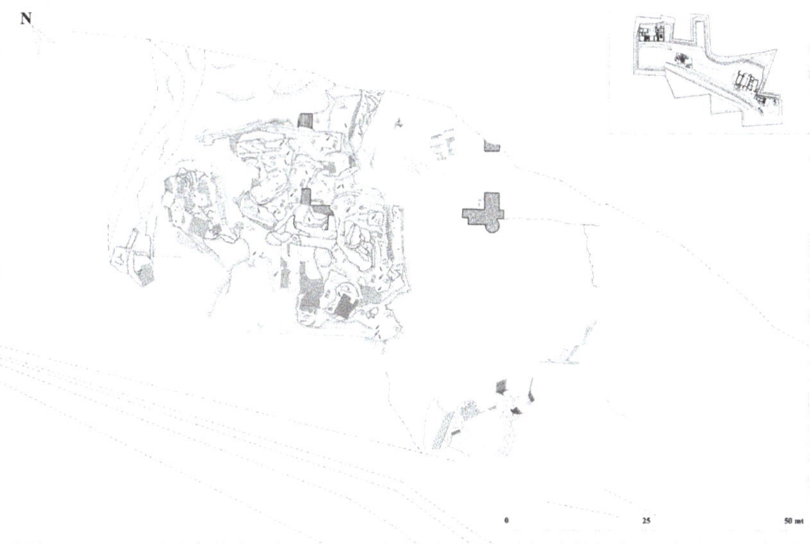

Fig. 34. Villa of the Papyri, VPSO area: plan.

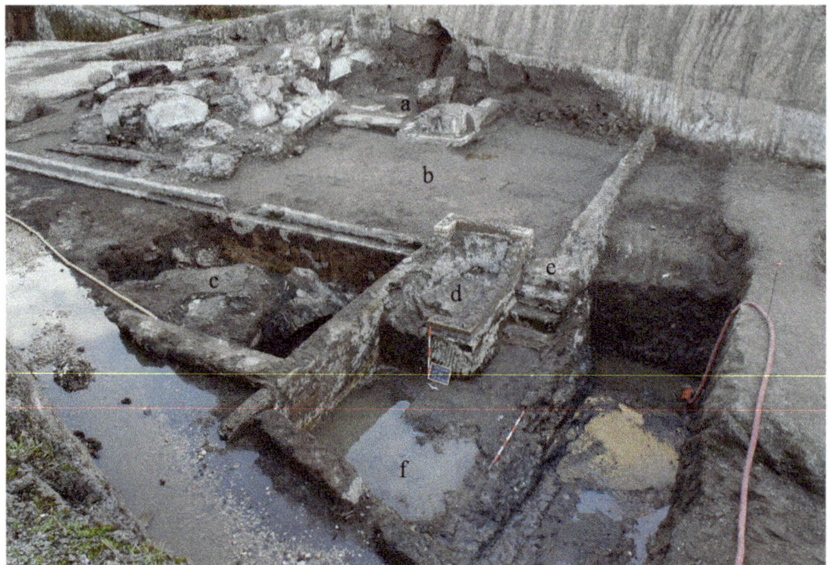

Fig. 35. Villa of the Papyri, panoramic view of VPSO area from the south: a) monumental hall; b) terrace; c) swimming pool; d) unidentified room; e) staircase f) ramp.

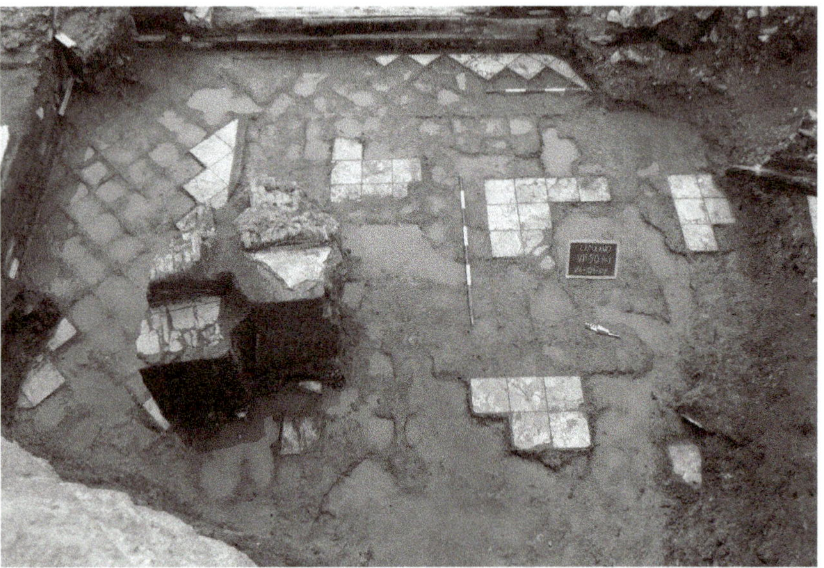

Fig. 36. Villa of the Papyri, VPSO area: panoramic view of the south-west part of room VPSO (a) from the north-east.

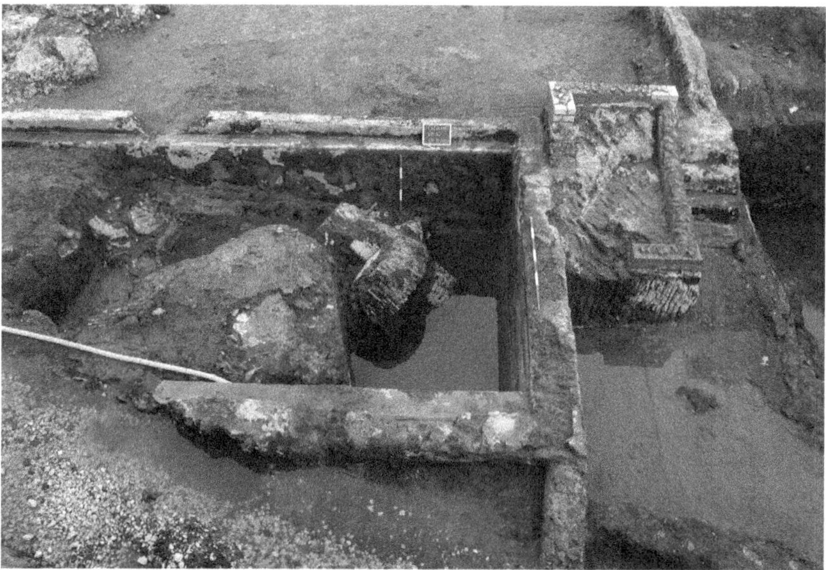

Fig. 37. Villa of the Papyri, VPSO area: panoramic view of swimming pool VPSO (c) from the south-west.

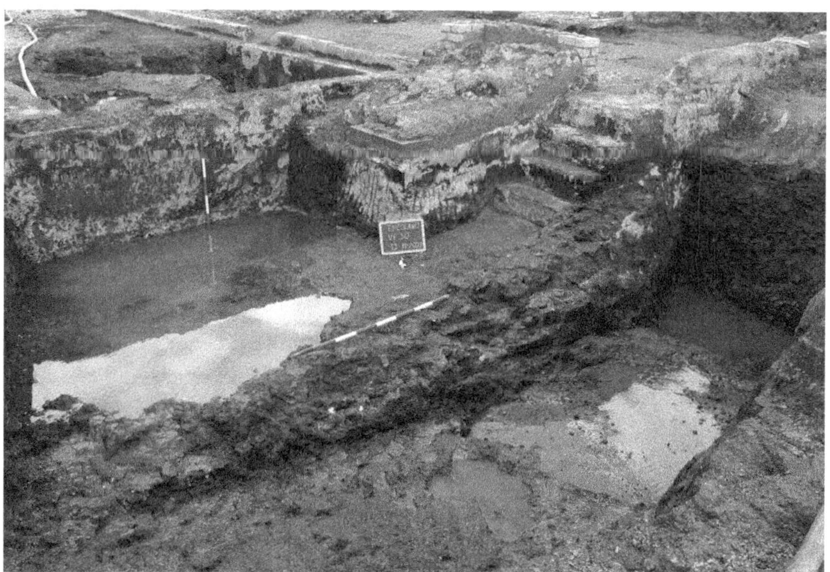

Fig. 38. Villa of the Papyri, VPSO area: panoramic view of ramp VPSO (e) from the south.

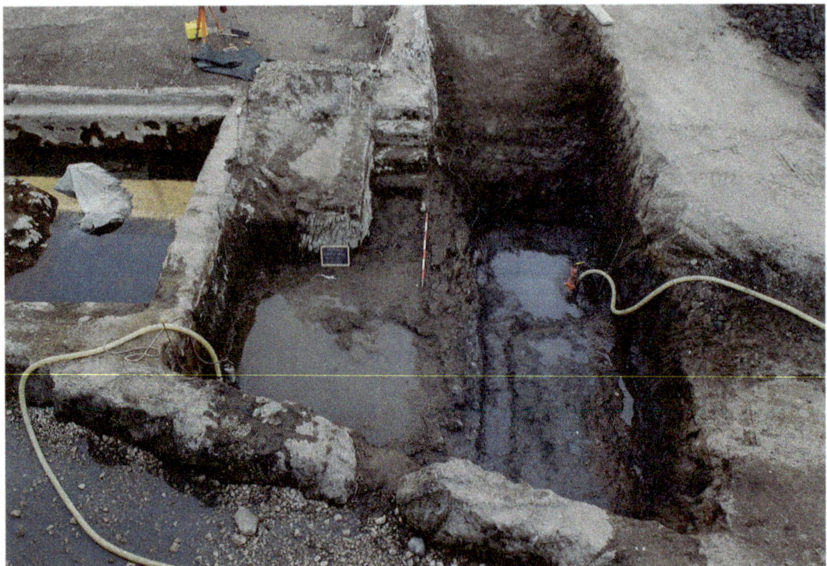

Fig. 39. Villa of the Papyri, VPSO area: panoramic view of ramp VPSO (e) and of the natural bank on which the structures of the VPSO area are erected.

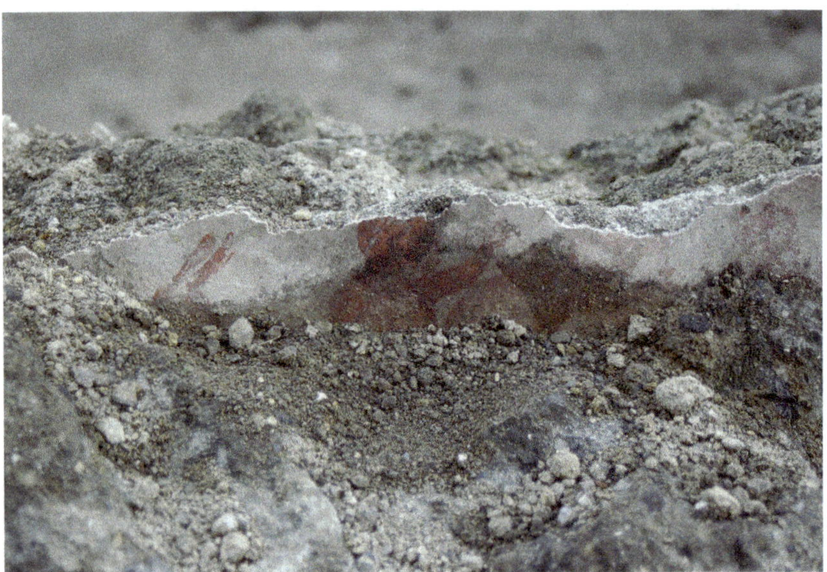

Fig. 40. Villa of the Papyri, VPSO area: room VPSO (d), detail of the red monochrome frieze with pygmies or dwarfs on the east wall.

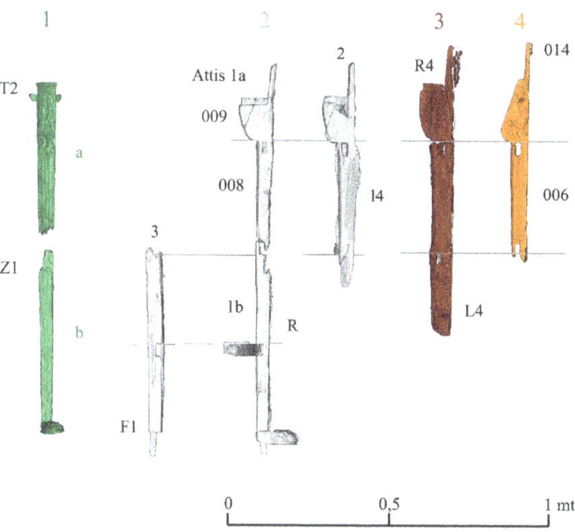

Fig. 41. Drawing of the wooden elements lined with ivory veneer by the Ditta Tebec at Priverno.

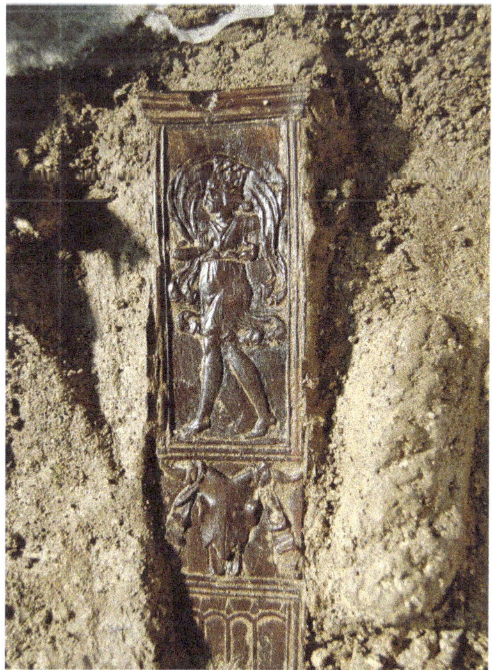

Fig. 42. Piece of furniture no.1, fragment a.

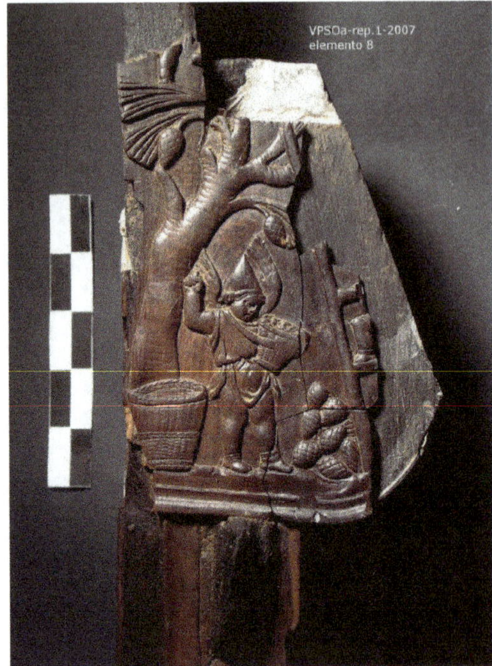

Fig. 43. Piece of furniture no. 2, component 1a, side b.

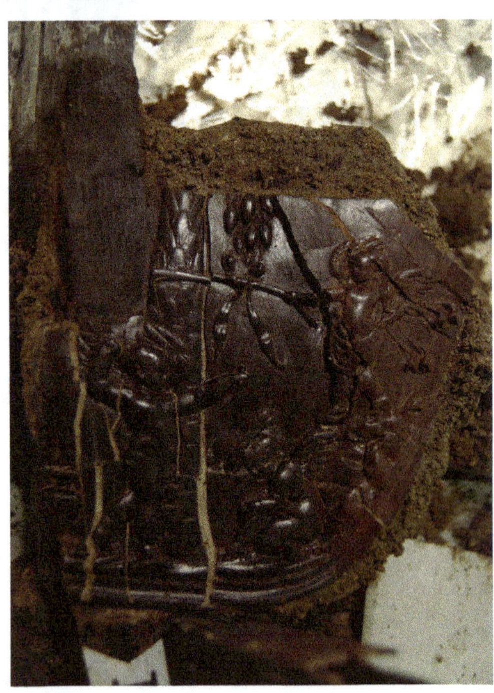

Fig. 44. Piece of furniture no. 2, component 2, side b.

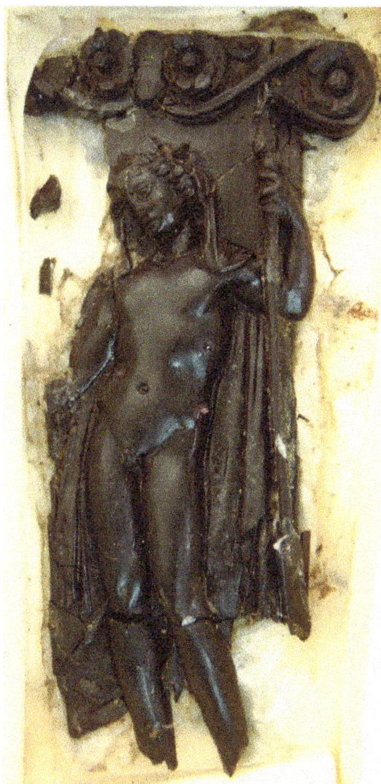

Fig. 45. Piece of furniture no. 2, component 2, side c.

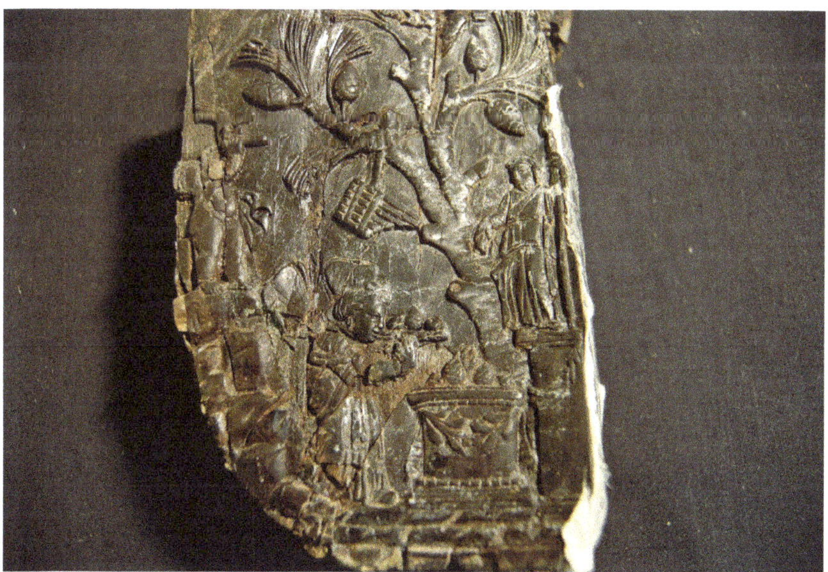

Fig. 46. Piece of furniture no. 3, component 1, side a.

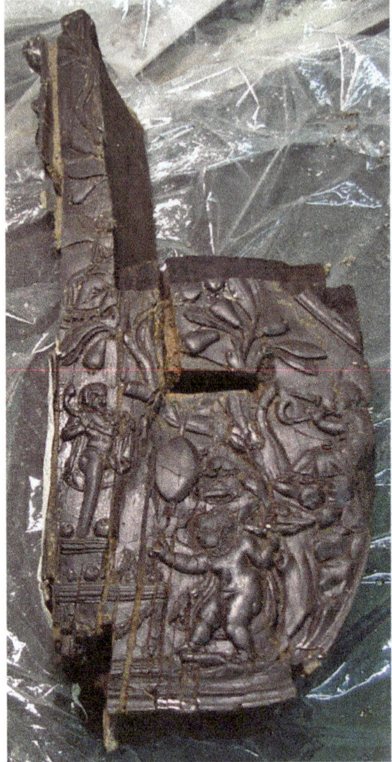

Fig. 47. Piece of furniture no. 3, component 1, side b.

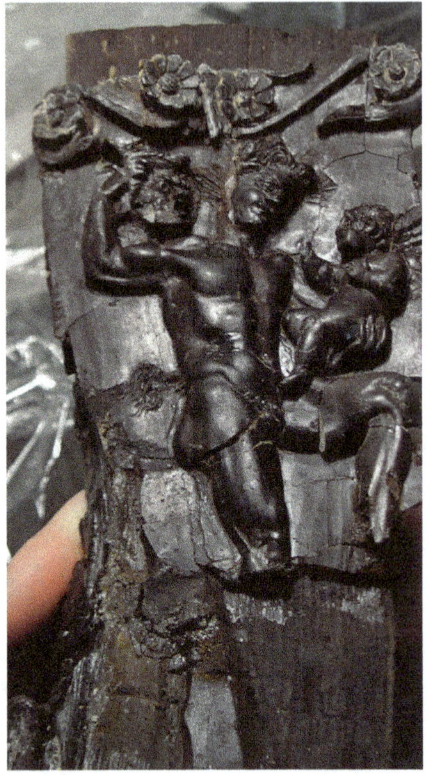

Fig. 48. Piece of furniture no. 3, component 1, side c.

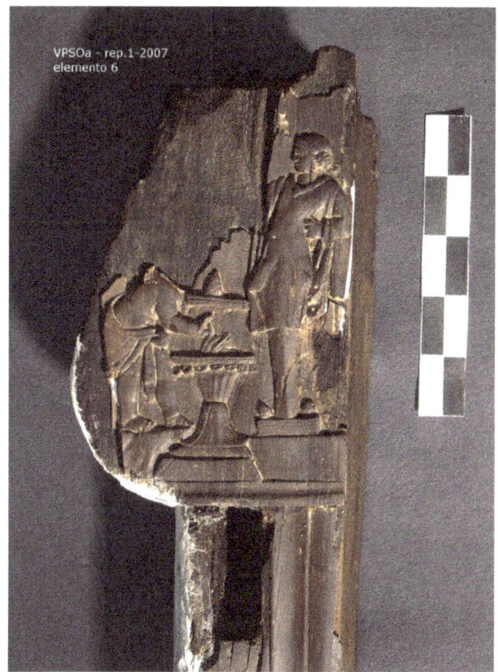

Fig. 49. Piece of furniture no. 4, component 1, side a.

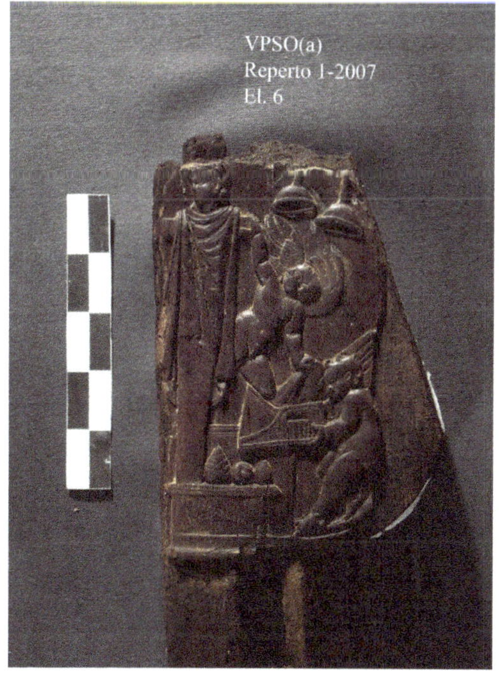

Fig. 50. Piece of furniture no. 4, component 1, side b.

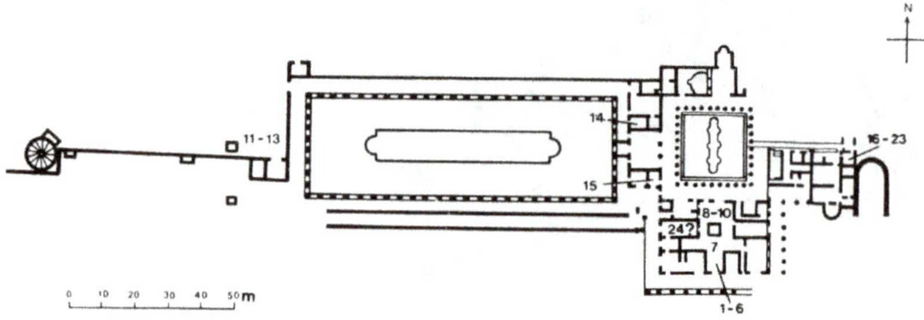

Fig. 1. Distribution of the fragments (after Moormann 1984, fig. 1).

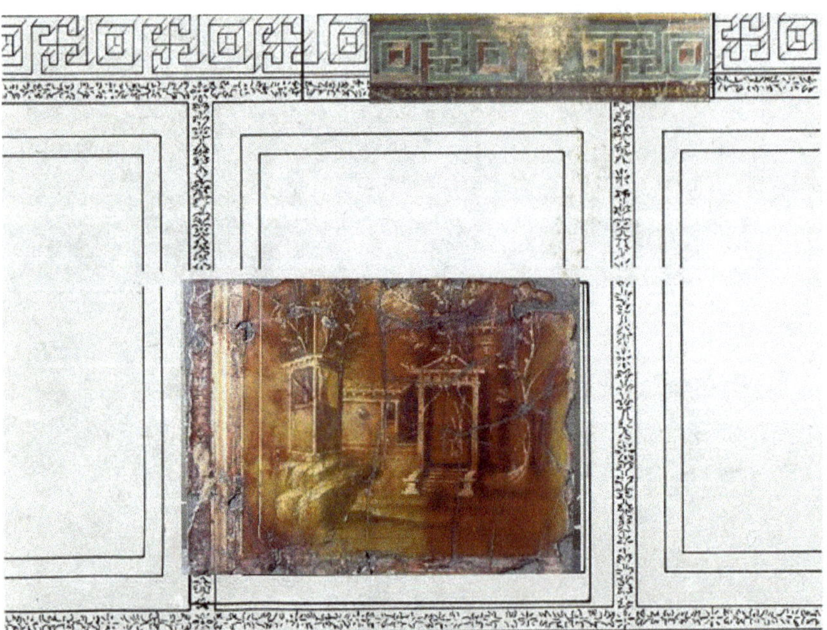

Fig. 2. 1984 reconstruction of wall painting fragments NM 9423 and NM 8548, (Moormann 1984, fig. 10).

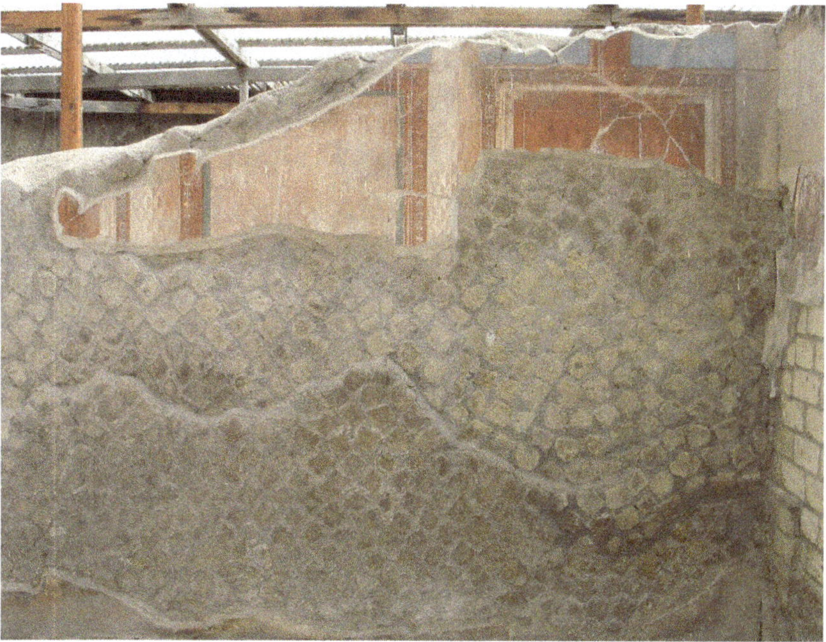

Fig. 3. *Ala* (e), north-east wall (photograph by S.T.A.M. Mols).

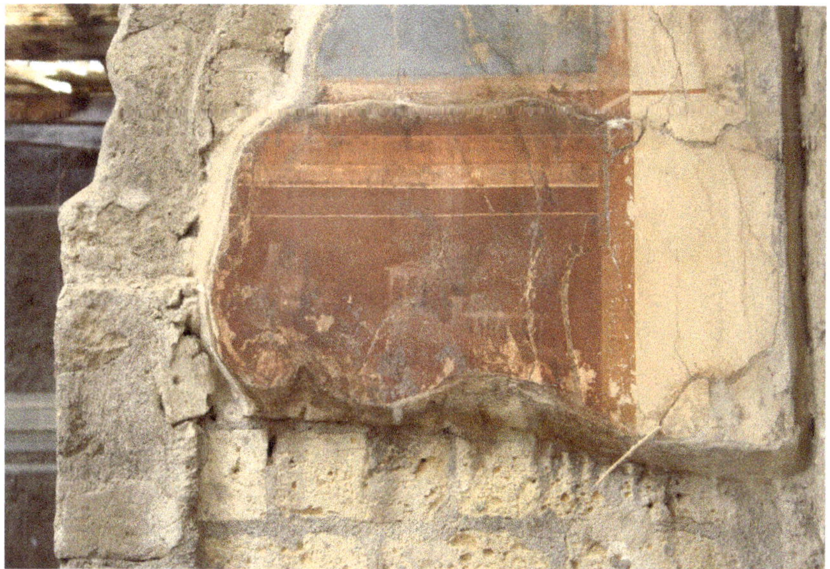

Fig. 4. *Ala* (d), north-west wall north section (photograph by S.T.A.M. Mols).

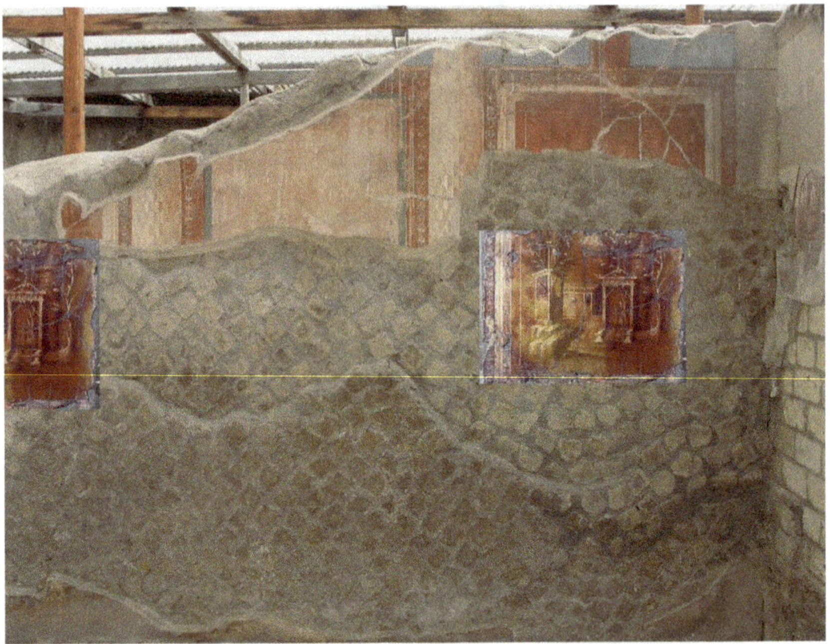

Fig. 5. Photo montage of the wall painting fragment NM 9423 on the north-east wall of *ala* (e).

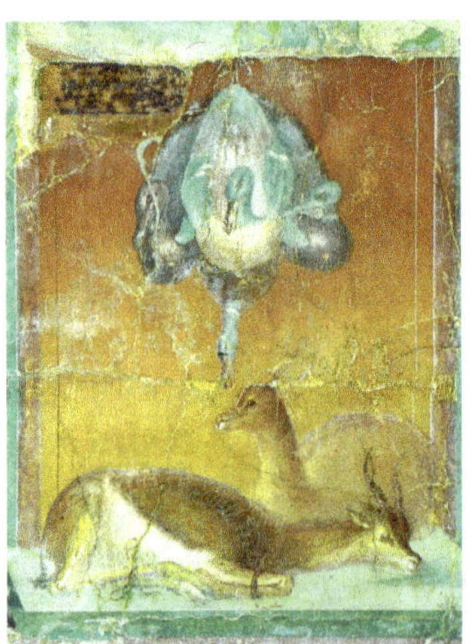

Fig. 6. Slab with the still life of deer and ducks, NM 8759, National Archaeological Museum, Naples (photograph by E.M. Moormann).

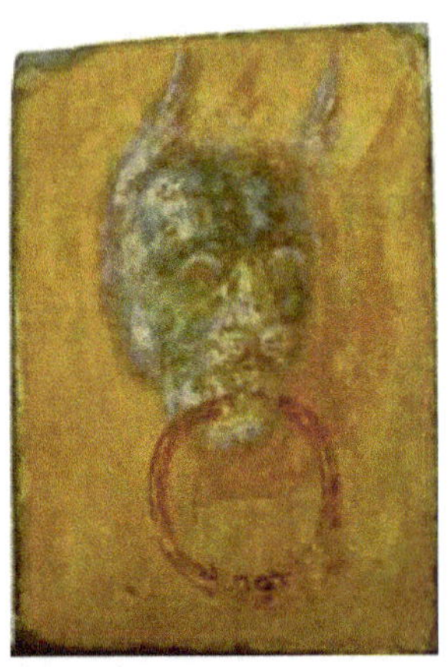

Fig. 7. Wall painting fragment with head of a panther, NM 9951, National Archaeological Museum, Naples (photograph by E.M. Moormann).

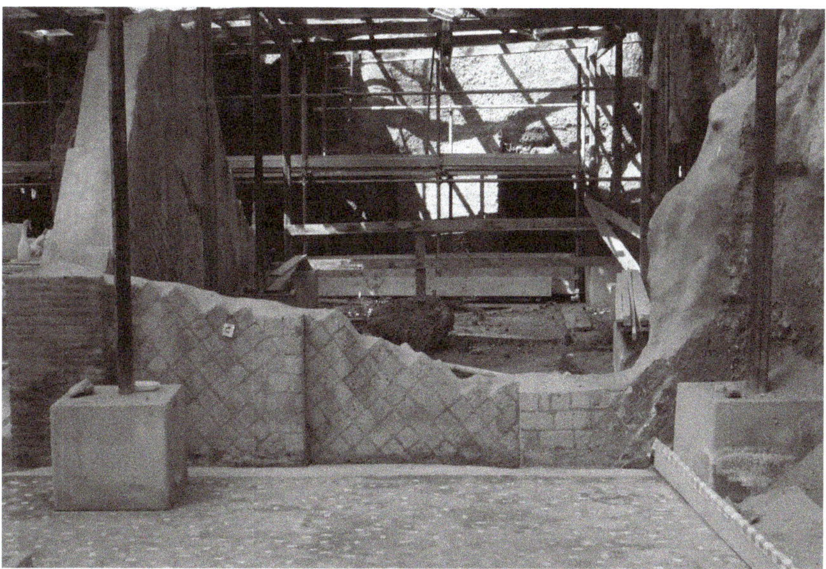

Fig. 8. North-west wall of the atrium, with remains of a fake door (photograph by S.T.A.M. Mols).

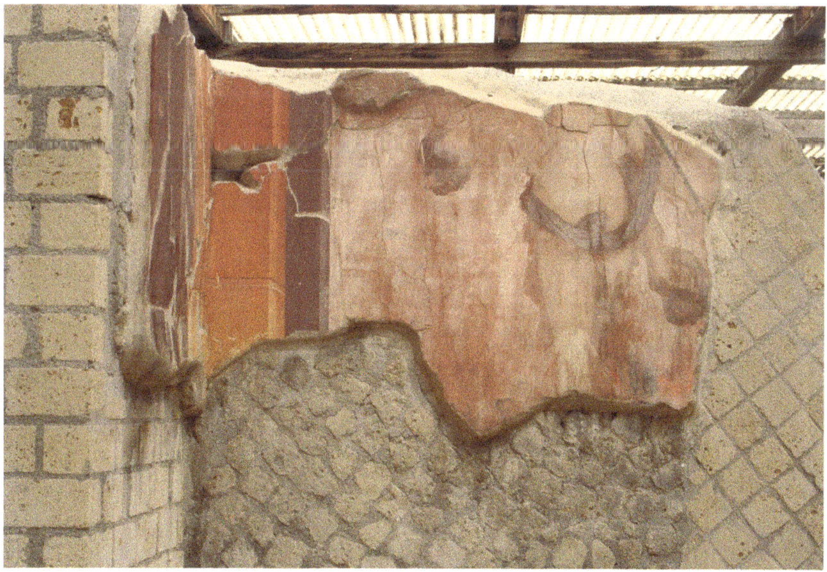

Fig. 9. Standing woman, part of a megalography from room (i) (photograph by S.T.A.M. Mols).

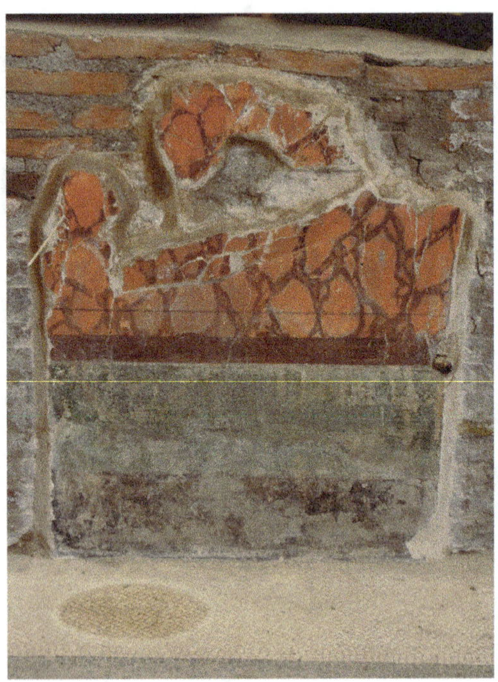

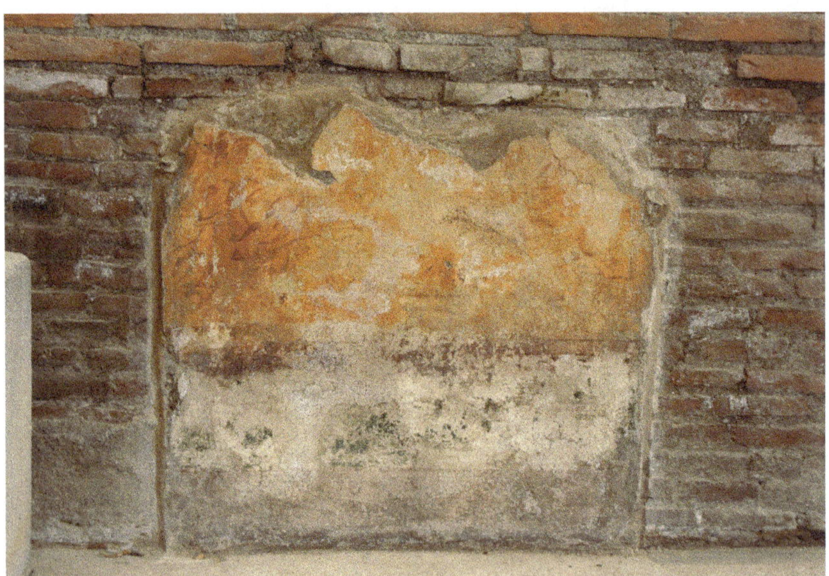

Fig. 10. Decorations in portico (a): imitations of marble veneer (photograph by S.T.A.M. Mols).

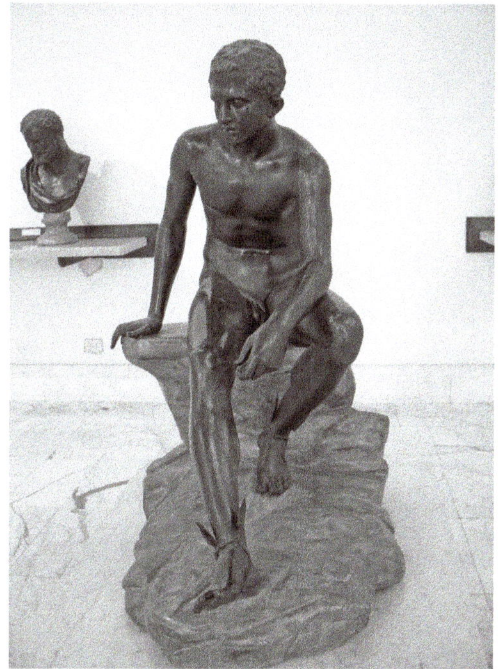

Fig. 1. Bronze Hermes, NM 5625, National Archaeological Museum, Naples.

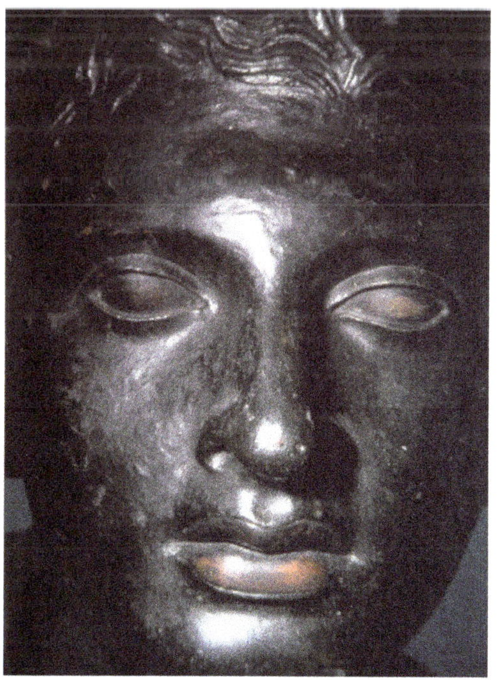

Fig. 2. Face of Hermes, NM 5625, National Archaeological Museum, Naples.

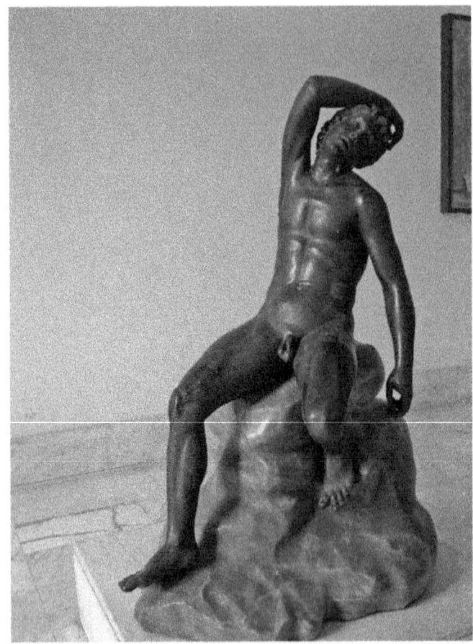

Fig. 3. Dozing bronze satyr, NM 5624, National Archaeological Museum, Naples.

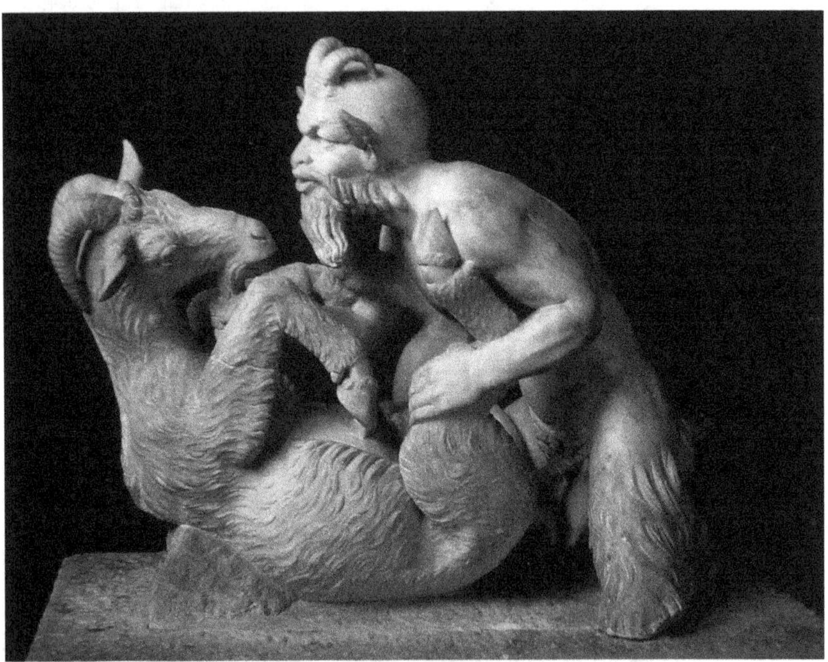

Fig. 4. Marble Pan and She-Goat, NM 27709, National Archaeological Museum, Naples. (photograph by L. Pedicini).

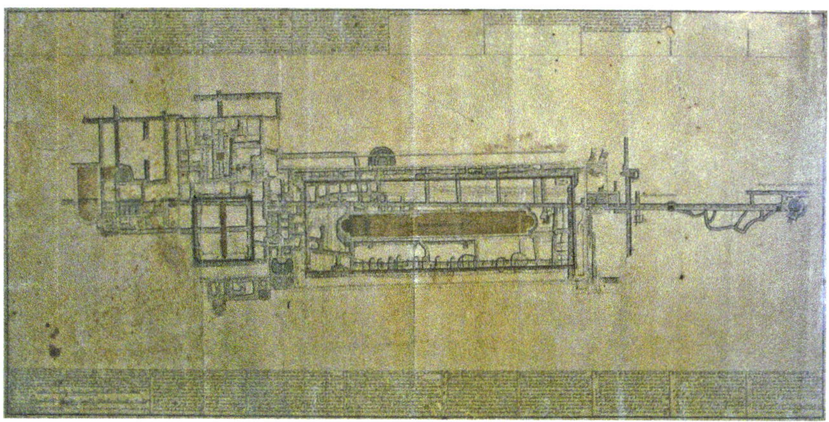

Fig. 5. Karl Weber, plan of the Villa of the Papyri, National Archaeological Museum, Naples.

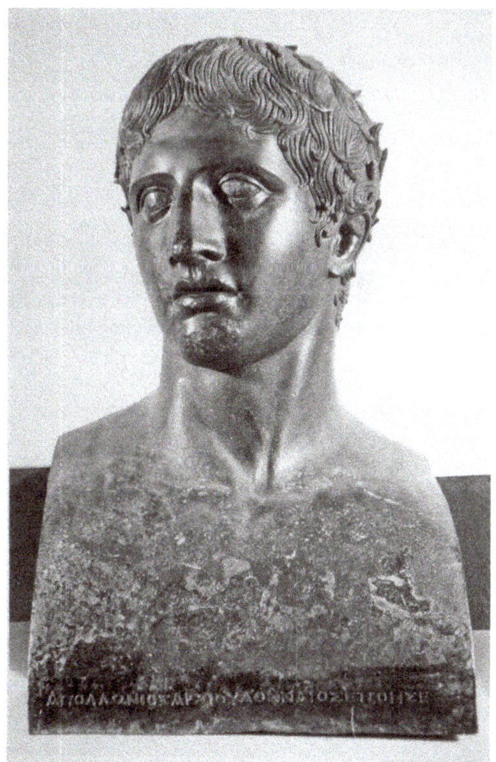

Fig. 6. Bronze herm-head of Doryphoros by Polykleitos, signed by Apollonios the Athenian, NM 4885, National Archaeological Museum, Naples.

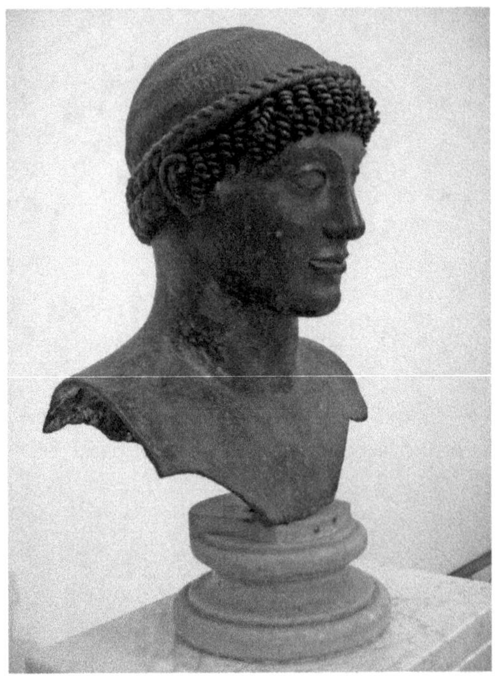

Fig. 7. Bronze "Archaic" head of kouros or Apollo, NM 5608, National Archaeological Museum, Naples.

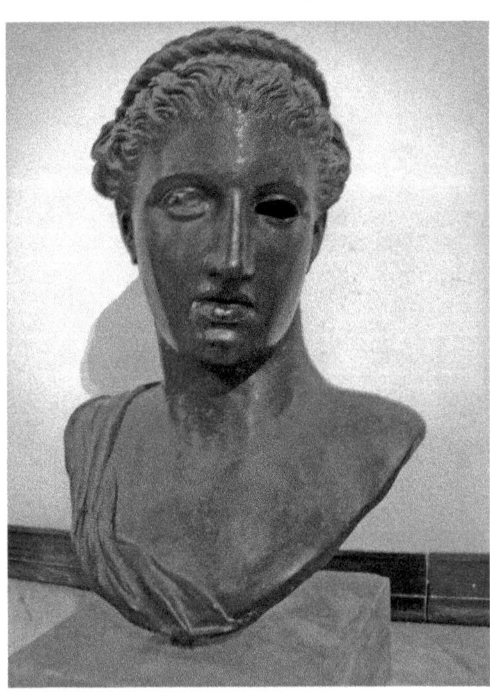

Fig. 8. Bronze classicizing head of young woman, NM 5592, National Archaeological Museum, Naples.

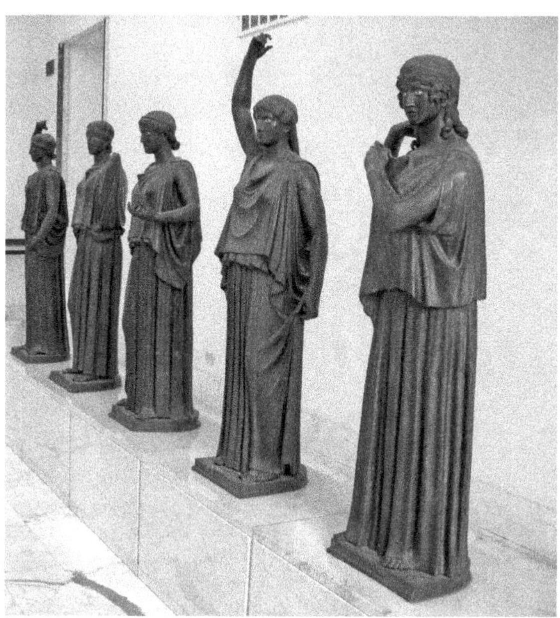

Fig. 9. Five bronze young women, NM 5604, 5605, 5619, 5620, 5621, National Archaeological Museum, Naples.

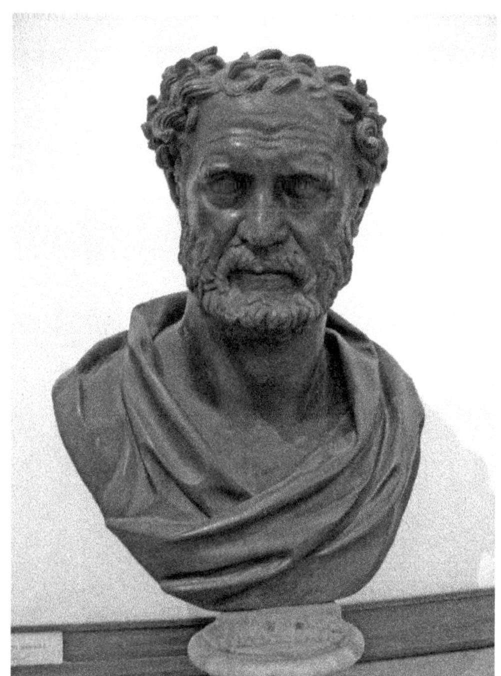

Fig. 10. Bronze bust of "Aristotle," NM 5623, National Archaeological Museum, Naples.

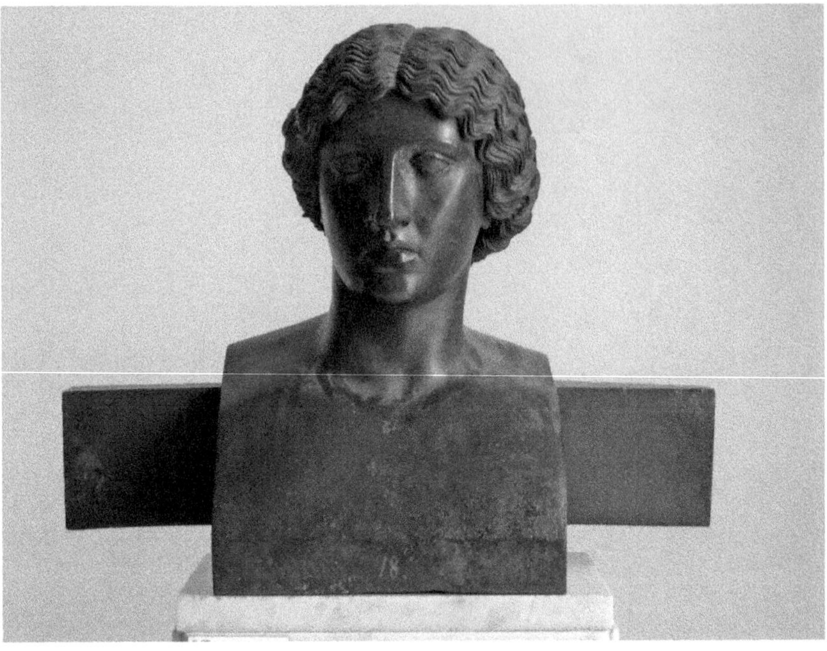

Fig. 11. Bronze herm-head of a "Polykleitan" woman, NM 4889, National Archaeological Museum, Naples (photograph by H. Lie).

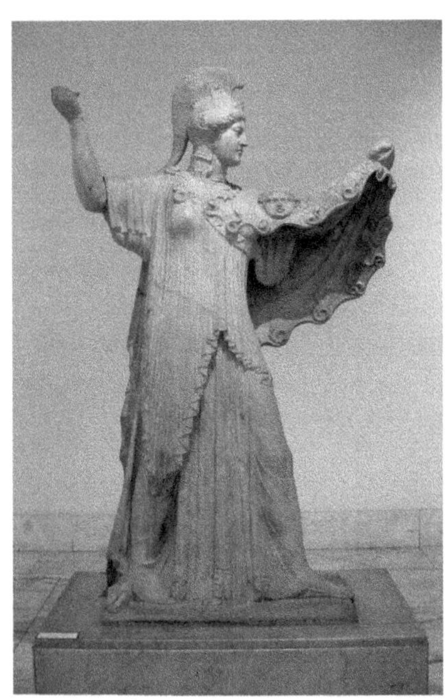

Fig. 12. Marble statue of Panathenaic Athena, NM 6007, National Archaeological Museum, Naples.

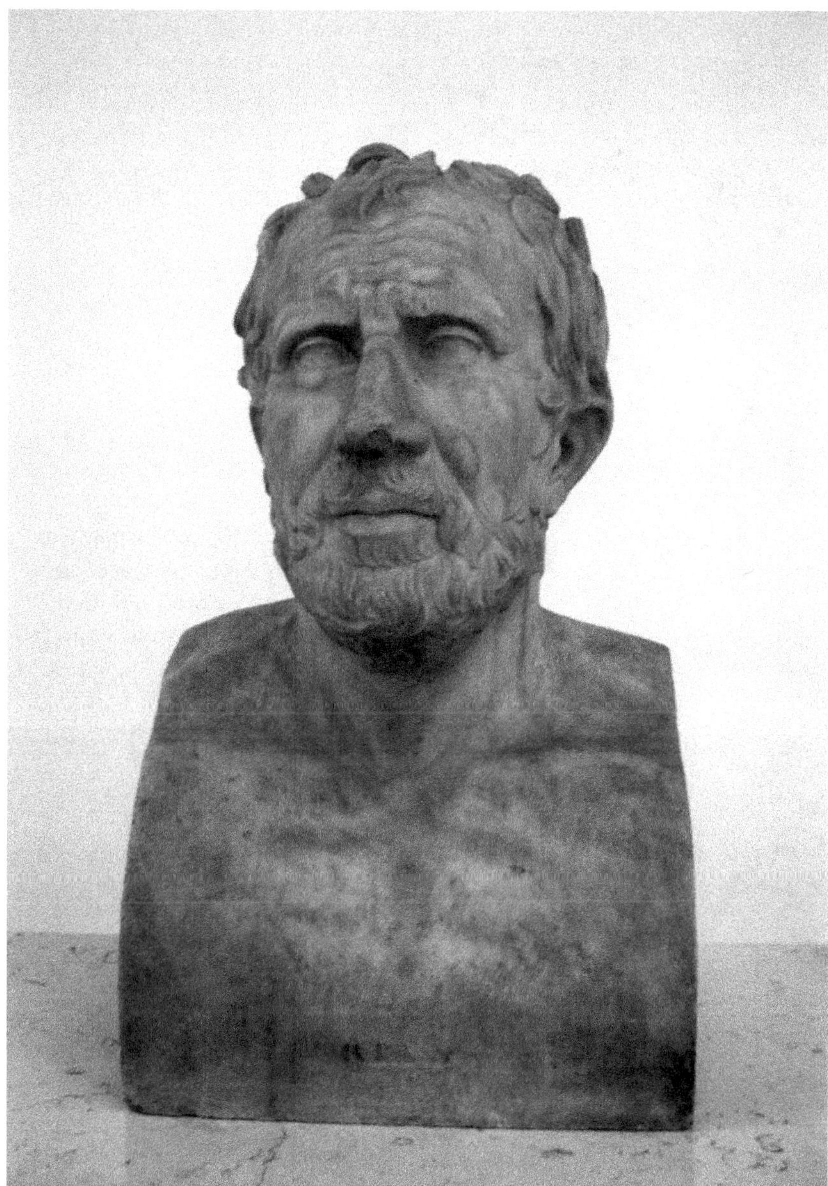

Fig. 13. Marble herm-portrait, NM 6152, National Archaeological Museum, Naples.

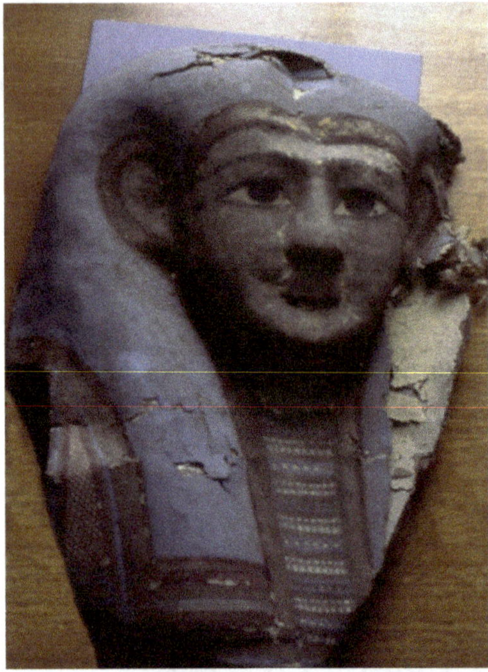

Fig. 1. Mummy cartonnage, Oxford (photograph courtesy Egypt Exploration Society and Imaging Papyri Project, Oxford).

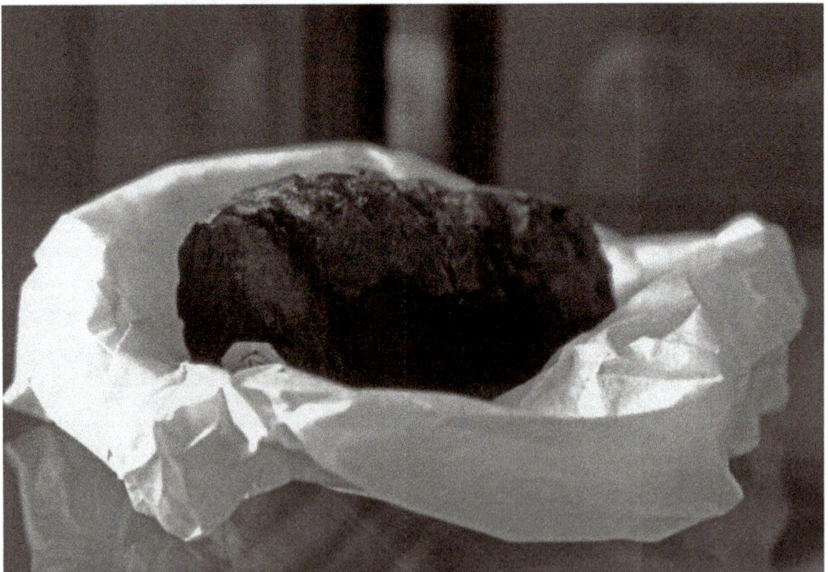

Fig. 2. Burnt papyrus scroll from Herculaneum (photograph by S. Sider: courtesy of the Egypt Exploration Society and Imaging Papyri Project Oxford).

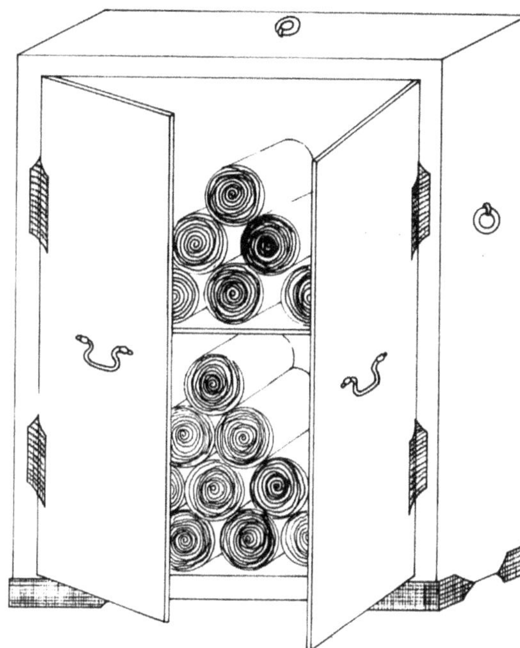

Fig. 3. Reconstruction of bookcase found in the Villa of the Papyri (source: Capasso 1991).

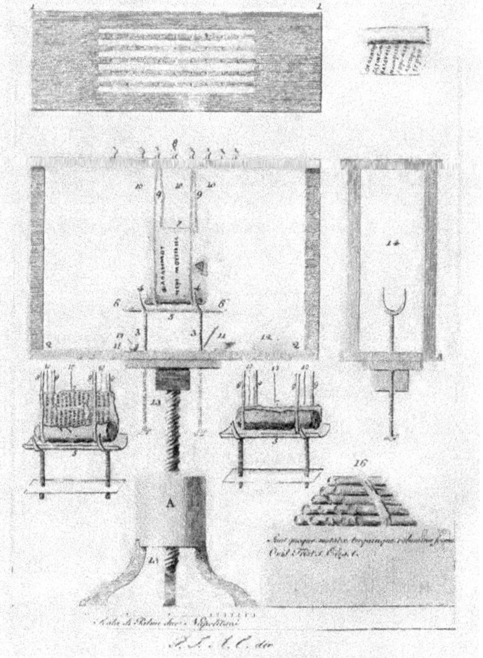

Fig. 4. Machine devised by Antonio Piaggio for the slow unrolling of charred papyri (source: Castrucci 1852, pl. IV).

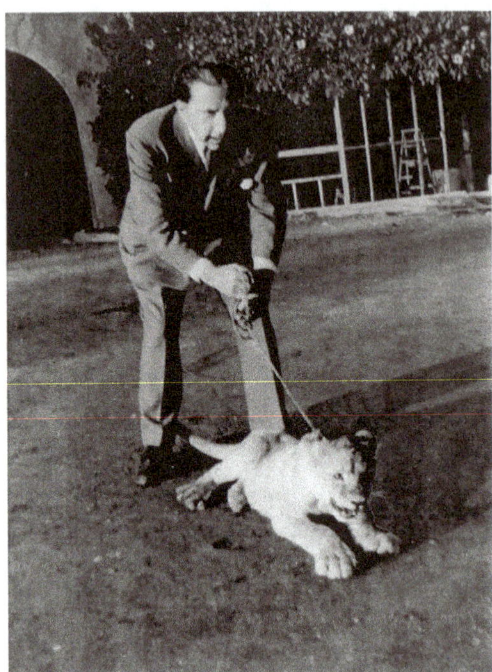

Fig. 1. J. Paul Getty with his pet lioness Tessa (source: Getty Research Institute, Institutional Archives of the J. Paul Getty Trust, BUI 10001).

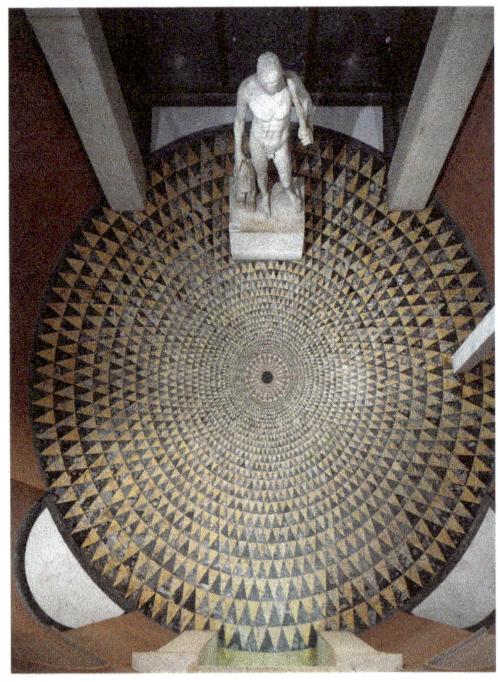

Fig. 2. The "Temple of Herakles" at the Getty Villa, Malibu, with polychrome marble floor copied after that of the belvedere of the Villa of the Papyri (photograph by Julius Schulman, courtesy of the J. Paul Getty Trust).

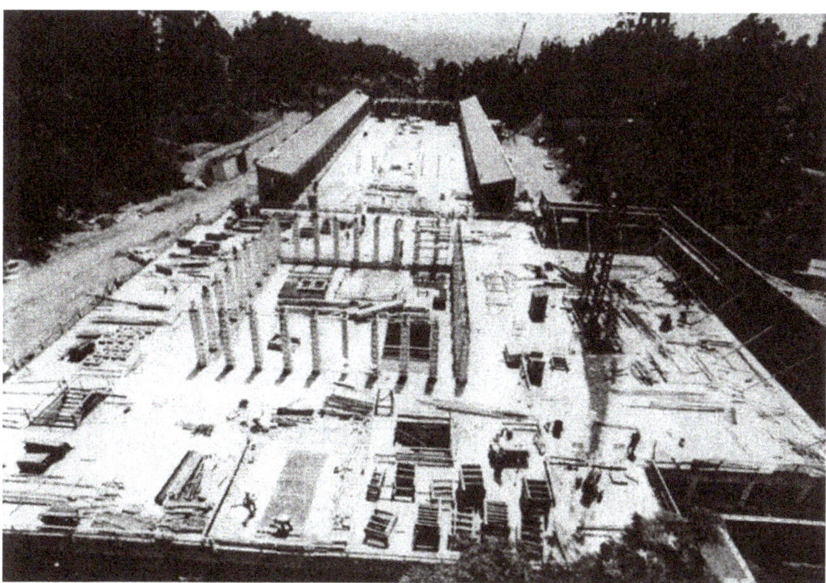

Fig. 3. The Getty Villa during construction in the early 1970s (source: Getty Research Institute, Institutional Archives of the J. Paul Getty Trust, BUI 10001).

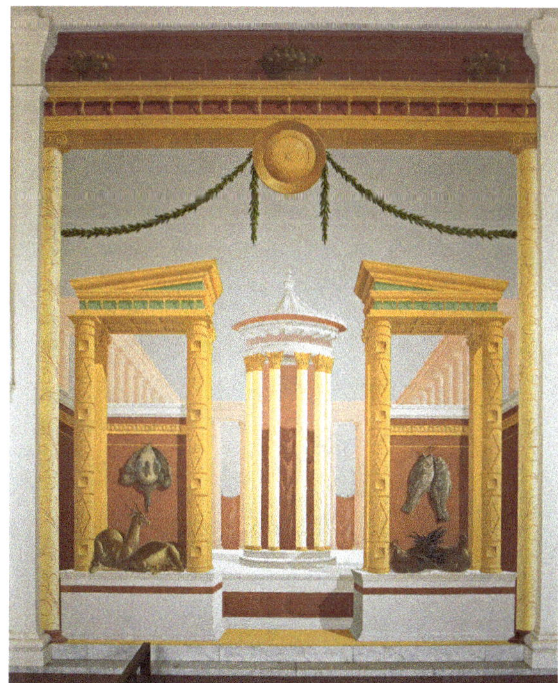

Fig. 4. Wall-painting by Garth Benton at the Getty Villa, copied in part after the Villa of the Papyri (source: Getty Research Institute, Institutional Archives of the J. Paul Getty Trust, BUI 10001).

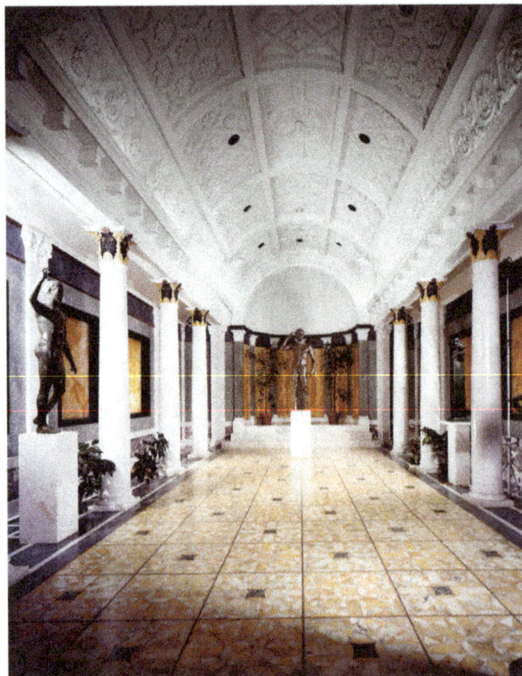

Fig. 5. The "Basilica" at the Getty Villa, with polychrome marble floor copied after the Villa of the Papyri (photograph by Julius Schulman, courtesy of the J. Paul Getty Trust).

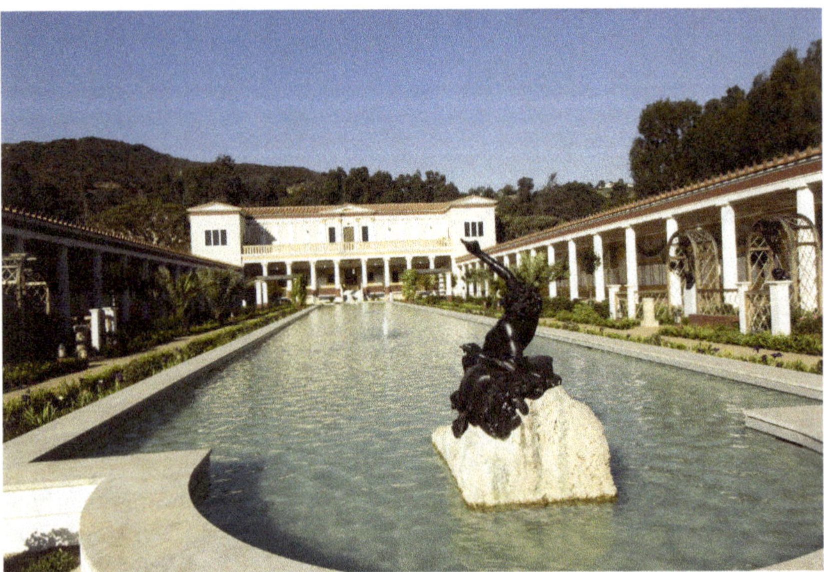

Fig. 6. Outer peristyle garden, the Getty Villa (photograph by Richard Ross, courtesy of the J. Paul Getty Trust).

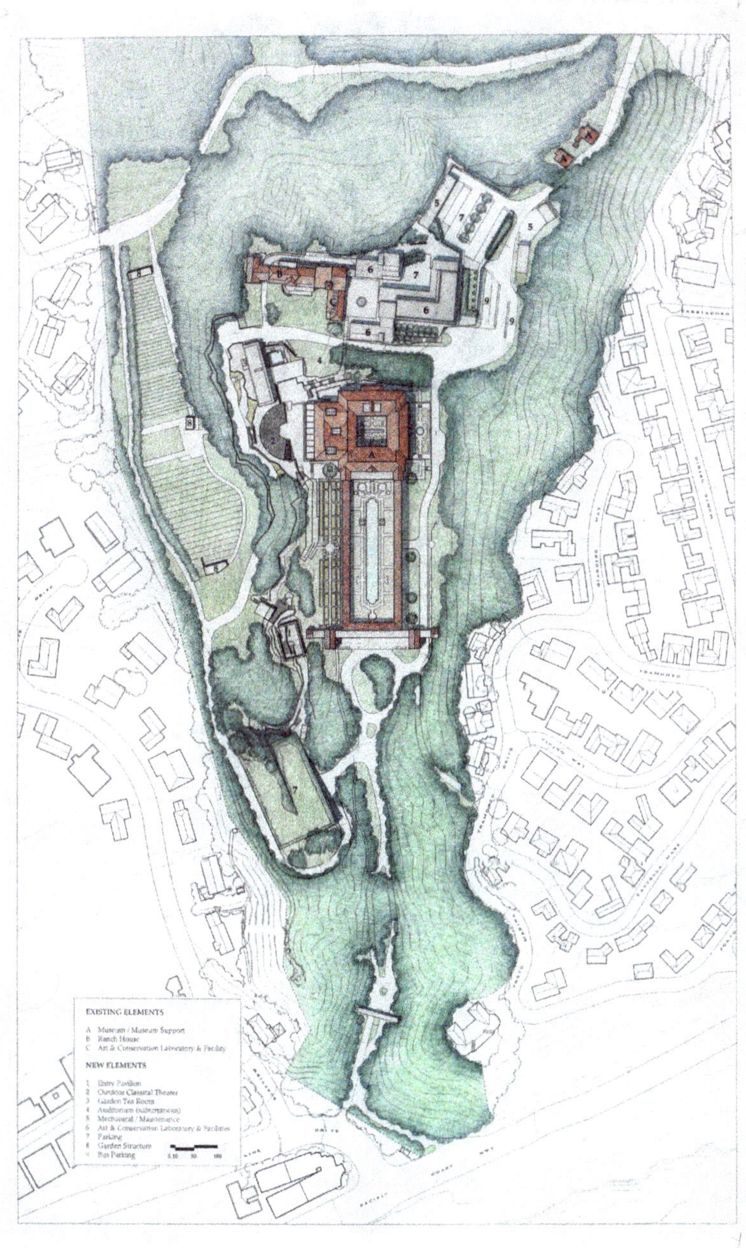

Fig. 7. Final site plan of the Getty Villa, by Machado and Silvetti (source: The Getty Research Institute, Institutional Archives of the J. Paul Getty Trust, 2004.IA.6).

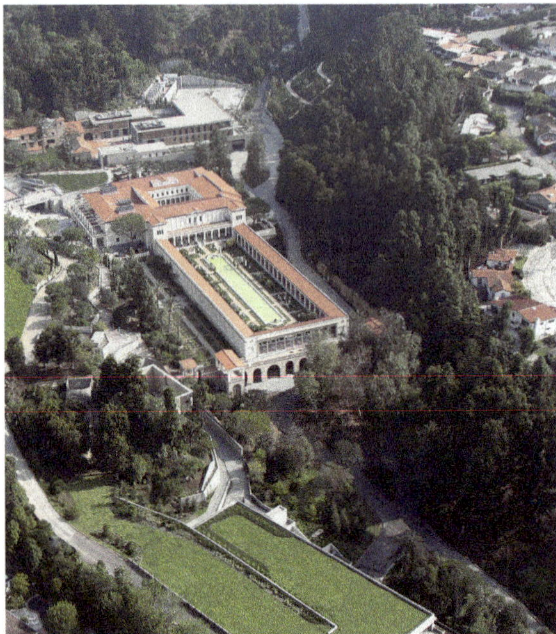

Fig. 8. Aerial view of the Getty Villa from the south (source: Morley Construction Company).

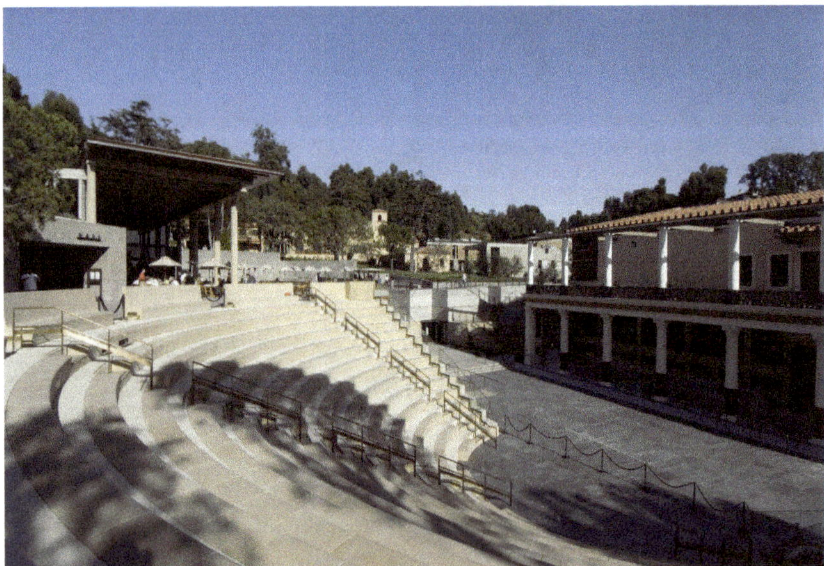

Fig. 9. The new outdoor classical theater opposite the west facade of the Getty Villa with the cafe, cafe terrace, and Ranch House in the distance (photograph by Richard Ross, courtesy of the J. Paul Getty Trust).

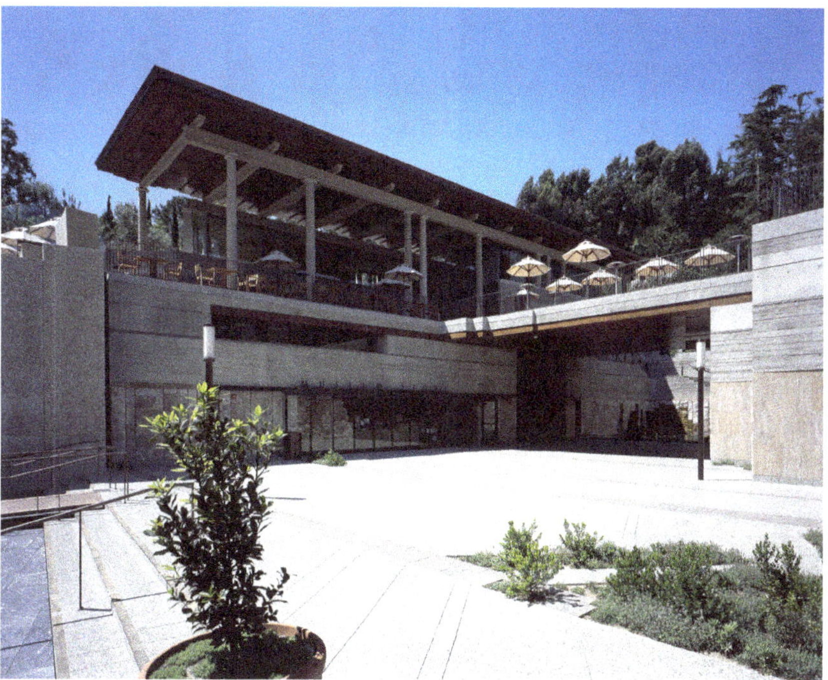

Fig. 10. The new cafe and cafe terrace at the Getty Villa (photograph by Julius Schulman and Juergen Nogai, courtesy of the J. Paul Getty Trust).).

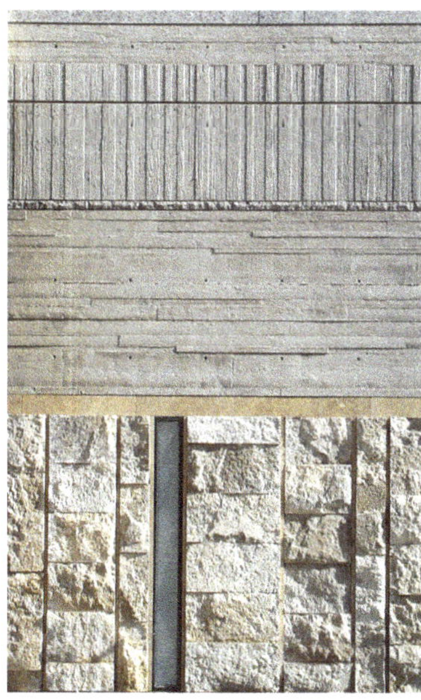

Fig. 11. A "strata" wall at the Getty Villa (source: Machado and Silvetti Associates).

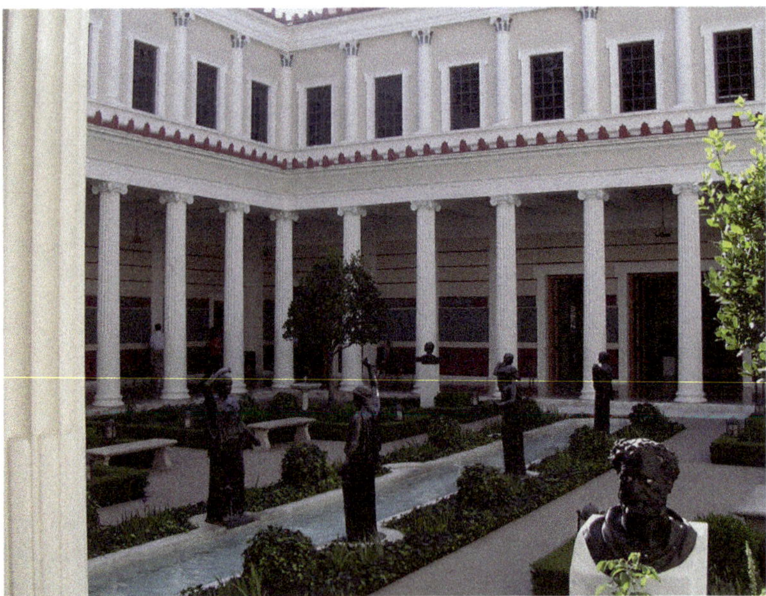

Fig. 12. Inner peristyle garden, the Getty Villa (photograph by Kenneth Lapatin).

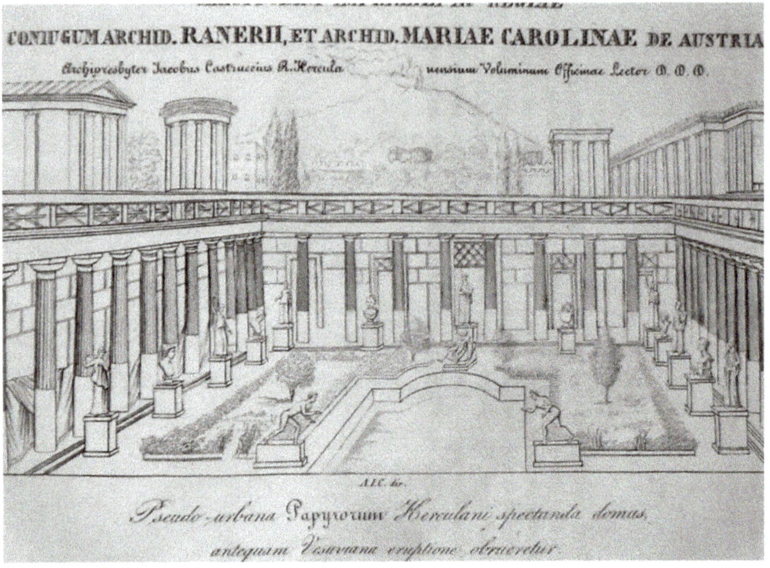

Fig. 13. The Villa of the Papyri at Herculaneum, as reconstructed in Castrucci 1852, plate XXI (source: Research Library, The Getty Research Institute, Los Angeles [88-B5582]).

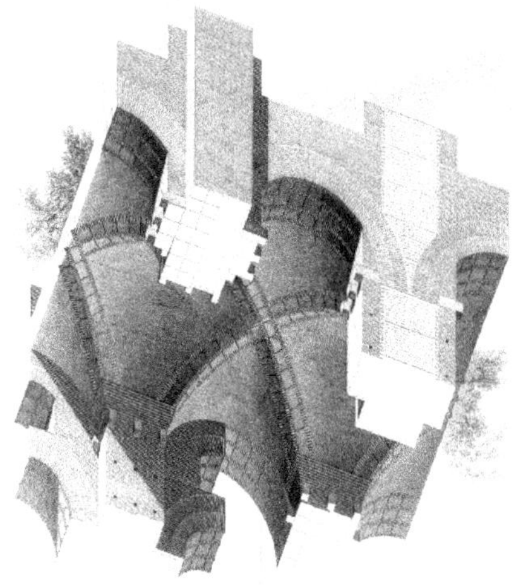

Fig. 1. "Frog's-eye-view" axonometric of reconstructed vaults from the Imperial Palace on the Palatine, Rome. Auguste Choisy (1873) as etched by G. Baranger.

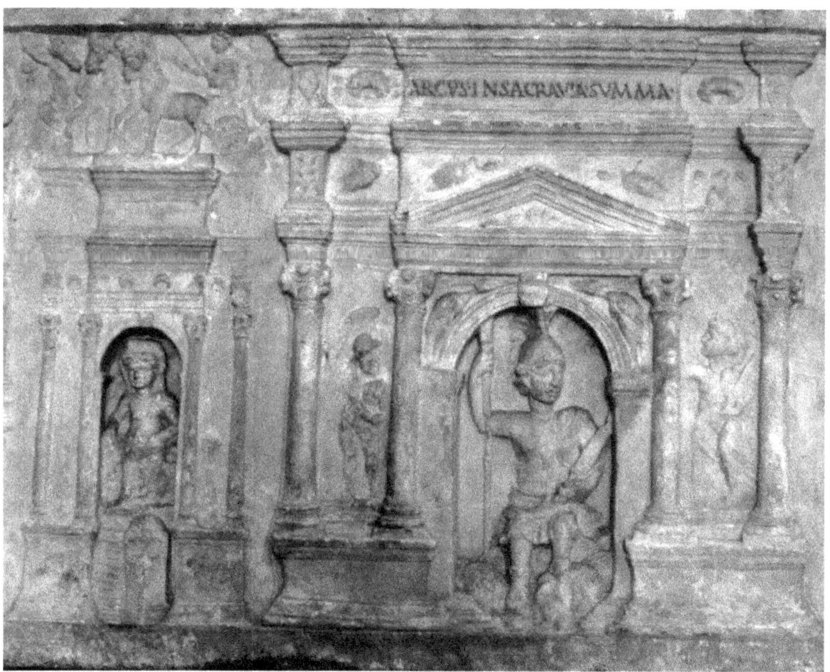

Fig. 2. Tomb of the Haterii, late first century CE, Vatican Museum (photograph by D. Favro).

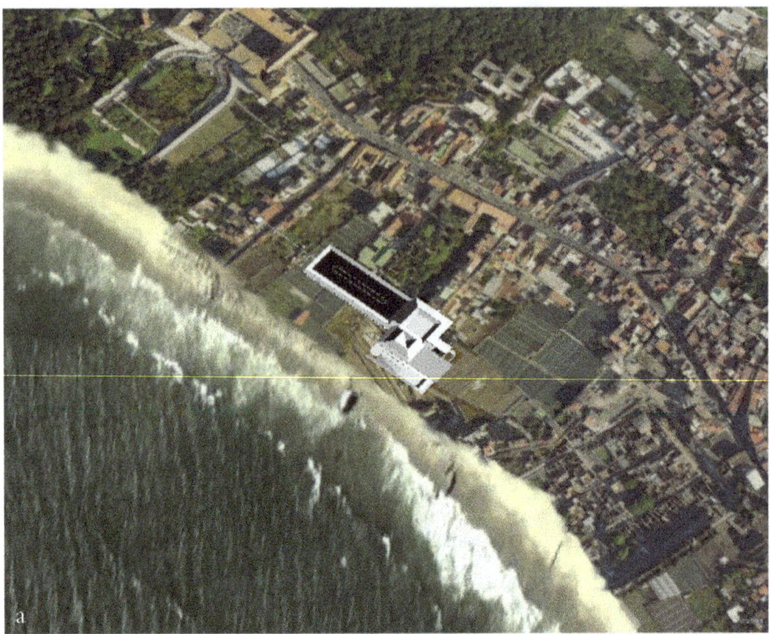

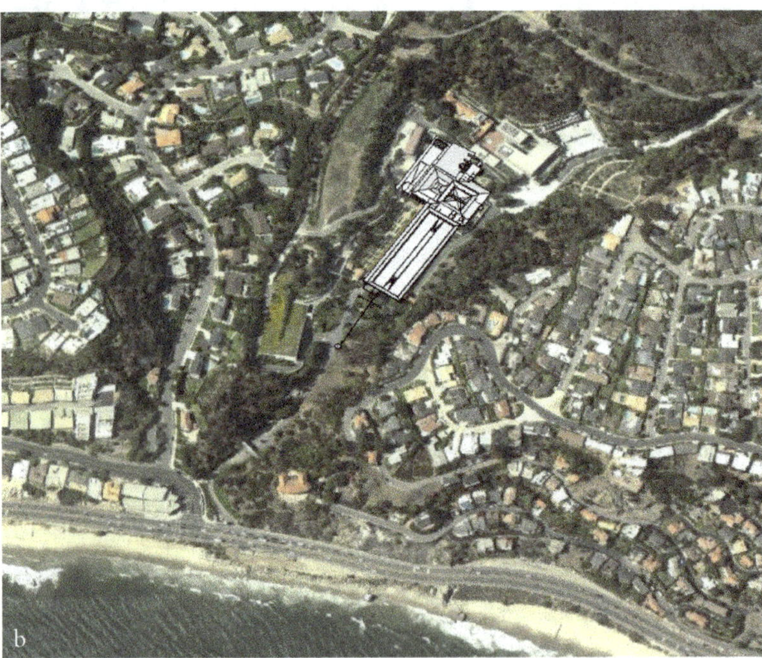

Fig. 3. Aerial view of a reconstruction model of the Villa of the Papyri situated in the modern context with imagined ancient coastline (3a), and of the Getty Villa (3b); images are oriented with north at the top (D. Favro)

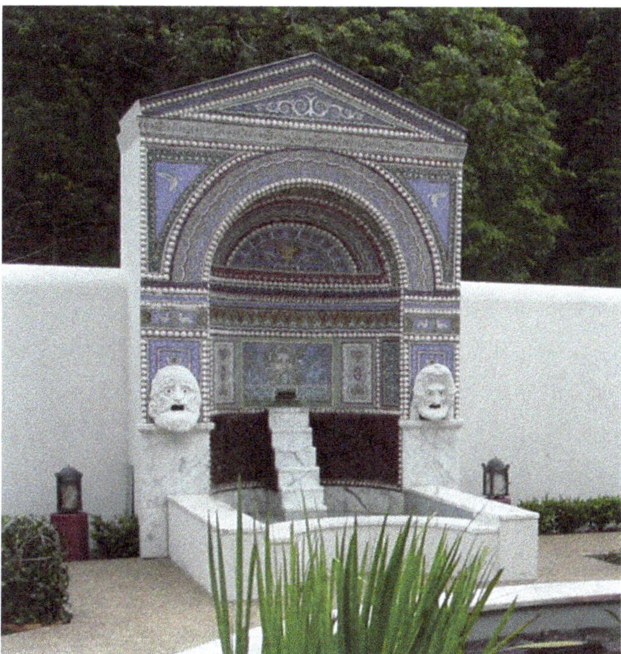

Fig. 4. The Getty Villa east garden with replica of the fountain from the House of the Great Fountain at Pompeii (photograph by D. Favro).

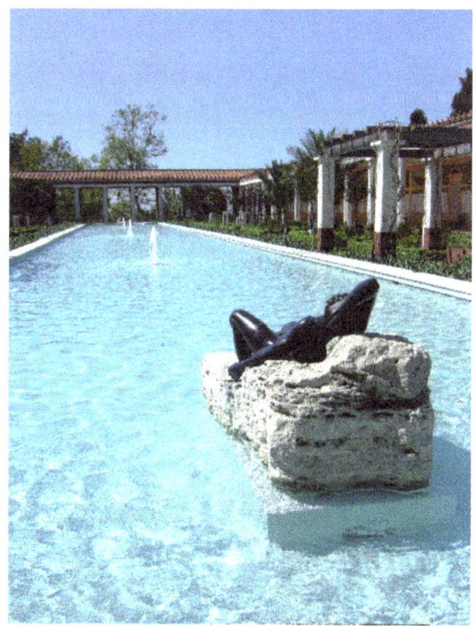

Fig. 5. View of the across the peristyle of the Getty Villa toward the sea (photograph by M. Harrsch).

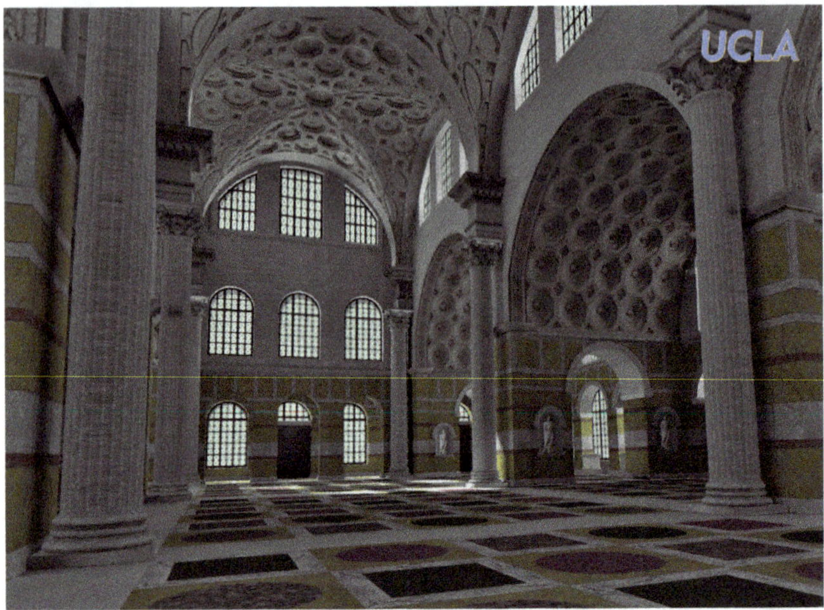

Fig. 6. Digital model depicting day-lighting inside the Basilica of Maxentius, copyright UCLA.

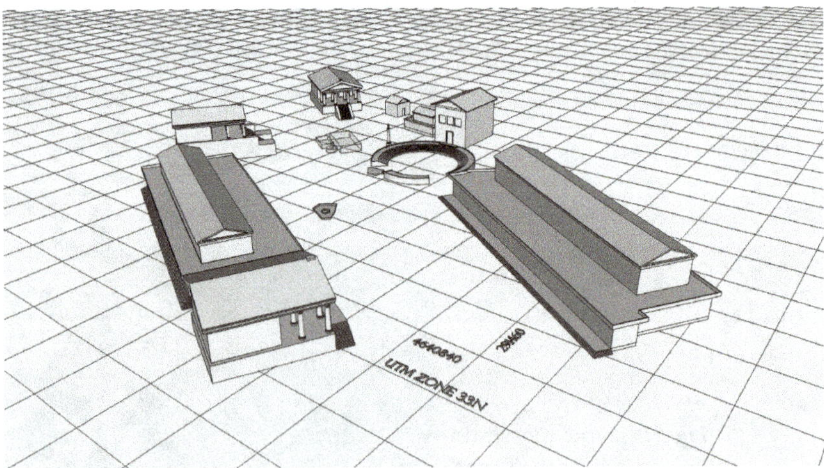

Fig. 7. Digital model of Republican Forum in Rome constructed on a Cartesian grid; model by C. Johanson.

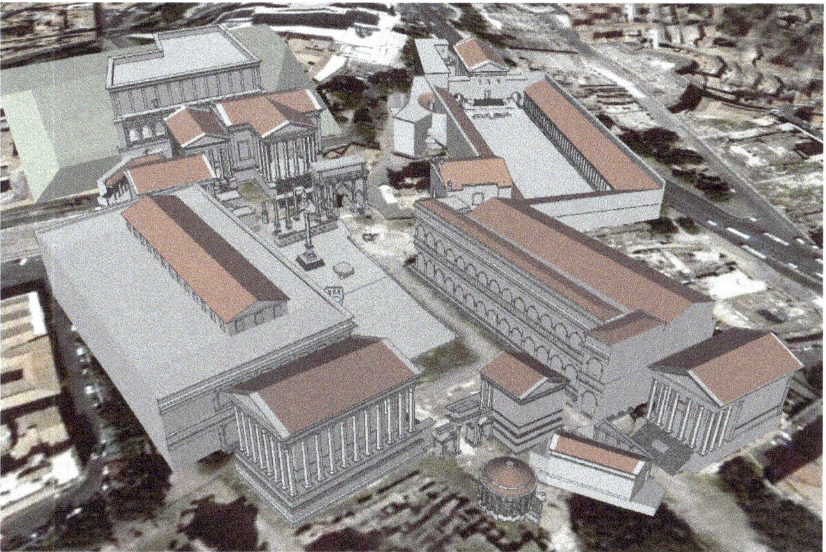

Fig. 8. Digital model of the Imperial Roman Forum situated in a geo-browser environment; Experiential Technologies Center, model copyright UCLA.

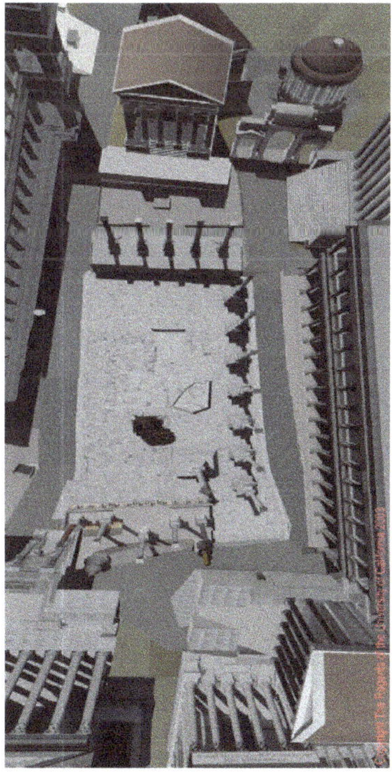

Fig. 9. Aerial view of the Imperial Roman Forum, Rome; digital model, copyright UCLA.

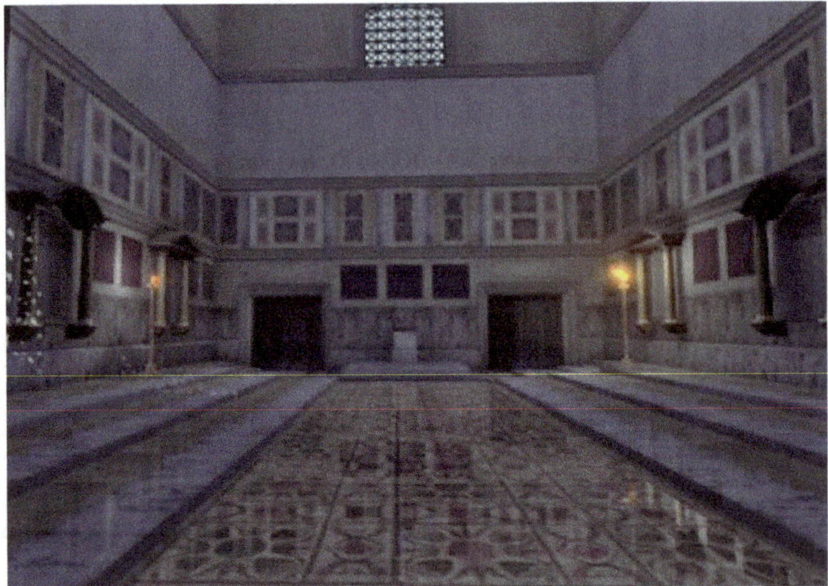

Fig. 10. Interior of Curia House, Rome, with recreated ancient lighting effects; digital model, copyright UCLA.

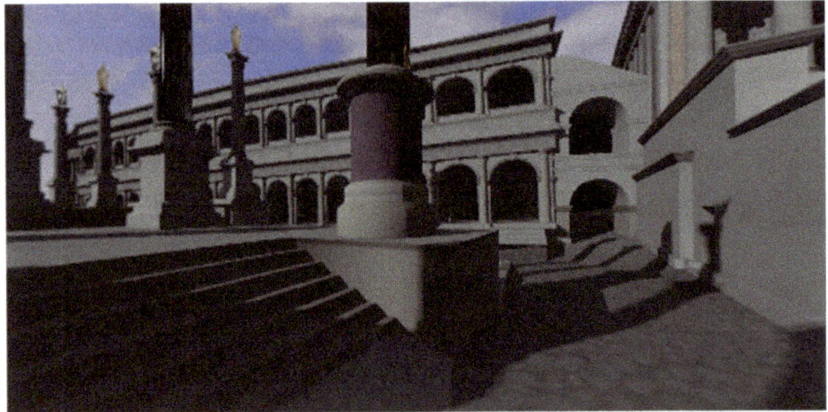

Fig. 11. Recreated lighting in ancient Roman Forum, 310 CE; digital model, copyright UCLA.

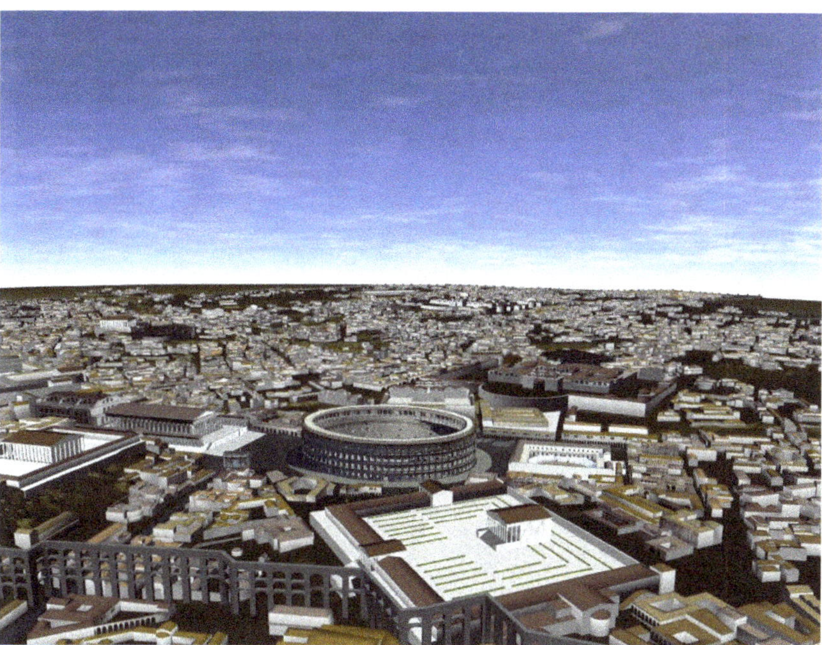

Fig. 12. View northward of the Imperial Rome; digital model copyright UCLA and University of Virginia.

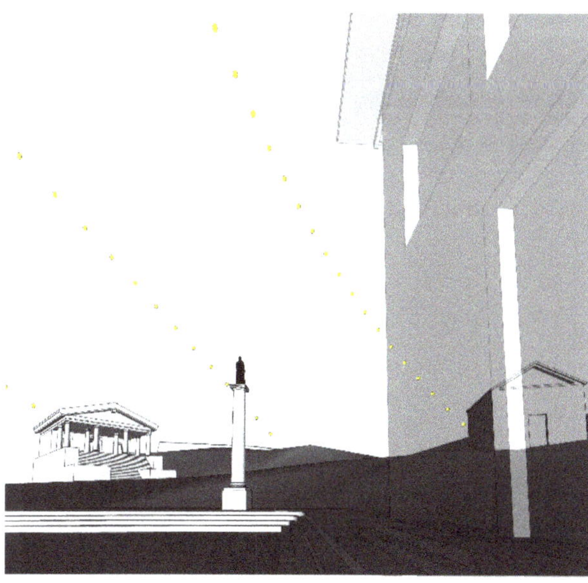

Fig. 13. Experimental analysis of the sun's movement in relation to a passage in Pliny (Pliny HN 7.212); model by C. Johanson.

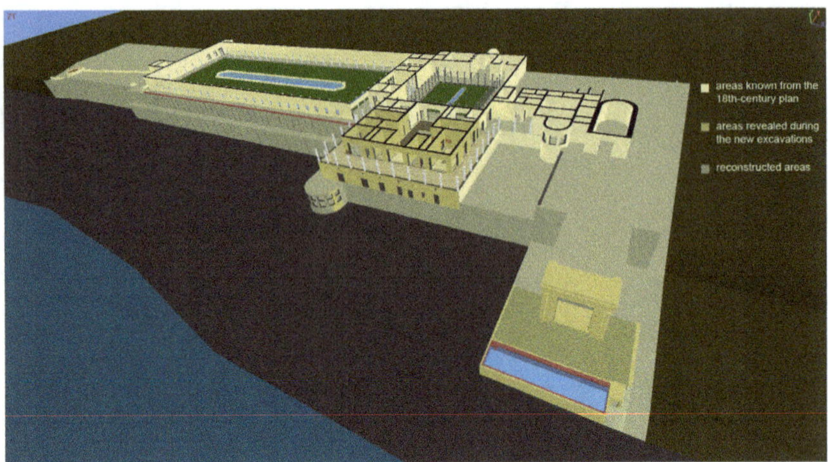

Fig. 1. Bird's eye view of the model of the Villa of the Papyri from the south.

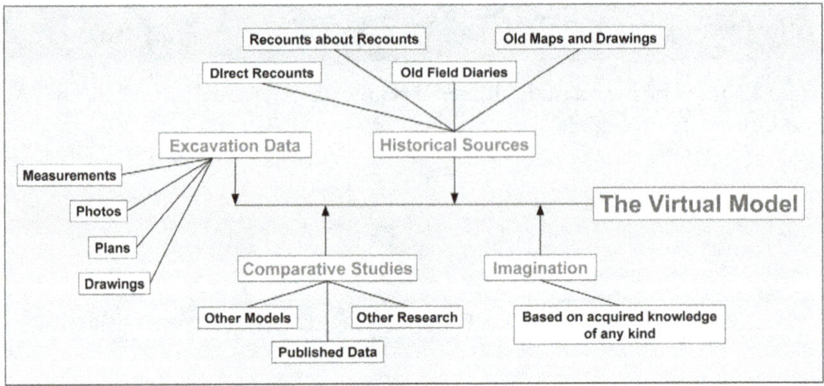

Fig. 2. Schematic diagram of 3D modeling stages (source: Hermon 2008, fig. 4).

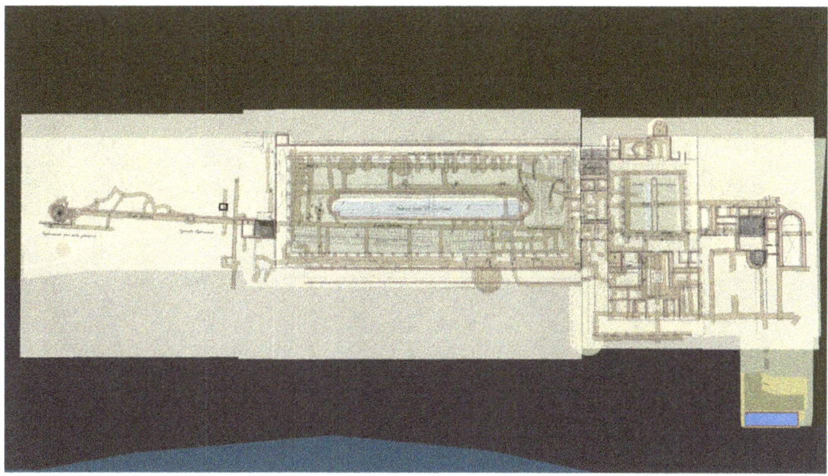

Fig. 3. Model of the Villa of the Papyri with Weber's plan superimposed.

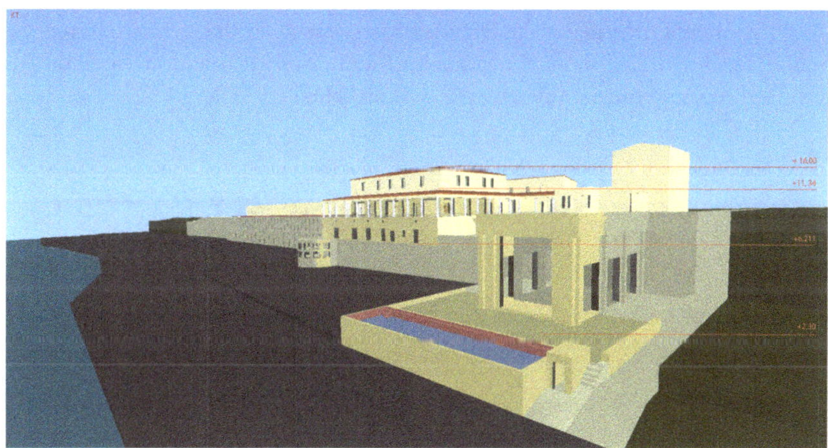

Fig. 4. View of the model of the Villa of the Papyri from the south with heights indicated.

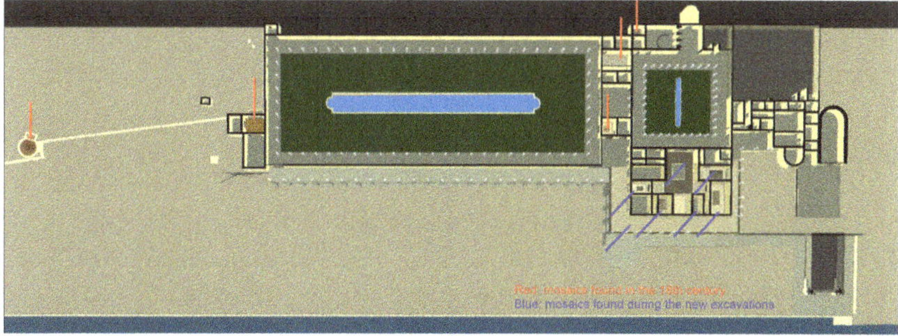

Fig. 5. Model of the Villa of the Papyri: plan indicating the mosaics found in the 18th century (red) and during the new excavations (blue).

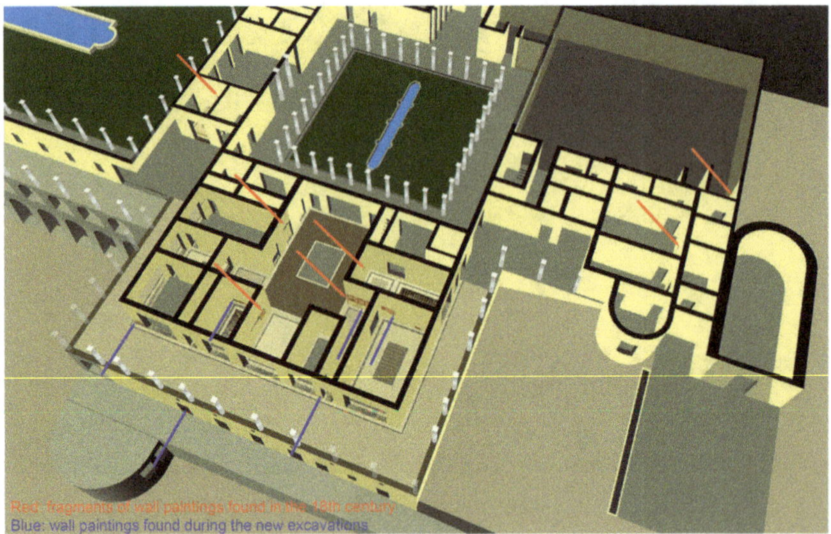

Fig. 6. Model of the Villa of the Papyri: bird's eye view of the atrium quarter indicating the finding spots of fragments of wall paintings found in the 18th century (red) and during the new excavations (blue).

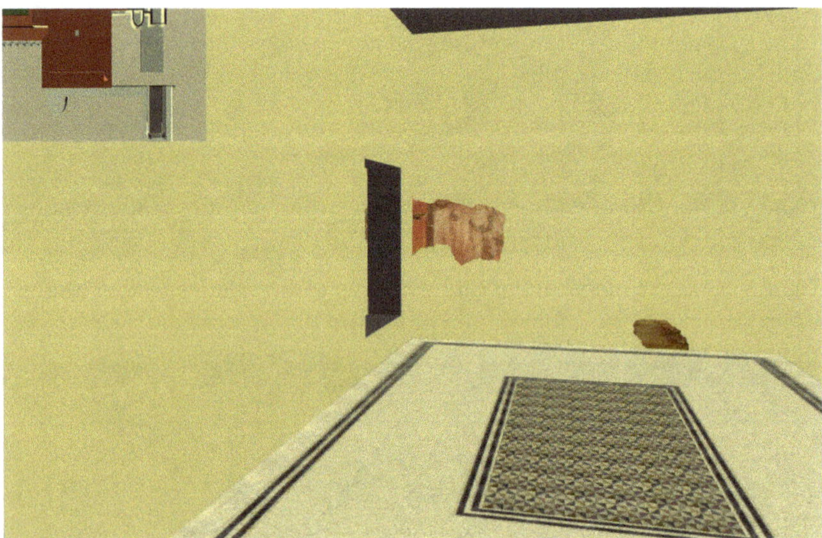

Fig. 7. Model of the Villa of the Papyri: view of fragment of megalography in room (i) (see also Moorman in this volume, fig. 9). At the upper left corner is a map of the model, a red arrow indicating the "viewer's" location.

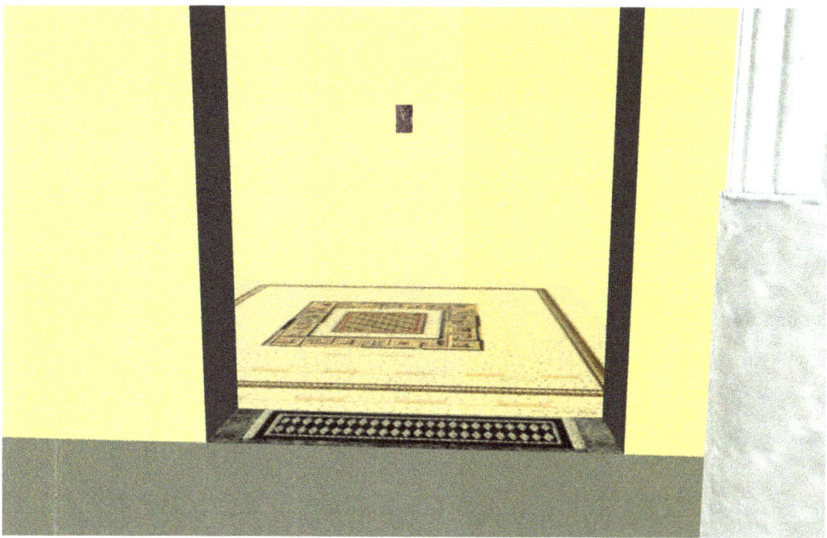

Fig. 8. Model of the Villa of the Papyri: view of room "XVI" in Weber's plan. At the far back is a fragment of wall painting (Inv. 9319) found in this room.

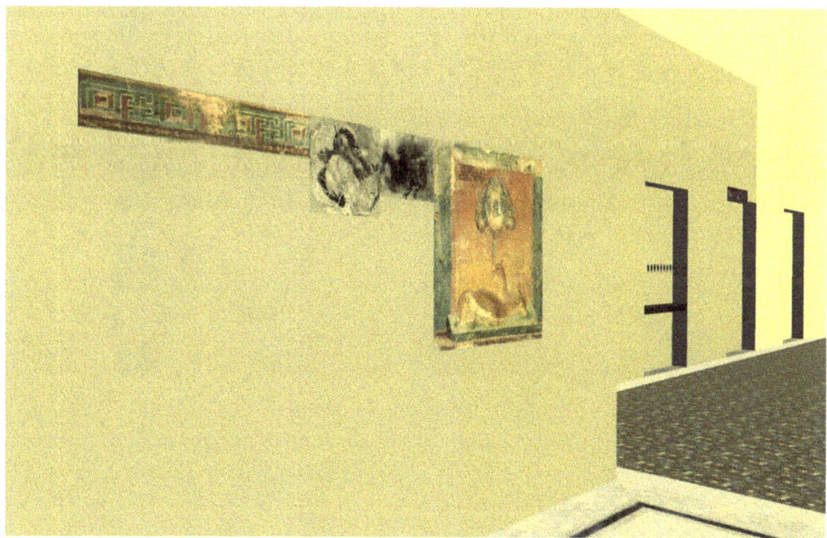

Fig. 9. Model of the Villa of the Papyri: view of the area of the atrium. The fragments found in this area have been placed on the model where their corresponding annotations occur on Weber's plan.

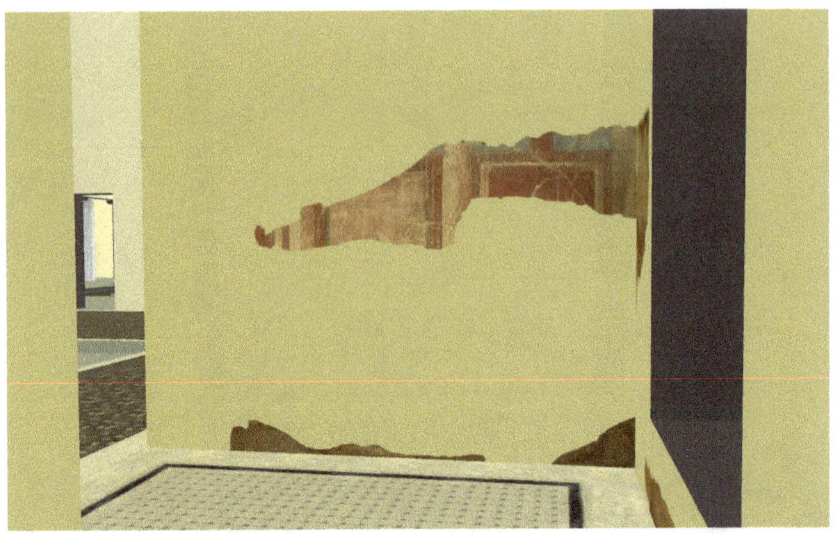

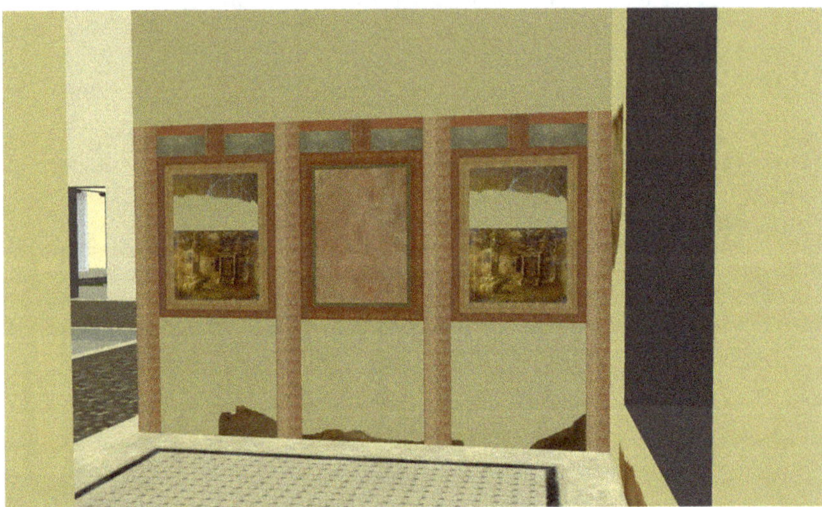

Fig. 10. Model of the Villa of the Papyri: view of north-east wall of *ala* (e) from the south-west; (a) existing state and (b) visualization of the restoration proposal by Moormann.

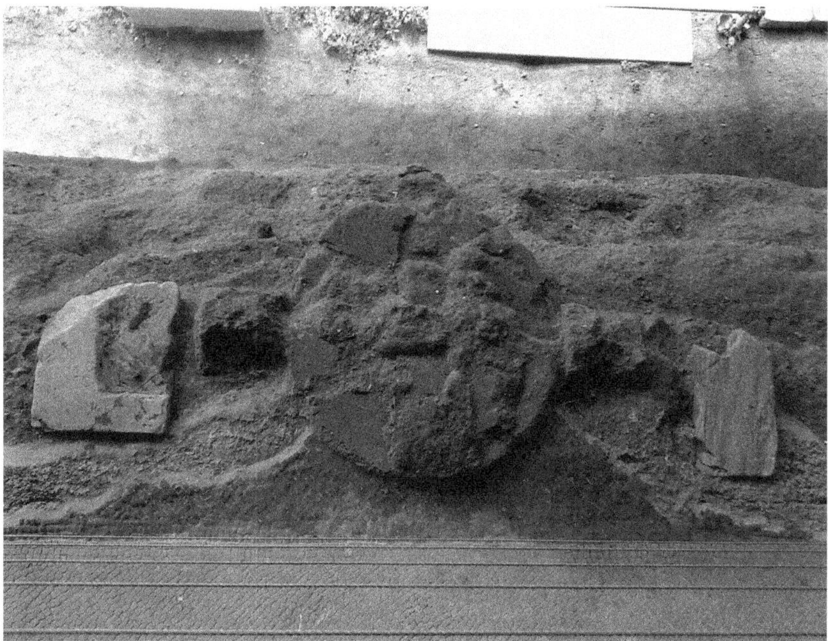

Fig. 11. Villa of the Papyri, portico (a): photograph of the footprint of a column. Flanking the column are the footprints of a fence or a doorpost.

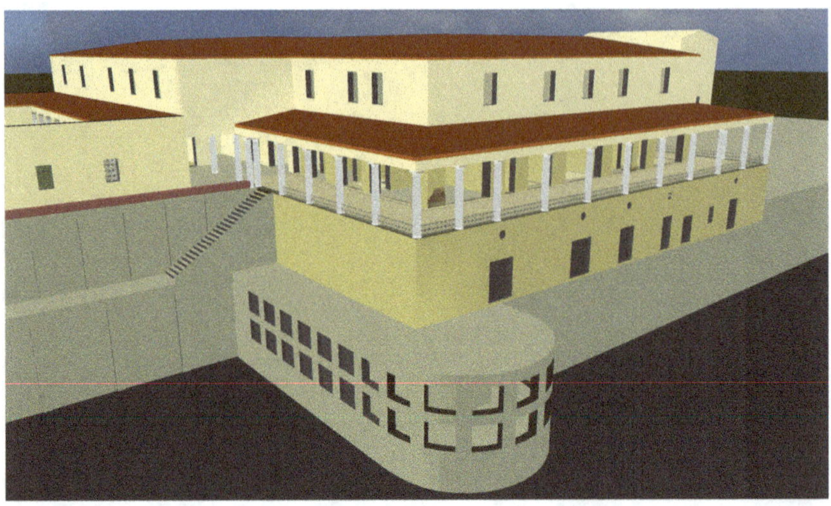

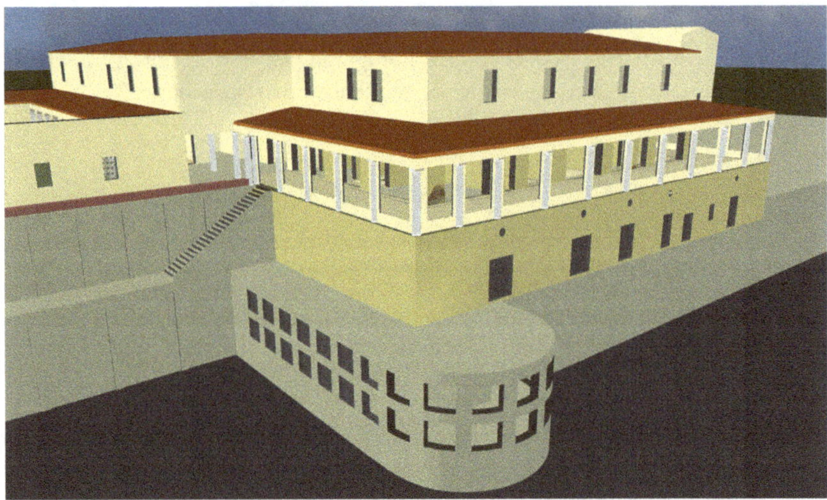

Fig. 12. Model of the Villa of the Papyri: view of the atrium quarter area from the south-west. Two alternative restoration proposals for the intercolumniations of the porticoes around the atrium quarter: above with a fence and below with a thin wall.

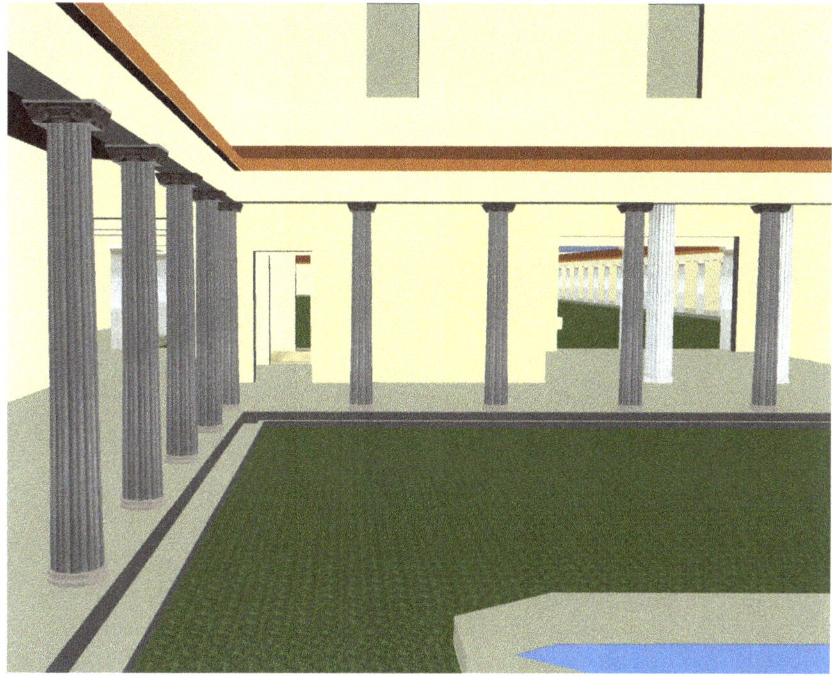

Fig. 13. Model of the Villa of the Papyri: view inside the square peristyle with the reconstructed columns from the south-east.

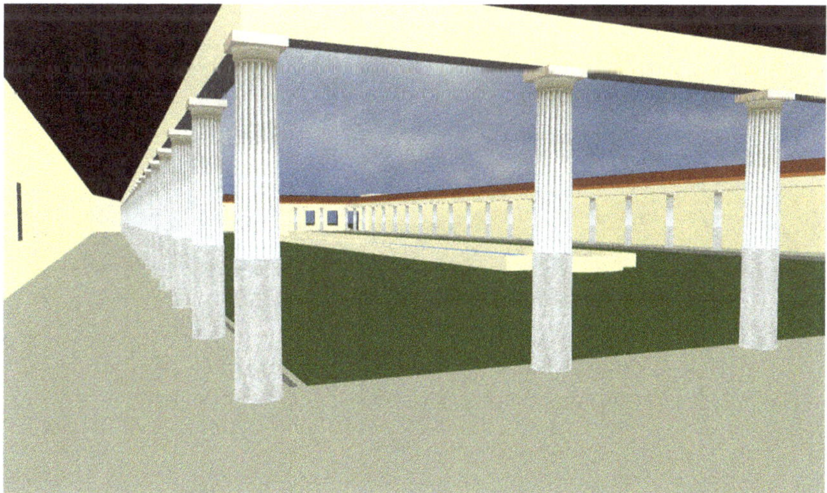

Fig. 14. Model of the Villa of the Papyri: view of the rectangular peristyle from the south-east. This reconstruction uses the columns of *porticus* 40 in Villa A at Torre Annunziata, which are plain up to 1.20 m and then fluted.

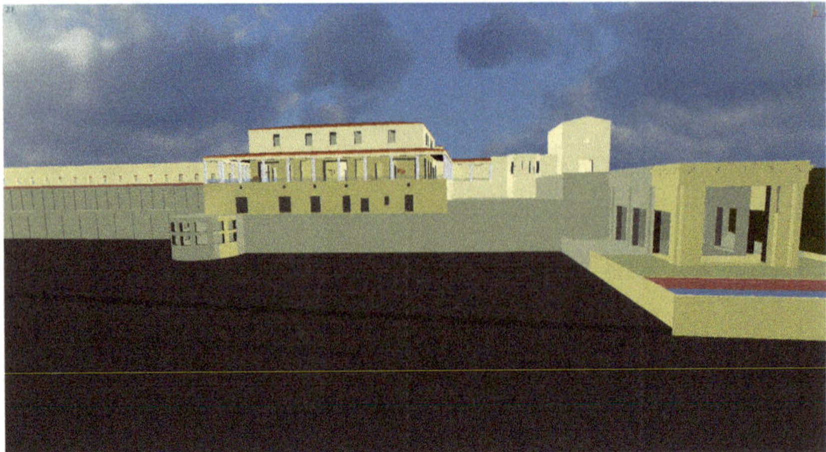

Fig. 15. Model of the Villa of the Papyri: view of the atrium quarter with its *basis villae* as well as the lower terrace structures (right) from the south-west.

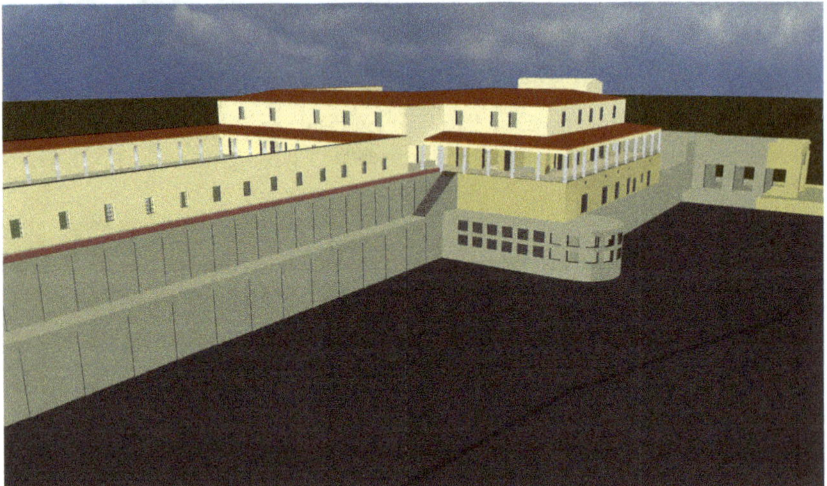

Fig. 16. Model of the Villa of the Papyri: view from the north-west. This restoration proposal of the substructures of the rectangular peristyle was formed by comparison to the south-east façade of a projecting structure of the north-west *Insula* of Herculaneum that features two rows of a series of niches.

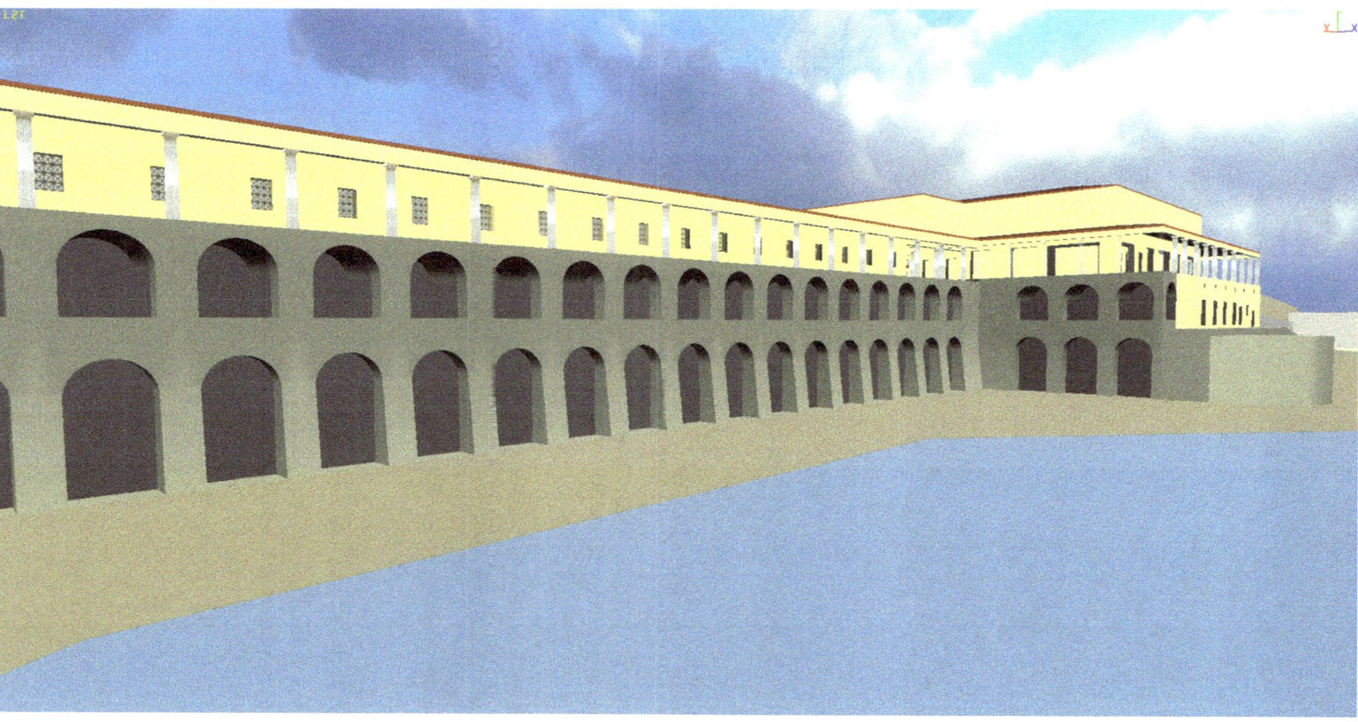

Fig. 17. Model of the Villa of the Papyri: view from the north-west presenting the façade of the substructures of the rectangular peristyle with two series of vaults. This restoration proposal was formed by comparison to the vaulted substructures of Villa Arianna A and Villa Arianna B in Stabiae.

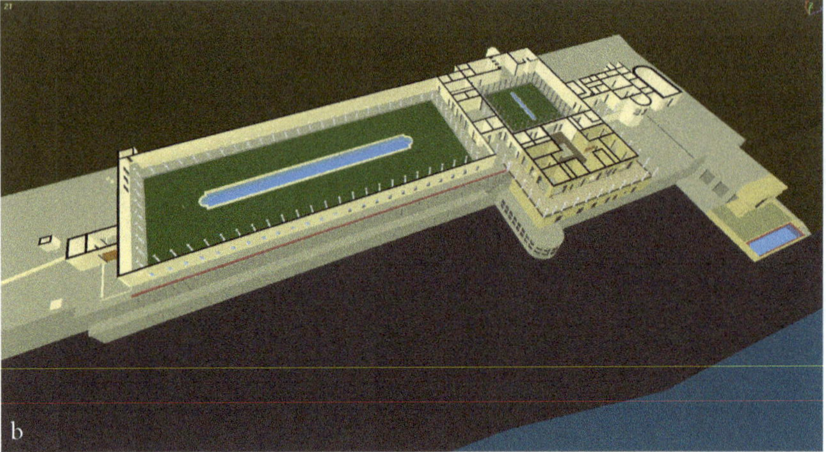

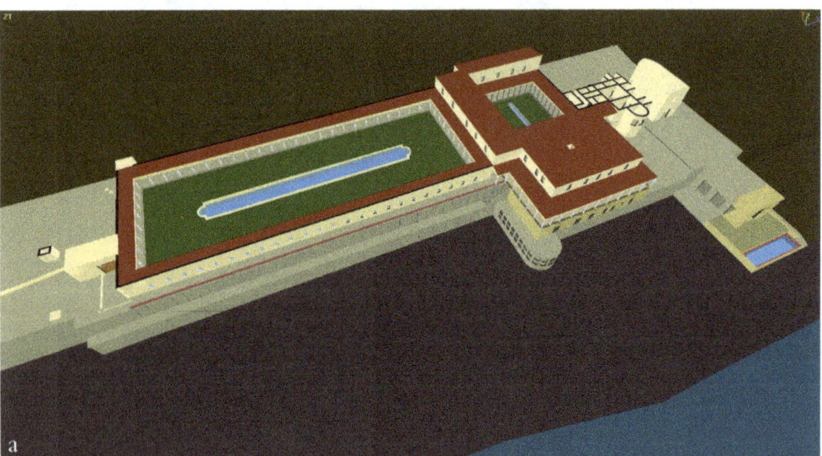

Fig. 18. Model of the Villa of the Papyri: bird's eye view from the north-west; (a) restoration proposal for the second storey above the areas of the atrium quarter and in between the square and rectangular peristyles and (b) without any restoration proposal for the second storey.

www.ingramcontent.com/pod-product-compliance
Lightning Source LLC
LaVergne TN
LVHW010853110826
845149LV00005B/1400
9783110482225